A Revolution of the Heart

Essays on the Catholic Worker

FRITZ EICHENBERG © 1951

THE LORD'S SUPPER 1951

A Revolution
of the Heart

ESSAYS ON THE
CATHOLIC WORKER

Edited by Patrick G. Coy

TEMPLE UNIVERSITY PRESS *Philadelphia*

Temple University Press, Philadelphia 19122
Copyright © 1988 by Temple University. All rights reserved
Published 1988
Printed in the United States of America

∞ The paper used in this publication meets the minimum
requirements of American National Standard for Information
Sciences—Permanence of Paper for Printed Library Materials,
ANSI Z39.48-1984

Library of Congress Cataloging-in-Publication Data

A Revolution of the heart: essays on the Catholic worker/edited by Patrick G. Coy.
  p. cm.
  Includes index.
  Contents: Peter Maurin/Marc H. Ellis—Peter Maurin and the future of
democracy/Geoffrey B. Gnuehs—Dorothy Day/Eileen Egan—Dorothy Day/Nancy
L. Roberts—The one-person revolution of Ammon Hennacy/Patrick G. Coy—The
politics of free obedience/Mel Piehl—The prophetic spirituality of the Catholic
worker/Daniel DiDomizio—Houses of hospitality/Angie O'Gorman & Patrick G.
Coy—War resistance and property destruction/Anne Klejment—Experiments in
truth/Janice Brandon-Falcone—The Chicago Catholic worker/Francis J. Sicius.
  ISBN 0-87722-531-1 (alk. paper)
  1. Catholic Worker. 2. Catholic Worker Movement. 3. Day, Dorothy, 1897–
1980. 4. Maurin, Peter. 5. Sociology, Christian (Catholic)—History—20th
century. 6. Peace—Religious aspects—Catholic Church—History of doctrines—
20th century. 7. Catholic Church—Doctrines—History—20th century. I. Coy,
Patrick G. II. Catholic worker.
BX801.C369653R48   1988   87-34910
267'.182—dc19   CIP

Woodcuts appearing in this book are credited as follows: frontispiece
by Fritz Eichenberg, chapter openers 1 and 3 through 10 by Adé Bethune,
Chapter 2 opener by Fritz Eichenberg, and Chapter 11 by Larry Nolte.
They appear courtesy of the artists.

All royalties from this book are being paid directly to the St. Louis
Catholic Worker to support their ongoing work.

For all Catholic Workers, past, present, and future

The greatest challenge of the day is: How to bring about a revolution of the heart, a revolution which has to start with each one of us?

—Dorothy Day,
Loaves and Fishes

CONTENTS

PART III
CATHOLIC WORKER COMMUNITIES:
TWO CASE HISTORIES

FOREWORD

Jim Douglass

READING THESE POWERFUL essays and reliving the story of the Catholic Worker, I am conscious of the impact the Worker has had upon me. I look out the window of our house at train tracks leading into the Trident submarine base. Shelley and I chose to live in this house by nuclear train tracks in order to experiment more deeply in the truth of nonviolence. As the weapons trains come weekly, shaking our house and our lives, we seek with our Ground Zero community the transforming power of nonviolence that is our only hope in the nuclear age. I was introduced to that power by Dorothy Day and the Catholic Worker, in the spring of 1957 at the University of Santa Clara.

Herb Burke was an English professor who taught our freshman class to think by refusing to tell us what to think. One day Herb asked us to read an article describing the act of civil disobedience now recounted in this book: Dorothy Day, Ammon Hennacy, and other Catholic Workers refused to go underground in New York City during a Civil Defense drill and were therefore arrested. When Herb Burke probed our thoughts on this action, I joined the other students in arguing against the example of the Catholic Worker. Herb listened, asked questions, and said little about his own opinion. We could tell, however, that Dorothy Day had his support. Without knowing it, I was already hooked by the Catholic Worker and the power of nonviolence. Through the spring of 1957, as I thought more about that electrifying act of conscience, I experienced a deep moral shock.

Although I had been in the U.S. army, I had remained unconscious of the evil of nuclear war. It took the power of nonviolence to awaken my conscience. The Catholic Worker's act of nonviolent resistance forced me to recognize in my heart the evil capacity we as humans have to annihilate life on earth by nuclear war. The example of the Worker also forced me to see the outlines of an alternative: the power of nonviolence proclaimed and lived by Jesus. Thirty years later alongside these nuclear train tracks, I am still struggling with those two realizations, the profound evil of nuclear war and the transforming power of the cross. Reading this book has brought it all home again to Dorothy Day and the Catholic Worker.

Christ *is* the poor. He is also our enemy. We are to love our enemies and the poor, and discover God through those encounters. This double scandal of the gospel has been lived out daily by the Catholic Worker. These essays on the Catholic Worker invite us to discover the transforming power of a nonviolent gospel through experiments in our own lives.

What the Catholic Worker holds up for all of us is a new way of living for the sake of life itself.

ACKNOWLEDGMENTS

IN OFFERING THIS initial acknowledgment, I trust I speak for all the contributors in thanking Marquette University archivist Phil Runkel. I know of no one who has done serious study of the Catholic Worker movement who has not been aided by him. His knowledge of the movement's history is encyclopedic, and his graciousness in responding to requests for help never falters. The Catholic Worker papers are in good and loving hands.

On a more personal level, I owe a debt of thanks to the secretaries of Campus Ministry at St. Louis University, who have generously lent their considerable clerical skills. Mary Ruth Ryan has been especially helpful, and characteristically patient with the often unwieldly nature of both this project and my longhand. While I am, of course, thankful for the help of all the contributors, Nancy Roberts and Anne Klejment have consistently provided me with support, encouragement, and sound advice. This would be a weaker collection without their keen interest and insights. I am fortunate to belong to a writers' support group dubbed "The Stinklings." Our gatherings have been a joy and a source of creative stimulation for me thanks to Belden Lane, Janice Brandon-Falcone, Bernhard Asen, and Jeannette Batz, who also lent her sharp editor's eye to early drafts of my sections of the collection. My editor at Temple, Jane Cullen, has been generous with her patience, enthusiasm, and valuable editorial advice. The same holds true for many of her colleagues at Temple, especially Jennifer French and Ann Marie Anderson. The beautiful artwork which graces these pages is the gift of three artists. My sincere thanks to Adé Bethune, Fritz Eichenberg, and Larry Nolte.

I am especially grateful for the guests and community members of the Karen Catholic Worker House in St. Louis with whom I have lived and worked these past five years. Ours is a community blessed with talented people willing to be vulnerable in Christian service and community. They have consistently both affirmed and challenged me, and I know of no greater gifts than these. In particular, I owe a deep debt of gratitude to Mark Scheu, a Catholic Worker of considerable integrity and devotion. Mark's friendship, support, and critical advice have been immeasurable over the four-year period it has taken to bring this book into being. Karin Tanquist has also provided encouragement but, more importantly, her patience and understanding of what this project has meant to me is of the sort that is only born of love.

Finally, my late father, Glenn Coy, gifted me with a love of knowledge, and an uncommon degree of trust, for which I will always be grateful.

INTRODUCTION

Patrick G. Coy

As I write from the kitchen of one of three Catholic Worker houses in the St. Louis ghetto, the sounds of the city filter up to our second-floor kitchen window, reminding me of the genesis of the Catholic Worker movement in New York City in 1933. A steady stream of street merchants pass by our house, pushing heavily laden grocery-store shopping carts. Their eyes dart to and fro on a vigilant search of the gutter and the vacant, deserted lots piled with urban rubble that lie behind the curb. It is not groceries that fill their supermarket carts, but the discarded aluminum cans they so diligently pursue among the dirt and trash of gutter and garbage can. They push a colorful kaleidoscope of cans, nearly matched by the clothes they wear. Their out-of-fashion and ill-fitting clothes were most likely obtained free from our clothing room at Karen House. Even though the clothing and the cans are both still quite serviceable, they are treated as castoffs, items deemed superfluous by our acquisitive, throwaway society. An indicting irony emerges: societal castoffs relegated to wearing and collecting castoffs.

The destination for these urban pilgrims is the recycling center located two blocks down Mullanphy Street in our old Irish-German neighborhood. There, they will exchange long days of hard, dirty labor—miles upon miles of street walking and hours of dumpster rummaging—for at most a couple of dollars. At an exchange rate of twenty cents per pound, their aluminum cans each fetch just a bit more than a penny a piece. Little more than crumbs thrown from a bountiful table, pennies hardly worth stooping over for, many would surely say.

This situation, this hard human reality, created by a society that values profits and production before people, evinces the continued need for the radical and ultimately timeless vision of the Catholic Worker movement. More than half a century ago, it was the desire to build a better system than this—to create both a personal and a social order where the spiritual was not subordinated to the material, and where it would consequently be easier for people to be good—that anchored the vision of Peter Maurin, the cofounder of the Catholic Worker.

In December 1932, Dorothy Day took a bus to Washington, D.C., to cover the Hunger March of the jobless. Still young in her conversion to Catholicism, the veteran journalist and activist was filled with emotion as thousands of the nation's unemployed marched in the communist-organized demonstration. She knew their demands for food, meaningful work, and a just wage had to be met; these were fundamental human rights. A deep sense of solidarity and compassion fueled her desire to serve those most precious in God's sight, the least of her sisters and brothers. But how was she—a recent convert—to do it? What path of service did the church offer her, and what promise did it speak to these poor hungry ones?

The next day was December 8, the feast of the Immaculate Conception. Nearly broken in spirit, Dorothy Day did what she was to do throughout her long life: she turned to the spiritual riches of the Christian tradition, and made a pilgrimage. It was to the National Shrine of the Immaculate Conception at Catholic University. There, in painful prayer, she searched her heart and her church. "I offered up a special prayer," she later wrote, "a prayer which came with tears and anguish, that some way would open up for me to use what talents I possessed for my fellow workers, for the poor."

Back home in New York City the very next day, Dorothy Day met Peter Maurin, and together they started the Catholic Worker movement. The history of the movement, and the biographical details of Maurin's and Day's lives, have been amply told in studies that are easily accessible elsewhere. Indeed, Dorothy Day and the Catholic Worker movement have spawned a growing body of secondary literature that is itself significant.

The present collection of essays is designed to fill some of the gaps in Catholic Worker scholarship, examining particular themes, events, and people in greater detail. Many who have studied the Catholic Worker movement would agree that its identity is often elusive, due in part to its personalist, decentralized nature. Consequently, generalizations about the Worker movement deserve some suspicion from the outset. The result is an ongoing need for fresh studies and approaches to even familiar dimensions of Worker history and practice.

Perhaps of greater significance is the fact that the Catholic Worker tradition is alive and growing. New manifestations continue to pop up across the land, like spongy toadstools responding to the moisture left by an early summer rain. The Catholic Worker remains a tradition in critical dialogue with the larger culture; it continues to evolve and be formed by this dialogue, just as the critique it offers continues to influence both church and society. As trenchant as Day's and Maurin's cultural critique was, Day especially retained a healthy respect for the larger culture. She had a deep appreciation of our worldliness, of the inescapable fact that we are embedded in the culture; and she delighted in and celebrated much of it. This mixture of critique and respect, this ongoing critical dialogue between the Worker ideal and society highlights the need to continue probing the movement's past and present, overturning both new and old stones, increasing our understanding of the ideas and lives of those who shape and attempt to live the Worker ideal.

The Worker has always been a movement in development, responding to new, concrete situations through the application of specific gospel principles. Of primary importance in the Catholic Worker's attempt to bring the social order to Christ, is the need for each individual to perform the spiritual and corporal works of mercy in a personalized manner, and with whatever sacrifice that entails. Complementing this first precept is the call to witness to the nonviolent love ethic of Jesus in relationships, in hospitality houses, on picket lines, and in politics. A third general principle is the mandate to live a life of relative simplicity in solidarity with the poor, those whom Peter Maurin called "the ambassadors of God."

The personalist emphasis of the first principle has resulted in a wide range of Worker communities, each with their own peculiar perspectives and particular ministries. This is perhaps truer today than it ever has been. There are growing numbers of communities focusing on such varied vocations as prison ministries, urban and rural land trusts, building resistance communities, providing legal and medical aid, working with Central American refugees through the sanctuary movement, building sustainable farms and cottage industries, working with the developmentally disabled, etc. And, of course, the long-held emphasis on providing food, shelter, and clothing to the urban homeless remains for many central to the Catholic Worker vocation.

This is a movement very much alive as it enters its mid-fifties, continuing to offer its cultural critique in a very concrete manner: through the broad daily work of its many communities. It is a developing tradition marked by openness and flexibility. People come and join in the work of the communities, are formed by the experience, and leave to become part of the larger, extended Catholic Worker family. Oftentimes these people continue to participate directly in the work of the houses; even more choose to contribute financially to allow the work to continue. Others, heeding a call to serve elsewhere, find new models, ones perhaps more appropriate for them to live out the gospel injunction of loving service. But they still often retain an abiding interest in the Worker, having been shaped and molded by it. They are replaced by new Workers, some long and some short in years, each bringing new life and energy to the work. Put another way, it is a dynamic and organic tradition, centered in the grassroots experience of the laity trying to work out their salvation in the modern world.

Given this open, dynamic nature of the movement, the need for and shape of the present anthology becomes clearer. By design, this collection draws on voices both inside and outside the movement and from the extended Worker family as well. The book is at once theoretical and concrete, providing a forum for both the scholar and the worker. The contributors have an analytical eye trained on the movement's past, but they ignore neither the present nor the future. Peter Maurin called for roundtable discussions for the clarification of thought and action. It is in this sense that I hope this book will itself be a contribution to and a participation in the Catholic Worker idea.

If a tradition is truly alive, it necessarily draws its life and sustenance from the intersection of its past with the present. We must know where we have come from in order to discern where we are heading. The aluminum can collectors shuffling down St. Louis's Mullanphy Street remind us that, in many ways, very little has changed in the socioeconomic world of the United States. Many of the same problems and tragic human realities that so moved both Day and Maurin remain today. The poor, it seems, we will always have with us. But the Catholic Worker solution of trying to literally follow the precepts of the Sermon on the Mount is a timeless one. Its truth transcends the particulars of historical circumstance. Like the poor, the truth of Christ's life and message will always be with us.

Yet the world of the latter 1980s is a different world than that of Day and Maurin. Peter died in 1949, Dorothy in 1981. Issues confronting Day and the rest of the Worker communities of her time are often less important now. In their places have arisen new problems, or newer versions of old problems. Perhaps most important is the fact that the U.S. Catholic church has changed so dramatically in the last half of the twentieth century. A good example of this is the long, persistent struggle of Day and her *Catholic Worker* paper to convince the immigrant and patriotically suspect U.S. Catholic church that pacifism is at the heart of Christ's call to unconditional love of friend and foe. In their 1983 pastoral letter, "The Challenge of Peace: God's Promise and Our Response," the U.S. Catholic bishops went partway and affirmed that pacifism is indeed a viable Catholic Christian stance toward war and violence. But so is nuclear deterrence a viable and moral approach, according to the bishops. So the problem remains, albeit in somewhat altered form. It is further complicated by the technological developments in first-strike weaponry and the obfuscation created by Ronald Reagan's "defensive" Strategic Defense Initiative, with its hollow promise of making nuclear deterrence obsolete.

Peter Maurin's vision was rooted in Catholic social teachings. He was a layman who developed a program of service and social change *within* the church. He took the church's teachings seriously and allowed them to make demands on his life. Dorothy Day had such a deep desire to serve God's poor within her chosen church that when she found no established vehicle to do that with, she moved ahead, in faith, and cofounded with Maurin her own lay movement. She created her own niche, publishing a paper and providing shelter for those on the street.

For Day and Maurin, the question of the role of the laity in the church was simply not of direct concern. They had created their movement, their vehicle for participation in the work of the gospel and the life of the church, so it was not a burning issue for them. But that is not true for many associated with the Worker today. The question of lay participation and the structure of the church stand in greater relief not just within the Worker but within the larger church as well. Because various Worker communities are struggling with such important issues as feminism, lay rights in the church, official church teachings on abortion and homosexuality, and what the "Catholic" in Catholic Worker means, this should be seen as a sign of health for a spiritually alive movement. Many of the same issues are, after all, on the cutting edge of the larger church. The Catholic Worker is not, and never has been, an island cut off from the church mainland. It is in many respects a microcosm of the larger church, reflecting the universal in the particular. To expect it to be otherwise would be unfair. For it, in fact, to be otherwise, would be a clear sign of danger to its continued health as a spiritual movement of any significance.

These are only a few examples of newer versions of old problems that face the Worker and the church. The central, timeless problem remains: how to give glory and honor to God by living a life centered on the love of God, self, and neighbor. All these questions, new and old, demand discussion and clarification. It is my hope that this collection will contribute to that important process by providing a historical perspective on certain elements of the movement and by conveying a small bit of its rich, collective wisdom.

In a broader framework, Harvey Cox persuasively argues in *Religion in the Secular City: Towards a Post Modern Theology* (1984), that much of what is currently vital in the religious world springs from small, voluntaristic groups and communities that come together both for a deepened spirituality and a passion for social justice.

Seven years after the death of Day, the Worker movement presses forward with its peculiar experiment in truth: trying to live out the gospel call to unconditional love in community with the poor and marginalized. It is as large a movement as it has ever been. A 1985 survey by the Des Moines Catholic Worker listed over ninety Catholic Worker houses of hospitality and farms scattered about the country. The Worker is, quite clearly, part of that broader movement afoot in the religious world that Cox names as especially vital. Its historical and ongoing witness has much to offer the contemporary world where many are forced to subsist by rummaging through trash for throw-away aluminum, and where peace and security are sought in the literally dead end of Star Wars technology.

THIS BOOK IS divided fairly clearly into three sections. The first, "The Individuals," focuses on three of the major figures in the movement's history. It begins with Peter Maurin, who provided much of the philosophical underpinnings of the movement's various programs. Marc Ellis's tightly argued lead essay reveals the continuing relevance of Maurin's incisive critique of modern culture. Reactionary in some aspects, progressive in others, Maurin is, for a variety of reasons, not easy to categorize. Ellis's method is to emphasize the spiritual roots of Maurin's thought, especially the foundational role that discipleship to Christ played in his life. In the process, the significant and too-little understood influence of Francis of Assisi on Maurin is highlighted. A detailed look at Maurin's storefront experiment in Harlem in 1934 buttresses Ellis's argument that it was Maurin's tendency to translate his vision into activity that defined both the uniqueness and limitations of his witness. Although Dorothy Day's views on violence and war are quite well known, Maurin's are much less so; Ellis opens a window onto Maurin's position on these crucial questions. He ends with a reflection on the contemporary relevance of Maurin's witness for community and commitment, situating the Catholic Worker in a broader movement of spiritual awakening that includes the Basic Christian Communities of the Third World.

Maurin was a synthetic thinker, deriving his program from a variety of sources. Deeply rooted in the spirituality of Francis, drawn to the simple life of voluntary poverty that so marked the man from Assisi, Maurin also relied on the philosophy of Thomas Aquinas. Geoffrey B. Gneuhs offers an essay that links Maurin's understanding of the primacy of the human person to the future of democracy. Drawing on Thomas Aquinas's doctrine of the common good, Maurin held that the human person, created in the image and likeness of God, must order all human activity, whether that be political, social, economic, or religious. Gneuhs argues that Maurin understood problems in any of these areas to be, ultimately, spiritual problems. He advocated a personalist decentralism and economic democracy as a vital prerequisite for a person's meaningful participation in the world of economics and labor. Maurin saw economic power as essential for each individual: without it, one was not free. In the final section of the essay, Gnuehs reveals the ongoing significance of Maurin's social philosophy. He suggests and explains three contemporary manifestations of Maurin's principles: the Solidarity movement in Poland; the Mondragon experiment in Spain; and the growing number of employee stock ownership programs in the United States.

Eileen Egan's wide-ranging essay on Dorothy Day gives an inside and very original view of Day's world travels on behalf of peace. Egan was her frequent companion on these peace pilgrimages, which included trips to Rome, Australia, London, Cuba, India, and California to be with the United Farm Workers. We are treated to some rich, concrete detail here, of experiences, conversations, and events that were crucially important to Dorothy Day. An especially significant section is Egan's recounting of Day's participation in the witness and fast in Rome for the peace and war discussions during the Second Vatican Council. The lobbying, church politicking, fasting, and prayer by church peace activists that eventually helped obtain a condemnation of nuclear war in the council documents make for particularly interesting reading. It is written with the verve that can come only from one who was in the thick of it with Day, as Egan was. But before taking us with her on her travels with Day, Egan sets an interpretive framework for Catholic Worker pacifism, examining the New Testament and early church influences on Day's spirituality. These roots are exposed through a detailed look at Day's position on the Spanish Civil War, conscription, and conscientious objection, and on her pacifist response to World War II and the Cold War. She argues that Day persisted in fidelity to pacifism as the foundation and heart of the Worker movement, and that ultimately it was this persistence that enabled Day and the Worker to revive the nonviolent tradition in the Catholic church.

Nancy Roberts follows with an essay focussing on Dorothy Day as a journalist and on the significance of the *Catholic Worker* in U.S. reform journalism history. Offering examples of Day's writing, she shows her to be a writer of considerable stature and diversity. Day could write muckraking pieces, analyses and commentaries, personal columns, and fiction. Always, she knew how to tell a story in a conversational style, with a grace and humor that had broad popular appeal. Roberts argues that the journalistic vocation was central to Day as a tool to achieve social and spiritual change. Through the written word, she sought to awaken people not only to the plight of the world but to their own spiritual condition. Hers was an advocacy journalism marked by a deep and distinctive religious faith. Roberts also examines and interprets Day's relations with church officials, particularly vis-à-vis her singular position as a radical Catholic journalist and a single parent laywoman convert.

The first section closes with my essay on Ammon Hennacy. Hennacy was a central figure in the Catholic Worker movement from the late 1940s to the late 1960s. A well-known Christian anarchist before joining the Worker, Hennacy was a classic American rebel, steeped in the rich history of U.S. social dissent. Tracing his evolution from socialism to Christian anarchism, I focus on the interlocking nature of his anarchism and pacifism; he simply couldn't be one without the other. Both his anarchism and pacifism achieved their attractiveness and moral weight in Hennacy's attempt to approximate in his daily life the ideals he so deeply cherished. I offer some critical reflections on the tenacious way he clung to his convictions and examine his relationship to the Catholic Worker, to the institutional church, and to the larger peace movement. Throughout, I try to let the man speak for himself, which he certainly did at great length, but always engagingly and with clever wit.

In Part II, entitled "Of Politics, Pacifism, and Spirituality," some of the most critically important themes of the Catholic Worker are explored. To make sense of the many ironies that attend the movement, Mel Piehl's erudite essay considers the Worker as an experiment in Christian free obedience. He situates the Worker in a series of broad yet specific interpretive categories, comparing and contrasting it to other religious, political, and ethical movements. Piehl answers the question: how is the Worker able to combine its spiritual and political witness in a way that asserts the autonomy and priority of religion, yet remain fully engaged with the most difficult and controversial affairs of actual political existence? This is a significant and recurring question in U.S. religious history. He argues that the Worker was singularly creative in its relation of politics and religion, and that this creative relation has been achieved through the movement's Catholic orthodoxy and obedience to the church. This orthodoxy was no constraint for the Worker; it was an expression of spiritual freedom, which resulted in the Worker being able to enjoy, as a lay movement, genuine political freedom. That political freedom, according to Piehl, is derived as well from the moral integrity of daily life at the Worker houses, where performing the works of mercy is the norm. Piehl shows how the Worker's hard-won spiritual and political freedom has been used to infuse uncompromised spiritual and ethical values directly into the heart of public life.

Daniel DiDomizio follows with a perceptive study of the spirituality of the Catholic Worker. He begins with a series of methodological questions: What are the sources proper to the study of a movement's spirituality? Are they voices, events, deeds and literature that are internal to the movement, external, or some combination? What is peculiar to a spirituality named "prophetic"; how does that determine one's methodology in studying and describing it? DiDomizio's own methodology is inclusive in scope, drawing on a wide range of sources as he examines how Catholic Worker spirituality has influenced U.S. Catholic culture and spirituality. He locates Worker spirituality in the life of voluntary poverty, hospitality, and pacifism, and in the intersection between a strong sense of community and a spirit of personal autonomy and responsibility. In his careful exposition of these central facets of Worker life, DiDomizio attends to both the successes and failures present in the attempt to live out this spirituality. In the process, he argues that each of them, whether realized or not, stands in stark contrast to the national ethos. He closes with some insightful reflections on the dilemna present in "evaluating" the successes or failures of prophetic spiritualities such as the Catholic Worker.

In the history of the United States, no other group or movement has experimented with the daily living out of the nonviolent ideal to the extent the Catholic Worker has in its hospitality houses. Day after day for more than fifty years, Catholic Workers have practiced the dynamics of nonviolence on soup lines and in alleyways, concretely applying nonviolent principles and reflecting on the results. In our essay, Angie O'Gorman and I have gathered some of the movement's collective wisdom on nonviolence. We maintain it is a wisdom both wide and deep, one born out of an elusive wedding of theory and praxis. In daily dealings with angry, violent guests, Workers have learned much about what contributes to either disarming or escalating violent encounters. The respective roles of personal vulnerability, sexual politics, physical touch, fear, paternalism, grace, the existence of a prior relationship with the adversary, trust, knowledge of when to intervene, and more are culled from the nonviolent experiments of individual Workers. The data is analyzed not only in terms of what has worked and what hasn't, but it is placed in the broader framework of Catholic Worker theology. We argue it is an incarnational theology, whose emphasis on the mystical body of Christ is integral to the Worker experiment in nonviolence.

We drew on our own personal experiences of living at the Worker, and gathered material from the newspapers of various houses. We also surveyed individuals directly by phone, letter, and taped interview. We deliberately avoided relying on the New York paper and community, believing that Catholic Worker scholarship has long suffered from an overemphasis on the New York houses. Such overemphasis, while understandable in certain respects, does its own sort of violence to the nature of the Worker movement: it is a decentralized movement founded on a doctrine of personal responsibility that has spawned a long litany of independent hospitality houses, each striving to live out the Worker ideal in its own way, within its own *Sitz im Leben*. To ignore the litany is to fail to enter into the spirit of the prayer.

The final essay in this section traces the evolution of Catholic Worker pacifism vis-à-vis the draftboard raid movement led by Philip and Daniel Berrigan in resistance to the Indochina War. Did the *Catholic Worker* support the draftboard raids and their resultant property destruction as a viable nonviolent tactic? What was Dorothy Day's position? Was it the same in public and private? How much did it change over time? These are only some of the questions Anne Klejment answers in a thought-provoking article that breaks significant new ground. After analyzing the Catholic Worker's relationship to the larger peace movement, Klejment probes the relationship of the Berrigan brothers and the draft-board raid movement to the Worker. Her analysis shows there were deep similarities in the aims of the two groups—to end the war and change U.S. society—and significant differences in the means and tactics employed to bring these goals about. The two movements had, according to Klejment, often conflicting approaches to questions on the role of community in resistance, the viability of state authority and the court system, the style of defense employed in trials, limits to property destruction, coercion and the role of individual conscience, and more.

The draft board raid movement has evolved into another resistance movement that the Berrigans play a central role in: the Plowshares, where nuclear warheads are symbolically damaged in nonviolent acts of civil disobedience. The Plowshares movement's emphasis on resistance in community is but one example of why Klejment says the current movement is much closer to the Worker than the Vietnam-era movement was. Given that many Plowshares activists are members of Catholic Worker communities, Klejment's chapter is a particularly timely and significant contribution.

Part III offers two case histories: one of the Catholic Worker presence in Chicago, the other of the St. Louis house before and during World War II. This section, though modest in size and scope, points to an untraveled path in Catholic Worker scholarship. Very little has been published on the life of the communities outside New York, even though their existence over the years has contributed markedly to the importance of the movement.

In the first essay, Janice Brandon-Falcone examines one community—the early St. Louis group—which is somewhat paradigmatic of many houses operating across the country in the 1930s and 1940s. They boasted shoestring beginnings and a large soupline, a failed farming venture and its dead dreams, involvement in labor issues and strike solidarity, a keen interest in the intersection between liturgy and social action, and a series of crisis and internal struggles that threatened their work. This is the stuff of which Catholic Worker history in the 1930s and 1940s was made. The fledgling experimental status of the movement was often reflected in the life of individual Worker communities. Relying on oral interviews with the members, Falcone looks at the hesitant beginnings of the group, examines their motivations, and follows these old-time Workers into the present, revealing the continuing influence Dorothy Day and the Catholic Worker have on them. In interpreting the St. Louis Worker, where an especially keen interest in prayer and liturgy was central to the group's aim, Falcone focuses on the sacramental nature of the experiment and on the dialectic between the works of mercy and the spiritual life.

The Chicago Catholic Worker presence has been much less paradigmatic. Frank Sicius reveals a pointed difference between the philosophy of the early Chicago house run by Dr. Arthur Falls, and the anarchistic thought of Dorothy Day and the larger movement. What was right for radical white Catholics imbued with a critical class consciousness was not right for a black medical doctor struggling to empower his people in the urban jungle of Chicago in the 1930s. Still, a Catholic Worker house it was, for over ten years. Sicius also documents the rise and fall of another, more well-known prewar Chicago house that counted among its community such notables as John Cogley, Tom Sullivan, Jim O'Gara, and Ed Marciniak. It, too, differed from Day's philosophy, most notably on the questions of the industrial union movement and pacifism. It was this group of young Workers who, with their paper, the *Chicago Catholic Worker*, publicly differed with Day on pacifism in the light of Hitler's Nazi Germany. Sicius notes that to attend to the existence of these differences and disagreements in the history of the Worker is simply to help define more fully the nature of the movement. His essay closes with a short look at the Chicago Worker's new beginnings during the Karl Meyer period of the 1960s and beyond. The entire piece reveals that the influence exerted both locally and nationally by the Chicago Catholic Worker was significant indeed.

Many have first been led to the Worker through reading about it. The various Catholic Worker papers, Day's books, and other books about the movement have long been an important part of the tradition, inviting and challenging many to examine the intersection between spirituality and politics in their own lives. In the final analysis, I hope this collection will do more than merely fill some gaps in Catholic Worker scholarship.

May the reading of this book be an occasion of grace, such that readers experience the invitation and challenge of the Catholic Worker idea, and are led to their own revolution of the heart. For as long as the hope of the poor is crushed by the immense weight of a U.S. military budget in excess of $300 billion annually, the voluntary poverty of Dorothy Day will remain a spiritual weapon of considerable import. As long as urban pilgrims shuffle down St. Louis's Mullanphy Street and are forced to "make a living" scavenging aluminum cans, the radical idea of the Catholic Worker remains relevant. And as long as people are given the grace to hear the gospel call to love and service, the Worker remains as a dwelling place for Christians in the modern world to heed that timeless call.

I

The Individuals

1. PETER MAURIN

To Bring the Social Order to Christ

Marc H. Ellis

FOR SOME TIME now, Peter Maurin and Dorothy Day, along with the Catholic Worker movement they founded, have been thought by many to exemplify the prophetic voice in the twentieth century. To the massive bureaucratic organization of industry and government, they propose a personal, decentralized society. To an urban-acquisitive economy, whether capitalist or secular communist, they propose a village-functional economy. To a secular and rights-oriented mentality, they propose the spiritual as the center of life and obligation to neighbor as its corollary. To a world armed to protect markets and national security, they propose disarmament and the refusal to harm even those who are "enemy." However, the Catholic Worker movement is not without critics. For some, despite respect for the people involved, the movement demonstrates the limitation of any such voice in the modern world. The problems raised are important. Does a small movement, founded in the Depression, emphasizing personalism and the land, hold any hope for the massive social reconstruction necessary in an urban-bureaucrat age? Does a movement that rejects the foundations of the modern world—government, bureaucratic institutions, industry—say anything of consequence to our time? Is a movement that speaks in the language of Roman Catholic faith able to communicate to a religiously pluralistic, even secular, nation and world?

The Catholic Worker's growth in American culture similarly raises important questions about the efficacy and survival of radical spirituality. If America is born of the Protestant Reformation and the Enlightenment, and if the West is still being shaped by these movements, what future do prophetic voices and movements have? A discussion of the orienting ideas of the Catholic Worker movement may shed light on these questions.

As COFOUNDERS OF the Catholic Worker movement, both Peter Maurin and Dorothy Day influenced its direction and spirit; but the impetus behind it, and the ideas the movement embodied, came from Maurin. He was a French peasant who emigrated to Canada and then the United States in search of his Christian vocation. His objective had eluded him in France despite his strong Catholic upbringing and his fitful tenure as a Christian Brother during the first decade of this century. Only in the aftermath of World War I and the subsequent world depression did Maurin find clarification of how Christian ideals could be realized in personal and social life.[1]

On the surface, Maurin's ideas seem idealistic, even simplistic; yet on another level they are almost prophetic. To an urban-industrial society in the midst of depression Maurin proposed embracing a village economy, where crafts, farming, and a personal way of life could be established. The foundation of this life is a religious affirmation from which flow prayer and communal sharing; it is centered in a simplicity that Maurin called voluntary poverty. Poverty, in Maurin's view, opened one to the call of God and neighbor and made the person and the community dependent on both.

Maurin's vision of community was neither evolutionary nor progressive, and the appetite of modernity in pursuit of power held no allure for him. Instead, Maurin's vision was to live in harmony with others, to share what manual and intellectual labor produced, to be silent and to worship in community. Maurin's sense of commitment was also a dissent. He did not share the hopes of secular radicals and liberals, for they were seeking to increase and distribute the material abundance of industrial life to a humanity freed from the spiritual. The basis of Maurin's commitment, in contrast, was renunciation and sacrifice exemplified in the life and crucifixion of Jesus. In this life of spirit and sacrifice Maurin saw the only possibility of recapturing the integrity of the person and bringing about authentic social reform.[2]

Still, to see Maurin simply as a dissenter against modernity is to miss the foundation of his mission and life. To enter into the life and death of Jesus is to affirm a spiritual reality, to become a disciple, and Maurin was, more than anything else, a disciple of Christ. His discipleship was the center from which his social apostolate arose rather than a peripheral attachment to an otherwise developed program of social reform. It formed the basis of his oft-repeated statement that his own word was tradition, not revolution—though, he would hasten to add, tradition made dynamic and faithful to its calling to represent Christ in the world.

For Maurin, the Catholic tradition illumined the darkness of the modern age by providing cultural continuity to the Western world, by critiquing the present, and by forming the basis for a new social order. The Catholic tradition first provided the Western world with a sense of continuity. The problems of modern life could be directly linked to the denial of the role of tradition in providing continuity; the Enlightenment, Maurin often said, was a prime example of such denial. Loss of tradition meant more than simply secularization, for with secularization, economic, military, and political systems were detached from the guidance of the spirit and thus free of the protection afforded the person by the canopy of eternity. For Maurin, tradition held worldly systems at bay, molding them to serve rather than oppress the person.

Tradition also contained the resources needed to critique the present, thus serving to upset the bias of contemporary culture. Modern society stresses competition and profit; the Hebrew prophets and the church fathers spoke for the poor and pronounced judgment on the affluent. The aim of modern life is to find ease and luxury even at the expense of others. Jesus exemplified the meaning of selfless suffering for neighbor as the path to salvation. The lure of modernity is the accumulation and organization of the material world; St. Francis abandoned everything to follow the spirit and to love more profoundly.[3]

For Maurin, however, the Catholic tradition offered more than continuity and critique as it provided the resources for personal and societal transformation. Jesus is at the center of this transformation, and to thus believe is to enter a new life of love and service. A person who follows Jesus is intimately involved in the life of a people who have been called to transform self and bid others to enter that transformation. Communities of Christians are formed precisely for these reasons; to praise God, to order personal life, and to reorder the large social life.

Maurin cited two examples from the past to demonstrate the efficacy of Christians gathering in community. The first was that of the early Christians who, in a hostile world, suffered for their beliefs and served neighbor at a personal sacrifice. They took seriously the counsel of Jesus to love and serve neighbor by doing the works of mercy—feeding the hungry, clothing the naked, sheltering the homeless, visiting the sick and the prisoner, and instructing the ignorant. As witnesses to truth and commitment, these communities attracted followers and finally triumphed over the surrounding hostile culture. The second example Maurin used was that of the Irish monks who, in the midst of a disintegrating and dying Roman culture, witnessed to a future beyond the chaos of their time. Through the establishment of agrarian and educational communities, they laid the foundations of a new society, medieval Christendom. Thus Maurin envisioned the seeds of change sprouting from below to subvert the dominant culture through witness and perseverance. These examples of societal transformation formed the foundations of Maurin's program to transform the social order: Roundtable discussions in community centers to clarify thought and initiate action; houses of hospitality to carry out works of mercy in service to the needs and as witness to the larger community; finally, farming communes to introduce urban civilization to the simplicity and spirituality of life on the land.[4]

Maurin's preoccupation with the social order needs to be placed in perspective. Though he lived his last years as an agitator, Maurin was distinct from many twentieth-century secular social activists. He thought that the social order had a singular mission: to protect and nurture the person's journey toward the mystery of God, thus promoting the possibility of salvation. The social order existed to mirror and express the spiritual dimensions of the person. The trappings of an order built for itself—large-scale industry, affluence, and militarism—were to disappear in Maurin's future society.

Maurin's final hope was that the tradition of the Catholic church— a tradition alive and dynamic—would provide the context within which the person might embody this message of salvation. Holding true to the word of Jesus and representing his voice in the world, the church could do nothing less and in effect could do nothing more, for there was nothing else to be done but to preach *and* embody this message.

Maurin took this understanding of the personal embodiment of the message of salvation so seriously that his last years were formed around it. By 1930, at the age of fifty-three, Maurin gave up everything—home, status, and comfort—to pursue a life of agitation and charity. When he came to New York City to speak on street corners, he came as a poor man and slept in Bowery hotels. Maurin insisted that the practice of poverty be the foundation of the Catholic Worker movement.[5]

THE INFLUENCE OF Francis of Assisi in Maurin's life was considerable. The "clarification" Maurin experienced in the 1920s, which
saw him change from a teacher of French in Chicago to an itinerant
philosopher and handyman in upstate New York, coincided with a
worldwide revival of interest in the life of Francis and his own reading of Johannes Jorgensen's *Saint Francis of Assisi,* G, K. Chesterton's *St. Francis of Assisi,* and a series of papal encyclicals on Francis
beginning with Leo XIII's *St. Francis and the Third Order.* Maurin
not only read these works, he reflected on them. In one of his essays,
Maurin used Jorgensen's understanding of Francis as a pilgrim, a life
that Maurin chose to adopt.

> According to Johannes Jorgensen
> a Danish convert living in Assisi
> St. Francis desired
> that men should give up
> superfluous possessions.
> St. Francis desired
> that men should work with their hands.
> St. Francis desired
> that men should offer their services
> as a gift.
> St. Francis desired
> that men should ask other people for help
> when work failed them.
> St. Francis desired
> that men should go through life
> giving thanks to God for His gifts.[6]

Maurin emulated Francis's way of life. When he traveled around
the country to spread his word, Maurin often depended on others for
hospitality. As much as anything, Maurin's adoption of Franciscan
poverty was designed to free him to preach the gospel and stand as a
witness to a culture that prized affluence. His emphasis on faith and
contemplation as the foundation for rebuilding the church in a time
of crisis was basically Franciscan, as was his emphasis on obedience
to the Catholic church, a theme he found crucial to Francis's ability
to maintain his radicalism while avoiding sectarianism. Above all,
Maurin's personalism, his patience with those afflicted, and his
sense of joy compared favorably to, and received instruction from,
the life of Francis. What he felt Francis "desired" of others, Maurin
tried to live. He gave away superfluous goods, worked with his

hands, offered his services as a gift, and went through life giving thanks to God.

However, Maurin thought Francis to be more than a personal model. With the papal encyclicals on Francis, Maurin asserted that the mobilization of the Third Order, a lay group devoted to the Franciscan ideals, could contribute significantly to the reconstruction of the social realm. The revitalization of Franciscan piety could occasion a rebirth of the dynamic lay faith for which Francis had hoped, and which through the centuries had been diluted. To this end, Maurin insisted that the evangelical counsels of the gospels were for everybody and that the new society would be built on Franciscan qualities of creed, systematic unselfishness, and gentle personalism.[7]

As a modern follower of Francis, Maurin was profoundly at odds with the times in which he lived. While his desire for a new social order was prophetic, the central place of poverty in this new order proved a stumbling block for many. It was one thing to talk about Christians of the first century and the monasteries sacrificing for their faith and community in the practice of poverty; it was quite another to bring the community face to face with the call to be poor in the present. Should poverty be pursued in a time of worldwide depression? Did not the first Christians, the Irish monks, and Francis himself sacrifice so as to make sacrifice unnecessary for future generations? Was not the taking on of poverty placing undue emphasis on suffering?

Though the questions were many, the answers in Maurin's view were clear. One became poor because Jesus gave everything, even his life, to serve humankind. In his preaching Jesus spoke of the difficulty of the rich entering the kingdom, and in his pilgrimage had made the poor his own. To become poor was to follow Jesus and thus embody the message of salvation he preached. This embodiment of the message of salvation was a witness to others of the importance of the spiritual, bidding them to follow. The personal and voluntary adoption of a life of poverty was a witness to the community as well and posed the prophetic question of the community's orientation: to the material or the spiritual. By adopting poverty, the community embodied the message of salvation.

For Maurin, personal and community poverty was the road to the spirit and to freedom. If there was suffering within freedom, Jesus had suffered, too. The person was free in giving up superfluous goods because life was ordered to its proper end: prayer and service, not sensuality and egoism. And the community was free because it was no longer consumed with the material. Instead of pursuing profit through competition, the community fulfilled its primary function of encouraging cooperation and nurturing the spirituality of the person.

The freedom and the spirit that came in voluntary poverty was the most radical orientation possible and, when implemented in centuries past, caused significant, sometimes violent attempts to restructure social reality. Like others who had sought to emulate the saint from Assisi, Maurin saw Francis's poverty as eschatological. For to Maurin, Francis's vision of life, when embodied in the person *and* the community, broke through the constraints of history and institutional forms, radically questioning the lethargy and "giveness" of personal and social life. Francis thus represented the transformation that Maurin sought: a return by the person and the community to a total dependence on God. For Maurin, this included freeing the Catholic church and the Franciscan orders themselves from the bureaucratization that had diluted the radical demands of Jesus. Through Francis, Maurin wanted to move to the beginning and the end: the following of Jesus Christ.[8]

To Maurin, fidelity to Christ in the spirit meant fidelity to the body of Christ in the world, and in a world filled with injustice this was hardly easy. Participation in the body of Christ called forth a love of neighbor out of whom radiates the presence of God. To recognize the worth of the person in relation to God is to enter a dilemma: the changing of a social order that hinders the spiritual development of the person becomes a necessity; at the same time, the worth of the person renders violence unacceptable even in the movement toward reform. Incarnation means both reform and nonviolence.

Maurin was hardly alone in living this dilemma of social change and nonviolence; such notable figures as Martin Buber and Mahatma Gandhi also explored these questions within their own traditions. Arrived at independently, the conclusions of all three were similar. The world was moving into darkness; only by charting a radically new direction could the world survive. Paradoxically, this direction came through revival of those traditions the modern world labored to forget, traditions that gave persons their proper due by placing them within eternity. Buber's synagogue and Gandhi's ashram were, like Maurin's church, places of faith where the seeds of personal and societal conversion might be nurtured.

To see Maurin in relation to Buber and Gandhi might be difficult for some, at least at first. Buber was a great Jewish scholar, Gandhi a world-renowned leader of the independence struggle in India. Maurin was a little-known agitator who spent much of his time and energy with the unemployed and dispossessed on the street corners of New York City. But viewed from a different perspective, their commonality is worth noting: Maurin participated with Buber and

Gandhi in the revival of the prophetic tradition in the twentieth century, the essential outlines of which include a willingness to address directly and openly the questions of the day, to refuse the political and economic alternatives presented as "realistic," to attempt to recover the personal aspects of social and private life, to serve as a witness to and advocate for the poor and oppressed, and, finally, to move within the political realm while maintaining a religious vision. In more specific terms, Maurin shared with Buber and Gandhi the emphasis on the person, simplicity, decentralism, nonviolence, faith, and the land as the foundations of renewal.[9]

Maurin sought to promote change in both society and the human heart through a three-part program that became the foundation of the Catholic Worker movement. First, roundtable discussions for the clarification of thought were specifically designed to move beyond cultural clichés and prejudice by bringing all elements of the community—scholar, middle class, and worker—together. The gathering of people with diverse backgrounds, talents, and perspectives provided the context for arriving at a common understanding of present and future possibilities. Discussions focused on learning the ills of the present, determining how things should be in the ideal, and finally, discerning a path to move the social order from where it was to where it ought to be. A community setting mitigated the divisive class and status distinctions that stymied efforts to change the present.

The second part of Maurin's program was the development of houses of hospitality, an idea he derived from the Christian hospices found among early and medieval Christian communities. In these communities the stranger and the poor, the widow and the orphan, had been served by the more fortunate. The revival of such hospices served a variety of needs. Immediate problems of the Depression years could be answered, such as the need for shelter, clothing, and food for the dispossessed. Members of the middle class who came to the hospice and joined in its atmosphere of service and sacrifice gained insight into the human costs of the present social order because they were no longer isolated from the sufferings of the unemployed and the poor; for them, the "givenness" of the social order was demystified. Finally, hospices served a spiritual function; the more affluent participated in their own salvation by fulfilling Christ's command to love and serve neighbor.

The development of what Maurin called "agronomic universities," or farming communes, was the third part of his program, and perhaps the most controversial. These were centers located in the country to train urban dwellers in farming and crafts in order to pave the way for a general return to the land and a village way of life. Typically, there were several levels to Maurin's proposal. Farming communes could fulfill the immediate needs of people in the Depression years by providing free fuel and food, which, while scarce in the city, were abundant in the country. A return to the land could mitigate the technological and cyclical unemployment Maurin thought inherent in an industrial economy, contributing to a more stable and just social order. Moreover, subsistence farming and crafts centered the forces of production once again on need rather than profit, and so provided a basis for recovering the value of cooperation and the spiritual dimension of human existence.[10]

Maurin evolved a program that continually raised the most radical questions about personal and corporate life. By binding the fortunate to the poor in the service of hospitality, Maurin profoundly challenged personal and social conscience. By deeming it worthwhile, even salvific, to care personally for those whom society had abandoned, Maurin challenged every abstract and institutional way of dealing with the afflicted. However, to care for others at a personal sacrifice was not only to challenge social and economic systems, it was also to challenge perceptions of life and progress at the heart of contemporary personal and corporate existence.

This context of suffering and service fostered freedom from both cynicism and naive optimism in the roundtable discussions. Hospices catalyzed personal and social conscience so that the powers of the day, which in other contexts seemed overwhelming, fell to insignificance. If the poor were no longer abstractions, the self was no longer immune to suffering, either its own or that of others. This suffering brought both person and society closer to the source of their origin in God.

Maurin took the question of salvation so seriously that he thought personal and social life had to be oriented around it. To give up what was superfluous and to live personal and community life centered on the spiritual was to follow the way of salvation as preached by Jesus. The question was, What form of life nurtured this message and what diverted attention from it. For Maurin, contemporary life, with its urban-industrial base, organizational propensities, and search for affluence, hindered rather than nurtured humankind's quest for salvation. Maurin's strong belief in human freedom to respond to the message of salvation allowed him to think that, once the message was posed, personal and community life could and would revolve around it.[11]

A COMPLEMENTARITY OF backgrounds and gifts made the meeting of Maurin and Dorothy Day providential. If Maurin, a French peasant-intellectual wandering in America, had come to conclusions about the primacy of the spiritual in the world and the need for a social reconstruction to nurture the spiritual, Day, a former socialist who had experienced the new freedoms in the urban centers of America, had wandered and come to conclusions as well: the integrity of the person, she had concluded, was bound up in spiritual affirmation. Maurin, through inheritance and study, was imbued with the history and spirituality of the Catholic tradition; Day, because of her journalistic talents, could facilitate the dissemination of his ideas through print and, because of her strength of character, translate his understandings into the concrete by founding the Catholic Worker movement. She also added an urban orientation and concern for the industrial worker that Maurin lacked. The prophetic quality of their encounter can be measured by the depth of their spiritual calling: their readiness to abandon self; their ability to stand in opposition to the present as they affirmed a future; their will to persevere in success and failure; their inclusion of others in the search for personal and social salvation.[12]

The Catholic Worker movement, along with its newspaper, grew out of this encounter. Over its next fifty years the movement remained steadfast in its positions: the spirit is at the center of radical activity and community; a personal, agrarian way of life provides meaningful labor and a sense of communal sharing that nurtures the interior dimensions of the person and the social order; a subsistence and cooperative order provides the context for true freedom as opposed to the illusory freedom promised by a consumer-oriented, competitive order. The program designed to move toward the ideal has not changed either: discussions for the clarification of thought; hospices to serve the needs and witness to the larger community; farming communes to instruct urban dwellers on the efficacy and spirituality of life lived in community on the land. However, members of the Catholic Worker do not simply repeat these positions; they live them. To be for the poor and the outcast, they become poor. To testify to the obligations of faith, they serve others voluntarily and at a personal sacrifice in hospices around the country. To affirm the mystical body, they refuse violence to protect nations or self. To begin the movement back to the land, they form agrarian communities. Like the founders, members combine theory and practice in daily works of justice and mercy; that is the key to the Worker's prophetic witness.

The optimism of a newborn venture, and the singularity of its views among American Catholics in the 1930s, made the initial impact of the movement far greater than its numbers. By the mid-1930s, circulation of the *Catholic Worker* passed the 100,000 mark and was climbing, influencing young and old alike who were interested in a dynamic Catholicism. *Orate Fratres* (later *Worship*) greeted the appearance of the *Worker* with satisfaction. "It appears a veritable godsend in our time of social disintegration and unrest." What impressed *Orate Fratres* particularly was the Christian foundation and the "thoroughly Catholic spirit that breathes through its pages." John Toomey, a Jesuit, wrote an enthusiastic article for *America*, noting that "the response to the paper has been simply tremendous. It seemed from the beginning to voice the unspoken thoughts of millions." Priests were ordering bundles of the newspaper for their churches and sisters were buying it for their schools. Farmers, miners, and textile workers were reading it. A priest in Hamburg, Germany, was distributing one hundred copies every month to American and English seamen he found on the Hamburg docks, and lay people in Australia were distributing it there. Toomey concluded that month by month the *Catholic Worker*, the "little Catholic monitor, is pouring Encyclical fire into red and reactionary merrimacs."[13]

Maurin himself was the subject of several articles. J. G. Brunini, writing in *Commonweal*, termed Maurin an apostle to the radicals. Brunini described his technique, which had now become familiar to those gathered in Union Square:

> Maurin does not employ a soap-box. From audiences he questions socialist or communist speakers and defends the position of the Catholic Church. Or he will initiate a discussion with one or two or three bystanders, gradually collect a crowd and address it although ostensibly talking only to his original listeners.

The presence of communists at Maurin's talks had the value of making Catholic workers who otherwise would remain silent "decidedly articulate." In Brunini's view, this had the effect of strengthening their faith. He concluded that Maurin had initiated discussion for the clarification of thought that had been advocated by the recent popes.[14]

John LaFarge wrote affectionately though critically of Maurin in an article in *America*. Describing him as an elderly, peaceful man who wanted to apply ethics to the complicated question of wealth, LaFarge thought Maurin's language perfectly familiar five centuries ago but confusing in the present:

> It is as when you cannot ring a bell without getting a jarring resonance from a cracked window pane. . . . In a conference, let us say, on social surveys, or some other finely graduated thesis, when discussion begins to languish, Peter stands up—not very high and conspicuously inconspicuous—and

without further preludes tells the audience that "in the first
centuries of Christianity the poor were fed, clothed and sheltered at a personal sacrifice."[15]

Maurin would continue:

And because the poor
were fed, clothed, and sheltered
at a personal sacrifice,
the pagans used to say
about the Christians
"See how they love each other."
In our own day
the poor are no longer
fed, clothed, and sheltered
at a personal sacrifice
but at the expense
of the taxpayers.
And because the poor
are no longer
fed, clothed and sheltered
the pagans say about the Christians
"See how they pass the buck."[16]

It was particularly important to LaFarge that Maurin lived the life
of simplicity and poverty that he preached. Yet, while recognizing
Maurin's voice as prophetic, LaFarge also raised piercing questions.
What would Maurin do if he had a wife and six children to support?
Could the ideals he proposed be seriously entertained as a general
solution to the world's economic malaise? Maurin replied that these
ideals were something to strive toward, and, furthermore, that the
movement toward ideals could be accomplished only through discussion and clarification. Instead of providing blueprints, Maurin
hoped to raise questions that could not be ignored. If his vocation
was to live the single life, his farming communes, especially, were
designed for families as well. Though these questions remained
problematic to LaFarge, they did not lessen his respect for Maurin
and he promised to pray for the success of Maurin's still theoretical
farming communes.[17]

Others were praying for the success of Maurin's venture. In November 1934, Jacques Maritain, the French Thomistic philosopher,
visited the Worker and had several discussions with Maurin. Upon
leaving he wrote to Maurin:

I wish I could have said all that was in my heart—never was I more vexed by inability to speak fluent English. It seemed as if I had found again in the Catholic Worker a little of the atmosphere of Peguy's office in the Rue de la Sorbonne. And so much good will, such courage, such generosity! It is thus, with meagre means and great love, that the future for which we long is prepared.[18]

Maurin's essays were also beginning to reach a wider audience. In January and July 1934, *Catholic Mind* reprinted several of his essays dealing with the role of Catholic Action and the call for social reconstruction. At the same time Maurin's essays began to appear in pamphlet form printed by the Catholic Worker Press. These were penny and two-penny pamphlets ranging from two to thirty pages in length and included essays on hospitality, usury, and the works of mercy. The latter pamphlets were briefly noted in *Commonweal.*[19]

Another avenue for Maurin's essays was the development of the *Daily Catholic Worker*, an extension of the monthly publication. Instead of a printed newspaper eight to twelve pages in length, this was a mimeographed sheet distributed daily at the rate of a thousand a day. The typical daily carried provocative statements on the news of the day and concluded with one of Maurin's essays, though usually in shortened form. This experiment for agitation proposed by Maurin himself lasted little more than a month. Yet despite the brevity of its duration the paper gained attention, with *America* citing it as the first Catholic daily in New York City and important for those interested in the laborer's plight and the claims of social justice.[20]

Maurin's "Easy Essays" were becoming the trademark of the Catholic Worker movement. Designed to communicate important ideas in an understandable manner, they often formed word plays that were memorable and easy to recite. In their essence, though, these essays contained energy and urgency and were not without a critical edge toward the social order and the church. Perhaps Maurin's most notable essay was that published in the first edition of the *Catholic Worker* in May 1933:

Writing about the Catholic Church, a radical writer says: "Rome will have to do more than to play a waiting game; she will have to use some of the dynamic inherent in her message."

To blow the dynamite of a message is the only way to make the message dynamic.

> If the Catholic Church is not today the dominant social, dynamic force, it is because Catholic scholars have failed to blow the dynamite of the Church.
>
> Catholic scholars have taken the dynamite of the Church, have wrapped it up in nice phraseology, placed it in an hermetic container; and sat on the lid.
>
> It is about time to blow the lid off so the Catholic Church may again become the dominant social dynamic force.[21]

For Maurin, both the clergy and the laity were to blame for the failure to blow the dynamite of the church. The laity told the clergy to mind their own business, particularly in economic and political matters and to retreat to an ever-diminishing sphere of doctrine and morals. By assenting to this retreat, the clergy divorced itself from the people, neglecting to acquaint itself with and be among the masses. Because it was separated from the people, the clergy lost touch with the social order and failed to provide a sociology that was grounded in theology, one that would join faith and social reform. This discouraged Maurin, for it meant that the clergy was not capable of or interested in a technique of leadership and thus was unable to provide leadership for Catholic Action. Because of this failure of leadership people were leaving the church and becoming interested in Marxism and fascism.[22]

Maurin's evolving message also indicated his disappointment with the failure of certain papal encyclicals, such as *Forty Years After*, which were more organizational in their approach and did not uphold the ideal of personal responsibility voiced by the encyclicals on St. Francis. It was as though "a sad and weary father said to his children who warred continually on one another: you will not follow the ideal so I will present to you another program—organization." During meetings at the Catholic Worker School, when speakers would affirm papal support for the New Deal, Maurin would rise and say, "The great danger of the present day is fascism and the tendency of all organization is to lead to fascism."[23]

Maurin's criticism was always balanced with pursuit of constructive proposals: blowing the dynamite had practical consequences and demanded a path which others could follow. Maurin's "Open Letter to the Bishops of the United States" published in the October 1933 issue of the *Catholic Worker*, points to this balance.

The Duty of Hospitality
People who are in need
and are not afraid to beg
give to people not in need

the occasion to do good
for goodness' sake.
Modern society calls the beggar
bum and panhandler
and gives him the bum's rush.
But the Greeks used to say
that people in need
are the ambassadors of the gods.
Although you may be called
bums and panhandlers
you are in fact the Ambassadors of God.
As God's Ambassadors
you should be given Food,
clothing and shelter
by those who are able to give it.
Mahometan teachers tell us
that God commands hospitality,
and hospitality is still practiced
in Mahometan countries.
But the duty of hospitality
is neither taught nor practiced
in Christian countries.

The Municipal Lodgings
That is why you who are in need
are not invited to spend the night
in the homes of the rich.
There are guest rooms today
in the homes of the rich
but they are not for those who need them.
And they are not for those who need them
because those who need them
are no longer considered
as the Ambassadors of God.
So people no longer consider
hospitality to the poor
as a personal duty.
And it does not disturb them a bit
to send them to the city,
where they are given the
hospitality of the "Muni"
at the expense of the taxpayer.
But the hospitality that the
"Muni" gives to the down and out

is no hospitality
because what comes from the
taxpayer's pocketbook
does not come from his heart.

Back to Hospitality
The Catholic unemployed
should not be sent to the "Muni."
The Catholic unemployed
should be given hospitality
in Catholic Houses of Hospitality.
Catholic Houses of Hospitality
are known in Europe
under the name of hospices.
There have been hospices in Europe
since the time of Constantine.
Hospices are free guest houses;
hotels are paying guest houses.
And paying guest houses or hotels
are as plentiful
as free guest houses or hospices
are scarce.
So hospitality, like everything else,
has been commercialized.
So hospitality, like everything else,
must now be idealized.

Houses of Hospitality
We need Houses of Hospitality
to give to the rich
the opportunity to serve the poor.
We need Houses of Hospitality
to bring the Bishops to the people
and the people to the Bishops.
We need Houses of Hospitality
to bring back to institutions
the technique of institutions.
We need Houses of Hospitality
to show what idealism looks like
when it is practiced.
We need Houses of Hospitality
to bring social justice
through Catholic Action
exercised in Catholic institutions.[24]

As with many of Maurin's letters, the bishops responded in neither word nor deed. Nonetheless Maurin continued to critique passivity and injustice and propose paths of peace and justice. He remained optimistic about the possibility of response, despite evidence to the contrary. In a simple but deeply moving essay Maurin outlined his understanding of the essence of what is human.

1. To give and not to take
   that is what makes man human.
2. To serve and not to rule,
   that is what makes man human.
3. To help and not to crush
   that is what makes man human.
4. To nourish and not to devour
   that is what makes man human.
5. And if need be
   to die and not to live
   that is what makes man human.
6. Ideals and not deals
   that is what makes man human.
7. Creed and not greed
   that is what makes man human.[25]

Yet, in the final analysis, it was Maurin's peculiar propensity to translate his vision into concrete activity that defined both the uniqueness and limitation of his advocacy. Maurin was always on the move, always experimenting and always risking failure. His presence in Harlem in 1934 again exemplifies the simplicity and complexity of his witness.

By 1934 the fate of blacks in America had become central in Maurin's thought. This was not a sudden consideration. He had roomed with a black in his years of wandering and had been in contact with blacks through Father LaFarge, and the *Catholic Worker* had run many articles decrying racial discrimination. Moreover, the Depression hit blacks particularly hard, and the Scottsboro Case, in which nine Alabama blacks had been convicted of rape, was then prominent. All this may have enhanced Maurin's sense of the urgency of the racial issue. In the final analysis, though, it was his sense of personal responsibility that sent him to Harlem.

In the May 1934 issue of the *Catholic Worker* Maurin first pronounced his concern for blacks, in a rephrasing of the bishops' annual statement of 1934. As stated by the bishops:

There is a very grave and subtle danger of infection from Communism. Special efforts are being made to win Negroes who are the victims of injustice. The Communists have as their objective a world war on God and the complete destruction of all supernatural and even natural religion.

Maurin rephrased the statement:

> The Negroes are beginning to find out
> that wage-slavery
> is no improvement
> on chattel-slavery.
> The Communists say
> that Christianity is a failure
> for the very good reason
> that Christianity has not been tried.[26]

With the donation of a store by Paul Daley, a Catholic attorney, Maurin made his home in Harlem, at 2070 Seventh Avenue just below 124th Street. Both the *Daily Catholic Worker* of May 22 and the June issue of the *Catholic Worker* announced the opening of the Harlem storefront with enthusiasm. It was to be not only a place where interested blacks could ask questions about Catholicism, but also a center for maintaining an active program of meetings emphasizing social justice and racial equality. Since the communist idea of a godless state had been concealed from the blacks, it was the object of the Harlem branch to show blacks that the church had a definite social program and that there was interest in all workers, black and white.[27]

The Harlem branch was anything but formal. A laundry sign hung over the door and the floor, though clean, was bare of any covering; someone needed to take a day to hammer down nails that had held down former layers of linoleum. There was no furniture until, some days after the opening, a neighbor donated a bed and covers. Soon to follow were donations of tables and chairs, pots and pans, a tool chest, and some boards for shelves. In the beginning there was no money for electricity or even candles, and Maurin received evening guests in the dark. One such guest was Father LaFarge, who remembered his visit because all he could see in the dark was Maurin's forefinger motioning in the air as he was making his points. Often, because of lack of funds, Maurin begged for food or money. Later a statue of a black Madonna that had hung in the Fifteenth Street house was delivered and hung in the Harlem storefront.

By the middle of September it was reported to the donor of the storefront that Maurin was living comfortably, holding meetings, and carrying on an educational campaign that had gained credibility through sharing the people's poverty. It was also reported that books, magazines, and blackboards lined the wall with Catholic teaching, and that Maurin was already taking in men off the street and sheltering them.

By October the Harlem program was in full swing. In the evenings there were discussions, with the leadership alternating among laity, priest, and black speakers. Maurin spoke on Saturday night. The afternoons featured art, catechetics, and story hours. Emile LaVallée, a professor of French, had joined the group in Harlem, and both he and Maurin conducted French classes as well.

Maurin discoursed on a variety of subjects in Harlem, but on the "Negro issue" his point was singular. If anthropologists divided the world into four kinds of people, with blacks being a distinct group, they added at the same time that there was nothing in science to prove one race superior to another race. Theologians made the same point: that Christ died for the redemption of all races. Blacks were created by the same God and enjoyed the same beatific vision. For Maurin the conclusion was obvious: all races were included in the mystical body of Christ. If there was a "Negro problem" in America, the solution was not the emulation of values whites had held out for blacks in slavery or capitalism but the development of black culture. The way for blacks to solve the Negro problem was to behave the way St. Augustine, a black man, wanted everyone to behave: as believers looking after each other. For Maurin, it was the power of example.

> The white people
> are in a mess
> and the Negro people
> will be in a mess as long as they try
> to keep up
> with white people.
> When the Negro people
> will have found the way
> out of their mess
> by evolving a technique
> in harmony
> with the ideology
> of Saint Augustine
> the white people will no longer
> look down
> on Negro people

but will look up
to Negro people.
When the white people
will look up
to the Negro people
they will imitate
the Negro people.
The power of Negro people
over white people
will then be the power of example.[28]

By the middle of October, initial enthusiasm was blunted by the difficulties of being white and Catholic in black and Protestant surroundings. Writing to a correspondent, Dorothy Day expressed dismay. "I wish you would drop in to see Peter when you have time. It is pretty hard sledding up there. There is great opposition to the work and it is hard to get along." The next day Day wrote to another correspondent in the same vein. "His school is not going well at all and only a few people show up. The place will just have to continue as an information and literature center and for the meeting of friendly groups." Day noted, however, one successful aspect of the venture: the arts and crafts classes conducted by Ade Bethune and Julia Porcelli were well received and thriving.

Maurin's venture in Harlem could not be faulted for lack of imagination. To spread his message one night, Maurin went on as an amateur performer at the famous Apollo Theater. He was announced as a comedian, and when he began reciting his essays, catcalls filled the theater. Maurin was escorted off the stage. Later he recalled that he really "got the hook that night." Maurin also conceived the idea of having "poster walks" in which a group of young men, each carrying a sign with an idea from one of his essays, would walk through the streets of Harlem. They would walk in a straight line, becoming something of a moving billboard. A group of students agreed to participate in the march, but marchers were abruptly dispersed by a barrage of insults and garbage hurled at them by members of the Harlem community. This was not the only such incident of violence for the Workers; one night Maurin was accosted by two thugs in Harlem who jumped him and gave him a severe beating. When he showed up at the office, his face was a mass of bruises.

Violence of yet greater magnitude was witnessed by people at the Harlem storefront. In March 1935, a riot broke out in Harlem, spurred by the Depression and rumors that a black child had been beaten to death by the police. One night, as the evening classes at the Harlem center drew to a close, the shattering of glass was heard. The door was locked and all sat in the rear of the house. At midnight the disturbance reached a climax as window after window in neighborhood houses fell to the sidewalk, and groups of angry blacks surrounded the storefront. Just as the destruction of the storefront seemed imminent, a man in the crowd shouted that these white people should be left alone, that they were "all right." The center was spared and the next day friends of the Worker, black and white, came to make sure all were safe.

"God's miracle," as it was described by a fellow Worker in Harlem, strengthened Maurin's determination but did not enhance black acceptance of the Worker's positions. Six months later, despite distribution of leaflets proclaiming the church's stand against war and fascism of any kind, there was still a marked reluctance to receive the paper. On several occasions the tabloid was torn up. Finally the Harlem center closed when the owner, a member of the National Guard, found out about the developing pacifist stand in the Worker movement and asked Maurin and his cohorts to leave.

Even before the riot in Harlem, many doubted the purpose of a Catholic Worker branch there. Some were skeptical of the usefulness of the work; others thought it wasted effort: "Teaching a few small children a few small things, they reasoned, would not remove the stench of race discrimination; handing out a few free copies of the *Catholic Worker* would not, they held, convince an oppressed people of the efficacy of Catholic Worker philosophy."[29] These understandings could not be easily dismissed. A willingness to go to the poorest, the least, was often an invitation to failure, and Maurin's Harlem work did precisely that—it failed.

BY THE EARLY 1940s the world and the Catholic Worker movement had changed considerably. To be sure, discussions for clarification of thought continued and hospices opened around the country, but the farming venture, the key to Maurin's vision of a new society, was failing. This failure was attributed to a variety of factors, not the least of which were the urban background common among those attempting to work the land and the poverty that the movement had adopted. Both mitigated against efficiency and planning. In addition, the refusal to discriminate among those who came to the farm meant that what began as an intentional community hoping to build a Catholic culture on the land ended as a refuge for many of the unemployed and the mentally disturbed fleeing the harshness of urban-industrial life.

But some reasons for failure must also be assigned to Maurin. Always willing to sacrifice order and success for the sake of making his point, he was even criticized by Dorothy Day.

> "Be what you want the other fellow to be," he kept saying. "Don't criticize what is not being done. See what there is to do, fit yourself to do it, then do it. . . . Everyone taking less, so that others can have more. The Worker a scholar, and the scholar a worker. Each being a servant of all, each taking the least place. A leader leading by example as well as by word."[30]

Leadership was also a problem. On the question of majority rule Maurin was clear: "I do not believe in majority rule. I do not believe in having meetings and elections. Then there would be confusion worse confounded, with lobbying, electioneering and people divided into factions." For Maurin, the ideal was the rule of the monasteries with an abbot who was accepted and obeyed by his subjects and whose decisions came after consultation with them. The problem with this concept of authority was that, while it fit the monastery in demanding the responsible independence of each monk, it did not fit the farming commune where many of the people had trouble just governing themselves. When Dorothy Day asked Maurin if he ever became discouraged over the failures he replied, "No, because I know how deep-rooted the evil is. I am a radical and know that we must get down to the roots of the evil."[31]

Equally significant was Dorothy Day's uncompromising opposition to America's participation in World War II. This opposition arose from her Christian pacifism and her desire to break the cycle of violence that enriched the wealthy and destroyed the innocent and the poor. It also effectively split the movement, for those who saw the war as justified disassociated themselves from the Catholic Worker.[32]

Maurin's stand on conscription and the war was less succinctly stated than Day's, and his general view of both can only be suggested through his own essays and his arrangements of the words of other authors on these subjects. However, his own choice was clear, as demonstrated in his earlier refusal to accept military duty in France and in his later emulation of the life of Francis of Assisi. Both showed a deepening fear of organization and coercion and a desire to follow the counsels of perfection, one of which was a refusal to do harm against neighbor even if endangered.

As early as May 1934, Maurin had written a short essay in response to a talk given by Carlton Hayes. In it, he questioned subservience of conscience to national aspirations by playing on the theme of supporting one's country regardless of the merit of its position. To stand up for your country regardless of its correctness was wrong. Sometimes, to correct that position, one had to say no. In the December 1937 issue of the *Catholic Worker*, he expanded the theme of conscience in reference to propaganda about the barbarian quality of the adversary. Indeed, in Maurin's view, the distinction between barbarians and civilized peoples was often blurred by the actions of the "civilized." If barbarians were those living on the other side of the border, the civilized were not ashamed to arm themselves for protection. And if the barbarians invaded, there was no hesitation in killing them before trying to civilize them. With this attitude, the persistence of calling one side civilized seemed ironic to Maurin. A classic example of this barbarian-civilized dichotomy was the Italian invasion of Ethiopia, ostensibly done to "civilize" Ethiopians. The Italians still retained the notion that "invaders can civilize the invaded." In Maurin's view, if Ethiopians needed to be civilized, the best way was to prepare the young men of Ethiopia for the priesthood. This example served to reinforce Maurin's major point that civilization came not through force but through religion.[33]

By April 1938, in an essay published in the *Catholic Worker* entitled "Peace Preparedness," Maurin was calling not only for physical disarmament but for disarmament of the heart.

They are increasing armaments
in the fallacious hope that they
will preserve peace by preparing for war.
Before 1914 they prepared for war and got it.
Nations have too long prepared
for war; it is about time they prepared for peace.[34]

Maurin quoted Archbishop McNicholas to the effect that governments had no fixed standards of morality and thus could scarcely settle the question of war for Christians. That Christians affirming the supreme domain of God knew the injustice of modern wars raised a very practical question: would such Christians form a league of conscientious objectors?

Maurin identified strongly with a lecture delivered by Cardinal Innitzer in Vienna, which he arranged and published in the September 1939 edition of the *Catholic Worker*. Innitzer believed the church did not bless arms, but peace. In the Sermon on the Mount, Christ had specifically blessed the poor and those who made peace, as he declared himself as the one who brings peace. He enjoined all to make peace with each other, to love enemies, and to be perfect in imitation of God's perfection. This call to perfection was Christ's wish to refuse every way of violence. Two passages in the New Testament were conclusive, the words of Jesus to Peter: "Put back your sword in the scabbard for he who draws the sword will perish by the sword" and "I give you peace, I leave you my peace, peace be with you." These words were sufficient to prove that the gospel excluded all violence and nothing in it could be interpreted as authorizing war.[35]

Three months later, Maurin published an arrangement of an address delivered by Eric Gill to the Council of Christian Pacifist Groups in September 1938. This address went beyond the call of conscience and the commands of Jesus to discuss the nature of modern warfare itself. Gill began by comparing modern work and war. As in work, war was made impersonal by modern machinery and weapons, which reduced the soldier to a subhuman condition. Because of technology, war was less ennobling than it was destructive and degrading. The entire structure of warfare had changed: instead of small professional armies manned by mercenaries fighting limited engagements, war had become mass war with entire populations mobilized. The result was that the vast majority who fought and were killed were involved in a struggle about which they knew little. If war had ever had a heroic aura about it, modern warfare had none. It was not a question of heroism, justice, or defense, but of plain and simple terrorism.[36]

Other evidence of Maurin's opposition to conscription and war is fragmentary, yet interesting. Two of Maurin's closest friends and disciples, Bill Gauchat and Arthur Sheehan, refused to cooperate with the war effort, and both saw this opposition as being in concert with Maurin's position on conscription and the war. With Maurin, they viewed their stance as the choice of the counsels of perfection as a higher calling but not an absolute duty. Sheehan, who was spending a great deal of time with Maurin, understood that Maurin's pacifism was the pacifism of the early church. At that time, church members refused to become judges because they might have to sentence men and women to death. Larry Heaney, a friend of Maurin, wrote to a priest in January 1942 that in regard to war, Maurin believed that the reestablishment of a rugged peasantry, with its common culture and unifying bond, would contribute much to peace. If Maurin personally opposed the war, he was also cognizant of its tremendous popularity. Realizing the difficulties Dorothy Day was having in her vocal opposition, Maurin counseled her that for a time silence would be better. The world was not ready to listen.[37]

The popularity of the war significantly decreased participation in and contributions to the movement; many hospices closed, and the circulation of the *Catholic Worker* dropped below fifty thousand. As the war years progressed, the question was no longer whether the movement would be a catalyst for social reconstruction but whether it would survive at all. A movement begun in hope entered into exile.

The movement, its basic position unchanged, from this time on saw itself in a new way. It might still hope ultimately to reconstruct the social order; but, in a more sober self-assessment, it knew it must and could bear constant witness to peace in a world scarred by massive dislocation and death. In this way the Worker represented the division of the century itself: before 1940, hope that a new order was about to arise; after 1945, the attempt to cope with a world poised on the brink of self-destruction.

The Worker's exile has not been a quiet one. The Worker community protested against the development and use of atomic weapons in the 1940s and 1950s by publishing lengthy articles in the *Catholic Worker* and organizing demonstrations in New York City. In the early 1960s when the Cuban revolution was the target of American foreign policy, Dorothy Day traveled to Cuba to witness the revolution firsthand. Like her stand against World War II and the atomic bomb, Day's report on the revolution was controversial and lends insight into the character of the Worker movement. She found the revolution to have problems, of course, but also hope; a genuine movement toward a communal life was taking place. To her fellow Catholics who wondered how she could condone an atheist revolution, she replied that if Catholicism was not in the forefront for the revolution it was because Marxists had taken seriously the needs of the people where Catholics had not. Of the revolution she wrote:

> The motive is love of brother, and we are commanded to love our brothers. If religion has so neglected the needs of the poor and of the great mass of workers and permitted them to live in the most horrible destitution while comforting them with the solace of a promise of a life after death when all tears shall be wiped away, then that religion is suspect. Who would believe such Job's comforters? On the other hand, if those professing religion shared the life of the poor and worked to better their lot and risked their lives as revolutionaries do, and trade union organizers have done in the past, then there is a ring of truth about the promises of the glory to come. The cross is followed by the resurrection.[38]

Day's trip to Cuba was just the beginning of a turbulent decade. The Worker wholeheartedly supported the civil rights movement and later initiated a Catholic, then American, dialogue on the Vietnam war. By the mid-1960s—to a new generation—the Catholic Worker became a symbol of good in the world. When Dorothy Day visited the universities and hospitality houses across the country, her talks drew large audiences. What seemed to many an ancient voice was rediscovered, an exile movement reborn.

DURING THE EXILE, the ideas of Peter Maurin, who had died in 1949, continued to illuminate the Worker's path. The vagabond peasant-intellectual had brought with him from France an intact and meaningful Catholic tradition capable of orienting the person toward transcendence. He had brought, too, the dissenting European Christian thought of the day—the ideas of Berdyaev, Christopher Dawson, Eric Gill, Maritain. As a result, the Worker saw (and sees) its struggle not in a parochial American context but within the larger framework of Western civilization.

The themes that Maurin preached and lived—the emphasis on a dynamic Catholicism, the social apostolate, and the role of the laity in social critique and reconstruction—came to fruition in the Second Vatican Council. He was one of the first Catholics to seriously entertain dialogue with Marxists, a dialogue that is being pursued with new vigor today. His understanding of hospitality as a Christian obligation is also flourishing, especially in the works of the contemporary theologian Henri Nouwen. Maurin's belief that decentralized political authority and simplicity of life provide not only the necessities for living but the context for research and freedom have similarly experienced a resurgence in recent years, most strikingly in E. F. Schumacher's popular book *Small is Beautiful.* So, too, Maurin's understanding of the Christian mission as a witness to faith and justice in a secular world has become central for many. Critical is Maurin's insistence on the role of faith and tradition in providing the context for nurturing both the person and the social order, and on the way of poverty and simplicity as a sign of judgment on a world in pursuit of affluence. Maurin's dream of the movement back to the land finds embodiment in small experimental communities in New York, West Virginia, and dozens of other places around the country.

But if Maurin's program has gained adherents, in the larger world his thought and program have been controversial and more often dismissed. To many, his insistence on a return to the land seemed then and seems today unrealistic. The question that Paul Hanly Furfey posed in 1939 in a series of articles in the *Catholic Worker* remains: is agrarianism, and those who espouse it, romantic both in content and possibility? Does it not reflect a bias against city life and a diversion from the necessary reforms of permanently urban civilization where most people will make their lives? Maurin's critique of industrialism, with its alienation of labor and the loss of personality in organized and bureaucratic processes, has similarly come under attack. The question that John Cort posed in 1948 in a series of a articles in *Commonweal* is relevant: is it not true that urban-industrial life with all its faults, can be humanized, even Christianized, through organization that has as its end the person and justice? Similarly, can a worldwide village economy with subsistence agriculture and crafts support a population curve that grows exponentially? Just as difficult is the predicament of religious traditions: is the form of religiosity that nurtured Maurin available to those who must struggle in the present?[39]

There is no denying the perhaps insurmountable difficulties involved in moving from a secular, urban-industrial society to a rural-village culture rooted in faith, even if that were desired by a majority of people. Maurin, in thought and experience, could hardly deny these difficulties. However, the criticism that Maurin's vision represented little more than a romanticized version of the Middle Ages is equally difficult to sustain. To be sure, Maurin's recitation of secular and church history suffers when compared with the complexities of historical investigation. His vision of reality, however, was never simplistically romantic. If Maurin's hope that personal and community witness could redirect, even dismantle, the power of modernity seems naive, his vision of the new social order was not superficial. If anything, Maurin was willing to confront what contemporary society, at its own peril, labors so hard to forget: the need for meaningful work; the development of the interior life; the connection between purpose and the mysteries of life found on the land and in worship; the importance of community; the reality of death.

For the powerful and the passive Maurin had the ability to function as a dangerous memory, to shock the contemporary world into a reassessment of its values and directions, to question "business as usual" in the midst of holocaust. Johannes Metz, a German Catholic theologian, describes a dangerous memory in a context that applies to the life and vision of Peter Maurin.

> There are memories in which earlier experiences break through to the center-point of our lives and reveal new and dangerous insights in the present. They illuminate for a few moments and with a harsh steady light the questionable nature of things we have apparently come to terms with, and show up the banality of our supposed realism. They break through the canon of all that is taken as self-evident, and unmask as deception the certainty of those "whose hour is always there." They seem to subvert our structures of plau-

sibility. Such memories are like dangerous and incalculable visitants from the past. They are memories we have to take into account: memories, as it were, with future content.[40]

In the final analysis, Maurin was in the unenviable position of all those who oppose the present: to oppose the present is to propose a reality that by definition does not as yet exist. However, Maurin compounded the problem by proposing for the future a society that had imperfectly existed in the past. This rendered his vision less accessible to the modern imagination used to seeing the future, progressive or not, as an extension of the present. The terror found in the modern imagination made it easier to contemplate the antiutopian writings of Aldous Huxley in *Brave New World* and George Orwell in *Animal Farm* and *1984* than to construct the radically human vision of the future proposed by Maurin.

For that was what Maurin was addressing: not how the present was to be reformed, not how the future was to be an extension of the present, but the need for a radical departure in order to ensure a future that could honestly be called human. To the complex questions of agrarianism and industrialism, Maurin replied with his own questions. Were material affluence and sensual desire the ends of life? Or were its ends involvement in the spirit and renunciation in service? Did the pursuit of affluence lead to the sharing of wealth, or to more and more destitution? Were the foundations of freedom and community found in the individual right to self-fulfillment, or were freedom and community found in the obligations of faith and service to neighbor? Did the pursuit of individual rights lead to securing these same rights for others, or to securing them from others? Did not the increasing organization of personal and institutional life to pursue affluence lead in its final form to totalitarianism on the left and the right? Was the function of the social order to ease the pursuit of materialism or to nurture souls bound for eternity? Maurin's most radical reversal of all was his understanding of poverty: to the world a sign of shame, to Maurin a sign of fidelity and salvation.

Despite obvious obstacles, Maurin's legacy, the Catholic Worker movement, continues to provide a way of life that addresses the seeming disjunction between contemporary life and the demands of Christian faith. This comes from the radical and thus freeing perspective of commitment, which Maurin articulated and lived. The essence of this commitment—being present among the poor and engaging in social critique—is both an affirmation and negation. It affirms the continuity of persons in community over time as it asserts the integrity of all persons, especially the outcast and the marginalized. It sees persons and history in a spiritual light: the movement of persons and community is not toward affluence and power but toward God. The commitment is to embody these beliefs. By acting, personally and at a sacrifice, the vision becomes a reality. The world is no loner foreign or abandoned; the people of the earth are no longer orphans. The negation is also clear. That which denies life and spirit is to be opposed, and in this affirmation and negation the presence of the spirit once again comes into focus.

At the close of the twentieth century one can hardly contemplate a more difficult and important task than embodying such a clarification, and it is fortunate that the Catholic Worker movement is not alone in this quest. The past fifteen years have seen a revival of prophetic thought and activity in the United States and throughout the world. The Basic Christian Communities of the Third World in particular carry this witness forward, and it is remarkable how similar the values and sensibilities of such diverse communities are to one another. Like the Catholic Worker, Basic Christian Communities have grown from the experience of dislocation and unemployment, from oppressive and misguided social, economic, and governmental policies and the desire among the poor and the middle class to address the situation from the perspective of a newly dynamic faith. We might say that Basic Communities and the Catholic Worker movement participate in a tradition that stretches back to the early Christians even as they now participate in the transformation of faith traditions. It is not too much to claim that there is now a worldwide rebirth of the message of commitment and community and, though chastened by the power of modern life, the movement toward a just world order grows stronger.

The struggle to be faithful to the holy events of the exodus and the coming of Jesus within the complexities of history is never easy. Despite a renewal of faith among the prophetic communities, there is a peculiar urgency about our age that threatens to overwhelm the transcendent forever. The victors and victims of the twentieth century, caught in the terrible spiral of hubris and abandonment, are breaking the tension that allows the search for meaning to continue. In such a time the struggle to be faithful is of critical importance because it holds forth, even in exile, a renewed connection between the divine and the human. Within our own history, exile is the fate of such a struggle, and yet it is precisely here that the seeds of clarity and reconstruction are stored and nurtured.

Notes

Note: The *Catholic Worker* is cited here as *CW.*

1. See Marc H. Ellis, *Peter Maurin: Prophet in the Twentieth Century* (New York: Paulist Press, 1981), 21–44.

2. Peter Maurin, "The Spirit for the Masses," *CW*, October 1933: 2.
3. Peter Maurin, "Easy Essays," *CW*, May 1933: 1, 8.
4. Peter Maurin, "Maurin's Program," *CW*, June–July 1933: 4.
5. For the years preceding the founding of the Catholic Worker movement, see Ellis, *Maurin*, 34–38.
6. Peter Maurin, "The Case for Utopia," *CW*, April 1934: 3. The encyclicals concerning St. Francis that Maurin read and quoted include those promulgated by Popes Leo XIII, Pius X, and Pius XI. They were compiled under the title *Rome Hath Spoken* (Chicago: Franciscan Herald Press, 1932).
7. See Stanley Vishnewski, "Days of Action: The Story of the Catholic Worker Movement," vol. 1, unpublished manuscript, ca. 1966, 55–56, Dorothy Day–Catholic Worker Collection, Stanley Vishnewski Papers, Memorial Library Archives, Marquette University, Milwaukee (hereafter cited as "CW Papers"), W-12.3, box 1. Also see Peter Maurin, "Go-Getters vs. Go-Givers," *CW*, August 1936, 4.
8. Peter Maurin, "The Case for Utopia," *CW*, April 1, 1934: 3.
9. For an interesting comparison see Martin Buber, *Paths in Utopia*, trans. R. F. C. Hull (Boston: Beacon Hill, 1949); and Mahatma Gandhi, *All Men are Brothers* (New York: Columbia University Press, 1958).
10. Peter Maurin, "Easy Essays," *CW*, June–July 1933: 1, 3; "To the Bishops of the U.S.," October 1933: 1; "Back to Christ!—Back to the Land!" November 1935: 1, 8.
11. Though I have emphasized the Franciscan quality of Maurin's thought, it is important to mention other intellectual influences as well. The intellectuals that Maurin read came from a variety of schools of thought: the English distributists who rejected machine technology and urban civilization for an agrarian, handicraft society; a revived Thomistic school of philosophy that sought to reassert the efficacy of metaphysics; the French personalist school, which attempted to reestablish the centrality of personhood in the individual and the social realms. Many of the intellectuals Maurin read and quoted were well known and included G. K. Chesterton, Christopher Dawson, Eric Gill, Jacques Maritain, and Emmanuel Mounier. Others, like Nicholas Berdyaev and Vincent McNabb, were less well known. Though the threads that ran through these writings were diverse, the basic conviction emerged that the revival of the spiritual dimension in the person and the culture could reverse the decline of civilization initiated with the triumph of secularism in the eighteenth century. For most, the dignity of the person could be affirmed only when this dimension was recognized. A humanism without God was to set forces into motion that would take humankind into a new dark age, where all would be possible and permissible and the person would count for nothing. Accordingly, these thinkers feared the power of modern life seen in industrialism, urbanism, and statism. Because of these fears, Edward Shapiro has labeled this group "decentralist intellectuals," and others, with less insight, have termed them reactionaries. Neither label, however, does justice to the motivation of their thought or their intellectual capabilities. Instead, these intellectuals might be better understood as dissenters against the confusion and violence of a world emerging into moderni-

ty. In the light of our century's subsequent experience they should be seen as protesting against a slaughter that was just beginning.

12. For a description of the meeting of Maurin and Day as well as the background that Day brought to their meeting, see William D. Miller, *A Harsh and Dreadful Love: Dorothy Day and the Catholic Worker Movement* (New York: Liveright, 1973), and his more recent biography *Dorothy Day: A Biography* (New York: Harper & Row, 1982).

13. "The Church and Social Problems, *Orate Fratres* 9 (April 1934): 227; John Toomey, S.J., "Radicals of the Right," *America* 52 (February 2, 1935): 399.

14. J. G. Brunini, "Catholic Paper vs. Communism," *Commonweal* 19 (November 24, 1933): 96–98. Maurin's discussions with communists were unusual in their day and controversial. He was attacked by conservative Catholics and communists alike. For the attack by Catholics see the *Brooklyn Tablet*, August 24, 1935: 6, 7. For the attack by communists see *Daily Worker*, August 18, 1934: 2.

15. John LaFarge, S.J., "Peter the Agitator Quotes the Prophets of Israel," *America* 55 (August 1, 1936): 395.

16. Peter Maurin, "Feeding the Poor," *CW*, May 1936: 4.

17. LaFarge, "Peter the Agitator," 395.

18. But if Maritain left with such an impression of the Worker movement, he also wanted to clarify a discussion he had had with Maurin, and stated: "I'm of the impression that I didn't make myself quite clear on the subject of the Pluralist State, when I replied to your explanation of it. I want to make it quite clear that such a state with its 'Federation' of diverse juridicial structures, would be not merely a simple collection, but would have a real moral unity of orientation. It would deserve the name of Christian because it would tend in a positive fashion, across these diverse structures toward an integral Christian ideal. Instead of being polarized by a materialistic conception of the world and of life, like the capitalist and the communist state, it would be polarized through the knowledge of the spiritual dignity of the human person and on the love which is due him" (Maritain to Maurin, November 11, 1934, CW Papers, W-10, box 1).

19. Peter Maurin, "Big Shots and Little Shots," *Catholic Mind* 32 (July 8, 1934): 260; "Action: Political or Catholic?" *Catholic Mind* 32 (July 22, 1934): 278. Numerous pamphlets were published by the Catholic Worker Press beginning in 1934; the one-penny pamphlets were mimeographed and the two-penny pamphlets were printed. See CW Papers, W-1, box 1. Also see "Catholic Worker Moves to New House of Hospitality on Charles Street," *Commonweal* 21 (March 1935): 627.

20. The *Daily Catholic Worker* began on May 1 and apparently ended on May 25. For the announcement of its beginning, see "Mimeograph Machines Urged by P. Maurin for Every Parish," *CW*, May 1934: 6.

21. Peter Maurin, "Easy Essays," *CW*, May 1933: 1, 8.

22. Peter Maurin, "For Catholic Action," *CW*, June 1, 1934: 5.

23. Dorothy Day, "Days with an End," *CW*, April 1, 1934: 3.

24. Peter Maurin, "To the Bishops of the United States," *CW*, October 1933: 1.

25. Peter Maurin, "Personalist Essays," in "Monthly Symposium on Personalist Democracy," January 1938: 5.6, CW Papers, W-10, box 1.

26. Peter Maurin, "The Bishops Message: Quotations and Comments," *CW*, May 1934: 2.

27. For continuing coverage of Maurin's Harlem experiment, see *CW*, May–October, 1934.

28. Peter Maurin, "The Race Problem," *CW*, May 1938: 8.

29. Herman Hergenhan, "Harlem Riot," *CW*, April 1935: 1. For the published and unpublished sources relating to the Harlem House, see Ellis, *Peter Maurin*, 182, 183 n. 20–30.

30. Dorothy Day, "Farming Commune," *CW*, February 1934: 1, 8.

31. Ibid., 8.

32. See Miller, *A Harsh and Dreadful Love*, 154–70.

33. Peter Maurin, "War and Peace," *CW*, December 1937: 1, 8.

34. Peter Maurin, "Peace Preparedness," *CW*, April 1938: 1.

35. Cardinal Innitzer, "Peace and War," arranged by Peter Maurin, *CW*, September 1939: 3.

36. Eric Gill, "Work and War," arranged by Peter Maurin, *CW*, December 1939: 6.

37. Arthur Sheehan, *Peter Maurin: Gay Believer* (New York: Hanover House, 1959), 199; Heaney to Father Kenpenny, January 2 [1942?], CW Papers, Nina Polcyn Moore Papers, W-17, box 1; Dorothy Day, *The Long Loneliness* (New York: Harper & Row, 1952), 180, 181.

38. Dorothy Day, *On Pilgrimage* (New York: Curtis, 1972), 100.

39. Paul Hanly Furfey, "Unemployment on the Land," *CW*, October 1939: 8; "There Are Two Kinds of Agrarians," *CW*, December 1939: 1, 8; John Cort, "Reform Begins at the Plant Level," *Commonweal* 48 (October 1, 1948): 597; "Is a Christian Industrialsim Possible?" *Commonweal* 49 (October 29, 1948): 60–62.

40. Johannes B. Metz, "The Future in the Memory of Suffering," *Consilium* 36 (1971): 15.

2. PETER MAURIN'S PERSONALIST DEMOCRACY

Geoffrey B. Gneuhs

TODAY'S WORLD IS one of extremes. Fundamentalism in various forms permeates life; dialogue decreases while the reach of mass media increases. Technology flourishes uncontrolled, bureaucracies dominate, surveillance is commonplace. As the United States has become more imperialistic in its use of economic and military power, its citizens have become more and more isolationist in their attitudes. There is actually little sense of the world as community, and there is lessened interest, desire, and responsibility to share with other countries. Political leaders reveal gross ignorance of other cultures and histories; smugness, condescension, and arrogance are the norm. Technology and materialism are becoming a type of totalitarianism, for they determine and control our capability for imagination and vision. Since World War II and the atomic bombing of Hiroshima in August 1945, government budgets and policies have reflected a war mentality, and official language often is a form of Orwellian newspeak.[1]

Of course much the same could be said of the Soviet Union. The two nations, as de Tocqueville presciently observed in 1835, were "marked out by the will of Heaven to sway the destinies of half the globe."[2] (The destinies of the entire globe, as it turned out.) And although I do not deny there are differences between the two empires, the fact remains that bureaucracy, technology, power, control, order, and dominance are present and intensifying in each state, Gorbachev and *glasnost* notwithstanding. What then is the future of the human person? What hope is there for democracy and the principles upon which it is based?

Great ideas often come from the unlikeliest of persons and places.

Peter Maurin, the Catholic peasant from Languedoc in the south of France, the soapbox orator of Union Square in New York, was one such unlikely person. Often mistaken for a ne'er-do-well from the Bowery, he was, as Dorothy Day said, "the saint and genius" who "showed the way" to her and many others. The essence of his thought revealed a keen appreciation of what it means to be a person and how we can make this world a better place where, in his words, it is "easier for people to be good."

I would like to consider what I call the vision of Peter Maurin, and then discuss the content of that vision in various forms and the possibility of its realization not just in the West, but in the East, not just in the northern hemisphere but in the southern hemisphere as well. If democracy is to survive, a recommitment to the person and all that that means is absolutely necessary.

The Roots of Maurin's Vision

Maurin (1877–1949) was born in the small village of Oultet near Mende in Languedoc in the southern part of France. He came from a large family who had lived on the same farm for hundreds of years. In 1895 he took vows as a religious brother in the Christian Brothers. While teaching in Paris he joined a study club and was introduced to Marc Sangnier (1873–1950), whose group Le Sillon (The Furrow) was particularly interested in reconciling Catholic ideas with democratic principles and various social and political reforms.[3] Maurin was intrigued with the ideas and example of Léon Harmel (1829–1915), a nineteenth-century industrialist from Val des Bois in the Champagne region of France, who had inherited his father's textile mills. Harmel introduced various reforms for his workers, setting up committees of employees who participated in the management of the mills. He chose to live among his workers and took them on pilgrimages to Rome. His closeness to the papacy contributed to the publication of Pope Leo XIII's seminal social encyclical *Rerum Novarum* (On the Condition of Workers) in 1891.[4] Maurin also read the works of Peter Kropotkin, the Russian naturalist and anarchist, author of *Fields, Factories, and Workshops* and *Mutual Aid*.

Maurin left France in 1909 (a few years earlier he had departed from the Christian Brothers congregation) and emigrated to Canada, where he homesteaded in Saskatchewan. He gave that up and drifted to the United States, taking on all sorts of jobs: building railroads, mining, tearing down concrete forms, janitorial work, and a stint on a freighter in Lake Michigan. During World War I he ended up in Chicago, where he supported himself by giving French lessons. This lasted about eight years, and although few details of his life at this time are known, clearly he did not give up his penchant for study, especially his interest in history and philosophy. It was in Chicago in the early 1920s that Maurin started to write down his ideas in neat, lettered script in the form of poems, which he duplicated and distributed on the streets. Later on, after he met Dorothy Day, these poems were collected and given the name Easy Essays.

Invited by a student, he moved to upstate New York in 1925, where he continued to give French lessons. One day, as he recalled in an interview, "I gave up the idea of charging for lessons. The whole world had gone crazy, and I decided to be crazy in my own way. They didn't let me starve."[5] This signaled a conversion that Maurin never elaborated upon but which nevertheless changed him and his outlook. Maurin's life took on a radical redirection; his years of wandering were to be no more, though he continued to be a peripatetic traveler, affectionately called an apostle on the bum. He now had a sense of vocation, the fullness of which, as for any of us, was known only to God: yet he was willing to take the awesome risk of submitting to the illumined unknown of God, of seeing through the glass darkly. He was fifty years old.

The key elements of Maurin's new-found vision were voluntary poverty, self-sacrifice, personal responsibility for the common good, and communal association. These latter two were especially to shape what might be termed his political and social outlook. His primary sources were the life of Christ and the social teaching of the Catholic church. From Léon Bloy (1846–1917), the French writer and author of *The Woman Who Was Poor*, Maurin got his trenchant critique of "bourgeois" culture and religion, in which security and material self-satisfaction take precedence over all else, distorting the radical Christian understanding of the human person as one endowed with freedom, the freedom (duty) to serve others, to do good.[6] In 1927 in a speech before the Rotary Club in Kingston, New York, Maurin suggested giving money to the poor, not just as an act of charity but as the means to increase their buying power and thereby their ability to function in the economic and political sphere. The group of business leaders laughed at him.

For the next few years, from 1927 to 1933. Maurin worked part time at a boys' camp near Woodstock, New York. He spent his free time in New York City at Union Square, debating philosophy and economics, and reading and studying at the public library. In December 1932, through George Shuster, editor of *Commonweal*, Maurin met Dorothy Day. In him, as she later wrote in her autobiography, she met "the French peasant whose spirit and ideas [would] dominate the rest of my life." Father Wilfred Parsons, S.J., one-time editor of *America*, considered Maurin the best-read person he had ever met. Maisie Ward, wife of Frank Sheed and cofounder of the publishing house of Sheed & Ward, later remembered, "At first glance you would probably overlook Peter, yet Peter Maurin was perhaps the greatest inspiration of Catholic America in our generation."[7] His pedagogy remained throughout his life the same: short, pithy poems, often repeated. At an initial reading these essays might seem simplistic, but in each there is a cogency and wisdom that doesn't let go of the reader.

Maurin was a derivative thinker, a synthesizer of the writings of other philosophers and scholars. To appreciate his vision and then to derive a certain application of that vision, it is necessary to look at those individuals whose ideas are the basis of Maurin's principles. Our starting point must be St. Thomas Aquinas's doctrine of the common good. Maurin wrote:

> According to St. Thomas Aquinas
> man is more
> than an individual
> with individual rights;
> he is a person
> with personal duties
> toward God,
> himself,
> and his fellow man.
> As a person
> man cannot serve God
> without serving
> the Common Good.[8]

Aquinas was first and foremost a theologian, who discusses various questions in his *Summa* in the context of scripture. Within his theological synthesis, he presents a social theology based on four fundamental realities: "the personal unity, dignity, and mystery of the human being; the naturalness of society; the primacy of the common good; and justice as the foundation of human fellowship."[9] Each person is created in the image and likeness of God. This radical truth revealed in scripture is thus the foundation for all human activity: social, political, and economic. All subsequent papal teaching and councils have recognized this truth as the starting point for a system of ordering human endeavors. It is the basis for an understanding of rights and duties (in contemporary American political discourse the latter is more often than not ignored).

The person signifies "what is most perfect in nature."[10] The thirteenth-century theologian stressed that each person is in a relationship with God, and together God and the person form a society. Likewise each person as a social being is related to other persons, and together they form a society with God. It is a society of friendship, of mutual love, activity, and responsibility. The trinitarian doctrine of the Godhead is the analogue for this understanding of society. It is a radically different view of the world from that which stresses individualism, materialism, and self-realization.

Aquinas considered the common good in relation to justice and firmly taught that the end of all law is the common good. Any law that is unjust is then not true law and one is not obligated to obey it. The common good, moreover, extends beyond the bounds and limits of any nation-state. For Maurin, this doctrine served as the unifying factor upon which society should be based. Maurin understood the common good as the context in which each person could most perfectly engage in living out the gospel demands of justice, forgiveness, compassion, and nonviolence. In this spirit one's own good does not come first but rather the good of the other. The common good is primary. In reality, often the emphasis is on one's own good first. Today, many ask, "Am *I* better off?" with no regard for society, for the good of the whole. Maurin was grounded in this traditional Catholic spirituality. He believed, contrary to popular notions of self and success, that one reaches perfection through love and sacrifice.

Paradoxically, as population has increased, as technology has bridged the gaps in communication, as economic interdependence through transnational corporations has grown, there is greater fragmentation, disunity, and antagonism among nations. The world is ruled more by competition rather than by cooperation. "Governments, when they are not dictatorships, are based on positivistic, contractural, and utilitarian conceptions of man [sic]. . . . Individual freedom can be challenged at any time on the grounds of 'party line' or 'national interest.'"[11] Today, we strive for immediate satisfaction, profoundly confused and determinedly cynical about what those interests are.

With his typical play of words, Maurin observed:

> America is all shot to pieces
> since the little shots
> are no longer able
> to become big shots.
> When the little shots
> are not satisfied
> to remain little shots
> and try to become
> big shots,

then the big shots
are not satisfied
to remain big shots
and try to become bigger shots.
And when the big shots
become bigger shots
then the little shots
become littler shots.
And when the little shots
become littler shots
because the big shots
become bigger shots
then the little shots
get mad at the big shots.
And when the little shots
get mad at the big shots
because the big shots
by becoming bigger shots
made the little shots
littler shots
they shoot the big shots
full of little shots.
But by shooting the big shots
full of little shots
the little shots
do not become big shots;
they make everything all shot.[12]

Fifteen years after Maurin's death the Second Vatican Council re-affirmed that "man's [sic] social nature makes it evident that the progress of the human person and the advance of society itself hinge on each other."[13] Maurin had proposed:

What a fine place
this world would be
if Dualist Humanists
tried to be human
to men.
What a fine place this world would be
if Personalist Theists
tried to be
their brother's keeper
as God wants them to be.
What a fine place this

world would be
if Fundamentalist Protestants
tried to exemplify
the Sermon on the Mount.
What a fine place
this world would be
if Roman Catholics
tried to keep up with
St. Francis of Assisi.[14]

According to Aquinas, "The common good is the end of each individual member of a community just as the good of the whole is the end of each part."[15] Consequently, a person's primary responsibility is to the common good, not to the state or to the political community per se. In other words, a person, who by nature has reason and free will, can in the context of the society of the common good reach divine perfection—the end of human existence.

This understanding of the person and society is a safeguard against the extremes of individualism and capitalism that ignore the proper use of goods and property, and the extremes of collectivism and socialism that deprive the person of ownership, responsibility, and freedom. Maurin excoriated both capitalism and socialism because both systems rely on materialism. Neither economic system incorporates or respects the true dignity of the person. Explained Maurin, "The Bourgeois Socialist does not believe in the profit system, but he does believe in the wage system. The Bourgeois Capitalists believe in getting all they can and not in giving all they can give."[16]

Ironically, by adhering to the wage system, state socialism helps to perpetuate capitalism. Hannah Arendt cogently pointed out that state capitalism and state socialism are twins, each wearing different hats. Under both, the masses, the people, are dispossessed of property and thus power and freedom. That is the central problem and one which Maurin attacked. He often cited Pope Pius XI's encyclical *Quadragesimo Anno:* "To each, therefore, must be given his own share of goods and the distribution of created goods." Today, there is an increasing gulf between the few exceedingly rich and the vast unnumbered propertyless. Under such conditions, justice and freedom are under siege. "When everybody is busy becoming more selfish we have classes and clashes."[17]

Maurin's constant recalling of the common good offers an alternative to the ideologies of capitalism and socialism. Its starting point is a moral perspective of the person and society. Quite frankly, today it is hard to distinguish the goals of the superpowers and the supercorporations. Their main concern is to keep going that which is already in place. There is no concern to try to *imagine* what should be, or the ultimate question: what is the purpose of our existence? Maurin answered this question by propounding the common good in this Easy Essay:

A personalist
is a go-giver,
not a go-getter.
He tries to give
what he has not,
and does not
try to get
what the other fellow has.
He tries to be good
by doing good
to the other fellow.
He is altro-centered,
not self-centered.
He has a social doctrine
of the common good.
He spreads the social doctrine
of the common good
through words and deeds.
He speaks through deeds
as well as words,
for he knows that deeds
speak louder than words.
Through words and deeds
he brings into existence
a common unity,
the common unity
of a community.[18]

Maurin's radical critique was strengthened by the observations of Nicholas Berdyaev (1874–1948), the Russian "prophet" of freedom and spirit. Born in 1874 in Kiev into an aristocratic family, Berdyaev as a young man attended military school. During his studies at the university, he engaged in political activity for which he spent time in jail. At the University of Heidelberg, he studied philosophy, concentrating on the thought of Immanuel Kant. In 1904, he moved to St. Petersburg, where he began a career of teaching and writing. For a brief period after the Bolshevik revolution, when there was still some pluralism in thought and policies, Berdyaev taught at the University of Moscow. In fact, he taught Marxist philosophy there. Intellectually honest, he was able to critique Marxism and point out its deficiencies. Consequently, he was arrested by the secret police in 1922; luckier than many others, he was deported and told never to return to Russia. He found refuge in suburban Paris, in Clarmant, where he lived to the end of his life.

In discussing his spiritual development, Berdyaev wrote that "the Grand Inquisitor passage of Dostoyevsky's *The Brothers Karamazov* was of supreme importance."[19] In that extraordinary passage of literature, Dostoyevsky presents Christianity as freedom incarnate in the person of Christ, the freedom of the spirit transcending material or economic rewards. That monologue in which the silence of Christ says more than all the words written about him is an invitation to a life of maximal Christianity. Like Berdyaev, Maurin understood history as ultimately more than facts, as being beyond time. Paradoxically, one can enter such history only by engaging in the human struggles of our time. It has nothing to do with progress or achievement or material satisfaction; rather it is radical commitment to the other, to one's fellow human beings. This is Christian existentialism, ontologically opposed to the liberal notion of history as progress and its Marxist counterpart.

Berdyaev acknowledged the absolute worth of the person as an end in itself. For him, human personality is the highest value. Personality belongs to eternity; government (the state) belongs to this world. History is a drama that necessarily centers on the mystery of the incarnation and the redemption, which are the fullness and completion of human personality. In *The Meaning of History* Berdyaev wrote, "Only for that reason there stands at its center God's suffering, for in truth God desired freedom, because the primal mystery and drama of the world are the mystery and drama of freedom in the relation between God and his other self which he loves and by which he desires to be loved; and the meaning of that love is only in freedom."[20] In the Christian view freedom ultimately is the freedom to love; moreover, we are free when we confirm freedom on others. Too often freedom is understood in a strictly positivistic, individualistic sense. For Berdyaev freedom is a spiritual disposition that should overflow into the realm of the physical.

Berdyaev stressed the person as subject over object. Objectification is idol making—power, lust, comfort—and is less than the highest aim of personality. It entails the loss of freedom, and is thus depersonalizing. It is a self-imposed form of slavery. Such a human being is bourgeois and stands outside the real world, the world of spiritual values. Berdyaev further described history as "the tragedy of the lack of agreement between what exists as human and personal on the one hand and all objectification which is always extra-personal, non-human, antipersonal and anti-human on the other."[24] History is an ongoing creation in which persons acting in freedom and love participate in the fullness of the incarnation and redemption. Berdyaev and Maurin embraced the goodness of God's creation. For Maurin, theology to the contrary would be anti-incarnational. Berdyaev and Maurin held that there is a dynamic interaction (and in all action upon action there is friction) between the divine and the human. It is a creative dialectic. As the Grand Inquisitor passage magnificently presents, this dynamic is impossible without "that irrational principle underling human freedom and the free creative subject."[21]

Christ stands at the center of history. The divine entrance into history is also the divine assertion, final and complete, that the human person is created in the image and likeness of God. Subsequently, all time is sacred; the now is eternal. The eternal is already now. Historical positivists and determinists, on the other hand, place all hope in the future and in fact look to the future as a solution of the human tragedy. Not surprisingly, with such a viewpoint freedom and love tend to lose value.

For Maurin, on the other hand, the Christian engages in the process of history most directly by engagement with the poor and by the works of mercy, by the works of liberation and justice, and by love; such is the divine fruition. *We* do not make that fruition; it is not a form of Pelagianism.[22] However, we are called through such works and actions to participate in the divine fruition, that is, Christian freedom. The Christian cannot resign from the world; rather, the Christian participates most properly by living out the precepts of the gospels. Thus, the justice of the state, when there is any, can never fully be the justice of the Sermon on the Mount. Those Christians who think that some form of the state (Marxist-Leninist, for instance) will embody justice are grossly mistaken and have been seduced by the allure of objectification. Spiritually, theologically, and historically they are mistaken; human beings cannot effect the final realization of the redemption.

Christianity, existential and prophetic, constantly nudges us out of our acquiescence, out of our illusions, out of our submission to ourselves. The kingdom of God can never be confused with or submerged by the kingdom of Caesar; this too often is the fallacy of so-called revolutionaries, whether of the right or the left. When tempted in the desert, Christ, as the Grand Inquisitor angrily recalled, forsook the offer of political power and the delusion that it could solve the problem of time—the tragedy of human existence. Instead Christ opted for freedom.

In the eschatological view of Berdyaev and Maurin, with their ethics of freedom and creativity, the role and function of the state should be minimal. The criterion for judging a system or state is how much it contributes toward the development of the highest spiritual values.[23]

Maurin derived his essay "Go-Getters vs. Go-Givers," describing the sameness of "Bourgeois Capitalists" and "Bolshevist Socialists," from Berdyaev's book *Christianity and Class War*, in which the Russian writes, "The socialist-communist ideal of man is the bourgeois ideal of the economic man, altogether depersonalized and soulless, assuming the image of a mechanized collective, and devoted exclusively to the economic and technical kind of life." Both systems are weighed down by what the economist Seymour Melman calls "managerialism" that further divorces those with power from the actual process of production and manufacturing and from those individuals who are more directly responsible for the work.[24]

The economic order should, ideally, benefit humankind; people should not be servants or slaves of the economic system. This is the major theme of Pope John Paul II's encyclical *Laborem Exercens*. Concentrated capitalism—he calls it "rigid capitalism"—denies any responsibility for the common good. The so-called trickle-down theory of supply-side economics basically implies that what is most beneficial for an individual or a few makes for the greatest good and happiness of society. In fact, under such a theory there is a moral jungle where the marginal and dispossessed are the prey of beasts. It is a world of expediency and utility. Likewise, Marxist-Leninist adherents of collectivism control power and property while the masses are subordinated to the whims of the state and the party. Alienation persists under both systems; despite Marx's analysis of alienation, the person remains object, rather than subject.

The ethics proposed by Berdyaev and Maurin—and by that other significant personalist philosopher of the 1930s, Emmanuel Mounier, founder of the French journal *Esprit*—are eschatological.[25] Berdyaev wrote: "In every moral act, an act of love, compassion, sacrifice, begins the end of this world in which reign hatred, cruelty, and avarice. In every creative act begins the end of this world in which reign necessity, inertia, and limitation and arises a new world, the 'other' world."[26]

Out of this ethical background Maurin derived his economic ideas, relying especially on Peter Kropotkin, Eric Gill, Arthur Penty, G. K. Chesterton and the English distributists, and Hilaire Belloc, author of the *Servile State*. Their emphasis is on broadened ownership of property and capital, direct participation in decision-making in economic and political affairs, and a greater cooperation between workers and managers. Maurin advocated a personalist decentralism and economic democracy. He summed up his economic ideas in a piece called "The Sixth Column":

> The Catholic Worker
> stands for co-operativism
> against capitalism.
> The Catholic Worker
> stands for personalism
> against socialism.
> The Catholic Worker
> stands for leadership
> against dictatorship.
> The Catholic Worker
> stands for agrarianism
> against industrialism.
> The Catholic Worker
> stands for decentralism
> against totalitarianism.[27]

He realized that, politically speaking, one cannot be free unless one has some economic power. A poor person on the Bowery in New York City may have the right to vote, but without some economic power or property that person is effectively ignored by the system. Real democracy requires participation, and this is most fairly achieved when each person has a "piece of the pie." Maurin believed that the economic problem cannot be separated from the spiritual, that is, from the ethical. A system of injustice diminishes the humanity of the person and makes any talk of freedom or democracy a sham.

In the mid-1930s Aldous Huxley, a proponent of a democratic, decentralized life, warned of the impending crisis the world today faces—the crisis of militarization: "A country which proposes to make use of modern war as an instrument of policy must possess a highly centralized, all-powerful executive, hence the absurdity of talking about the defense of democracy by force of arms. A democracy which makes or effectively prepares for modern, scientific war must necessarily cease to be democratic."[28]

The challenge remains: how to arrange matters so that the masses dispossessed by industrial society in capitalist and socialist systems can regain property and thus freedom. Maurin's personalist democracy incorporates the principle of subsidiarity enunciated by Pius XI:

"Nothing should be done by a larger and higher institution that can be done equally well by a smaller and lower institution." A passage from Chesterton's *Outline of Sanity* sums up what such a political-economic system would entail:

> We do not propose that in a healthy society all land should be held in the same way; or that all property should be owned in the same conditions; or that all citizens should have the same relation to the city. It is our whole point that the central power needs lesser powers to balance and check it, and that these must be many kinds; some individual, some communal, some official, and so on. Some of them will probably abuse their privileges, but we prefer this risk to that of the state or the Trust which abuses its omnipotence.

In our day Pope John Paul II reiterated that the church has always taught "the principle of the priority of the laborer over capital"; in other words the priority of persons over profit, over machines, over progress, over efficiency.[29]

As a matter of justice, Maurin also condemned usury, excessive interest charged on money. Such "legalized usury" he considered to be at the base of the acquisitive society. He wrote:

> Because the State has legalized
> money-lending at interest,
> in spite of the teachings
> of the Prophets of Israel
> and the Fathers of the Church
> home owners have mortgaged their homes,
> farm owners have mortgaged their farms,
> institutions have mortgaged
> their buildings,
> governments have mortgaged
> their budgets.

This terse analysis is even more telling today. The propertyless for the most part now, however, cannot even get a mortgage because of high interest rates. The consuming public is left with an enormous debt not just in the developing nations of the world but in the United States itself, which now is the largest debtor nation in the world. This financial albatross is threatening the very stability of the world's economy, with ominous implications politically and militarily. Although he was referring to the Great Depression, Maurin's observation is prophetic for our time: "We made the mistake of running business on credit and credit has run into debts and debts are leading us to bankruptcy."[30]

Maurin's criticism of excessive interest was rooted in the teaching of St. Thomas Aquinas, who wrote that to take interest on money is "to sell what does not exist, and this evidently leads to inequality which is contrary to justice."[31] It is asking for *extra* payment when in fact return in equal measure is all that is required. In other words, it puts the debtor in double jeopardy. To be sure, some interest on money loaned is necessary to cover risk involved. On the other hand, as Aristotle said in *Nicomachean Ethics*, money is for exchange; it has a functional and practical purpose since bartering is not always possible or realistic. Money, according to the view of Aristotle, Aquinas, and Maurin, is not to be used for speculation because such speculation creates an illusion of wealth and prosperity, causing an unfair and large burden of debt for which the masses suffer, for which the common good suffers. Such a system of speculation and usury further dispossesses people from the real, active participation in economic and thus political life.

The implications of Maurin's vision are radical. He liked to think that when the ethical and spiritual underpinnings of the person and society were exposed, then, and only then, could society address the economic, political, and social issues of humankind.

PERSONALIST DEMOCRACY: SOME CONTEMPORARY EXAMPLES

Over the years Maurin has been amply criticized for his emphasis on agrarianism and his dislike of industrialism.[32] To focus on those aspects is to lose sight of his greater concern and his real contribution to ethical thought and the problems of our modern age. Maurin never worked out in detail a specific plan or program; that would have been contrary to his own disposition, intellectually and personally. His role was to provoke us into thinking and to illuminate fundamental principles. He once said that if collective bargaining leads to collectivism he was against it; however, if it led to personalist democracy it was an acceptable means.[33]

There are three contemporary examples that, I believe, illustrate a valid application of Maurin's social and political ethics. Moreover, each draws upon the personalist principles that Maurin so uniquely promoted in the 1930s. The three are employee-ownership plans in the United States, the Mondragon experiment in Spain, and the Solidarity movement in Poland.

Worker Ownership. In the United States slightly more than 2 percent of all families own 80 percent of all the nation's productive capital (stocks, bonds); approximately 8 percent owns the balance.

In short, about 10 percent of the U.S. population owns the corporate capital wealth and thus has the real power.[34] The rich borrow to make more money; the middle class and poor cannot afford to borrow, and so their ability to participate is severely curtailed. America extols "free enterprise," yet if 10 percent of the population owns the vast majority of the capital then in reality the majority of the people are virtually excluded from economic opportunity and from engaging in free enterprise.

Louis Kelso, a lawyer and an economist, is concerned about this inequity and its dire implications for democracy. Presently, he points out, working people are in a bind (to say nothing of those who are unemployed); they are unable to pay bills, to pay off mortgages, or even to take vacations. Kelso believes that although each worker cannot own a factory or business, each can at least own part of a business or factory. As industry has become more and more mechanized, the machines have become the producers and the makers of the profits. Kelso rightly says that whoever owns the machines is going to make the money. Whoever makes the money will have power and will exercise political freedom.

Kelso also notes that the banking system, as it currently operates, "denies credit to the man who needs it and gives it to the man who doesn't."[35] He proposes that banks should be limited to a modest fee for work done, rather than high, erratic interest rates that cut into the natural profits. Of course to effect such changes would require reform of banking legislation and of Federal Reserve policy. The point is to distribute the opportunities for capital and, therefore, the possibilities for broadened ownership. If such changes were implemented, over a period of time the concentration of capital and of power would gradually be dispersed. The great corporate conglomerates would cease to exist. Small farmers, who are being squeezed out of agriculture, would also benefit.

One remedy that encourages broadened ownership is called employee stock ownership plans (ESOP). An ESOP is essentially a form of trust into which the employer contributes stocks or turns over cash to employees to buy company stock. The stock is deferred compensation for the employee. The plan can assure the continuation of the company without the worry of a possible takeover from an outside firm. There are now more than 6,000 ESOPs in the United States (in 1965 there were only a dozen).

According to Norman Kurland, a consultant for ESOPs, these plans offer a real and radical reordering of the present gross imbalance in the American economy. However, for ESOPs to work, a change of attitude by both managers and workers is necessary, besides the legal and financial changes. A whole new understanding of work and the meaning of production and ownership is required. Kurland explains: "In the long run, management of a worker-owned company can ignore the participatory rights of worker-owners only at the expense of the company and everyone with a stake in its success."[36] What is required is a program to reinforce the gradual building of "worker consciousness." Managers, to be effective, must begin to think like teachers rather than like bosses. Besides education, this approach should include frequent economic feedback in the form of cash productivity bonuses linked to a formula based on profits. In addition, there must be a "just wage differential" between the highest- and lowest-paid employee. A 6 to 1 ratio is often cited; a new employee would receive one-sixth the salary of the highest-paid person in the business, from the assembly-line worker to the president. (In many corporations, at present, the ratio exceeds 50 to 1!)

Ideally, ESOPs should come from the bottom up. Realistically, in the years to come as more and more see the wisdom of ESOPs and the necessary legislative and banking reforms take place, the changeover will be multidimensional, from those starting a new concern to large corporations transforming themselves. Unions, though generally rather conservative and locked into a "wage system, class conflict" mentality, could play a key role in this transformation of the U.S. economy. Right now they could begin to lobby for more legislation enabling ESOPs (the first ESOP law was passed by Congress in 1973). They could educate workers about the relationship between property and power and the virtues of economic democracy. As wage earners they remain a kind of "slave"—propertyless—like the workers under a collectivist system. The unions could also promote ownership participation, self-management, accountability systems, and voting rights.

With ESOPs there is the beginning of the redistribution of opportunities to acquire new wealth. It is a method for a nonviolent, nonvindictive way to adjust the future for past concentration of wealth. Kurland notes, "Just as society can structure its monetary and tax policies to concentrate on ownership, society can reform its laws and institutions to decentralize future ownership."[37] The Federal Reserve, for instance, could establish a "two-tier" interest rate policy. The higher tier would rise to market rates; the lower tier would be reserved exclusively for loans that promote real growth and use ESOPs as the vehicle. In other words, the Federal Reserve could begin to offer low-cost capital credit at, say, 3 percent to those committed to starting ESOP businesses. Such a move would suddenly make capital available to millions. For example, if a steel company wants to install a new continuous caster and knows it would be a good investment, it could approach a local bank with access to the discount windows of the regional Federal Reserve bank and apply for a loan at the lower tier rate, as long as it is willing to devise an ESOP plan.

Participation without power is a hoax; there is a need to universalize access to power, to capital in America. The only way to do this is by expanded ownership opportunities, not by concentration in the state or by a few individuals and corporations.

Mondragon. Another significant example of an alternative economic structure based upon personalist-decentralist principles is Mondragon, a city in the Basque country in the north of Spain. Perhaps the most striking example of a worker cooperative in the world, it involves a whole city and began "from below," very organically, by a few individuals. Mondragon is an example of cooperation in production for the common good.

The Mondragon Group was founded in 1956 by a priest, Father Jose Maria Arizmendi.[38] It was originally begun as a business to repair refrigerators, with the name Ulgor; today this company is the largest producer of electrical refrigerators and stoves in all of Spain. There are now cooperatives for foundry products, for machine tools, and for consumers. There are seventy-six industrial cooperatives with 15,621 members. There are also five service cooperatives and a bank and research center, as well as housing, educational, and agricultural cooperatives. In all there are 28,000 working members with salaries in a 3 to 1 ratio. The cooperatives are organized democratically throughout. Members elect the board of directors, and the board appoints a general manager for a term of four years.

Father Arizmendi had for years studied the social encyclicals *Rerum Novarum* and *Quadragesimo Anno.* Those two documents inspired him to gather a few unemployed workers together in the early 1950's to study those teachings and try to apply them to practical life. Those same papal teachings had moved Peter Maurin to write nearly twenty years earlier: "The high ethics of the Canon Law are embodied in the encyclicals of Pius XI and Leo XXII on the social problems. To apply the ethics of the encyclicals to the problems of today, such is the purpose of Catholic Action."[39]

Solidarity. A third expression of the principles of Peter Maurin's vision is the Solidarity movement in Poland.[40] Solidarity began spontaneously (though with several historical antecedents) in August 1980 with the worker strikes in Gdansk. The election of Karol Wojtyla as Pope John Paul II in 1978 and his subsequent visit to his homeland in 1979 gave impetus and renewed confidence to the religious and national yearnings of the Polish people, yearnings that over the centuries of occupation, partition, and repression have never been quenched.

In a sermon delivered October 19, 1980, at Wawel Hill in Krakow on the Vistula River, Father Josef Tischner, the theologian-philosopher of the Solidarity movement, preached, "Solidarity does not need to be imposed from the outside force. This virtue is born of itself spontaneously, from the heart. . . . The virtue of Solidarity is an expression of human goodwill. In essence, we are all in Solidarity, because in the depth of our souls we are people of goodwill. Solidarity is born out of goodwill and awakens the goodwill in human beings." In the same vein, Lech Walesa, the Solidarity leader, has explained, "Solidarity is a communion of the people who do not wish to participate in a lie. This is the simplest ethic of the common people."[41]

Solidarity stands for the truth of human dignity and freedom. Although an actual program has not been explicitly developed by Solidarity, the essence of that movement is concerned with justice for workers, for all the people, and for the right to make decisions and to participate in formulating policies that affect their lives, politically, socially, and intellectually. It is quite evident that Solidarity wishes to change the centralized, bureaucratized one-party rule of the Polish state. It favors a decentralized order with economic democracy. Some in the West have tried to use Solidarity as a signal of desire for a capitalist system in Poland; they are grossly mistaken. Solidarity is a Polish movement coming out of a long history and culture with religious and social traditions rooted in the vision of the common good.

In *Laborem Exercens* Pope John Paul II expressed this particular perspective: "Work has the characteristic of binding people—this is the essence of social power, the power of building a communion. Ultimately those who work and those who govern the means of production or own them must some how join with each other in this communion." Such an understanding is diametrically opposed to a self-interested, unrestrained capitalist view. John Paul offers the personalist argument: the priority of persons, of the laborer, over capital. "When man [sic] works, using all the means of production he also wishes the fruit of this work to be used by himself and others and he wishes to be able to take part in the very work process as a sharer in responsibility and creativity at the workbench to which he applies himself. . . . The Church's teaching has always expressed the strong and deep conviction that man's work concerns not only the economy, but also, and especially, personal values. In the mind of St. Thomas Aquinas this is the principle reason in favor of private ownership of the means of production."[42] In such a milieu the economic system and the production process will benefit.

These three examples acknowledge the person as the starting

point for devising economic and political structures as Peter Maurin envisioned. The common good is recognized as the proper form for society, a society in which persons are responsible for the good of the whole and in which the goods of the whole, including natural resources, are held for the good of all.

Maurin's understanding of the personalist nature of society stresses that for democracy to be vital it requires far more than voting or the outward forms of constitutional government. His personalist ethics can be realized only if freedom is understood as the core of human personality; the person is then free to serve others. There can be no freedom without justice, and without freedom there can be no justice.

NOTES

1. Countless examples abound. In the 1987 episode known as the Iran-Contra Affair, millions of dollars were given illegally to Nicaraguan forces (the Contras) attempting to overthrow the Nicaraguan government, with whom the United States has full diplomatic relations.

2. Alexis de Tocqueville, *Democracy in America* (1835; reprinted New York: New American Library, 1956), 20.

3. Sangnier had been a student of Maurice Blondel. Le Sillon emphasized democracy as that forum in which people can develop, exercise their conscience, and engage in social and civic responsibility. Sangnier established cooperatives and made contacts with socialists, anarchists, and trade unionists. He also started a political party. At one point Pope Pius X had praised the work of Sangnier, but by 1910 Pius had decided that the group's ideas were too "modern"—it promoted tolerance, ecumenism, and stressed the humanity of Christ and the human origin of authority. It is hardly surprising that a man of Pius's narrow intellectual scope, his fear of the changing world, and his abhorrence of democracy would suppress such a group. Charles Maurras, a leader of the reactionary group L'action française and a royalist, was instrumental in persuading the Vatican to condemn Le Sillon. It is an episode in the church's checkered history in which politics and ideology overrode other considerations. Maurras was an atheist who viewed the church as the only institution capable of halting the advance of democracy and various social reforms.

As if a sign of divine justice, when Sangnier died in 1950 the church had already begun in its social teaching to recognize the worth of democratic principles and the need for social justice. (By the 1980s Pope John Paul II was actively promoting democracy and reforms on visits to Chile and other politically oppressed countries.) Sangnier's funeral was held at Notre Dame with the hierarchy in attendance and the eulogy given by Georges Bidault, premier of the French republic. Two years later Maurras died ignominiously, having served five years of a life imprisonment sentence for collaboration with the Nazis. See Jean de Fabregues, *Le Sillon de Marc Sangnier* (Paris: Librairie Academique Perrin, 1964) and Simone Galliot *Marc Sangnier 1873–1950* (LeMans: Impr. commerciale, 1960).

4.   Henri Rollet, *L'action sociale des Catholiques en France 1871–1914*, (Paris: Boivin, 1947).

5.   Joseph Brieg, "Apostle on the Bum," *Commonweal*, April 29, 1938: 10.

6.   The word *bourgeois* is often casually bandied about by radicals and leftists. Maurin realized, however, that the bourgeois spirit has nothing to do with class, and is in fact an attitude, an inner disposition.

7.   Dorothy Day, *The Long Loneliness* (New York: Curtis Books, 1972), 189; Arthur Sheehan, *Peter Maurin: Gay Believer* (Garden City, N.Y.: Hanover House, 1959), 104; Maisie Ward, *Unfinished Business* (New York: Sheed & Ward, 1964), 194.

8.   Peter Maurin, *Easy Essays* (Chicago: Franciscan Herald Press, 1984), 44. In at least six of his essays Maurin cites St. Thomas Aquinas.

9.   Janko Zagar, "Aquinas and the Social Teaching of the Church," *The Thomist* 28 (1974): 832.

10.   Thomas Aquinas, *Summa Theologiae*, I.q.29.a.3.

11.   Zagar, "Aquinas and the Social Teaching," 829.

12.   Maurin, *Easy Essays*, 115–18.

13.   Walter Abbott, ed., "Gaudium et Spes," no. 25 in *The Documents of Vatican II* (New York: America Press, 1966).

14.   Maurin, *Easy Essays*, 193.

15.   Aquinas, *Summa*, II-II, q.58. a.9.

16.   Maurin, *Easy Essays*, 115–18.

17.   Hannah Arendt, *Crises of the Republic* (New York: Harcourt Brace Jovanovich, 1972), 214; Maurin, *Easy Essays*, 85.

18.   Maurin, *Easy Essays*, 116–17.

19.   Matthew Spinka, *Nicolas Berdyaev: Captive of Freedom* (Philadelphia: Westminster Press, 1950), 19ff.

20.   Nicolas Berdyaev, *The Meaning of History* (New York: Charles Scribner's Sons, 1936), 58.

21.   Nicolas Berdyaev, *The Fate of Man in the Modern World* (New York: Morehouse, 1935), 4; *Meaning of History*, 30.

22.   To try to live this ideal is the aim of each Catholic Worker community. Although each community is autonomous, they all try to do the works of mercy in some form and to live voluntary poverty. The houses, however, do not quite express Maurin's ideal as training centers, as places to learn craft labor, etc. Historically, there has been a lack of coordination, organization, and accountability. Rule by the few has too often been the norm, contrary to Maurin's idea of communitarianism and participatory democracy. Individualism can be mistaken for freedom, or as an expression of "anarchism," which in fact is only an excuse for egoism. Because of this "organized disorganization," there is usually no recourse for appeal. Power and authority end up being used as arbitrarily as in any other setting that does not profess personalism and communitarianism. On the other hand the houses remain perhaps one of the most unique settings for the gathering of the whole spectrum of humanity, where the most unlikely come together and where those who might not find acceptance or tolerance elsewhere may at a Catholic Worker house. In this respect there is a freedom and brutal honesty that

confounds and astounds the world and what we might imagine to be our own capabilities and possibilities, or lack thereof, for being more human.

23. Spinka, *Nicolas Berdyaev*, 174.

24. Nicolas Berdyaev, *Christianity and Class War*, (London: Sheed & Ward, 1933), 81; Seymour Melman, *Profits Without Production*, (New York: Alfred Knopf, 1983), especially Chapter 4.

25. Mounier's influence on Maurin and the Catholic Worker has been significant. In getting *Esprit* started, Mounier was assisted by Jacques Maritain, who not only influenced Maurin but visited the Catholic Worker when it was located on Mott Street in New York in the 1930s. Maurin, however, did not derive his personalism from Mounier. By the time Mounier had started *Esprit* in 1932, Maurin had already devised his philosophy. Mounier's personalism expressed what Maurin had already been writing in his *Essays*. With the help of Dom Virgil Michel, O.S.B., Maurin was able to get Mounier's books published in America. In addition, the *Catholic Worker* published articles by Mounier.

26. Nicolas Berdyaev, *Samopoznanie* [Self-knowledge] (Paris: YMCA Press, 1949), 327.

27. Maurin, *Easy Essays*, 170.

28. Aldous Huxley, *Ends and Means* (New York: Harper & Row, 1937), 71.

29. Pope Pius XI, *Quadragesimo Anno* (1931); Gilbert K. Chesterton, *The Outline of Sanity* (New York: Dodd, Mead, 1927), 145; Pope John Paul II, *Laborem Exercens* (1981). John Paul's awareness and understanding of personalism came from two sources. Jerzy Turowicz, publisher of the courageous Catholic journal *Tygodnik Powszechny* in Krakow and a close friend of the pope, as a young man in 1937 attended *Esprit's* international conference in France. In 1946 Emmanuel Mounier visited Poland and lectured at the Jagiellonian University, where the then Karol Wojtyla was studying. After his ordination Wojtyla went to Rome to study and wrote his doctoral dissertation under the Dominican Reginald Garrigou-LaGrange, friend of Jacques Maritain and the early *Esprit* circle. See John Hellman, "The Prophets of Solidarity," *America*, November 6, 1982: 266–70.

30. Maurin, *Easy Essays*, 24.

31. Aquinas, *Summa*, II-II, q.78, a.1.

32. John Cort, "The Labor Movement," *Commonweal*, October 1, 1948: 597.

33. Joseph Brieg, "Apostel on the Bum," *Commonweal*, April 29, 1938: 12.

34. Report of the Joint Economic Committee, Congress of the United States, 1972 and 1985, esp. 33–35.

35. Nicholas Von Hoffman, "What Will Save Us from Poverty?" *Esquire*, December 1973: 234–36. Louis Kelso and Mortimer Adler, the Thomist philosopher, co-authored *The Capitalist Manifesto* (New York: Random House, 1958). The title is inappropriate since the authors are deeply committed to a society based on justice and fairness and respect for the dignity of the person.

The Individuals

36.   Norman Kurland, "Practical Guidelines for Building Justice in the Workplace," unpublished paper, April 12, 1982.

37.   Ibid.

38.   John Cort, "The Marvels of Mondragon," *Commonweal*, June 18, 1982: 369ff.

39.   Maurin, *Easy Essays*, 4.

40.   Stefania Szlek Miller, "Catholic Personalism and Pluralist Democracy in Poland," *Revue Canadienne des Slavistes*, September 1983: 425–39.

41.   Josef Tischner, *The Spirit of Solidarity* (San Francisco: Harper & Row, 1982), 3, 106.

42.   Pope John Paul II, *Laborem Exercens* (1981).

3. DOROTHY DAY
Pilgrim of Peace

Eileen Egan

DOROTHY DAY STOOD before an audience of eight thousand persons, mostly women, at the International Eucharistic Congress of 1976 in Philadelphia. The congress was timed to be a part of the American Catholic celebration of the two hundredth anniversary of the founding of the United States of America. The theme of the gathering, to which four women, among them Mother Teresa of Calcutta, had already addressed themselves, was "Women and the Eucharist." The date was August 6.

Dorothy Day was seventy-nine years old, and her white hair was wrapped in a kerchief of blue cotton. Her tall frame was slightly stooped, and her blue-checked cotton dress hung loosely upon it. She appeared frail, but not too frail or too old to challenge the establishment. *The Enquirer*, a daily of Washington, D.C., headlined her challenge: "Pacifist Assails Timing of Military Mass." The organizers of the congress had chosen August 6, the anniversary of the atomic destruction of Hiroshima, as the day to honor those in the armed services.

At the Cathedral of Sts. Peter and Paul, a mass was bringing together large elements of the army, navy, and air force in full service regalia. That morning, as Dorothy Day, Mother Teresa, and I made our way together from a convent that had given us hospitality, Dorothy confided to me that she dreaded the talk. She felt in conscience that she had to chide publicly the organizers of the Eucharistic Congress.

It was with visible effort that she made her way to the podium. She began by confessing to the audience, "It is almost easier to stand before a judge and go to jail than to come before you. I am usually very diffuse," she continued, "but today, because of the seriousness of this day, I wrote out my paper."[1] In point of fact, when she had ascertained that there was to be no mention of Hiroshima but instead an honor to the military, she had composed her talk with special care. It was the only occasion, in all the years I knew her, that Dorothy Day came to a meeting with a typewritten text.

Before the words of censure, Dorothy Day declared her gratitude to and love of the Catholic church. It was the church, she read, that taught her that before approaching the eucharist, there must be reconciliation with one's fellows and penance for wrongs committed. "And here we are on August 6th," she said, as though the words were being wrung from her, "the day the first atomic bomb was dropped, which ended the Second World War. There had been holocausts before—massacres after the First World War of the Armenians, all but forgotten now, and the holocaust of the Jews, God's chosen people. . . . It is a fearful thought that unless we do penance, we will perish. Our Creator gave us life, and the eucharist to sustain our life. But we have given the world instruments of death of inconceivable magnitude. Today we are celebrating—how strange a word—a mass for the military, the 'armed forces.' "

Dorothy expressed wonder at the fact that those in charge of the congress had not realized what August 6 meant to those dedicated to the work of peace. Thirty-one years earlier, after the nuclear holocaust of August 6, 1945, Dorothy Day had gone on record in the pages of the *Catholic Worker*, deploring the bomb and the jubilation its use evoked. "Mr. Truman was jubilant," she had written then. "Truman is a true man of his time in that he was jubilant. . . . We have killed 318,000 Japanese. . . . They die vaporized, our Japanese brothers, scattered, man, woman and children, to the four winds, over the seven seas. Perhaps we will breathe their dust into our nostrils, feel them in the fog of New York on our faces, feel them in the rain on the hills of Easton. . . . 'We have spent two billion on the greatest scientific gamtle in history and won,' said President Truman jubilantly."[2]

When she asked the audience before her, "Why not a mass for the military on some other day?" there was a burst of applause. "I plead," she asked the participants, "that we regard the military mass, and all the masses today, as an act of penance, begging God to forgive us."[3]

An ovation lasting several minutes broke out after Day finished her speech. Mother Teresa and all on the platform joined with the audience in the acclamation, perhaps realizing that there might not be many more occasions when Dorothy Day would appear on a public stage.

The talk on Hiroshima Day 1976 was indeed the last time Dorothy Day spoke in public. To the end of her life, she was committed to a prophetic witness for peace. It was a witness that would move individuals to become peacemakers. It also helped the Catholic church to see the peace of Jesus as central to its message. As a witness for peace in a church that over the centuries had accommodated itself to war, she still loved that church as "Christ made visible." Calling her church to task when she saw its course as a scandal to the gospel, she did so out of an overpowering and transparent love. "Though she is a harlot at times, she is our Mother," she would say.[4]

By a special gift, she was able to direct attention to issues rather than engage in naked confrontation with the ecclesiastical institution. It was because love undergirded all her positions of dissent, in particular her dissent on the issue of peace and war, that this one woman was able to influence the U.S. Catholic church in a deeper way than any Catholic lay person of the twentieth century. The charisma of this love and the blazing quality of her dream sparked generations of Catholics, especially the young, to respond to the ideals lived out before them by Dorothy Day and the Catholic Worker movement.

This chapter deals with one strand of the movement founded by Dorothy Day, a strand that was distinctly her contribution, in contrast to that of her cofounder and mentor, Peter Maurin. It was this strand, namely absolute pacifism, that gave rise to Dorothy Day's "loving disagreement"—to use a Quaker term—with the Catholic church.

Dorothy Day derived her absolute pacifism from the teachings of the New Testament, and in particular from the unconditional love that Jesus taught his followers, a love that embraced even enemies. (Other sources of her pacifism will be discussed later.) As a young woman, seventeen years old at the beginning of World War I, she found herself drawn to socialism. She became a comrade of the left, and though her friends were socialists and communists, she never actually joined a political party. She took part in antiwar demonstrations and actively opposed U.S. participation in World War I. She described her position as "pacifist in what I considered an imperialist war though not pacifist as a revolutionist."[5]

When Day was converted to Catholicism on December 28, 1927, she came into a church in thrall to a teaching of justified warfare. It was an unusual and even daring act to assert that one was at the same time a practicing Catholic and an absolute pacifist. As late as 1967, the article on pacifism in the *New Catholic Encyclopedia* stated, "It is clear from what has been said that absolute pacifism is irreconcilable with traditional Catholic doctrine."[6]

Traditional teaching on peace and war was considered to begin and end with the conditions of the just war, developed by St. Augustine of Hippo (354–430 A.D.). Augustine accepted from Cicero that war is fought to secure peace and must be declared by lawful authority. Justice was a basic concern of Augustine and he defined as just those wars undertaken to avenge injuries and restore justice. In such wars, he asserted in "Aginst Faustus," soldiers should perform their military duties in behalf of the peace and safety of the community."[7]

The theologians, guardians of the "just war" conditions, were not consulted as wars were unleashed, and the most they could do was to remonstrate after the slaughter was over. Since every nation declaring a war declares it just, the unintended effect of "just war" teaching was to allow Christians to be rented out for combat in every war declared by every ruler or nation. Once the war was announced as just, nations and rulers could and did use any means at their disposal, from siege and boiling oil to nuclear bombs. Noncombatant immunity was a victim of war. War, in effect, became an enterprise divorced from morality.

The witness to a theology of peace was left, in the main, to the "peace churches," the Mennonites, Brethren, and the Society of Friends, the Quakers. The "just war" tradition had the effect of impeding the development of a coherent theology of peace, not only in the Catholic church but in the major Christian churches, sharers of this "just war" tradition. It is worth noting that the "just war" tradition never became a creedal matter in the Catholic church.

Day buttressed her own pacifist position by carrying statements by the early fathers of the church in the *Catholic Worker*. She also opened its pages to priests who discussed the incompatibility of war, especially modern war, with the teachings of Jesus. Among them were Franziskus Stratmann of Germany, Johannes Ude of Austria, W. E. Orchard and Canon F. H. Drinkwater of England, and Michael J. Deacy of the United States.[8]

It was Dorothy Day, however, who by her year-in-year-out writings on the centrality of love—including love of enemy—and by her acts of prophetic witness against preparations for war, helped bring to the forefront of the Catholic church an ancient and valid teaching on peace. It was often called pacifism, and Dorothy Day used the term freely, aware of its derivation from peacemaking. Others who shared her views used the word more sparingly, and only with an explanation, since it was a term little understood in the Catholic community. When it was used, it carried a pejorative connotation of passivity, and in particular passivity in the face of injustice and oppression. For many it implied an unwillingness to go to the aid of a person attacked. For some in the Catholic community, the term *gospel nonviolence* served to open more doors to understanding. The teaching of gospel nonviolence, or pacifism, was of overarching importance when war had escaped all moral boundaries and threatened the future of humankind.

WHAT DOROTHY DAY, along with Peter Maurin, cofounder of the Catholic Worker movement, brought to the U.S. Catholic church was a revolution on many levels. Significantly, it was a lay revolution rising from below. Dorothy Day's commitment to pacifism came in a matrix of personalism, which called for a heightened sense of personal responsibility for one's neighbors and involvement in struggle for justice on their behalf. Personalism, as developed by Peter Maurin, was expressed in the "daily practice of the works of mercy," the corporal works of feeding the hungry, clothing the naked, and sheltering the shelterless, and the spiritual works of mercy, including consoling the afflicted and instructing those in need of it.[9] These works of mercy were to be carried out even at the cost of personal sacrifice and rested on a bedrock of voluntary poverty.

During the early days of the Catholic Worker, days of a savage Depression, strictures against the competitive and depersonalized spirit of capitalism won respect, as did Peter Maurin's insistence on finding "concordances" in a time of confrontation. The teaching and policy of the Catholic Worker on the rejection of interest, the very life blood of modern capitalism, was too shocking to be considered, although it had been a firm teaching of the Catholic church at an earlier age. Peter Maurin's revolution, gentle, communitarian, and tied to right use of the land, was adopted by Dorothy Day. Maurin was convinced that such a revolution could remake twentieth-century society "during and after the fall of modern empires," as it had after the fall of the Roman empire. Dorothy Day decided that as a journalist, coming from a family of journalists, her part in the revolution would be to edit a newspaper. Her special contribution would be pacifism. Many students of the movement agree with Mel Piehl that "after 1945, it was the issue of pacifism that most effectively represented the Catholic Worker's gospel idealism."[10]

When Dorothy Day stood among the 50,000 communist demonstrators massed in Union Square on May Day 1933, with the first issue of the *Catholic Worker* under her arm, she could hardly have envisioned the sequel. From that first tiny printing of 2,500, the *Catholic Worker* leapt to 100,000 by the end of the year. Before 1936 was out, the circulation had reached 150,000, counting the bundles sent to parishes and schools.[11] The movement was heeded, not only because it spoke to the burning issues of the day, but because those in the community actually lived out what they proposed to others. Dorothy and Peter, together with those who joined them, lived in the same poverty as those they served, except that their poverty was chosen. In 1936, the movement was given a headquarters at 115 Mott Street, abutting New York's Chinatown. It was a five-story tenement, with two storefronts and in the rear, another house of sixteen rooms. Rarely did sunlight reach the rear house, hemmed in as it was by surrounding tenements. Yet in its dark, heatless apartments, into which Irish immigrants had poured in the nineteenth century, lived the homeless and a band of young people on fire to remake the world.

In the same year, 1936, violent conflict exploded in Europe; it was to halt the impetus of the Catholic Worker movement. The issue was raised on which Dorothy Day had taken her stand and from which she would not move—pacifism. It was an issue for which the U.S. Catholic church was not ready.

THE EVENT THAT precipitated a division in the Catholic Worker movement was the outbreak, in July 1936, of a savage civil war in Spain. It was to last thirty-three months and cost as many as a million lives. Catholic publications were filled with accounts of outrages against priests and nuns, including tortures and executions, and burnings of churches. Except for some Basque Catholics who sided with the loyalists, the church in Spain put its hopes in a victory of the insurgents, led by General Francisco Franco. The U.S. church followed the lead of the church in Spain. Support of the insurgents took on the overheated rhetoric of a crusade.

The *Catholic Worker* delivered a shock to the U.S. Catholic community by announcing its neutrality between the warring sides. Careful readers of the paper should not have been surprised, since the *Catholic Worker* had announced in the May 1936 issue, shortly before the outbreak of the Spanish conflict, that it was a pacifist paper, opposing also class war, class hatred, and imperialist war.

> A pacifist who is willing to endure the scorn of the unthinking mob, the ignominy of jail, the pain of stripes and the threat of death cannot be lightly dismissed as a coward afraid of physical pain.

A pacifist even now must be prepared for the opposition of the mob who think violence is bravery. A pacifist in the next war must be ready for martyrdom.[12]

The Spanish Civil War was discussed in November 1936 in an editorial entitled "The Use of Force." After describing how immensely difficult it was for Jesus' disciples to learn the truth of the "hard saying" that they must imitate Jesus in "laying down their lives for their friends," Dorothy wrote,"

> And now the whole world is turning to "force" to conquer. Fascist and Communist alike believe that only by the shedding of blood can they achieve victory.
>
> Christians, when they are seeking to defend their faith by arms, by force and violence, are like those who said to Our Lord, "Come down from the Cross. If you are the Son of God, save Yourself."
>
> But Christ did not come down from the Cross. He drank to the last drop the agony of His suffering, and was not part of the agony, the hopelessness, the unbelief, of his own disciples.
>
> If 2,000 have suffered martyrdom in Spain, is that suffering atoned for by the death of 90,000 in the Civil War? Would not these martyrs themselves have cried out against more shedding of blood?[13]

Dorothy's prayer was that all, including the priests and people in Spain, would have the courage to accept suffering and become "a spectacle to the world and to angels and to man." She never closed her eyes to the persecution of the church by the loyalist side in blood-drenched Spain. "In the light of this fact," she wrote, in 1938 at the height of the carnage,

> it is inconceivably difficult to write as we do. It is folly—it seems madness—to say as we do, "we are opposed to force as a means of settling personal, national or international disputes. . . ."
>
> We pray those martyrs of Spain to help us, to pray for us, to guide us in this stand we take. We speak in their name. Their blood cries out against a spirit of hatred and savagery. . . . And did they not rather pray, when the light of Christ burst upon them, that love would overcome hatred, that men dying for the faith, rather than killing for their faith, would save the world? . . . As long as men trust in the use of

force—only a more savage and brutal force will overcome the enemy. . . .

While we take this stand we are not condemning those who have seized arms and engaged in war. Who of us as individuals if we were in Spain today, would tell what he would do? . . .

We are afraid of the word love, and yet love is stronger than death, stronger than hatred. If we do not, as the press, emphasize the law of love, we betray our trust, our vocation. We must stand opposed to the use of force.[14]

The vocation of the Catholic Worker was thus spelled out.

Dorothy Day had some European cohorts in her stand against the violence of both sides in the Spanish conflict. One person who shared her views was Emmanuel Mounier, editor of the influential Catholic review *Esprit*. It was from Mounier's writings that Peter Maurin had adopted the key concept of personalism. In November 1936, Mounier published a long article by a Spanish Catholic condemning the bloodletting of each side, and mailed it to the *Catholic Worker*. The article appeared on the first page of the paper for December 1936.[15] A few well-known French Catholics spoke out in the same vein, including Georges Bernanos, François Mauriac and Jacques Maritain.

The formation of a Catholic peace group in England called Pax was reported in the *Catholic Worker*. One of the founders, E. I. Watkin, was quoted as stating that in any modern war, the evils unleashed would be greater than any good that might be accomplished. Pax also supported the right of conscientious objection to war. Among the Pax founders was Eric Gill, artist, craftsman, and pacifist, who developed social concepts strikingly similar to those of Peter Maurin. Gill pointed to war and usury as the great evils of modern times. By February 1937, the paper announced the formation of an American Pax with Joseph Zarrella and William Callahan as leaders.[16] English Pax, which faltered during World War II when its pacifist views were muted, came alive at war's end. With Dorothy Day as sponsor, it branched out in the United States in 1962.

The young Catholic Workers associated with Pax pledged themselves not to bear arms or assist in any way in carrying out a war. They seemed to echo the pledge of those who joined the Third Order of St. Francis not to "take up lethal weapons or bear them against anybody." Membership in the Third Order released them from the feudal oath, making it possible for them to be, in effect, conscientious objectors in the unending wars declared by princes and lords in the Middle Ages.

Peter Maurin, by insisting on "the daily practices of the works of mercy," was actually excluding the option of war. He gave depth to the pacifist vocation of the Catholic Worker without stating explicitly that he espoused pacifism. In Easy Essay after Easy Essay, he pointed to the evil and futility of war. His own experience as a conscript while a member of an order of Christian brothers served to turn him against militarism. He became active in Le Sillon, a movement with an antimilitarist position. On the subject of the Spanish Civil War, Maurin did not speak out, though he made it clear that his way was the Franciscan way, a way that excluded violence. For a man intent on finding "concordances," the confrontation of the Worker movement with modern war, and the bitter criticism it evoked, was hard to bear. "Perhaps silence would be better for a time than to continue our opposition to war," he said to Dorothy Day as World War II began. "Men are not ready to listen."[17]

Some saw Dorothy Day's refusal to support the Spanish insurgent cause as the result of her leftist past and attacked her as a communist. On the other hand, her old comrades of the left saw her position of neutrality as a betrayal. Dorothy was stung by the fact that one of her oldest and dearest friends, Mike Gold, a committed communist, considered her pro-Franco. She mentioned this only after his death. None of the partisans glimpsed her vision, a vision that rose above the issues that divide and embitter humankind.[18]

> We believe that all men are members or potential members of the Mystical Body of Christ. This means Jews, Gentiles, Black and White. This means our enemies as well as our friends. Since there is no time with God, and since we are told that all men are members or potential members of Christ's Mystical Body, that means that now at the present time we must look upon all men with love. We must overcome all evil with good, hatred with love.
>
> Hence our work to combat anti-Semitism; to combat the use of force as a means of settling disputes between men and nations.[19]

BY JULY 1940 there were unmistakable signs that the United States would soon be engaged in war. Preparations for universal military conscription had already begun. Dorothy Day became the lone lay Catholic voice raised to official Washington on behalf of the right of conscientious objection for the Catholic laity. News reached her that month that hearings were being held in Washington before the Military Affairs Committee of the Congress to discuss the Burke-Wadsworth Compulsory Military Training Law. Joseph Zarrella, a young man who had joined the Catholic Worker in 1935, related, "Miss Day told me we would have to rush down to Washington right away."[20] Obtaining the text of the proposed law, they hurriedly prepared testimony and found a typist to make presentable copies for the Senate panel.

Dorothy learned that there had been testimony on the part of the Catholic church. Monsignor Michael J. Ready, secretary of the National Catholic Welfare Conference, asserted that Catholics were patriots and considered patriotism a virtue. He pointed out that the bishops were opposed to provisions in the bill that might include compulsory military service for seminary students and religious brothers under vows. All ministers of religion were exempt from the draft. In speaking for seminarians and religious brothers, Ready adverted to the damage the law, as proposed, would cause to the religious, educational and charitable institutions of the church, as well as to civil society.

In testimony before Senator Burke and the panel members, Dorothy Day stated:

> We are a paper that is edited by lay people. It is an expression of lay Catholic opinion in regard to matters in the social order. . . . In New York City we have a house that feeds about one thousand people a day, the unemployed who come to us.
>
> Both Mr. Zarrella and I are speaking of the bill in relation to the unemployed especially, with whom we have so much to do. I for one feel that any arming of youth will result in the future in a real army of the unemployed, disillusioned, unemployed still, beginning all over again the degrading hunt for work.

She challenged the panel on two points, the threat to civil rights and its limitation of conscientious objection. "Section 10 of this bill," she pointed out, "does more than hint at doing away with free speech, free press, free assembly, even free conscience. Anyone who aids or abets another in evading conscription is liable to fine and imprisonment." She added that if Catholic Workers felt obliged in conscience to oppose a law they considered unjust, "then we are in danger of having our work wiped out, of imprisonment and fine."

Senator Burke explained that penalties would come into effect only if the bill became law. While it was possible to urge objection to the passage of the law, he asked Dorothy Day whether the law, when written into statute, should be evaded. She referred to the rights of conscience "which we, as all Americans, believe in. Well, if we consider that there is an unjust law passed, we would consider it our duty not to follow that law."

On the question of conscientious objection to military service, Senator Burke explained that it was taken care of in the bill. There would be exemption from combat for any member of a "religious sect whose creed or principles forbid its members to participate in war in any form." The Senator asked Dorothy Day, "Does not that protect the situation?"

"It does not protect Catholics; no," Dorothy replied, "it may protect the Quakers, the Mennonites, the Dunkards, but not Catholics. . . . There is nothing in the Catholic creed which would entitle us to that exemption. It does not deal with Catholics."[21]

A cleric from the National Catholic Welfare Conference who happened to be at the hearings questioned Dorothy's right to speak for Catholics on the issue. She answered in a few words: "We are speaking for lay people, and they are the ones who fight the wars."[22]

In the summer of 1940 the *Catholic Worker* featured a front page article on conscription, unmistakably in Dorothy's style. It stated, "In addition to imperilling man's natural and sacred rights, conscription contributes to an 'armed peace' a fallacy which has been pointed out by Pope Pius XI. The biggest issue in the world today is the work for peace. We continue to work for justice at home, charity for all and personal responsibility."

The article noted that fines and imprisonment faced those aiding or abetting young men in resisting conscription, acknowledging that this meant a crisis for the Catholic Worker. It would, however, continue to oppose conscription. "How can we sacrifice our principles? We ask the right to call attention to the precious counsels of Jesus Christ, our Brother."[23]

Dorothy Day's Washington testimony was of no avail. The Selective Service Act, passed in August 1940, ignored recommendations from her and from representatives of mainline churches that the right of conscientious objection should apply to those whose beliefs might include the possibility of a just war. This has been called selective objection. Selective Service made a theological decision, which it was hardly in a position to make, that the only conscientious objectors recognized under the law would be religious "all-war" objectors whose position arose from religious training and belief. It has been pointed out by many that the position of selective objection demands more from the indivdual objector than does the blanket rejection of all wars. It calls for the objector to examine a particular war and determine whether it meets certain conditions that harmonize with the objector's conscientious beliefs.

As early as 1936, the *Catholic Worker* had been warning of the war that was to be unleashed in Europe. To the pacifist, the time to oppose war is before it breaks out. "War Imminent: Catholics Must Judge It Now" was the headline. After asserting that "there will be another war," the article urged Catholics to make up their minds about what they would do in the war. "Know the teachings of the Catholic Church on war," they were urged. "But do more than know them: apply them. The Church presents a stronger case for conscientious objection than any other group on the face of the earth."[24]

From the beginning of the movement, Dorothy Day had written or accepted articles exposing the things that made for war: hatred, especially anti-Semitism, all forms of injustice, and growing totalitarianism. As Hitler's grip on Germany strengthened in the 1930s, a Catholic Worker group picketed the German consulate in New York City. Dorothy Day was one of the organizers of the Committee of Catholics to Fight Anti-Semitism, which brought out its own publication, *The Voice.*

With Europe engulfed in war, Dorothy stated in September 1939:

> We must choose sides now; not between nations at war but between the world's way and Christ's way. The world hates; Christ loves. The world's way brings chaos and destruction. Christ's way brings peace and justice. Pray for Poland, pray for England, pray for France, pray for Germany. If this seems like a madman's advice, we can only say again that Christians must be fools for Christ's sake. We believe or we do not believe and we are now given our chance to bear witness. Pray for peace.[25]

Dorothy Day drove home her point in the editorial "Our Stand" in June 1940.

> "And if we are invaded" is another question asked. We say again that we are opposed to all but the use of nonviolent means to resist an invader. We are urging what is a seeming impossibility—a training in the use of nonviolent means of opposing injustice, servitude and a deprivation of the means of holding fast to the faith. It is again the folly of the cross. But how else is the Word of God to be kept alive in the world. That word is Love, and we are bidden to love God and to love one another. It is the whole law; it is all of life.[26]

Not even key members of the Catholic Worker community, to say nothing of the larger Catholic community, could accept absolute Christian nonviolence. Some Catholic Worker houses refused to distribute the New York *Catholic Worker* and one group actually burned it. Dorothy Day took action, sending a letter to all thirty houses of the Catholic Worker throughout the country. Her letter of August 10, 1941, is famous in the movement, mentioned over and over again to new arrivals. She wrote that she realized that not all members of the Catholic Worker movement stood with her on the issue of pacifism, and admitted that she had been unsuccessful in attempts at changing their views. While groups, she added, could maintain their disagreement on the issue, they must continue to distribute the New York *Catholic Worker*. If they refused, they should separate themselves from the Catholic Worker movement and "not use the name of a movement with which they are in such fundamental disagreement."

A week-long retreat later that same month brought together members of Catholic Worker houses at Maryfarm, the Catholic Worker farm in Easton, Pennsylvania. They prayed, worshipped, and discussed the movement, and some returned to their houses still opposed to pacifism. Dorothy Day's letter and the retreat made two crucial points. First, the vocation of the Catholic Worker movement was indissolubly linked to pacifism, or at least the freedom to disseminate pacifist views to other houses through the New York paper. Secondly, the New York Catholic Worker had a special role in asserting what the movement stood for. In a way, Dorothy Day had staked the coherent future of the movement on the issue of pacifism.

Much correspondence ensued as Catholic Workers broke with the movement and responded to the draft for combat in World War II. Among them were John Cogley and Tom Sullivan of the Chicago house. That Christian pacifism was commonly viewed in terms of heresy is clear in a letter from Cogley to Dorothy Day written after the Chicago paper was discontinued in August 1941: "Profound disagreement is a wall between people and it rears higher every day. How I wish you weren't a heretic. And sometimes how I wish that I were one, too."[27]

AT THE ENTRY of the United States into World War II on December 7, 1941, Dorothy Day went to the Church of the Transfiguration on Mott Street, prayed, and wrote: "Dear Fellow Workers in Christ: Lord God, merciful God, Our Father, shall we keep silent or shall we speak? And if we speak, what shall we say?"

These words were carried on the front page of the January 1942 issue of the *Catholic Worker* under a stark black headline with half-inch-high letters: "Our Country Passes from Undeclared to Declared War: We Continue Our Pacifist Stand." In the center of the page was a graphic of St. Francis of Assisi with the words "Peace Without Victory." Her letter continued:

> I am sitting here in the church . . . writing this in your presence. Out on the streets it is quiet, but You are there, too, in the Chinese, in the Italians, these neighbors we love. We love them because they are our brothers, as Christ is our Brother, and God our Father. . . .
>
> We will print the words of Christ, who is with us always, even to the end of the world. "Love your enemies, do good to those who hate you and pray for those who persecute and calumniate you, so that you may be children of your Father in heaven, who makes His sun to rise on the good and the evil, and sends rain on the just and the unjust." . . .
>
> In the *Catholic Worker* we will quote our Pope, our saints, our priests. We will go on printing the articles of Father Hugo, who reminds us today that we are all called to be saints, that we are other Christs, reminding us of the priesthood of the laity.
>
> We are still pacifists. Our manifesto is the Sermon on the Mount, which means that we will try to be peacemakers. Speaking for many of our conscientious objectors, we will not participate in armed warfare or in making munitions, or by buying government bonds to prosecute the war, or by urging others to these efforts.

After appealing for daily, hourly prayer, she went on, "Let us add that unless we continue this prayer with almsgiving, in giving to the least of God's children, and fasting in order that we may help feed the hungry, and penance in recognition of our share in the guilt, our prayer may become empty words."

Dorothy Day realized that the government might take some action against her and the whole movement. She concluded, "But we trust in the generosity and understanding of our government and our friends, to permit us to continue, to use our paper to preach Christ crucified."[28]

In addition to her front-page letter, Dorothy Day contributed a column, announcing, "Since this is the only paper published by Catholic pacifists in the world, and since we are trying to print as much material as possible which throws light on our point of view, we may seem to be overly crowded with one subject."[29] That she took complete responsibility for the position taken by the paper was clear from the masthead, adorned by her solitary name as editor and publisher, with Peter Maurin as founder.

DOROTHY KEPT TO her promise to print the articles of the Reverend John J. Hugo and to quote from the saints. Hugo provided a half-dozen articles, later published under the title "Weapons of the Spirit." He elaborated on the theme of St. Paul: "Though we walk in the flesh, we do not war according to the flesh. For the weapons of our warfare are not carnal, but mighty to God, unto the pulling down of fortifications, destroying counsels."[30] Hugo began a second series of articles under the title "The Gospel of Peace" in the September 1942 issue; they were published later as a Catholic Worker pamphlet. He developed at length his thesis that "the supernatural principles of Christ are considered irrelevant to war. When they participate in war Christians set aside revelation and evangelical principles."[31]

Dorothy Day consistently invited to the pages of the *Catholic Worker* theologians of like mind, including Father Paul Hanly Furfey and Monsignor G. Barry O'Toole. In later years, these were joined by such articulate exponents of Christian peacemaking as Robert Ludlow, Gordon Zahn, Thomas Merton, James Douglass, and Patrick Jordan.[32]

In an editorial clearly in her style, Dorothy Day challenged all to admit guilt for "our participation in the social order which has resulted in this monstrous crime of war. That should be our cry with every mouthful we eat. 'We are starving in Europe.' When we look to our comfort in a warm bed, in a warm home, we must cry, 'My brother, my mother, my child is dying of the cold.' "[33]

At the height of World War II, the Catholic Worker printed testimonies to pacifism from the early fathers of the church. The period of the early church fathers is considered by some historians to have extended to about 600 A.D. These testimonies were all given before 450 A.D. Under the title "Patristics and Peace," spiritual nourishment for pacifists came from St. Clement of Alexandria, St. Justin Martyr, St. Cyril of Alexandria, St. Gregory Nazianzen, St. John Chrysostom, and St. Martin of Tours. St. Gregory Nazianzen reminded Christians of every age that only one war should be waged, the war against the powers of evil. "As to those who have attacked us," he admonished, "let us call even them by the name of brothers."

Featured was the famous refusal to kill by St. Martin of Tours. Martin had carried out soldierly duties, actually akin to police duties, until called upon to face an enemy in battle. He refused to kill. "A soldier of Christ I am," he told his commander. "To fight is not allowable for me." An armistice called a halt to the fighting and Martin, escaping execution, lived to become the bishop of Tours.

A citation from the third-century canons of Hippolytus clarified the situation of Christians who found themselves in the Roman army. "Soldiers are not to kill even if this is commanded to them."[34]

Dorothy Day uncovered for ordinary Christians a stream of nonviolence coming from the Christian gospels and from the great spiritual teachers of the early church. The stream, subterranean at times but surfacing in certain historical periods, ran, nevertheless, an unceasing course. Even in the teaching of St. Augustine, grafted from Cicero and seminal for just-war thinking, killing was justified only in defense of the community. Against a personal attacker, the Christian was to accept death rather than inflict it on the attacker. By joining the peace message with a life of poverty and merciful service, Dorothy Day revived a nonviolent tradition that had never died; with the Catholic Worker movement, she put flesh on the ancient maxim, "the church abhors bloodshed."

DESPITE THE FACT that the Selective Service legislation provided for "all-war objection" as the only basis for conscientious objection, some Catholic conscripts received the classification of CO. In general, draft boards ruled against the claim of those who held to the possibility of a just war but objected to the war in question; these objectors were sent to prison. However, some boards ruled in favor of this claim; those whose claims were sustained either entered CO camps or participated in alternative service, involving service to others and works of mercy. Some Catholics asserted their objection to all wars. Joseph Zarrella and Gerald Griffin of the New York Catholic Worker obtained the CO classification as total pacifists. They joined the American Field Service and became ambulance drivers in the Middle East war zone.

Having testified publicly on the right to conscientious objection and continuing to support it, Dorothy Day spent herself on practical programs on behalf of objectors. In 1940 she sponsored the formation of the Association of Catholic Conscientious Objectors. It replaced the Pax group, founded earlier, and was led by Arthur Sheehan, an editor of the paper. Sheehan, a pacifist, was exempted from the draft as a recovered tuberculosis patient.

The Friends, Mennonites, and other groups operated camps for COs in an arrangement with the National Service Board for Religious Objectors. Why not a camp for Catholic COs, sponsored by the Association for Catholic Conscientious Objectors? With immense effort, such a camp was opened in July 1941 in a ramshackle former Forest Service camp in Stoddard, New Hampshire. Enormous difficulties soon came to the surface, from inadequate financing to meaningless make-work programs. The men were poorly fed and lacked sufficient clothing to protect them against the New Hampshire winter. An appeal in the *Catholic Worker* for canned food and clothing yielded some results. The camp was moved to an improved site in Warner, New Hampshire, but nothing, not even the heroic work of Dorothy Day and Arthur Sheehan, could save the experiment. The Warner camp was closed in March 1943.

Just over sixty Catholic COs passed through Stoddard and Warner, including Gordon Zahn, whose book, *Another Part of the War: The Camp Simon Story,* recalled the experience.[35] Catholic COs were hardly heroes in their own community, but some Catholic institutions accepted them for alternative civilian service. The Alexian Brothers employed many Catholic COs in their hospital in Chicago. Gordon Zahn, among others, found meaningful work in the Rosewood Training School for the mentally handicapped in Maryland.

Arthur Sheehan, with the help of Dorothy Day, edited a quarterly called the *Catholic CO* for the Association of Catholic Conscientious Objectors. In "Women and War," Dorothy Day addressed the role of women in urging war resistance and conscientious objection. She faced the charge that she, as a woman, was "placing burdens on the backs of others that I did not have to bear myself." Her response was that women should intensify their antiwar, anticonscription efforts. "In World War I," she pointed out, "there were two Catholic COs. In World War II, there were 154 Catholic COs in jail and 200 in Civilian Public Service, and many more who were not called were registered with us." In any other war, she hoped to see a "mighty army of Catholic COs using the weapons of the spirit."[36]

SUDDENLY, IN 1943, with World War II bringing death and desolation to large areas of the globe, Dorothy Day decided to absent herself from the Catholic Worker. She announced that she would give a year to solitude and prayer, removing herself from the responsibility of the movement. She turned over editorship of the paper to Arthur Sheehan and took her name from the masthead.

Dorothy explained that the impulse for such a decision had come to her during a retreat given by the Reverend John J. Hugo at Maryfarm in Easton, Pennsylvania. Those of us who made the retreat, which was given repeatedly, knew that in the five days of silence, the focus was on the ascetic life, on the need to "give up" what was dearest in our lives. The retreat, discouraged in Canada where it had originated, was controversial in the Catholic Worker movement, and seemed unsettling to those with a tendency to scrupulosity.[37]

For Dorothy Day, the retreat was food for the strong, and she took from it the strength to "give up" the Catholic Worker for a year. The year started in September 1943 in Farmingdale, Long Island, where she was given hospitality by the sisters of St. Dominic. Dorothy attended early mass with the sisters and spent time during the day in their chapel. Her daughter, Tamar, had joined her friend Mabel Egan at the Farmingdale State School of Applied Agriculture. Dorothy was now able to give more time to her daughter, now eighteen. She was in fact a mother to both Tamar and Mabel, who were roommates in Mott House on campus. They were both in love and planning to marry the following year; eventually each became the mother of nine children. On weekends, Dorothy could visit her own mother in nearby Minneola.

Dorothy was able to absent herself from the Catholic Worker because the flow of invitations to speak that had formerly taken her around the country, to parishes, schools, seminaries, had petered out. News of destruction in far parts of the world fed headlines, and grief over sacrificed lives filled hearts. For Dorothy Day, the hours of solitude, when she took her three meals alone, were a severe and even painful change from the days at the Catholic Worker or on the road. She made a little community with the two young women and relished the hour in the evening when they came to her room. Still in their barn clothes and often smelling of the goatherd, they would sit down with her for hot cocoa and for the bread she often baked. The young women, who seldom cleaned their room, would return from the cow barn to find that Dorothy had slipped into their room and set it to rights.

During the Christmas season of 1943, I visited Farmingdale to see Mabel Egan and spent some time with Dorothy Day. She seemed glad to have company, and we sat and talked in her "cell," a long, dim room with many sinks and a stove. It had once been used for cooking classes. In the corner was her sleeping cot. I was on a short leave from work at a Mexican camp for Polish refugees. They had survived the massive deportations from eastern Poland during the Hitler-Stalin pact and had been given temporary shelter in a corner of the Mexican countryside.

On the day before Christmas, we sat and talked about the sufferings inflicted on ordinary people by wars whose causes they did not understand. Dorothy was concerned not only with the terrible anguish of each day, but with the hunger and homelessness after the killing had stopped. Devastated by my experience with simple people who had seen their families die before their eyes in Siberia, I wondered if the end of the war would not bring a tidal wave of refugees, especially in Europe. We agreed that only an immense explosion of compassion and practical works of mercy could help those victimized and displaced by the works of war.

I reminded Dorothy that I, in company with many others, owed our pacifist convictions to her. She wondered what in particular had moved me to a sudden about-face in my acceptance of war, and I told her it was her eloquent stand against the violence of both sides in the Spanish Civil War. I still did not use the word *pacifism*, I explained, finding the term *gospel nonviolence* easier to defend among my friends who considered me unpatriotic if not a traitor.

As twilight fell, we did not turn on the light, but went on talking about war and peace and human anguish until it was time for midnight mass in the little Farmingdale church. I counted it a blessing that I was able to attend the mass on Christmas Eve with Dorothy Day. The message of peace (and, as we saw it, Christian pacifism), so small, so unheard while millions were engaged in the works of war, was still being announced at altars throughout the world. I had met Dorothy earlier, but it was on that Christmas visit that our friendship began.

Dorothy Day's year of solitude turned out, not surprisingly, to be less than a time of solitude and less than a year in length. In April 1944, after six months away from the Catholic Worker, she was back on Mott Street in New York's teeming Lower East Side. A life even of partial solitude was not for her. As she was to say many times, "We hear about desert fathers, but we never hear about desert mothers. Women are meant for community."

World War II had a year to run, and the paper carried the message of love, of overcoming evil with the weapons of the spirit, to the last day of bloodletting. When peace was declared in Europe in May 1945, the *Catholic Worker* carried in the center column of the front page the Beatitudes from the Sermon on the Mount: "Happy the merciful, Happy the meek, Happy the peacemakers, children of God." Also on the front page was a headline, "Peace Now with Japan." During May, June, and July of 1945, it might have been possible to negotiate a peace with Japan, already on its knees from conventional bombing, that would have forestalled the unleashing of atomic terror on humankind.

The war that wounded the world and took more than 50,000,000 men, women, and children through the doors of death, also left its wounds on the Worker movement. The circulation of the paper, including bulk mailings, was reduced to about 50,000 and only ten Catholic Worker houses managed to keep open, some of them feebly.[38]

In the letter composed in the Church of the Transfiguration at the outbreak of World War II, Dorothy Day acknowledged that she and others in the movement might face difficulties as a result of their dissent from the war and service in it. This did not happen. Dorothy

Day, however, was considered so dangerous that in 1941 she was put on a U.S. government list to "consider for custodial detention in the event of a national emergency."[39]

With the end of war's indiscriminate slaughter in Europe came the heart-stopping evidence of the Holocaust, the unspeakably discriminate slaughter of Europe's Jews. Across U.S. newspapers were spread photographs of piled-high bodies, the cadaverous remnants of those not consumed in the ovens of Auschwitz or other annihilation camps. Dorothy's closeness to Jews was part of her life. From her college days her treasured friends had been Jewish. She recalled in particular her friend Rayna, a girl with bright red hair and a glowing personality. In 1927, Rayna chose her life path by enrolling in Moscow's Lenin Institute; in the same year, Dorothy chose hers by entering the Catholic church. She often mentioned her shock at Rayna's early death. Dorothy talked of Mike Gold and of many others with whom she felt at home because of their sense of world mission and their willingness to suffer hardship to change the world.

The revelation on television and in cold print of what had been done to the Jews shook Dorothy Day to the core of her being. One day in 1945 she turned to me, her face a mask of suffering, and pondered aloud, "If I had known all this, known it while it was happening, would I have been able to maintain my pacifism?" A while later she added, "But all the violence didn't save the Jews."[40]

Dorothy Day's tragic awareness of the fragility of life after World War II and the advent of nuclear weaponry was expressed many times. She wrote in November 1945:

> Wherever we go, there is talk of the atomic bomb. All are impressed with the imminence of death, not only for themselves but for their dear ones. . . . We can only suggest one thing—destroy the two billion dollars worth of equipment that was built to make the atomic bomb, destroy all the formulas, put on sackcloth and ashes, weep and repent.[41]

THE CATHOLIC WORKER took on new life after 1945. Dorothy was joined by young men returned from war, including Tom Sullivan of the Chicago house and Jack English of the Cleveland house, who was released from a prisoner of war camp in Rumania. Robert Ludlow and Gerry Griffin came to Mott Street from service as conscientious objectors. In 1952, Ammon Hennacy, the "one-man revolution," arrived, to remain for a decade a creative and vociferous member of the Catholic Worker community. Stanley Vishnewski, always sunny and unobtrusively helpful, was a continuing presence throughout the war years. He had obtained CO status in his own way. "When they called me for a hearing, I took my advocate. I told them, 'I want to have my advocate, my lawyer, here with me.' I unwrapped a statue of Our Lady and put it down. They looked at it and at me, and they made a decision in my favor."[42] Peter Maurin, after 1945, was hardly more than a physical presence; he had suffered a stroke. The man who loved to talk and "make a point" was now almost mute, and had only four more years to live.

The circulation of the *Catholic Worker* was gaining, and new houses and farms began to sprout across the country. The *Catholic Worker* addressed itself to the needs of the postwar world, to a Europe pockmarked with the camps of the uprooted as it had been earlier with concentration camps. It ran appeals from missions whose hospitals, schools, and orphanages were without resources.[43] A front-page call to "Feed the Hungry Children! Clothe the Naked Children!" carried the biting attack, "We are Herods; we kill children. There is no peace while the world starves."[44]

It soon became clear that the peace that followed World War II was only a continuation of war by other means, chief of which was fear of an ally now seen as an enemy. It did not take long to see the outlines of the Cold War, and Dorothy Day expressed her opposition as she had to the "hot" war. As early as 1947, the *Catholic Worker* asked, "What is our stand on Russia?" and quite predictably the answer was, "The Russians are our neighbors, our brother in Christ." Dorothy wrote, "To those who call us isolationist, we must remind them that the Good Samaritan did not leave the poor traveler by the road and run after the robbers. He ministered to the wounded, fed and sheltered him."[45]

When the Cold War exploded into a hot war at the other side of the world, Korea, Dorothy expressed her heartbreak at seeing once more the lists of casualties in the *New York Times*. She sensed the fear in people's hearts that the conflict would become more widespread, but she repeated unequivocally her peacemaking vocation. "Once again, we must reiterate our absolute pacifisit position. We believe that not only atomic weapons must be outlawed, but all war, and that the social order must be restored in Christ."[46]

In the early 1950s, even "peaceful coexistence" with the Russians was ruled out as dangerous; some claimed that Joseph Stalin invented the term. Dorothy read an article entitled "Coexistence and Christian Conscience" in *Integrity* magazine, and felt it expressed the stand of the Worker; it was then featured in two issues of the *Catholic Worker*. "Coexistence is no more than a modus vivendi as opposed to a modus moriendi. . . . If coexistence with Communism is 'shameful appeasement,' then what alternative is there? The most obvious one would be a shooting war. A shooting war today means total war, and total war means the use of thermo-nuclear bombs."[47]

"Massive retaliation" described the American response to a possible Russian attack during the Cold War 1950s. Air raid drills were supposed to prepare Americans for the destruction the Russians could unleash over their cities. By 1955 the drills had become mandatory, and on June 15 Dorothy Day decided to take part in civil disobedience, first signing a broadside with Ammon Hennacy, instigator of the protests. When the siren went off for everyone to take cover, Dorothy Day, with a group of Catholic Workers and members of other peace groups, planted herself in the open park directly in front of New York's City Hall. By the act of sitting unmovable in New York's City Hall Park, Dorothy asserted, "We were setting our faces against things as they are. But especially we wanted to act against war and getting ready for war, nerve gas, germ warfare, guided missiles, testing and stockpiling of nuclear bombs, conscription, the collection of income tax—against the militarization of the state."[48]

Each act of civil disobedience was carried out according to the concept of *satyagraha,* defined by Gandhi as "the argument of suffering." The persons choosing *satyagraha* must announce it in advance, must perform it without hatred of the opponent, and must be ready to suffer for it. In the June 1957 action, the Civil Defense Office was duly informed in advance and a letter was delivered to the mayor's office in City Hall. The protesters were ready to accept the penalty for their disobedience. The judge handed down a sentence of thirty days, and Dorothy Day found herself in the Women's House of Detention in lower Manhattan. Along with Deane Mary Mowrer of the Catholic Worker and Judith Malina of the Living Theater, she plunged into a city prison crowded with more than five hundred women, many of them prostitutes and drug abusers.

Only Dorothy Day would have seen the sentence as a work of mercy, visiting those in prison. "We visited prisoners by becoming prisoners ourselves," she said. The women found themselves in cells that resembled cages, with gates composed of five heavy steel bars. Four women in the same corridor were awaiting trial for murder. Dorothy knelt with one of them at her cot in the evening for prayer.

"Here we are treated like animals, so why should we not act like animals" one woman prisoner asked Dorothy.

"Animals, however," Dorothy commented sadly, "are not capable of the unmentionable filth that punctuates the conversation of prisoners, so these prisoners are, in a way, pushed below the animal level. I can only hint at the daily, hourly obscenity that pervades a prison."

The job assigned to Dorothy was in the prison laundry, a stifling place in the torrid heat of the New York summer. The noise assaulted her whole being; the clamor of steel gates, seventy to a floor, the blaring of the television from the recreation room, the banging of pots, pans and dishes and the incessant shouting, even screeching, of the women began to unsettle her nerves. Yet she found the energy to talk to the women, sometimes to console them. Dorothy was reminded of the words of St. Catherine of Siena: "I have placed you in the midst of your fellows that you may do to them what you cannot do to Me . . . and what you do to them, I count as done to Me." The warden, a Catholic, could understand neither her pacifism nor her loving concern for the women around her. It seemed to him that Dorothy Day was not admitting the reality of evil. "The evil was there, all right," she wrote in *Loaves and Fishes*. "It was inside and outside the jail. But he did not know what we meant when we spoke of finding Christ in our prison companions."[49] Civil disobedience continued until 1961 when the Civil Defense authorities dropped the compulsory drills.

Judith Malina, Dorothy Day's cellmate in the House of Detention, was profoundly moved by Dorothy's spirit of love and compassion. In 1987, she remarked, "Not a month has passed since those days with Dorothy that I have not reflected on my experience with her. I live with her example of compassion for all. I remember her vision that each person is a gift of God. Her extreme optimism encourages me. It reminds me that whatever we do counts—and that sometimes we can move mountains. When my compassion falters, I feel that I have failed Dorothy."[50]

Daniel Berrigan, the Jesuit poet and peace activist who is a veteran prisoner for civil disobedience, spoke after her death of the importance of Dorothy Day's example. "Without Dorothy, without that exemplary patience, moral modesty, without this woman pounding at the locked doors behind which the powerful mock the powerless with games of triage, the resistance we offered would be unthinkable. . . . The best tribute we could offer Dorothy is that we too would stand somewhere or sit down."[51]

THE DECADE OF the 1960s was for Dorothy Day an international period. Her travels were related to peace. She loved to travel, and to travel for peace was the dearest delight of her soul. It was a decade that highlighted how far the Catholic Worker witness, in particular its witness for peace, had penetrated. Besides talks at the Spode House conferences of English Pax, Dorothy went to Rome three times, once for a peace witness during the Second Vatican Council.

The decade was climaxed by an invitation in 1970 to speak in Australia, which then had conscripts fighting in Vietnam.

Dorothy Day's first visit, in 1962, was to Cuba, and many found it less than easy to view the trip as she did, as a sort of peace pilgrimage. She was one of the last American journalists allowed into Cuba during that period. In her extensive reporting, she described the ordinary Cuban people in human terms at a time when Cuba was being delineated as an enemy of the United States. In the effort to find concordances rather than confrontations, she emerged as uncritical of the regime of Fidel Castro. When asked what she herself would do under Castro, she replied that she would "speak in terms of the generosity and sacrifice of Jesus Christ." Only in this way, she felt, could there be a real revolution, where revolutionaries might be opened to the message of Jesus. "This is a dream, worth dreaming," she wrote, "and the only kind of vision powerful enough to stand side-by-side with Marxist-Leninism."[52]

The peace movement in England took Dorothy Day to its heart when she arrived in October 1963, forty years after her last visit to Britain. Simon Blake, a Dominican priest and chairman of the Pax conference, welcomed Dorothy and termed the conference memorable because of her presence. The conference took place at Spode House, a former residence of the Spode family (of Spode china fame), near Birmingham. The conference theme was "Peace Through Reconciliation," and Dorothy took as her topic "Fear in Our Time." Participants came from all parts of England, Wales, and Ireland.

Dorothy's talk covered community, poverty, draft resistance, civil rights, and the refusal to play the war game by cooperating with civil defense drills. She dwelt on death in a way I had never heard before, giving examples of her prison visits to inmates on death row. Each example led to dispelling the fear of death through faith in the resurrection of Jesus. Toward the end of her talk, Dorothy said that it was not worthwhile talking at all unless one says what is in one's heart.

> This is what converts expect when they come into the Church. They find it in the lives of the saints who accept the idea of death in whatever form it takes. We say all these things in our prayers and do not mean them. But God takes us at our word, fortunately, and so we are saved in spite of ourselves. We are just dragged in by the hair of the head. This is the message we try to give at the Catholic Worker. It is painful to speak of and that is one of the reasons we rejoice in tribulation. We rejoice in suffering and so we can speak in these terms. It is not morbid. We have been called necrophiliacs. We have been accused of having a sordid and morbid

delight in the gutter and so on, the worship of ash cans. The fact of the matter is that God transforms it all, so out of this junk heap comes beauty.[53]

The occasional references in the *Catholic Worker* to Peter Kropotkin's brand of anarchism was known to the Anarchist Society of London. During the October visit to London, Dorothy Day was the speaker at the society's meeting, which filled the ancient Dryden Room. Her anarchism meant turning away from dependence on the state to carrying out personal responsibility for others through voluntary associations. Dorothy Day's fear of the intrusive power of the state, in particular its warmaking power, was with her to the end of her days. Nationalism she saw as a consuming evil, an idolatry that too often replaced religion. "The greatest enemy of the church today is the state," she told a surprised Catholic gathering in 1975.[54]

London in 1963 was ablaze with antiwar activities. Protesters maintained a vigilant presence at the U.S. embassy to signal their opposition to nuclear stockpiling. Hugh Brock, editor of the pacifist weekly *Peace News*, invited Dorothy to tea. The paper, founded in 1936, covered news of peace, nonviolent activism, and resistance around the world. Brock himself was at the center of the ferment in those heady days. *Peace News* promoted the Easter peace marches of the Committee for Nuclear Disarmament, which brought thousands on the roads to Aldermaston to protest Britain's nuclear arsenal. The marches, which began in 1958, grew in numbers each year, and did not disband after reaching Aldermaston. On their return to London, the protesters massed in Trafalgar Square. "In 1961, we had over 50,000 people in Trafalgar Square," Brock told us. He showed us a *Peace News* publication, known as "The Black Paper"; it was entitled *H-Bomb War: What It Would Be Like*. The response was so overwhelming that 130,000 copies were printed.[55] Brock told Dorothy that he was at her service for anything she wanted to do in Britain. What Dorothy wanted above all was to meet with Muriel Lester, whom she had known from her visits to the United States with the Fellowship of Reconciliation.

Muriel Lester's life dramatically paralleled Dorothy's. She became a champion of the poor and opened a community center in London's teeming East End. A devout Anglican, she pledged herself to a life of voluntary poverty. Her pacifism and opposition to England's imperialism and militarism led to a friendship with Gandhi. When he came to London in 1931 and the Round Table Conference, Gandhi stayed at Lester's community center, Kingsley Hall, a center similar to a Catholic Worker house of hospitality.

The close facial resemblance of the two women was uncanny.

Muriel Lester was in her seventies, Dorothy was close to her sixty-sixth birthday. Both had finely chiseled faces with high cheekbones. Lester's eyes were clear, like Dorothy's, but a bright, sapphire blue. Visiting in Lester's tiny retirement cottage, the women talked, like two old campaigners, of campaigns long gone, World War I, anti-imperialism, and Gandhian work, and the continuing effort for conscientious objection and gospel nonviolence.

Dorothy eagerly accepted an invitation to the Taena Community, a craft and work community modeled on the ideas of Eric Gill and founded decades earlier by Dom Bede Griffiths. Peter Maurin's unrealized dream of self-sufficiency on the land was in actual practice at Taena. There was a working farm, with well-cared-for animals in sturdy barns; disciplined craftspeople fashioned saleable pottery and silver objects.

Dorothy's history of the Worker movement, *Loaves and Fishes*, was published by Victor Gollancz during her stay in London. To a gathering in Dorothy's honor, Gollancz invited Vera Brittain, whose *Testament of Youth* recounted her personal tragedies during World War I. Because her sufferings spoke for a whole generation whose youth was blighted and shattered by that war, it sold in the millions. In the 1980s it was dramatized by *Masterpiece Theatre* and shown worldwide.

Two young Pax activists invited Dorothy to attend their wedding. For the reception they had rented a simple facility in Highgate Park. A goodly representation of London's peace community was there and Dorothy was in her element. Angela and Adrian Cunningham made Dorothy feel a part of the family. I remembered that Karl Marx was buried in Highgate Cemetery and I asked if the cemetery was far from where we were. One of the guests offered to walk with us. Through a gentle mist, we made our way to the cemetery and stood in front of the ponderous marble base with its immense carved head of Marx. Fresh red roses lay on the marble slab. Dorothy stood in prayer. She related afterward that she prayed for all those named on the grave plot, but especially for Jenny, Marx's wife, who lacked money for a coffin to bury a dead child, and his daughter Eleanor, who committed suicide. We pondered those unforgettable last sentences from the "Thesis on Feuerbach" carved into the marble base:

The philosophers have only interpreted the world
in various ways.
The point, however, is to change it.

DOROTHY DAY ARRIVED in Rome in September 1965 to be present during the peace and war discussion at the fourth and last session of the Second Vatican Council. The peace issue had been raised briefly at the third session, in November 1964, when Maximos IV, patriarch of Antioch and Jerusalem, had called on the Catholic bishops of the world to speak out on peace. "A threat of destruction hangs over humanity: nuclear armaments," the bearded patriarch told the fathers of the Council. As always, he spoke in French. "The intervention of two thousand bishops from all parts of the world on behalf of peace could change the course of history and safeguard the fate of humanity." He begged the bishops to see themselves as "defenders of the earthly city."[56]

The church had not addressed itself to a specific method of warfare since the Second Lateran Council in the twelfth century. At that time the cross-bow was condemned as a weapon for use against human beings. The ban lapsed during the later Crusades. Although Pope Paul VI had called nuclear weapons used over Japan "nefarious and dishonorable," no church body had specifically addressed itself to them. One bishop remarked, "The silence of the church after the atomic attack on Japan in 1945 was scandalous. If the Americans had dropped contraceptives, a howl would have gone up from Rome to Alaska."[57]

She brought with her three hundred copies of the special summer issue of the *Catholic Worker*, devoted to war and peace at the council. It was her second visit to Rome during the 1960's, the first in April 1963 with a women's peace pilgrimage to express gratitude to Pope John XXIII for his encyclical *Pacem in Terris*.

Dorothy came by ship in 1965, since up to that time, she had never taken a plane. When I arrived by plane about a week later, she was comfortably lodged in a small room in the home of an ordinary Italian family, who charged her $1 a day. Barbara Wall of English Pax was of special help to Dorothy. Barbara's press card gave her entry to ceremonies at St. Peter's Basilica, to meetings and press briefings. Dorothy had already met with key council fathers, including Patriarch Maximos, Archbishop T. D. Roberts, former archbishop of Bombay, and Bishop Reginald Delargy of New Zealand. Gordon Zahn, who had taken part in fruitful discussions on modern war with English bishops, and James Douglass, who had lobbied for peace throughout the council, had left Rome before my arrival, as had Hermene and Dr. Joseph Evans. Richard Carbray, professor, Latinist, and peace activist, was still in Rome, serving as volunteer secretary to Archbishop Roberts as he had in the earlier sessions.

Dorothy's presence in Rome was not designed to be one of lobbying, but rather one of prayer and fasting. She joined nineteen women from five countries on a ten-day fast in Rome's Cenacle Convent. The fast was organized by Lanza del Vasto, founder of the Community of the Ark in France. His wife, Chanterelle, was one of the fasters. The communal fast was not a protest, but a way of begging the Lord to inspire the council fathers with the gospel solution for war and peace and all human conflict. The group pointed to the Sermon on the Mount as not only a way to personal perfection but a power capable of transforming institutions.

The peace witness of Dorothy Day and other Americans at the final council session was given impetus by a group of lay persons belonging to the Catholic Association for International Peace (CAIP). They had urged in November 1964 that in any pronouncement on war and peace, the recommendations of qualified experts in military matters by taken into account. One part of the statement sounded almost like a warning to the council: They asserted that too adverse a declaration against nuclear war and nuclear weapons would "place close to fifty million American Catholics in an awesome dilemma as to whether to listen to the solemn findings of a Vatican Council or to the hitherto acccepted assurances of their government that America's nuclear deterrent is the foundation for international stability and the sine qua non of the defense of the United States."[58]

Shocked into action by this statement, which seemed to assume that all Americans accepted the morality of the deterrent, with its power to destroy human beings and even whole cities indiscriminately, some of us felt we had to take action. We learned that the CAIP members had submitted actual paragraphs as their recommendations for the peace statement to the Vatican Council commissions preparing the peace/war document. In effect, their statement constituted a defense of the nuclear deterrent as possessed by the United States. In contrast to the peace statement of Patriarch Maximos, an American bishop rose to the defense of nuclear weaponry, asserting that a draft calling nuclear arms "uncontrollable" was not correct. "It is false to say that nuclear arms cannot be controlled," he said. "There now exist some weapons of very precise limitation. . . . Their goal is to defend freedom from aggression." Nuclear weaponry, in his view, might be required for legitimate defense.[59]

As U.S. Catholics dedicated to peace, we felt we had been faced with a challenge. We had to find a way to let the council bishops know that there was another strand of opinion in U.S. Catholicism. We wanted to prevent a reversal of Pope John XXIII's *Pacem in Terris,* which had urged the banning of nuclear weapons. The question was how to reach the bishops with an alternative position on modern nuclear war, on gospel nonviolence and the right of conscientious objection. Dorothy and I discussed the issues with Bishop John Taylor, a U.S. missionary bishop in Sweden. Would he speak to the question of modern war in opposition to the American defenders of deterrence? He promised he would, even if he had to make it in written form rather than on the floor of St. Peter's Basilica. He fulfilled his promise, incorporating some sentences by James Douglass which were reflected in the final draft.

Friends in Rome kept us up to date with the various drafts of Schema 13 dealing with peace and war. Some formulations, shared with us privately, gave rise to alarm. One draft asserted, "When the law of God is not manifestly clear, presumption of right must be acknowledged to lawful authority and its commands must be obeyed." In concrete terms, one could wonder when the average person called to war service could claim that the law of God was manifestly clear. When warring governments exact punishment, and even death, from those who refuse the "presumption of right" to their strategies, the door is opened to the age-old resort of the abdication of conscience. The government, especially a totalitarian government, which does not divulge to its citizen soldiers its plans for mass destruction could hardly ask for more than such a formulation as the "presumption of right."

Another formulation that raised questions was one that englobed nuclear weaponry. "As long as international associations are not able sufficiently to safeguard peace, the possession of these weapons as a means of deterring an enemy equipped with the same weapons cannot be branded as in itself immoral." Since no international associations were likely to be empowered to safeguard the peace in the foreseeable future, the possession of nuclear weapons could continue to be considered moral. An unstated corollary could also be considered moral: the threat to put nuclear weapons to use.

Given all this, we decided to produce a special issue of the *Catholic Worker* on the subject of war and peace. Dorothy entrusted me with the task of editing the special issue. The July–August issue of the *Catholic Worker* was ready early in June 1965. Valerie Delacorte and Hermene Evans of Pax came forward with funds. The eight-page paper was airmailed to the Catholic bishops of the entire world so that they could receive it in time for the last council session.

Its first page carried an article by James W. Douglass, "The Council and the Bomb." With it went the latest draft of the war/peace section of Schema 13. Dorothy Day, in her "On Pilgrimage" column, wrote about Pope John XXIII's "Journey of a Soul," in which he described his brief life as an army chaplain as his "Babylonian captivity." He revealed that after his experience with barracks life, he knew what hell was like. She also reviewed Gordon Zahn's *In Solitary Witness*, the account of Franz Jägerstätter, the Austrian who was beheaded for his conscientious objection to Hitler's war. There were boxes citing Pope John's pastoral letter, *Pacem in Terris*, including the crucial sentence: *The same moral law which governs relations between individual human beings serves also to regulate the relations of political communities.*

Philip Scharper, then editor at Sheed & Ward Publishers, contributed a cogent essay entitled "The Church and the Nation." George H. Dunne, S.J., of Georgetown University, asserted that neither the manufacture nor the use of nuclear or other indiscriminate weaponry could be morally justified. John L. McKenzie, S.J., of Loyola University, stated, "If the warfare based on the deterrent is not immoral warfare, then there is no immoral warfare." Dr. Benjamin Spock of SANE, the Committee for a Sane Nuclear Policy, joined many in asking the world's bishops "for a strong statement for the good of mankind."

It was my task to write the editorial. "We are all under the judgment of love," it pointed out. "If all of us, lay and clerical alike, must meet the same judgment, we should look with terror at any human activity which makes it impossible to perform the works of mercy. . . . It is at this fact of modern war that we ask our Shepherd to look." The editorial drew attention to Thomas Merton's heart-stopping assertion that "total nuclear war would be a sin of mankind second only to the crucifixion" and concluded with the statement, "It is in order to avoid that great sin that we beg clear words and deed from the Fathers of the Council."

Howard Everngam, Pax chairman, contributed "Questions on Modern Warfare," noting that a moral position should stress the effects of nuclear weaponry rather than deal with the technical aspects of the weaponry. He posed the question: "Is not any act or policy of direct or indiscriminate killing of innocent or noncombatant civilian populations to be condemned?" He also asked whether individuals had the right to abstain from war or killing that was repugnant to their conscience.[60]

CAIP was supicious of Pax, as a letter from its president revealed. "The European pacifist influence in Rome may need to be offset. Here, too, we need to speak out because of Pax. Like all extremists, they may have the most persistent, devoted and persuasive adherents."[61]

On October 1 Dorothy Day was to start the ten-day fast. The evening before, we enjoyed a feast with an Indian bishop at one of Rome's good restaurants. The next morning, we met Barbara Wall for a mass in the ancient Syriac rite in St. Peter's Basilica. Before the mass, Dorothy went to confession. Then we joined Dorothy for her last cup of coffee. The lack of coffee to start the day would be one of Dorothy's most difficult sacrifices, since she never traveled without instant coffee for her morning cup. Fast organizer Lanza del Vasto, tall and patriarchal with a flowing white beard, met us in the Cenacle garden. All nineteen women were assembled. The fast began with prayer, the Our Father, the Franciscan peace prayer, and the reciting of the Beatitudes. Four days later, on October 5, the issue of war and peace was initiated in the Vatican Council.

It was the day after Pope Paul VI addressed the United Nations in New York, telling the world's peoples, "No more war. War never again!"

Barbara Wall came out of the basilica on October 5, her eyes brimming with tears of gratitude. She called it a *dies mirabilis* for peace. Two English bishops had come out strongly for a peace statement, and had supported Cardinal Alfrink, president of Pax Christi International, in asking that the passage legitimizing the nuclear deterrent be eliminated. The women's action of prayer and fasting was announced in St. Peter's by Bishop Pierre Boillon of Verdun. In a moving address, he reminded his brother bishops that in his diocese 1,300,000 human beings had perished during World War I.[62] We came to give Dorothy bulletins on the progress of the debate.

Dorothy was offering up her fasting for the victims of famine in the world as well as for peace. She called it a small thing in the face of world suffering, "a widow's mite." Her special pain was something she had never before experienced, and it attacked her most when she lay down at night. In the afternoons, when she saw us, she was eager and cheerful, and the doctor who examined the women daily found that she was reacting well.

One of Dorothy's visitors was the Benedictine abbot Christopher Butler, a gentle but firm man who was one of the drafters of Schema 13. We told him we had a statement entitled "Will Nationalism Spoil the Schema?" in which some U.S. Catholics took issue with the defense of the nuclear deterrent voiced by other U.S. Catholics.[63] We wondered if it could be distributed as a piece of information to the drafters. He said it could, but it would have to be in Latin as well as English. Richard Carbray, treasured among the peace lobbyists for many qualities, including his facility in Latin, speedily turned the statement into Latin. His solution for the word *overkill* was his own coinage, *superhomocidium*. Butler distributed 150 copies to the drafters.

Archbishop Roberts asked to take the floor in the peace debate. To speak, a bishop needed the signatures of seventy of his fellow bishops; he had collected eighty-eight. He showed us his statement, which dealt with the rights of conscience in wartime. He described the case of Franz Jägerstätter as a reminder to the bishops that in the twentieth century a citizen could be sent to the beheading block for refusing war service. Roberts made the point that national hierarchies of Catholic bishops had become the moral arm of government in nearly every war.[64]

Cardinals could rise to speak at any time, and we decided to do what we could to assure that they would support a strong peace statement. Barbara Wall, Richard Carbray, and I sped around Rome to confer with three cardinals, Konig of Vienna, Leger of Montreal, and Ritter of St. Louis. All were reassuring, telling us that their views were close to ours. When we saw Patriarch Maximos, we expressed our hope that he would make one more plea for peace on the floor of St. Peter's. We told him about the progress of the fast, stressing the fact that the women were limiting themselves to water. The old man looked into the distance and said in a far-off voice, "L'eau nourrit." Water nourishes. It was a response that could only come from one acquainted with parched land. As for speaking again before the council, he said simply, "I have already spoken."

The next day, cloture was declared just before Roberts was to speak. His written statement was on the record. The interventions were distributed to the various commissions, and the final drafting, which was expected to take many weeks, was begun.

THE FAST OVER, Dorothy Day returned to New York in mid-October to find less than harmony at the Catholic Worker. The Vietnam conflict had energized the entire U.S. peace movement and had brought new blood to the Catholic Worker. The circulation of the paper topped 70,000.[65] But other currents were in the air. The young volunteers were searching out ways to express their disaffection with what Emmanuel Mounier referred to as the established disorder; word went out not to trust anyone over thirty. This was the spirit that met Dorothy Day at the Catholic Worker. Some suggested she should cede her authority to the young militants.

The witness that mattered to the militants was one that was out on the streets, that "hit the bricks," as they put it. The action that counted was one that publicly challenged the religious and political establishment. It had to reach the headlines and television screens. Actions without visible drama, "within the system," actions such as that in Rome, even though aimed at moving a worldwide church closer to being a peace church, seemed to the young people of little account. The church itself seemed irrelevant to many of them and the tenor of their lives reflected a freedom from its constraints.

I did not return from Rome until early November, and I found Dorothy alarmingly drained of energy, her face white and drawn. She had not been prepared for the almost savage reception by some of the young people at the house. Hostility to her was one thing, but hostility to the institutional Catholic church and its rules of conduct was something else, and it affected her deeply. Her spirits, buoyed up during October by the experience with the Rome community of prayer and dedication, plummeted. About three weeks after her return from Rome, on November 6, 1965, she stood on a platform in support of young men involved in the anti-Vietnam protest of burning their draft cards. Thomas Cornell of the Catholic Worker was among them. A law had been passed threatening prison for such an act.

"I speak today as one who is old," she told the group, "and who must endorse the courage of the young men who themselves are willing to give up their freedom." Cries of "Moscow Mary" assailed her from counter-demonstrators. "I speak as one who is old." It was not Dorothy Day's usual enspiriting style. The place was Union Square, on the Lower East Side, where on a spring day more than three decades earlier, the young Dorothy Day had launched the movement with the first issue of the *Catholic Worker.* Two days later, on November 8, 1965, she entered her seventieth year.[66]

Just before dawn the following day, November 9, Roger LaPorte, twenty-two years old, sat in front of the United Nations, drenched himself in gasoline, and made a flaming torch of his body. He said he was a Catholic Worker, antiwar and against all wars. Attempts to save the mortally burned young man were fruitless. The press and television newsmen besieged the Catholic Worker. Dorothy Day had never met Roger LaPorte, who was not a member of the Catholic Worker community but rather an occasional volunteer. She herself and the movement came in for bitter attack and questioning, even from friends like Thomas Merton. Exactly twelve hours after LaPorte had pierced the dawn with the flames of his body, a total blackout due to a power failure descended on New York City. During the darkness, Dorothy Day had time to reflect on LaPorte's act, and the responses to it.

When I saw Dorothy, I tried to console her, to raise her flagging spirits. She turned to me with a leaden look. "These times are hard," she said. "I have never felt so low, so rejected, in my entire life."

DISCUSSIONS AT THE Vatican Council on the document containing the peace statement continued through November and into the beginning of December 1965. Things seemed to be going smoothly, and we were informed that the right of conscientious objection was secure. We awaited word on the treatment given the issue of indiscriminate warfare. Just before the document was to be put to the vote, a U.S. bishop brought in objections. In a letter signed by ten

U.S. bishops, including himself, he asserted that the possession of *arma scientifica* (nuclear arms) had helped preserve freedom. "In today's world," the letter stated, "there is no adequate self-defense for the largest nations without the possession of nuclear arms."[67] The letter, distributed to the council fathers in six languages, asked that the peace section of the document be voted down. If the objections were not taken into account, then the whole document should be voted down and turned over to a synod of bishops for study and correction. Since the council was due to close within a week, this seemed an extreme proposal.

This last-ditch effort did not succeed in delaying consideration of the Schema. The voting proceeded as scheduled and on December 6, 1965, the entire document, with the peace statement, received a favorable vote. "The Church in the Modern World," in a section entitled "The Fostering of Peace," contained a validation of gospel nonviolence and a pronouncement on the right of conscientious objection to military service. It singled out blind obedience for censure and called the arms race "a treacherous trap for humanity."

Section 80, which called for the "evaluation of war with an entirely new attitude," carried the crucial condemnation of modern warfare: "Any act of war aimed indiscriminately at the destruction of entire cities or extensive areas along with their inhabitants is a crime against God and man himself. It merits unequivocal and unhesitating condemnation." This, the one condemnation of the Second Vatican Council, became the cornerstone of the twentieth-century Catholic peace movement, anchoring activities against indiscriminate warfare, whether so-called conventional or nuclear.

News of the final vote on "The Church in the Modern World" came over the radio early on December 7, 1965. Dorothy Day's usual resilience reasserted itself. She commented, "The happy news on the radio this morning is that the Vatican Council has passed with an overwhelming majority vote the Schema on 'The Church in the Modern World,' included in which is the unequivocal condemnation of nuclear warfare. It was a statement for which we have been working and praying."[68]

Whether the witness of prayer and fasting or the mailing of the *Catholic Worker* to the world's bishops had any effect on the final outcome can never be assessed or known. What is important is that it occurred, and that it took place as a lay action.

Dorothy Day was in Rome again in 1967 to take part in the Congress of the Laity. As usual, her way was paid by a generous friend. She took part in workshops on poverty and peace, and was chosen as one of two Americans to receive the eucharist from Pope Paul VI in St. Peter's Basilica. Perhaps to indicate that the Vatican was not leaning too much to the pacifist side, the other recipient was a member of the U.S. military, a well-known astronaut.

During our stay in Rome, I took off by air to spend a week in Israel, but could not persuade Dorothy to take a plane. While I was gone, she pondered with regret the fact that her fear had prevented her from visiting the holy places. She had also longed to visit Israel's kibbutzim and moshavim settlements. When it came time to return to New York, with a stopover in England for a Pax meeting, she took to the air for the first time in her life, and never hesitated again to take planes.

WHEN DOROTHY DAY was invited to be the main speaker at an anti-Vietnam rally in Sydney, Australia, in August 1970, she accepted with alacrity. With the invitation came round-the-world airline tickets for Dorothy Day and me; if she harbored any lingering distaste for flying, she did not express it. Australia had troops battling in Vietnam and opposition to military involvement was building up there as it had in the United States. Dorothy had been invited from across the world to encourage the opposition. I was invited as a representative of Pax.

An incident of the plane trip stays in my memory. As we flew over the Pacific, we crossed the international date line. The day we lost was August 6, 1970. When I rejoiced that we were going to miss the anniversary of Hiroshima, Dorothy remonstrated, "Don't rejoice. We are missing the feast of the Transfiguration of Our Lord."

Members of the Vietnam Moratorium Committee were at the Sydney airport to meet us, and one confided to me that Dorothy might be disappointed at the size of the audience in Sydney's Town Hall. It was, he said, a cavernous structure with several balconies, not easy to fill to capacity; the moratorium committee hoped to fill the main floor. The fears proved groundless. Dorothy faced a full house, with every seat taken and the balconies overflowing with people, mostly young and often vociferous. Everyone seemed jubilant at the success of the moratorium. The streets had been filled with marchers carrying antiwar banners and lighted candles. The organizers saw the turnout as a blow to the government's war policy and a step toward Australia's disengagement from Vietnam.

Shortly after its founding in New York, the Catholic Worker had been started in Australia. For thirty-five years, the group had published a lively monthly magazine, elaborating on the themes of work, poverty, liturgy, and nonviolence. An urgent theme there, as in the U.S. Catholic Worker, was resistance to compulsory military service, since in the 1960s the Australian government had resorted to military conscription. The magazine had kept the group cohesive without community living. Another group, headed by the Reverend John Heffey, expressed the communitarian ideas in a community at Gaddysdale, some distance from Sydney. They were faithful followers of Peter Maurin and Eric Gill. Community members had designed and hand-lettered the posters announcing Dorothy's talks.

When Dorothy stood up on the stage of Sydney's Town Hall, the audience cheered her long and loudly. Her war resistance and civil disobedience had been featured in the daily press. A seventy-three-year-old woman from half a world away seemed a powerful symbol of resistance to war and dissent from governmental policies. Dorothy did not confine her speech to war, but told of the ideas of the Catholic Worker, of the need for community, of love as expressed by the works of mercy. Feeding and sheltering the poor were direct, revolutionary action when they challenged the dehumanized, competitive economic system that people took for granted. The Catholic Worker, she explained, was against class war and race war and had actively opposed the four major wars unleashed since the founding of the movement. She talked of the need to support absolutist resisters as well as conscientious objectors. She was voicing what peace and resistance groups were anxious to hear.

At Harbord, near Sydney, Roger Pryke had arranged a series of seminars on peace and justice with Dorothy as discussion leader. People representing many groups and various religious affiliations attended. Dorothy had a deep interest in the rights of Australia's aborigines and met not only leaders from the aboriginal group but young people who were conducting a public fast to support the land rights of Australia's first inhabitants.

Young people came to consult with us on the U.S. experience with conscription and the right to conscientious objection. The Catholics among them were heartened by the acceptance given conscientious objection by the world's bishops at the Second Vatican Council. Too few had realized the implications of the council documents.

Dorothy found the daily schedule of seminars, speeches, and interviews, though stimulating, a heavy one. It was decided that I would take just about all the evening engagements. There was no doubt that Dorothy Day's presence had encouraged the mounting anti-war sentiment in Australia, and that her forthright support of conscientious objection had helped many young men. Little more than two years later, in December 1972, Australia responded to public sentiment by disengaging itself from the Vietnam conflict and bringing its troops home.

One of the gifts of the Australian invitation was that it permitted Dorothy Day her only visit to India. Since I had worked with Mother

Teresa, I sent word ahead about our arrival. At Calcutta's Dum Dum Airport, Mother Teresa was waiting to garland Dorothy Day with the traditional welcome of a necklace of fresh flowers. She had arranged hospitality for us with a staff person at the U.S. consulate. When Dorothy Day talked to the novices at the Missionaries of Charity, it was clear to me that a like vision animated the two women. Mother Teresa served the dying of a scourged city, seeing each one "as Jesus in a distressing disguise." Dorothy Day stated that Jesus linked salvation to "how we act toward him in his disguise of commonplace, frail, ordinary humanity."[69]

In Delhi, Devendra Kumar Gupta of the Gandhi Centenary Committee welcomed Dorothy Day. As a young man, he had been a member of Gandhi's ashram at Wardha. Later, at Vinobha Bhave's suggestion, he had taken his family for work in a poor village. He told us the Gandhians had received and read the *Catholic Worker* for many years, and were gratified by the concordances between the ideas of Gandhi and Peter Maurin. Devendra took us to the Gandhi Museum and to the Rajghat, the cremation place of Mahatma Gandhi. We stood in bright sunlight before a slab of black marble and read the Gandhi talisman. "Recall the face of the poorest and most helpless man you may have seen and ask yourself if the step you contemplate is going to be of any assistance to him. Will he be able to gain anything by it?" Devendra's parting gift to Dorothy was a significant one. Gandhi saw the spinning wheel as a symbol of Indian self-reliance and of the nonviolent movement for self-rule. The Gandhian movement presented her with the newest and most compact spinning wheel yet developed.

DOROTHY DAY'S LAST prison witness was in 1973 when she spent ten days in a California prison farm in solidarity with Cesar Chavez and the United Farm Workers. Dorothy and I had taken a plane to San Francisco on July 30 with several purposes in mind, one of which was attendance at the fiftieth anniversary gathering of the War Resisters League at Asilomar, California. Joan Baez had invited Dorothy to spend a week with leaders of the farm workers at the Institute for the Study of Nonviolence. Everything changed when Chavez sent a message to Dorothy to tell her that the future of the union was at stake. A strike had been called at the vineyards and the growers had obtained injunctions against picketing in some areas. We met with Joan Baez at the institute and then we all threw ourselves into the program of "La Causa," the cause of the farm workers.

The United Farm Workers won the Catholic Worker to its cause from the beginning. An early group of farmworkers who came to

New York in 1968 to promote the grape boycott found warm hospitality at the New York house. The boycott, as a method of nonviolent resistance and weapons of the poor and powerless, was taken from the example of the deprived Irish peasants who had nothing with which to bargain but their labor. Dorothy saw the United Farm Worker movement as one that pointed to a new social order and was, at the same time, part of the peace movement. "Cesar Chavez and the Farm Workers' movement," she wrote, "is also part of the peace movement, committed to nonviolence, even while they resist, fighting for their lives and their families' lives."[70] "Nonviolence," Cesar Chavez told the workers, "tests our patience, our power to love."

Dorothy and I put ourselves at the disposal of the strikers, and on July 31 drove down to Delano and from there to Bakersfield for an open-air mass. The reverent air during the mass gave way to jubilant singing and chanting of "Viva la Causa" at its close. Banners were held aloft and the singing continued as the strikers dispersed.

We were given sleeping space on mattresses at farmworker clinics and began picketing at vineyards where the injunction was not in force. We got up at farmworkers' time, before 3:00 A.M., and made our way before the light of dawn along the road at the edge of the vineyards. Before us, as far as the eye could see, were straight rows of carefully tended vines. Soon, the men and women performing "stoop labor" were at their task of grape picking.

At one vineyard, we joined in the call to the nonstrikers to come out of the fields. "Come out to join your brothers and sisters. Come out for 'La Causa.' Come out for your children," challenged the organizers through their bullhorns. Dorothy and I tried to reach those nearest us. "Have courage. Stand with the union." To our immense joy, one morning, fourteen farmworkers walked out of the vineyard right then and there and stood with us.

The Teamsters, contesting with the United Farm Workers for contracts in the fields, were very much in evidence. A powerfully built Teamster carrying a long stave rushed up to Dorothy. He fixed his eyes on her and shouted in emotional tones, "Jesus Christ was not nonviolent, Dorothy Day."

Joining the picket line were Joan Baez and Daniel Ellsberg. Baez often took out her guitar and sang "De Colores," the Cursillo anthem, to encourage the strikers. Ellsberg was grateful for the inspiration he drew from Chavez during his two-year struggle with the law after making public the Pentagon papers on Vietnam. Dorothy had brought with her a gift she had received for her birthday on one of our Pax trips to England. It was a folding chair-cane such as the English take to the races. At times, she would sit on the picket line and chat with the police who stood in imposing lines at the struck vineyards. One day, she told the police that the next day she would read the Sermon on the Mount to them. A photograph of Dorothy Day on her chair-cane, calmly facing two policemen whose burly backs framed her right and left, was widely reprinted. It became a symbol of nonviolent patience.

Dorothy did not return to those policemen, since the next day she was arrested, along with Cesar Chavez. At Cesar's request, she picketed with him at a vineyard where the injunction was in force. She was carrying her chair-cane when she was led off to the police van. She had asked me to cover the War Resisters League anniversary meeting for the paper instead of being arrested. Thousands were now in jail for resisting what they considered an unconstitutional ban on picketing.

The Fresno jail was full, so Dorothy, with about a hundred others, was taken to a prison farm located on agricultural land not far from Fresno. There were priests and religious sisters as well as women farm workers in the group. She rejoiced in daily mass and recitation of the rosary. There were prayer vigils at night for the outcome of the meetings between Cesar Chavez and the Teamsters Union. When Joan Baez came to the prison farm she was allowed to give impromptu concerts. Her pure soprano reached the strikers and all the prisoners from the open-air courtyard. At visiting time, the children of the strikers filled the air with sounds of their brief reunions. One of Dorothy Day's most treasured possessions was the green prison uniform she was allowed to keep on her release on August 13. Farmworkers had borrowed it to trace their names on it so that their seventy-five-year-old prisonmate would not forget them.

Immediately after release, Dorothy and her prisonmates were brought to join a great crowd of farm workers and their friends in front of the Fresno courthouse. Banners for "La Causa," "La Huelga," and the Virgin of Guadalupe were everywhere like outlandishly colored flowers. Priests from many parts of the country, who had come to California to make common cause with the United Farm Workers, concelebrated an open-air mass.

When Cesar Chavez came to Dorothy's funeral, he wrote in a tribute, "It makes me very proud that Dorothy's last trip to jail took place in Fresno, California, with the farmworkers. The picture that was taken of her that day, sitting amongst the strikers and the police, is a classic portrayal of her internal peace and strength in the midst of turmoil and conflict."[71]

DOROTHY DAY LIVED long enough to see notable changes in the U.S. Catholic church's attitude to peace and war. In 1940, she had been the lone voice for the right of conscientious objection for lay people; in 1968, the entire church hierarchy of the United States spoke out in favor of this right.[72] Their statement reflected the Vatican II document, "The Church in the Modern World," for which she had fasted and prayed.

She did not live long enough to see in May 1983 the 40,000-word pastoral letter of the U.S. bishops devoted solely to peace and war. *God's Promise and Our Response* contained a thousand-word section titled "The Value of Nonviolence," in which the bishops stated, "The nonviolent witness of such figures as Dorothy Day and Martin Luther King has had a profound effect upon the life of the Church in the United States." Dorothy Day's life-long commitment to peacemaking, despite misunderstanding, opposition and attack, was validated in the bishops' declaration that "peacemaking is not an optional commitment; it is a requirement of our faith." She would have rejoiced at a prophetic statement toward the end of the pastoral letter:

> To be a Christian, according to the New Testament, is not simply to believe with one's mind, but also to become a doer of the word, a wayfarer and witness to Jesus. This means, of course, that we can never expect complete success within history and that we must regard as normal even the path of persecution and the possibility of martyrdom.[73]

Certainly, Dorothy Day stood out in the U.S. Catholic church of the twentieth century as a wayfaring pilgrim and witness to the peace of Jesus. Her passionate commitment to peace, and the things that make for peace, set many hearts on fire long before she exerted any influence on the institutional Catholic church. In addition to the Catholic Worker, she inspired the founders of the Catholic Peace Fellowship, begun in the early 1960s as an affiliate of the Fellowship of Reconciliation. At the same time, she was godparent to Pax, which held annual assemblies at the Catholic Worker farm in Tivoli, New York. Dorothy Day was the centerpiece for those gatherings, which took place every summer from 1964 to 1970 and drew many peace leaders and hundreds of participants.[74] Dorothy was the sponsor when in 1972 Pax metamorphosed into Pax Christi by becoming the U.S. branch of the International Catholic Movement for Peace. Within a decade and a half, Pax Christi counted 350 local groups operating throughout the United States.

Dorothy Day never tired of pointing to the need to see Christ in every person, but particularly in the disguise of the poor, the homeless, the despised and humiliated. It was these she loved and with them she chose to live and carry out the "daily practice of the works of mercy." This was part of her incarnational vision. She said:

> We felt a respect for the poor and destitute, as those nearest to God, as those chosen by God for His compassion. Christ lived among men. The great mystery of the Incarnation, which meant that God became man so that men might become God, was a joy that made us want to kiss the earth in worship because his feet once trod that same earth.[75]

This incarnational vision did not separate her from those who did not share it, nor narrow her views in any way. It rather buttressed her deep sense of human solidarity, undergirded by the conviction of the divinity inhabiting each human person. In the struggle for peace and justice, she counted cohorts among those far distant in outlook from the Catholic Worker. As for pacifism, she made common cause with people who came to that position through many paths other than religion, including humanists, agnostics, and atheists, many of them moved by a strong conviction of the unity of humankind. "We welcome *all* pacifist actions against war and imperialism," announced the *Catholic Worker* during the Vietnam conflict. Relying on the gospel, "we must lay down our arms and love one another for in every man we meet, we meet Christ."[76]

Dorothy Day repeatedly made it clear that her pacifism was fed by another disguise of Christ, a disguise even harder for many to penetrate, namely the disguise of "the enemy." She joined those who have been called "Sermon on the Mount Pacifists" for taking literally Christ's words, "Love your enemies: do good to those that hate you" and pray for those that persecute and calumniate you." Love inspires the works of mercy, since mercy is only love under the aspect of need. For the followers of Jesus, the duty to enemies consists of giving them to eat, and providing clothing and shelter, the reverse of the works of war.

Dorothy Day's pacifism, however, can only be fully understood in a specifically Catholic context: the bread and wine in the eucharist. Besides prayer, reading the psalms of David, and other spiritual nourishment, Dorothy Day attended mass and took communion daily. She joined with the Catholic faithful in accepting the awesome reality that partakers of the eucharist become one with Jesus and with each other. For her, the daily sacrifice of the mass was the reminder that at the Last Supper, Christ, the passover lamb, offered his life for the redemption of the world. He left to his followers his own weapon against evil, innocent suffering. Catholics believe that he gave them, too, his body and blood as spiritual food for the journey of life. Dorothy Day could never understand how Christians could come from the table of the Lord and rend the bodies of the human family in violence and war. She identified with the role of lamb or sheep, meek in the face of attack and willing to suffer, like Jesus, without retaliation. During World War II she wrote, "One reader writes to protest our 'frail' voices 'blatantly' crying out against war. (The word 'blatant' comes from 'bleat,' and we are indeed poor sheep crying out to the Good Shepherd to save us from these horrors.)"[77]

The Christian faithful in the role of lambs and sheep formed the heart of the peace message of St. John Chrysostom (347–407) blazoned on the pages of the paper at the height of World War II. He urged the followers of Jesus to go out meek as lambs, even though they are to face wolves, for it is only in this way that the power of God may be shown through them.

> Certainly it is a greater work and much more marvelous to change the minds of opponents and to bring about a change of soul than to kill them. We ought to be ashamed, therefore, who act far differently when as wolves we rush upon our opponents. For as long as we are lambs, we conquer.[78]

John Chrysostom warned that those who act as wolves deprive themselves of the shepherd's help. He pointed out that those fed with the sacred flesh of the Lamb have no excuse to become wolves. "This mystery," he added, "requires that we should be innocent not only of violence, but of all enmity, however slight, for it is the mystery of peace."

From the heart of the Christian gospel and from the works of those who echoed the gospel, Dorothy Day challenged the fifteen-hundred-year-old tradition of justified warfare and became the luminous center for Catholic peacemakers in the United States and beyond its borders. The mystery of her strength is the mystery of grace, that enabling grace that comes through the Sanctifying Spirit. She lived with the poor, she prayed and suffered, she fasted and went to prison as witness to the reconciling message of Jesus, which she hoped would be the message of a reconciling, peacemaking church. Essentially, the aim was to prevent the displacement of the love imperative from its centrality in Christian living, above all, in conflict and war; and love and God could not be separated.

In her struggle, and the struggle of the Catholic Worker movement, Dorothy Day was moved to assert, "Our very faith in love has been tried through fire."[79] Others in her spirit have come and are coming through this fire. The struggle continues.

NOTES

Note: The *Catholic Worker* is here cited as *CW.*
1. Dorothy Day, "Bread for the Hungry," *CW,* September 1976: 1, 5.
2. Day, "We Go on Record," *CW,* September 1945: 1.
3. Day, "Bread for the Hungry," 5.
4. Day, "In Peace Is My Bitterness Not Bitter," *CW,* January 1967: 1–2.
5. Dorothy Day, *The Long Loneliness* (New York: Curtis Books, 1972), 99.
6. *New Catholic Encyclopedia,* 1967 edition, 10:856. I owe this reference to Ronald G. Musto, *The Catholic Peace Tradition* (Maryknoll, N.Y.: Orbis, 1986), 9.
7. As quoted in Albert Marrin, *War and the Christian Conscience* (Chicago: Henry Regnery, 1971), 61.
8. Stratmann first appeared in *CW* with "Lest Christ Accuse Us," April 1941: 5. A review of Stratmann's groundbreaking work *The Church and War,* appeared in *CW* for April 1934: 5. Ude contributed eleven pieces to *CW,* including "The Fundamental Alternative: Christ or the Bomb," January 1960: 3, 7. Drinkwater contributed "Some Reasons for Regretting the Attitude of our Catholic Newspapers in Regard to the Spanish War," July 1937: 1, and "Unilateralism," February 1964: 8. Among Orchard's articles, "Cut the Roots of War," May 1942: 1, 5–6. Among Deacy's half-dozen articles, see "Mass Manslaughter and the Mass," February 1948: p. 4.
9. Peter Maurin, *Easy Essays* (Chicago: Franciscan Herald Press, 1984), 208–9 and *passim.*
10. Mel Piehl, *Breaking Bread: The Catholic Worker and the Origin of Catholic Radicalism* (Philadelphia: Temple University Press, 1982), 198.
11. Day, *Long Loneliness,* 207.
12. "Pacifism," *CW,* May 1936: 8.
13. Day, "The Use of Force," *CW,* November 1936: 4.
14. Day, "Explains CW Stand on the Use of Force," *CW,* September 1938: 1, 4, 7.
15. "Spanish Catholic Flays Both Sides," *CW,* December 1938: 1, 8. (Originally credited to "A Spanish Catholic," the article was later attributed to Alfredo Mendizabal.)
16. "PAX: A Group of Catholic Conscientious Objectors," part 1, *CW,* December 1936: 2; part 2, February 1937: 3.
17. Day, *Long Loneliness,* 205.
18. Day, "Michael Gold," *CW,* June 1967: 2, 8.
19. "Aims and Purposes," *CW,* January 1939: 7.
20. Joseph Zarrella, conversation with author, New York, December 1980.
21. U.S. Congress, Hearings of the House Committee on Military Affairs, July 30, 1940.
22. Dorothy Day, conversation with author, Tivoli, New York, August 1964.
23. "CW's Position," *CW,* July–August 1940: 1, 4.

24. "War Imminent: Catholics Must Judge It Now," *CW*, April 1936: 1, 6.

25. "We Are to Blame for the War in Europe," *CW*, September 1939: 1, 4.

26. "Our Stand," *CW*, June 1940: 1, 4.

27. John Cogley to Dorothy Day, November 1941, Dorothy Day–Catholic Worker Collection, Memorial Library Archives, Marquette University, Milwaukee (hereafter cited as "CW Papers"), W-4.

28. Day, "Our Country Passes from Undeclared to Declared War: We Continue Our Pacifist Stand," *CW*, January 1942: 1, 4.

29. Day, "Day After Day," *CW*, January 1942: 1, 4.

30. John J. Hugo, "In the Vineyard," part 4: "The Cause of the Trouble," *CW*, January 1942: 1, 6.

31. John J. Hugo, *The Gospel of Peace* (New York, Catholic Worker, 1944), 1. Reprinted privately in 1986: obtainable from C. Hugo, 30 North Sprague Avenue, Pittsburgh, PA 15202.

32. Furfey's several contributions during the 1930s included "Christ and the Patriot," *CW*, March 1935: 3. O'Toole's articles, many on conscientious objection, included "Peacetime Conscription: A Catholic View," October 1940: 1, 3. Ludlow, as editor, gave prominence to Gandhian nonviolence: see "Satyagraha (A Christian Way)," May 1949: 3, 8. Zahn's many contributions included "The Church and the Arms Race," May 1978: 1, 4, 9–10. Merton's more than thirty contributions included "St. Maximus the Confessor on Nonviolence," September 1965: 1–2. Among Douglass's many articles, "Theology of Resistance," December 1969: 1, 6. Jordan as editor contributed many articles including "Vietnam: Our Peace Is Christ," February 1973: 1, 8.

33. Editors, "Why Do Members of Christ Tear One Another?" *CW*, February 1942: 1, 4.

34. "Patristics and Peace," *CW*, June 1943: 2–3.

35. Gordon C. Zahn, *Another Part of the War: The Camp Simon Story* (Amherst: University of Massachusetts, 1979).

36. Day, "Women and War," *The Catholic C.O.*, quarterly of The Association of Catholic Conscientious Objectors, Fall 1946: 4.

37. John J. Hugo, *Your Ways Are Not My Ways: The Radical Christianity of the Gospel* (Pittsburgh: privately printed, 1986). Available from C. Hugo, 30 North Sprague Avenue, Pittsburgh, PA 15202. Two volumes describe retreat-conferences given by the Reverend John J. Hugo.

38. Nancy L. Roberts, *Dorothy Day and the Catholic Worker* (Albany: State University of New York Press, 1984), 180.

39. An FBI file of over five hundred pages was built up on Dorothy Day; summarized by Robert Ellsberg, "An Unusual History from the FBI," *CW*, June 1979: 1, 8.

40. Dorothy Day, conversation with author, New York City, October 1945.

41. Day, "We Go On Record," *CW*, September 1945: 1.

42. Stanley Vishnewski (Vishnauskas), conversation with author, New York, February 1946.

43. Doris Ann Doran, "Christ's Winter Agony," *CW*, January 1942; one

of several articles by Doran on the needs and sufferings of war-afflicted peoples.

44. "Feed the Hungry Children! Clothe the Naked Children!" *CW*, February 1946: 1, 7.

45. "The Russian People," *CW*, February 1947: 1, 4.

46. Day, "On Pilgrimage," *CW*, July–August 1950.

47. Jerem O'Sullivan-Barra (pseud. for Eileen Egan), "Coexistence and Christian Conscience," *CW*, June 1956: 3; July–August 1956: 3.

48. Day, *Loaves and Fishes*, 161.

49. Day, *Loaves and Fishes* (New York: Curtis Books, 1972), p. 160, 163, 173.

50. Judith Malina, conversation with author, New York, March 1987.

51. Daniel Berrigan, S.J., "Introduction," *The Long Loneliness: The Autobiography of Dorothy Day* (San Francisco, Harper & Row, 1982), xxiii.

52. William D. Miller, *A Harsh and Dreadful Love: Dorothy Day and the Catholic Worker Movement* (New York: Liveright, 1973), 307.

53. Day, "Fear in Our Time," from *Peace Through Reconciliation*, proceedings of Pax Conference, Spode House, near Birmingham, England, October 1963, CW Papers.

54. Day, testimony at "A Call to Action" hearings, Newark, New Jersey, December 6, 1975. CW Papers, D-5, box 9.

55. Hugh Brock, conversation, London, *Peace News*, Caledonian Road, October 1963.

56. Patriarch Maximos IV of Antioch and Jerusalem, "Bishops as Defenders of the Earthly City," *The War That Is Forbidden: Peace Beyond Vatican II*, ed. Eileen Egan (New York: American Pax Publication, 1968), 60, CW Papers.

57. Attributed to Archbishop T. D. Roberts in Rome during Second Vatican Council, 1963.

58. Gordon C. Zahn, "American Experts and Schema XIII," *CW*, July–August 1965: 6, 8.

59. Xavier Rynne (pseud.), *Vatican Council II* (New York: Farrar, Strauss and Giroux, 1968), 381.

60. The issues raised by Everngam in "Questions on Modern Warfare" were directly addressed in *The Church in the Modern World*, the pastoral constitution issued by the bishops at the close of the Vatican Council.

61. Piehl, *Breaking Bread*, 228.

62. Bishop Pierre Boillon, "Man Must Be Trained in Evangelical Education," *The War That is Forbidden*, 80, CW Papers.

63. "Will Nationalism Spoil the Schema?," editorial, *Peace* 11 (Summer 1965): 19, CW Papers.

64. Archbishop T. D. Roberts, S.J., "Nearly Every National Hierarchy in Nearly Every War Has Allowed Itself to Become the Moral Arm of Its Own Government," *The War That Is Forbidden*, 74, CW Papers.

65. Roberts, *Dorothy Day and the Catholic Worker*, 181.

66. Miller, *Harsh and Dreadful Love*, 320–21.

67. Rynne, *Vatican Council II*, 564–67.

68. Day, *On Pilgrimage: The Sixties* (New York: Curtis Books, 1972), 253.

69. Eileen Egan, *Such a Vision of the Street: Mother Teresa, the Spirit and the Work* (New York: Image Books–Doubleday, 1986), 57; Dorothy Day, *By Little and By Little: The Selected Writings of Dorothy Day* ed. Robert Ellsberg (New York: Alfred A. Knopf, 1983), 97.

70. Day, *By Little*, 347.

71. Ibid., 253.

72. *Human Life in Our Day*, statement of U.S. Catholic bishops, November 15, 1968 (Washington, D.C.: United States Catholic Conference, 1968).

73. *The Challenge of Peace: God's Promise and Our Response*, pastoral letter of U.S. Catholic Bishops (Washington, D.C.: United States Catholic Conference, 1983), Sections 21 and 50.

74. Among the speakers at the Pax Tivoli Conference were Walter Stein, Archbishop T. D. Roberts, Gordon Zahn, Dr. Tom Stonier, and Seymour Melman. Thomas Merton, before leaving for Bangkok, sent his last article, "Peace and Revolution: A Footnote to Ulysses," to the 1968 Pax Conference. Articles by these and other participants at Pax Tivoli Conferences in *Peace* Magazine, CW Papers.

75. Day, *The Long Loneliness*, 231.

76. "Vietnam Horror," *CW*, May 1973: 1.

77. Day, "Day After Day," *CW*, February 1942: 1, 4, 7.

78. St. John Chrysostom, *Homily on Matthew* 34, n. 1, Blackfriars. "Patristics and Peace," *CW*, June 1943: 2–3.

79. Day, *The Long Loneliness*, 317.

4. DOROTHY DAY

Editor and
Advocacy Journalist

Nancy L. Roberts

WHEN DOROTHY DAY and her colleagues hawked the inaugural
issue of the *Catholic Worker* in Union Square on May Day 1933, the
reception among communists and socialists was fairly hostile.[1]
Catholics were thought to embrace an otherworldly spirituality that
discouraged their interest in social reform. But despite the name
"Catholic," this small tabloid stood apart from the rest of the contemporary religious press. Its purpose was bold: to tell the jobless,
the poor, and the forgotten that the "Catholic Church has a special
program—to let them know that there are men [sic] of God who are
working not only for their spiritual, but for their material welfare."[2]
Indeed, the *Catholic Worker* espoused something that seemed revolutionary to many at that time: the infusion of Catholicism with a
concern for social reform, as the first editorial indicated:

Is it not possible to be radical and not atheist?
Is it not possible to protest, to expose, to complain,
to point out abuses and demand reforms
without desiring the overthrow of religion?[3]

This chapter is based in part on the research used for *Dorothy Day and the* Catholic
Worker, by Nancy L. Roberts (Albany: State University of New York Press, 1984).

115

Certainly this is advocacy journalism, as defined by Everette Dennis and William Rivers. For advocacy journalists, they write, it is essential "to be involved, to be *engaged.*" No passive recorders of reality, advocacy journalists participate in the very events they cover. They "write with an unabashed commitment to particular points of view, casting their reporting of events along the lines of their beliefs."[4]

Advocacy journalism in the United States has a long history, starting with the colonial pamphleteers. Later practitioners include activists such as Henry David Thoreau and Eugene Debs, nineteenth-century editors who wrote in a highly personalized style such as Edwin L. Godkin of the *Nation* and the New York *Post* and Horace Greeley of the New York *Tribune,* and to various degrees, turn-of-the-century muckrakers such as Ida Tarbell and Lincoln Steffens.

The *Catholic Worker* might also be seen as part of the trend toward a more interpretive reporting that many scholars, including Dennis and Rivers, trace to the early 1930s as a journalistic response to an increasingly complex world.[5] But it was also much more. Often in times of social crises, a journalism that goes beyond interpretation to advocate reform thrives.[6] Thus at the turn of the century, when social and political problems loomed, the muckrakers' exposés sprang into print. Similarly, the underground press and the "new journalism" of Joan Didion, Gloria Steinem, Tom Wolfe, and others blossomed in the midst of the 1960s social upheaval. It should not be surprising, then, that the *Catholic Worker* began at the depth of the Depression's harsh realities. Desperate citizens were ready to consider radical sources, even one that sounded suspiciously close to the communist *Daily Worker:* the *Catholic Worker.*

Yet how fittingly that name captured Dorothy Day's historic fusion of two key elements: the secular social activism of her youth with the devout Catholicism of her later adulthood. This was a uniquely personal, and at the time most unusual, combination. In the days of jazz and bathtub gin, Dorothy Day had hobnobbed with the New York avant-garde. Often, after filing her articles with such publications as the socialist *Call,* the *Masses,* and the *Liberator* (on whose staffs she served), she might listen to aspiring playwright Gene O'Neill recite "The Hound of Heaven" in a Greenwich Village speakeasy. Or she would rendezvous with other friends such as Michael Gold, Malcolm and Peggy Baird Cowley, Caroline Gordon, Hart Crane, Allen Tate, and John Dos Passos. A card-carrying Wobbly with ties to socialism and communism, Day seemed destined for an editorial career among Old Left publications.[7]

All this changed in 1927 when she joined the Roman Catholic church.[8] Thereafter, until her death in 1980 at the age of eighty-three, Day sought to unite her devout Catholic faith with the passionate concern for social justice she had developed as a young American secular radical. In some ways the Catholic church of 1927, so conservative about women's roles, seemed an odd choice for one such as Day. She was, after all, a single parent and a career woman, not to mention a veteran of the Old Left. But Catholicism compelled her, because it was the church of the poor. And she felt its continuity. "No matter how corrupt or rotten" it had become, no matter how allied with capitalists and imperialists, she sensed that "it had the mark of Jesus Christ on it."[9]

If Day's conversion seemed incongruous to her old radical friends, some five years later she did something equally remarkable. It was the Depression decade, a time of reactionary public opinion against any change in women's traditional roles of homemaker and mother. During the prevailing economic disaster, women who worked outside the home were often accused of depriving men of jobs they needed to support their families. Although these women were actually working most often in such typically non-male, low-paying fields as clerical work and domestic service, legislatures enacted laws restricting the employment of married women. Labor, government, and the mass media all urged women as a patriotic duty not to take jobs. The equal-pay rules written into the National Recovery Administration industry codes in 1933 were hardly enforced. Women's economic and social status plummeted.[10] In the midst of this milieu, Dorothy Day—single parent, career woman, and convert—sought to start a radical movement and paper in a conservative church.

Only a profound spiritual faith could have propelled her—along with the courage of conviction supplied by a partner. In 1932, the thirty-five-year-old Day met the person who would inspire her life to make a dramatic turn: a saintly, eccentric, French Catholic hobo-philosopher named Peter Maurin.[11] He had been sent to her door by George Shuster, managing editor of *Commonweal*, who had guessed that the pair would get along intellectually. And in many ways, the two were perfect complements. Maurin, always more visionary than practical, had developed a plan for a utopian Christian communism that embraced voluntary poverty, feeding the hungry, sheltering the homeless, and "personalism" (personal activism) to achieve non-violent social justice and peace. He also envisioned a paper to spread his ideas. Dorothy Day supplied the journalistic and organizational talent, the practical approach, and the public relations skills necessary to translate his vision into everyday action.

The story of the many Catholic Worker Houses of Hospitality established in the United States and abroad since 1933 has often been told. Less well known is the history of the movement's organ, the *Catholic Worker*, a leader among the advocacy press. In several ways, today's *Catholic Worker* resembles the original May Day 1933 issue. It is still tabloid-sized, with the densely printed columns and striking illustrations by Fritz Eichenberg and Adé Bethune so familiar to long-time readers. The fixed penny price as well as the name have become proletarian trademarks of the paper. For its first fifty years, the *Catholic Worker*'s page-one emblem, designed by Bethune, consisted of two brawny male workers, one white, one black (at the suggestion of an early reader). They held pick and shovel and shook hands in solidarity, while Christ stretched his arms over their shoulders. In May 1985, a new Bethune masthead appeared: a white female holding a bowl of produce, with a baby strapped to her back, replaced the white male. In an article in that issue, Bethune explained that the addition of this mother and agricultural worker was intended to counteract the sexism of the old masthead, as well as to express Dorothy Day's "love of little children, of the land, of feeding people."[12] Late in its fifty-first year, in 1983, the *Catholic Worker* made the only other major visual innovation of its history: neater type and columns, resulting from a switch from letterpress to offset printing.

Content seems largely unchanged. Much of each issue includes reports of happenings in the Catholic Worker "family," often related by old-time members such as Deane Mowrer, who write in a chatty, easygoing style. Typically, there are articles of considerable intellectual depth on such topics as poverty in America, the nuclear arms race, military tax resistance, the U.S. military presence in Central America, and the relevance of Dostoevsky, Marx, and Kropotkin to Christianity.

The *Catholic Worker*'s editorial offices are still located at the first house of hospitality, St. Joseph's, currently situated in New York City on the fringes of the Bowery at 36 East First Street.[13] Thus there is no gap between theory and practice. Every month, as they have for more than fifty years, street people who have stopped by for the daily meal of soup help address and fold 104,000 eight-, ten-, and occasionally twelve-page copies of the paper. The *Catholic Worker* was a monthly until the early 1980s, when it began to publish eight issues annually, usually combining editions for January and February, March and April, June and July, and October and November.[14] This helps defray rising printing and postage costs. More important, according to Frank Donovan, the Catholic Worker who handles the paper's finances, such a schedule frees the editors to perform the works of mercy, an activity to which they are at least equally committed.[15]

Like most advocacy publications, the *Catholic Worker* has always been funded by faith, hope, and charity. To pay for the second issue, Dorothy Day, in an act of faith, pawned her typewriter. Precarious Catholic Worker finances have often called for such measures. Although the paper's price more than doubles with a subscription, which costs a quarter a year, subscriptions and street sales scarcely cover the printing bill, which ranges between $4,000 and $5,000 per issue.[16] Yet the *Catholic Worker* has always refused paid advertising. Only occasionally has it exchanged an ad at the request of others, usually social justice groups. Catholic Workers do not solicit foundation grants, and turn away both government assistance and stocks and bonds.[17] Practicing the decentralism it preaches, the Catholic Worker movement is not legally incorporated. Thus it receives neither bequests nor tax breaks for its charity. Dorothy Day always believed that "it is better that we remain poor and dependent on the small contributions of those who can send a dollar now and then. That keeps us humble."[18]

To raise funds, the *Catholic Worker* editor appealed mainly to individuals. Once or twice a year she wrote an eloquent appeal, which was printed in the paper. Copies were also sent to others interested in the work. Often, clergy and nuns responded with checks, but most of the money trickled in (as it still does) in small amounts from individual subscribers, often on the verge of destitution themselves, who had been touched by Day's moving portraits of poverty. The Dorothy Day–Catholic Worker Collection at Marquette University contains many letters of support from such benefactors.[19]

In its first few years, much of the *Catholic Worker*'s news, features, and editorials dealt with labor issues—strikes, unions, wages, unemployment, the exploitation of black workers. Such content, in the reform-minded years of the Depression, won the *Catholic Worker* an impressive following. From 2,500 copies of its premiere issue, circulation jumped to 20,000 by November 1933, 40,000 by December 1934, and 110,000 by May 1935.[20]

Peace soon emerged as a strong theme, for Catholic Workers link it to all other issues of social justice.[21] Content analysis reveals that from 1933 through 1981, about 16 percent of all the items in the *Catholic Worker* (excluding short boxed notices) have emphasized the issue of pacifism. Content analysis also indicates the paper's editorial consistency throughout its existence. Today, as in 1933, the *Catholic Worker* still emphasizes pacifism and a radical social reconstruction based on the gospels of the New Testament. Such editorial consistency, for so long, is rare in American journalism history.[22]

Reflecting the *Catholic Worker*'s tandem focus on the everyday and the eternal, its contributors have included both the famous—such as Jacques Maritain, Martin Buber, Thomas Merton, Maria Montessori, and J. F. Powers—and the unknown. Catholic Workers in the United States and abroad often send in reports from their Houses of Hospitality. Readers are vigorously encouraged to write in, making the Letters column a regular feature.

Articles also come from cardinals, bishops, and priests. But Dorothy Day always made sure the paper was written and edited largely by laypeople, without official endorsement by the Catholic church. She realized that the lay group could afford to make mistakes that clergy and bishops could not. As one entry in her diary reads: "Press day—late again but good issue. . . . Too long center article by Merton. After all we are a layman's paper—for workers not men [sic] of letters." And after she viewed the October 1962 issue, which included articles by three priests, she bawled out Thomas Cornell, one of the editors. "What are you trying to do, let them take over? This is a layman's paper!"[23]

From recruiting writers and readers to determining its content, appearance, and circulation, Dorothy Day was primarily responsible for setting and maintaining the quality and consistent tone of the *Catholic Worker*, as well as for its survival as a pacifist paper through several major war periods. Yet few have recognized or emphasized the importance of the journalistic vocation to her. Day grew up in a newspapering family; her father, John I. Day, was an itinerant sportswriter who helped found the Hialeah racetrack in Florida, was sports editor of Chicago's *Inter Ocean*, and later become racing editor of New York's *Morning Telegraph*. Like their father, her three brothers had newspaper careers. Two achieved considerable distinction: Sam Houston Day eventually became managing editor of the New York *Journal American*; Donald Day worked on E. W. Scripps's experimental adless newspaper, Chicago's *Day Book*, became sports editor of the New York *Journal American* and the Baltic correspondent for the *Chicago Tribune*. But the senior Day thought women were constitutionally unsuited for journalism. When in 1916 his daughter began to search for a job on a New York paper, he asked his city editor friends to lecture her on the subject of women's proper place and show her the door. Finally, when Dorothy found a job on the socialist *Call*—whose editor was hardly a crony of her Republican father—she had to leave home. John Day made it plain that no daughter of his would work and live in his household.[24]

Despite such discouragement, the young Dorothy Day clearly sensed that journalism was her vocation. Somewhat shy, she never really enjoyed public speaking, although she made countless speeches for the Catholic Worker movement. Her abilities and interests led her to the medium of print journalism.[25] It seemed tailor-made for the communication of her ideas. Like many writers of the Depression decade, she wished her work to be morally significant and to inspire social change. Like her friends Elizabeth Gurley Flynn and Mary Heaton Vorse, she served her apprenticeship in socialist journalism. But after becoming a Catholic, Day aimed to awaken people not only to this world's problems, but also to their own spiritual condition. Her advocacy journalism was driven by a distinctive and profound religious faith.

No one will ever know exactly how many articles she wrote for the *Catholic Worker* in her lifetime, because many of the paper's unsigned pieces were also hers, but there can be no doubt that she was a prolific contributor. In the *Catholic Worker*'s early years, Day wrote investigative, muckraking reports of such topics as the 1930s seamen's strikes, the 1936 Vermont marbleworkers' strike, tenant evictions, and the Republic Steel massacre. Her flair for description, developed when she was a young radical reporter, was very evident in her 1936 series of articles on Arkansas sharecroppers, which appeared both in the *Catholic Worker* and in *America*.[26]

Dorothy Day also wrote some outstanding pieces for the *Catholic Worker* on the Depression-era labor movement.[27] In 1936 she covered a speech by the Reverend Stephen Kazincy, the "labor priest," in Braddock, Pennsylvania. Through sharp detail and well-chosen quotation, she communicated the heart and soul of the event. Her straightforward, unsentimental tone underscored the gravity of the steelworkers' plight:

> The steel workers spoke first and the sun broiled down and the men and their wives stood there motionless, grave, unsmiling, used to hardship, and thinking of the hardships to come if the steel masters locked them out.
>
> And then Father Kazincy was announced. He got up before the microphone, a broad, straight man of about sixty. His hair was snow white, his head held high . . . his words came abrupt, forceful, and unhesitating. . . .
>
> "Remember that you have an immortal soul," he told them. "Remember your dignity as men.
>
> "Do not let the Carnegie Steel Company crush you."[28]

In articles like this, it was plain that she cared not only about content but also about the technique she would use to communicate her ideas. This strategy only strengthened the impact of her message, as Day surely knew. She had learned her lessons well at the *Masses*, where literary brillance had likewise illuminated radical commentary.

Once Day established the *Catholic Worker's* tradition of muckraking, she would eventually leave such writing more to others. But she never lost the journalist's sense for telling quote and evocative detail that she developed early in her career. Throughout her life she kept her ability to write informative, compelling muckraking and advocacy journalism, whether describing the Scottsboro trials, the Rosenberg executions, or Cesar Chavez's struggles in the California vineyards.

These skills also enriched her occasional analytical background pieces.[29] Sometimes she also contributed thoughtful spiritual commentaries and critiques of sophisticated theological and literary works.[30] Her 1946 three-part series on the Catholic church and work is a masterpiece. Synthesizing the ideas of Pope Pius XI, G. K. Chesterton, Eric Gill, the Reverend Vincent McNabb, Eugene Debs, John L. Lewis, John Steinbeck, and others, she presented an array of Christian responses to the issues posed by the modern industrial workplace.[31]

In the March 1957 issue, she typically began such an analytical piece with a story. As she had walked home from mass, she had passed "a man lying dying on the Bowery pitifully bony and dirty." As she waited for priest and police to arrive, she reflected on all she had observed as a guest at the annual convention of the Communist Party of America, in session just around the corner. The rest of her essay discussed the problem of poverty and the differences—and similarities—in the solutions suggested by Catholic Workers and communists. "Decentralists and distributists as we are," she wrote, "we find ourselves just as often in opposition to the ends as to the means of the Communist Party. But being pacifists, we believe in sitting down to discussion with them." Quoting from such texts as Bertram Wolff's *Three Who Made a Revolution* and Abbé Combes's *The Mission of St. Thérèse,* she made a persuasive case for "incorporating social thinking into the works of mercy." This was where Day thought communists and Catholic Workers could meet.

While Day rejected Marxists' atheism and acceptance of violence to achieve their ends, she applauded their love of the poor. "Believing in the works of mercy as we do, to show our love for God and our brother, we would undoubtedly always be more in sympathy with the great mass of the poor, . . . than we would with imperialists, the colonials, the industrial capitalist, the monopolists." Catholic Workers would remain "interested in the Communists as human beings, creatures of body and soul, made to the image and likeness of God." And besides, she added with characteristic practicality, "in the struggle ahead is it the capitalist or the Communist who will be easier to convert?"[32]

As the years went on, Day directed her writing energies increasingly to her column, originally called "Day by Day," shortly changed to "All in a Day," then to "On Pilgrimage" in 1946. Today her column is still frequently reprinted, and then it forms the heart of the paper. Dwight Macdonald once aptly described it as a marriage of Pascal's *Pensées* and Eleanor Roosevelt's "My Day." In her column, Day was exceptionally warm, conversational, and appealing. She ruminated on subjects as diverse as children, visitors to St. Joseph's, animals, the saints, the weather, the soup line, prayer, pacifism, publishing the paper—sometimes mentioning them all in the same paragraph. Day's writing tended to be personal, discursive, and slightly repetitive, but in "On Pilgrimage," it was especially so. She took full advantage of the column format's creative freedom. Frequently, she conversed about her role as mother and grandmother, adding to the personal effect. "I may repeat myself," she acknowledged in the foreword to the collection of her 1948 columns, *On Pilgrimage*, but mothers always do that to be heard."[33] Her adoption of the first-person voice gave the column a personal immediacy, as did the many vivid details, dialogue, and quotation.

Her *Catholic Worker* columns alone suggest that, if she had so desired, Dorothy Day could have been a successful writer of fiction. She had the ability to evoke strong sense impressions, the scene-setting and storytelling skills, the ear for authentic speech, and a delightful sense of the comic. By lightening the depressing scenes she sketched, her humor actually served to intensify her message. Her description of the death-bed days of one of the Catholic Worker's most irascible visitors is a fine example of comic irony. In the 1930s, an angry racist named Edward J. Breen, "his dirty white hair tossing, his eyes bulging out of his apoplectic face," had long been a cross for all at St. Joseph's House of Hospitality to bear. Now he lay dying. "As the end drew near," Day reminisced, "we all sat around his bedside, taking turns saying the rosary." With comic understatement, she recorded Mr. Breen's final words to her: " 'I have only one possession left in the world—my cane. I want you to have it. Take it—take it and wrap it around the necks of these bastards around here.' Then," Day continued, "he turned on us a beatific smile. In his weak voice he whispered, 'God has been good to me.' And smiling, he died."[34]

Doubtless Day's sense of humor helped her through the daily tribulations of living on the edge of the Bowery. In her personal life as in her writing, Dorothy Day communicated her commitment to Catholic Worker personalism, which stresses the importance of individual actions to remake society. "You can't write about things without doing them," she remarked in an interview in 1971. "You just have to live that same way."[35] Because she lived a life of voluntary poverty herself, she could write of it in the most personal and vivid terms. She knew too well the indignities of destitution: mismatched skirts and stockings from the common clothing bin, stale bread and watered-down coffee, having to beg for another week to pay the rent. Many readers found her firsthand accounts of hope and despair uncommonly moving. She was at her best when writing about some of the everyday people who frequented the Catholic Worker house. Day deftly characterized ordinary men and women, sympathetically and unsentimentally.[36] She always introduced them by their first names—Bill, Anna, Millie—as if to say, "They are one of us." The effect was haunting.

In sum, Day's conversational, unpretentious writing provided a necessary balance to the more sophisticated, theoretical articles (sometimes also hers) elsewhere in the *Catholic Worker*. Readers loved her style, as many letters in the Catholic Worker Papers attest. One found such inspiration in Day's "vivid journalistic accounts" that he helped to start a House of Hospitality in South Bend, Indiana, in the early 1940s. "Before we ever met her," he said, "we knew her holiness and love of the poor which she expressed so well in words."[37]

From 1933 until several heart attacks sickened her in the late 1970s, Day reigned as editor and publisher—and movement leader. Only once, for about a year beginning in the fall of 1943, did she take a leave of absence, spending her sabbatical in religious retreat. Even when illness mandated her retirement in her last years, colleagues still felt her presence keenly.[38] From the start, the paper was Day's special endeavor. She chose the content, wrote much of the copy, and carefully assigned the rest. At times, she even prepared the makeup and headlines. A forceful editor and publisher, a shrewd manager, Day evoked an apprehension of her strong personality by her bearing. Michael Harrington, a *Catholic Worker* editor in the early 1950s, described her simply as "a presence. When she comes into a room even a stranger who had never heard of her would realize that someone significant had just entered."[39] Independently of each other, many of Day's other associates have emphasized her commanding demeanor, her ability to hearten others.[40]

But what of Peter Maurin's role? Maurin's major contribution, and his significance, lies in his act of communicating to Day his idea for the Catholic Worker movement. He also represented elements whose lack Day acutely felt in her own life. She was a veteran of the Old Left and an American Catholic convert. He was a French "cradle Catholic" who could trace his agrarian roots back 1,500 years, a link to the older, more established European church, soundly educated in the classical Catholic tradition. He lived a life of voluntary poverty modeled on that of Christ himself. And Maurin exuded confidence, repeating his ideas over and over until Day appreciated them. The Frenchman gave Day a feeling of psychological security. He gave a sense of legitimacy and direction to her life, inspiring her with a plan that addressed her longing to serve the masses as a Catholic.[41]

Day's affection and respect for Maurin were genuine. He continually called her to faithfulness, his presence inspiring her to disregard the trials of daily life at St. Joseph's in order to achieve a greater purpose. Yet Day was never blind to Maurin's imperfections. She once confessed that although she was "sure that he was a saint and a great teacher," sometimes she wasn't quite sure that she liked Peter Maurin: "He was twenty years older than I, he spoke with an accent so thick it was hard to penetrate to the thought beneath, he had a one-track mind, he did not like music, he did not read Dickens or Dostoevsky, and he did not bathe."[42] Day had a few of her own ideas, too. She did not devote the *Catholic Worker* exclusively to Maurin's writings, but included varied material with much wider appeal. She did not publicize other tendencies in his thought that she feared might hinder the success of the movement. For example, like many other European Catholic social activists, Maurin sometimes took an anticlerical tone. Day made sure no hint of this ever saw print.

Once it became clear, after the first issue, that his partner would be operating the *Catholic Worker*, Maurin was more of a symbolic than an actual helpmate for her, until his death in 1949. He seemed to be content with a lesser role in the movement, often traveling by bus around the country to address religious and social organizations. As a single parent, a career woman, and a convert, trying to start an unprecedented, radical Catholic publication in a sexist, male-dominated church during the 1930s, a decade that saw perhaps the century's most repressive antiwomen legislation, Day must have found Maurin's presence comforting. "I know the Catholic Worker movement would not have had the cooperation it has had from so many brilliant young men had it not been for Peter's influence," she once remarked. "Far be it from men to follow a woman."[43] She could point to a male cofounder and mostly male editors (especially in the paper's early years) and achieve a greater credibility and acceptance in the Catholic church than if she were operating alone.[44]

Dorothy Day had all the convert's zeal for her religion, frequently attending mass and rising daily before dawn to pray in solitude. She was a conventional Catholic in theological and spiritual matters. "I am afraid I am a traditionalist," she once remarked, "in that I do not like to see mass offered with a large coffee cup for a chalice."[45] Although she was a widely acknowledged inspiration for the Catholic Left of the mid-1960s and early 1970s, whose style was protest, civil disobedience, and sometimes even violence, the latter was never her style. And although its pacifism put the *Catholic Worker* outside mainstream Catholicism, Day always frequented the humble, conventional, working-class Catholic churches of her Lower East Side neighborhood.

Many of the Catholic radicals who acknowledge an intellectual debt to her have disagreed with her seemingly unquestioning obedience to the church hierarchy and her refusal to challenge church tradition in areas such as birth control, abortion, and liturgy. For it is true that Day subjected herself to the direction of Catholic clergy. Many times during her life she avowed that "if the Cardinal asked me to stop publishing the *Catholic Worker* tomorrow, I would."[46] When a worried *Catholic Worker* editor asked Day if such a spirit of obedience might cause the paper eventually to abandon its pacifism, she replied: "Not at all. But it means then we only use quotations from the Bible, the words of Jesus, the sayings of the saints, the encyclicals of the Popes—nothing of our own." She added, "I'm Catholic, not Quaker. If you want to edit the *Quaker Worker* you're at the wrong place."[47]

In the *Catholic Worker's* early years, Catholic church authorities viewed Day with intense suspicion, as "a borderline heretic who rightly belonged in the prison cells she so often inhabited."[48] Conservative publications such as the *Brooklyn Tablet* and the (St. Paul) *Wanderer* often attacked Day and her work. And in 1935 the *American Mercury* described her as a "former Greenwich Village habituée and recent convert of the Church," an unmistakable sign of the downfall of the Catholic church in the United States.[49]

But as the decades showed Day to be a loyal Catholic, obedient to and reverent toward the church hierarchy, she was increasingly accepted. She never criticized what the church taught, only its failure to live up to its teachings. Thus she served as a conscience. No one could ever truthfully charge Day and her paper with undermining Catholic doctrine. Her sources were unimpeachable authorities: the papal encyclicals, the Bible, the sayings of the saints, the very words of Jesus.

The relationship between Dorothy Day as editor and publisher of the *Catholic Worker* and Catholic authorities was complex.[50] As might be expected, it grew more so during times of war. For example, in World War II the paper's support of pacifism, including sponsorship of the first real group of Catholic conscientious objectors, was quite a departure from the mainstream.[51] It is true that during World War II and at other times, several bishops forbade Dorothy Day from speaking to religious groups in their dioceses, the paper was sometimes banned from churches, and she was even sharply criticized by some clergy. But the Catholic church never actually halted her work, primarily for two reasons: the doctrinal purity of her Catholic Worker philosophy with its irrefutable sources, the same as the church's; and Day's personal manner, including her sincerely loyal support for the hierarchy. She once remarked, "I think you approach a bishop as a human being and a member of the human family."[52]

Her many carefully composed letters answering clerical criticism, collected in the Catholic Worker Papers, show great diplomacy. "We are going to concentrate on peace and the land in all the coming issues of our paper to try to keep these ideals alive," Day wrote to an archbishop in 1942. She assured him that "if our Bishop asks us to cease we will, of course, obey immediately," but then gently reminded him that church authorities "permitted us to continue in the Spanish Civil War, when we were again opposed to use of force in spite of widespread controversy here over our refusal to uphold war as holy."[53] In other letters, her use of the editorial "we" and her mention of her cofounder's name, dispelled any doubt that a lone, irrational woman was subverting the church.

Always a Catholic first and an activist second, Day was an old-style radical who adhered to the traditional forms while she tried to change them. By the time of the church's Second Vatican Council in 1964, Day was respected not only among Catholic clergy, but worldwide.[54] In 1972, Notre Dame University honored Day as an outstanding American Catholic with its prestigious Laetare Medal; on her eightieth birthday in 1977, Terence Cardinal Cooke personally delivered a greeting from Pope Paul VI; and when Day died in 1980, the acclaim from the Catholic church was impressive.[55]

It had not always been so. Day's refusal to compromise the *Catholic Worker*'s pacifist principles during World War II had accelerated the decline in circulation that had started during the Spanish Civil War, when the *Catholic Worker* had also decried the use of force. Subscriptions fell from 190,000 in May 1938 to 50,500 in November 1944.[56] "The pacifism you preach is false, unpatriotic, and dangerous," wrote one offended reader.[57] Some Catholics even beat *Catholic Worker* salespeople in the streets. But Day remained staunchly pacifist, and the movement's stress on personal responsibility and direct action fostered a self-censorship. Those who disagreed with the paper's basic stand were encouraged, Quaker fashion, not to argue but to secede.[58] For example, during World War II, the editors of the *Chicago Catholic Worker* did not advocate pacifism, but rather supported participation in the war effort.

At the end of World War II, the *Catholic Worker* was bruised but not broken. During the 1950s, Day and her paper inspired pacifists to commit acts of civil disobedience to protest the prevailing Cold

War mentality of war preparations, for which she herself was jailed four times.⁵⁹ In the 1960s, always stressing that protests be non-violent, Day and the *Catholic Worker* rallied Catholic conscientious objectors to oppose the Vietnam war. In 1972, at the age of seventy-five, Day was arrested for the eighth time, for defying the law by picketing with Cesar Chavez and the United Farm Workers in California. Through such personal actions but especially through the *Catholic Worker*, she challenged several generations of Americans to consider the value of peace and social justice activism.

While her *Catholic Worker* never spoke for a mass movement or enjoyed a circulation larger than that of a major daily newspaper, it has reached influential channels. Catholic Workers have expressed their movement's philosophy in numerous publications. An important example is Michael Harrington's *The Other America*, which came to the attention of President John Kennedy and inspired his antipoverty programs. Catholic Worker ideas have inspired the work of Arthur Sheehan and J. F. Powers; John Cort, Edward Skillin, John Cogley, and James O'Gara of *Commonweal*; peace activists and authors Gordon Zahn, James Douglass, and Robert Ellsberg; Thomas Cornell of the Catholic Peace Fellowship; Eileen Egan of Pax Christi; James Forest of the International Fellowship of Reconciliation; the Reverend Daniel Berrigan and Philip Berrigan; Abigail McCarthy; and Eugene McCarthy.

Dorothy Day's *Catholic Worker* has been the catalyst for several significant offshoot publications, including: *Liturgy and Sociology*, the first *Christian Front*, *Work* (founded in 1943 by Edward Marciniak as the official publication of the Catholic Labor Alliance of Chicago), *Today*, and *Integrity*. Also, the publications of the many Houses of Hospitality around the country have helped diffuse Catholic Worker ideas. Examples include the *Chicago Catholic Worker*, the *Catholic Agitator* (Los Angeles), the Minneapolis *Catholic Worker*, *Agape* (Rochester, New York), the Melbourne, Australia *Catholic Worker*, the *Catholic Family Farmer* (Quebec), and the *Canadian Social Forum*.⁶⁰ Then there are the writings of Dorothy Day herself, both her books and her articles in such publications as *Commonweal*, *Sign*, *Blackfriars*, *Jubilee*, *Preservation of the Faith*, *Ave Maria*, *Liberation*, and the *New Republic*, which have introduced many to the movement's philosophy. Catholic Worker activism has directly inspired a number of organizations, including the Association of Catholic Trade Unionists, the Association of Catholic Conscientious Objectors, Pax Christi, and the Catholic Peace Fellowship.

Perhaps the *Worker*'s most discernible impact has been on the Catholic church's position on issues of war and peace. Long before it was even considered possible to be both a Catholic and a pacifist,

Dorothy Day was, as the *National Catholic Reporter* wrote in 1981, "plucking the U.S. church's peace and justice base string, sounding that lonely note."[61] In their 1983 pastoral letter, which condemned the use of nuclear weapons as immoral (a historic shift in their viewpoint), the American Catholic bishops praised Dorothy Day's exemplary peace activism.[62]

Her *Catholic Worker* is a significant achievement in advocacy journalism, on the basis of its impact on American consciences, its editorial viewpoint representing the first viable journalistic union of Catholic traditionalism with social radicalism, and its singular editorial consistency. It remains to be seen if the paper can sustain the quality and vigor it knew under Day's exacting editorship, but certainly it has enjoyed an influence much greater than its circulation size might suggest.

Dorothy Day stands as one of U.S. history's major advocacy journalist-activists. Like Henry David Thoreau and Eugene Debs, she combined journalism with civil disobedience in a vital, effective way. In doing so, she sustained pacifism through challenging times. From the start of the *Catholic Worker* during the Depression, when circulation peaked at 190,000, through the Spanish Civil War and World War II, when subscriptions fell to 50,500, and then through the McCarthy era, the Korean War, and Vietnam, Dorothy Day maintained the paper's commitment to peace and social justice activism.

Like the lives of Thoreau and Debs, Day's life showed no separation between her beliefs and her actions. Intertwined, her journalism and activism were greater than their sum. Through them she not only revitalized the ideal of peace in a church that had all but abandoned this tradition since the time of Constantine, but among all those who read her writing and thus came to know of her life. The achievement of this lay woman—to revitalize pacifism and social activism in a church not only long out of touch with these traditions, but with a heritage of male clerical leadership—is significant indeed.

NOTES

Note: The Catholic Worker is cited here as *CW.*

Acknowledgements: I would like to thank Professor Anne Klejment, Department of History, College of St. Thomas, St. Paul, Minnesota, for her helpful criticism of drafts of this chapter.

1. Dorothy Day, *Loaves and Fishes* (New York: Harper & Row, 1963), 18.
2. "To Our Readers," *CW,* May 1933: 4.
3. "Filling a Need," *CW,* May 1933: 4.
4. Everette Dennis and William Rivers, *Other Voices: The New Journalism in America* (San Francisco: Canfield Press, 1974), 8.

5. Ibid., 2.

6. Carey McWilliams, "Is Muckraking Coming Back?" *Columbia Journalism Review*, Fall 1970: 8.

7. The best sources for the details of Day's life are William D. Miller, *A Harsh and Dreadful Love: Dorothy Day and the Catholic Worker Movement* (New York: Liveright, 1973), and *Dorothy Day: A Biography* (New York: Harper & Row, 1982). Three recent works are Robert Coles, *Dorothy Day: A Radical Devotion* (Reading, Mass.: Addison-Wesley, 1987); a popular biography by James Forest, *Love Is the Measure: A Biography of Dorothy Day* (New York: Paulist Press, 1986); and William D. Miller, *All Is Grace: The Spirituality of Dorothy Day* (New York: Doubleday, 1987). Other sources are listed in Anne Klejment and Alice Klejment, *Dorothy Day and "The Catholic Worker," A Bibliography and Index* (New York: Garland, 1986).

8. Dorothy Day, *The Long Loneliness: The Autobiography of Dorothy Day* (New York: Harper & Row, 1952), 146.

9. Quoted by Jeff Dietrich and Susan Pollack, "An Interview with Dorothy Day," *Catholic Agitator* (publication of the Los Angeles Catholic Worker House), December 1971: 1.

10. William Chafe, *The American Woman, Her Changing Social, Economic, and Political Roles, 1920–1970* (New York: Oxford University Press, 1972), 107–9.

11. The standard biography is Arthur Sheehan, *Peter Maurin, Gay Believer* (Garden City, New York: Hanover House, 1959), especially valuable for details of Maurin's early life. For interpretation of Maurin's thought, compare Marc H. Ellis, *Peter Maurin: Prophet in the Twentieth Century* (New York: Paulist Press, 1981) with Anthony Novitsky, "The Ideological Development of Peter Maurin's Green Revolution," Ph.D. dissertation, State University of New York at Buffalo, 1976.

12. Adé Bethune, "How I Met Dorothy Day," *CW*, May 1985: 5.

13. For a description of daily life at St. Joseph's House of Hospitality, see Marc H. Ellis, *A Year at the Catholic Worker* (New York: Paulist Press, 1978).

14. Throughout its history, the paper has occasionally combined issues (usually July–August and October–November).

15. Telephone interview, January 11, 1984.

16. Ibid.

17. "Going to the Roots," *CW*, May 1978: 7.

18. Dorothy Day, "Catholic Worker Appeal," *CW*, May 1944: 8. Also see Milton Mayer, "A Dollar for Dorothy," *Progressive*, November 1977: 40–41.

19. A list of research materials available in the Dorothy Day–Catholic Worker Collection (hereafter referred to as "CW Papers") can be obtained by writing to Memorial Library Archives, Marquette University, Milwaukee, WI 53233.

20. *CW*, April 1934: 2, November 1933: 1, December 1934: 1, May 1935: 1. The circulation of the *Catholic Worker* is difficult to pinpoint. Occasionally, especially in its first few years, the paper has reported its circulation, but usually it has not specified how many copies included in these figures have constituted bundle orders to churches and other organizations. In

1960, when postal authorities required all publications to print their circulation annually in the Statement of Ownership, Management, and Circulation, the *Catholic Worker* began to total its circulation more exactly.

21. Dorothy Day, "Catholic Worker Positions," in *Peace and Nonviolence*, ed. Edward Guinan (New York: Paulist Press, 1973), 51–54.

22. Nancy L. Roberts, *Dorothy Day and the "Catholic Worker"* (Albany, N.Y.: State University of New York Press, 1984), 52–55, 59–65.

23. Dorothy Day, diary entry, December 16, 1966, CW Papers; Thomas Cornell, interviews with author, Milwaukee, November 6, 1981; Waterbury, Conn., May 15, 1983.

24. Miller, *Dorothy Day*, 7–8, 55.

25. Day, *The Long Loneliness*, 91. Day's books on her Catholic Worker experiences include several collections: *From Union Square to Rome* (Silver Spring: Preservation of the Faith Press, 1938); *House of Hospitality* (New York: Catholic Worker Books, 1939); *Loaves and Fishes; The Long Loneliness; On Pilgrimage: The Sixties* (New York: Curtis Books, 1972). Her selected writings, edited and with an excellent introduction by Robert Ellsberg, are collected in *By Little and By Little: The Selected Writings of Dorothy Day* (New York: Alfred A. Knopf, 1983).

26. Dorothy Day, "Masked Men Plough Under Poor—Families Starve in Arkansas," *CW*, April 1936: 2, 7; "Sharecroppers," *America*, March 7, 1936: 516–17.

27. See, for example, Dorothy Day, "Experiences of C.W. Editor in Steel Towns with C.I.O.," *CW*, August 1936: 1, 2.

28. Dorothy Day, "Father Kazincy, Workers' Friend, Speaks for Labor," *CW*, August 1936: 4.

29. For example, "Khrushchev and Alexander Nevsky," *CW*, October 1960: 1, 3; "Theophane Vernard and Ho Chi Minh," *CW*, May 1954: 1, 6.

30. For example, "More About Holy Poverty, Which Is Voluntary Poverty," *CW*, February 1945: 1, 2; "On Distributism," *CW*, December 1948: 1, 3; "The Pope and Peace," *CW*, February 1954: 1, 7; "Worship of Money," *CW*, October 1954: 8; "Distributism Is Not Dead," *CW*, July–August 1956: 5.

31. "The Church and Work," *CW*, September 1946: 1, 3, 7, 8; "Reflections on Work," *CW*, November 1946: 1, 4 and December 1946: 1, 4.

32. "On Pilgrimage," *CW*, March 1957: 3, 6.

33. Day, *On Pilgrimage*, 2.

34. Day, *Loaves and Fishes*, 37–38.

35. Quoted by Dietrich and Pollack, "An Interview with Dorothy Day," 2.

36. Day wrote many memorable obituaries for the poor who lived and died at the Catholic Worker houses; for example, "For These Dear Dead," *CW*, November 1946: 1, 2, 6.

37. Julian Pleasants, quoted in "Admirers Express Sadness, Gratitude," *National Catholic Reporter*, December 12, 1980: 8.

38. Peggy Scherer (recent co-editor of the *Catholic Worker*), interview with author, Milwaukee, November 5, 1981; Miller, *Dorothy Day*, 378–79.

39. Michael Harrington, *Fragments of the Century* (New York: Simon and Schuster, 1972), 19.

40. Interviews with author, (Milwaukee, November 4–6, 1981): Thomas Cornell, Joseph and Mary Alice Zarrella, Florence Weinfurter, and Nina Polcyn Moore.

41. I am indebted to Mel Piehl's analysis of Day and Maurin's relationship in *Breaking Bread: The Catholic Worker and the Origin of Catholic Radicalism in America* (Philadelphia: Temple University Press, 1982), 61–70.

42. Day, *Loaves and Fishes*, 101.

43. Quoted by Dwight Macdonald, introduction to the Greenwood reprint edition of the *Catholic Worker* (Westport, Conn., 1970), 12.

44. Piehl, *Breaking Bread*, 65.

45. Dorothy Day, "On Pilgrimage," *CW*, March 1966: 6.

46. Quoted by Dwight Macdonald, "Profiles: The Foolish Things of the World—I," *New Yorker*, October 4, 1952: 39.

47. Quoted by James Forest, "Dorothy Day: Witness to the Kingdom," *Catholic Agitator*, November 1981: 2.

48. James Forest, "There Was Always Bread," *Sojourners*, December 1976: 12.

49. Lester P. Eliot, "The Troubles with American Catholicism," *American Mercury*, March 1935: 295.

50. William D. Miller's "The Church and Dorothy Day" (*Critic*, Fall 1976: 63–70) is an excellent summary of this topic, and I have relied upon it for much of this section. Also see Dorothy Day, "The Case of Cardinal McIntyre," *CW*, July–August 1964: 1, 6, 8.

51. For a discussion of the movement's survival as a pacifist organization through the years, see John Leo LeBrun, "The Role of the Catholic Worker Movement in American Pacifism, 1933–1972," Ph.D. dissertation, Case Western Reserve University, 1973.

52. Quoted by Dietrich and Pollack, "An Interview with Dorothy Day," 1.

53. Dorothy Day to Archbishop Doherty, January 26, 1942, CW Papers.

54. Donald R. Campion, "Of Many Things," *America*, October 19, 1968, inside back cover.

55. For example, David J. O'Brien, "The Pilgrimage of Dorothy Day," *Commonweal*, December 19, 1980: 711–15; William D. Miller, "All Was Grace," *America*, December 13, 1980, inside cover and 382–86.

56. *Catholic Worker*, May 1945: 2 and April 1948: 3.

57. Quoted by Miller, *A Harsh and Dreadful Love*, 167–68.

58. Interviews with author, Milwaukee, November 5–6, 1981: Joseph Zarrella, Thomas Cornell.

59. See Nancy L. Roberts, "Journalism and Activism: Dorothy Day's Response to the Cold War," *Peace and Change: A Journal of Peace Research*, vol. 12, no. 1–2 (1987), 13–27.

60. The history of the *Chicago Catholic Worker*, which was edited by John Cogley, James O'Gara, and others, is detailed in Francis J. Sicius, "The Chicago Catholic Worker Movement, 1935 to the Present," Ph.D. dissertation, Loyola University (Chicago), 1979.

61. Arthur Jones, "U.S. Catholic War Resistance Growth 'Historic'; Building on Catholic Worker Image," *National Catholic Reporter,* October 30, 1981: 1, 20.

62. "The Challenge of Peace: God's Promise and Our Response," section I, C-4, paragraph 9.

5. THE ONE-PERSON REVOLUTION OF AMMON HENNACY

Patrick G. Coy

You see the beauty of my proposal is
It needn't wait on a general revolution.
I bid you to a one man revolution—
The only revolution that is coming.

—Robert Frost[1]

AMMON HENNACY ENDEAVORED to be the one-person revolution in the United States. His life of radicalism spanned two world wars, and when he died in 1970 he was still working to prevent a third. A good portion of his time was spent in association with the Catholic Worker movement, an association that made considerable impact on both him and the Worker. He was born into a Baptist family in Negley, Ohio, on July 24, 1893. His father held local elective office as a Democrat in Republican territory. Young Hennacy was exposed early on to the political side of life. On the first page of his autobiography, he proudly relates that "a bewhiskered picture of John Brown hung in the [family] parlor and I was ten years old before I knew the difference between God, Moses, and John Brown."[2] He came from early Scots-Irish stock, from a family with a history of progressive political activity. His mother had fed "Coxey's Army," a band of jobless men who, after the Panic of 1893, were led on a cross-country march for jobs by the social reformer Jacob Coxey. Earlier, at the risk of losing the family farm, his grandmother helped fugitive slaves cross the Ohio River and aided them in their long trek north to Canada.

At the tender age of sixteen, Hennacy joined both the Socialist Party and the Industrial Workers of the World. His life-long proclivity to jump feet first into the fray apparently already marked his character. He was elected secretary of the socialist local, and after reading Upton Sinclair's socialist apologetic and exposé of the meat-packing industry, *The Jungle,* the impressionable young radical found himself in possession of clearer reasons for having become both socialist and vegetarian.

On a cold winter's day in eastern Ohio in 1912, an old-guard radical met the new, making quite an impact in the process. The legendary labor organizer Mother Bloor had come to town. Hitching up his grandfather's horse and buggy, eighteen-year-old Ammon drove Mother Bloor throughout the Ohio mining district, organizing the first socialist locals in the area. In between stops, sitting high in the bouncing buckboard, the old socialist instructed Ammon in the faith. She had much to teach the young radical as they traveled the quiet countryside, for she had earlier been a social worker and now journeyed throughout the nation, helping out wherever there was labor trouble. She had even been appointed by Teddy Roosevelt to work in the Chicago meat-packing plants to discover the conditions there. (Roosevelt had read *The Jungle* too.) She had earned other stripes in the radical army as an organizer and laborer in the textile industry, fighting the exploitation of children. Mother Bloor's young escort found her to be a wonderful person and a great inspiration for his own burgeoning radicalism. Burgeoning indeed.[3]

While still in high school, Ammon brashly put up a sign on the public square near the Civil War cannon. The plainly lettered sign outlined definitions of socialism. It stood for several years as a lone sentry in the staid southern Ohio republican town of Lisbon. Hennacy went off to college, bouncing from one school to the next. In three years (1913–1915), he attended three separate universities. The middle year was spent at the University of Wisconsin where he continued organizing, giving up his bed to Randolph Bourne on his visit to campus and introducing Emma Goldman when she spoke there.

Hennacy claimed that he was instructed in the virtues of pacifism at a very early age. "My first memory is that of my Quaker great-grandmother in her bonnet sitting in the east room by her Franklin stove and telling my three-year-old younger sister Julia and myself of how the peaceful Quakers loved the Indians and were not hurt by them." This early instruction did not immediately take root. While at the university, he was a socialist but not yet a pacifist. He therefore had no objections to taking military drill. Looking back at that period of his life, he proffered a bare explanation: "I wanted to know how to shoot, come the revolution."[4]

In between his studies and activism, he supported himself selling breakfast cereal, aluminum ware, and brushes. His breezy air of self-confidence, quick wit, and silver tongue served him equally well as a soapbox salesman of socialism or a door-to-door pusher of pots and pans. He sold plenty of both. World events moved quickly in the prewar years; so did Hennacy. During the 1916 presidential campaign, while selling cornflakes throughout New England and Ohio, Hennacy also spoke on soapboxes scores of times for Allan Benson, the Socialist Party candidate. This early soapbox training emboldened him later at the New York Catholic Worker in the 1950s, where making street-corner speeches and hawking the *Catholic Worker* were part of his disciplined daily regimen.

As he had been in 1912, he was a delegate to the socialist state convention in 1916. It was a heady time for the young agitator, made only more so by his being in love with Selma Melms, the daughter of the socialist sheriff in Milwaukee, Wisconsin. But romance, schooling, and other plans would have to wait, for he was caught up in the fast pace of world politics immediately prior to U.S. entry into World War I. His financial help was needed at home with his seven younger siblings, so he dropped out of school and moved back to Ohio. This time around he sold bakery goods, all the while staying active in local Socialist Party electoral campaigns. But as World War I grew in its scope and intensity, so did Hennacy's opposition to it.

Although not all socialists perceived the war as an imperialist conflict, Hennacy was one of the many who did, demonstrating and remonstrating against the U.S. entry into the war. As chair of the local Socialist Party chapter, Hennacy spearheaded an antiwar and anticonscription campaign. Using organizing techniques popular at the time, he designed posters and leaflets to be pasted on storefronts. In stark language, the material encouragingly asked, "Young men, are you going to refuse to register for military service in a foreign country while the rich men who have brought on this war stay at home and get richer by gambling in food stuffs? We would rather die or be imprisoned for the sake of justice, than kill our fellow men in this unjust war."[5] Hennacy would soon enough have his chance to act on his boldly-stated closing proposition, for he was about to learn the terrible truth of the personalist Emmanuel Mounier's statement uttered many years later: "It is a deprivation for a person not to have known illness, misfortune, or prison."[6]

136

Hennacy not only refused to register for the draft, but in April 1917 he was arrested for "attempting to defraud the government in its experiment of the Selective Service Act." The arrest followed a rather serious cat-and-mouse game across a number of states, which saw Hennacy distributing his and other Socialist Party leaflets and posters in town after town in Ohio, Pennsylvania, and West Virginia. Somehow, he always managed to stay precious few steps ahead of the police, vigilante citizens, and what he termed "turncoat Socialists."

Finally, he returned to Columbus, Ohio, in time to stand trial for an earlier arrest stemming from his leadership role in an antiwar rally that, according to Hennacy's personal account, had attracted some 10,000 participants.[7] He was arrested again, this time at 2:30 A.M. after an evening of postering downtown storefronts. He was held in solitary confinement (ostensibly for his own protection) for six weeks while he awaited trial. The considerable wrath of a nation-state at war came fully down upon him. He was told that unless he registered for the draft, he was to be shot on orders from Washington. He was shown newspaper headlines screaming "Extreme Penalty for Traitors." He was falsely told that all of his young socialist comrades who had also been arrested for refusing to register had given in and registered.

The only bright and emboldening note was struck by a Wobbly who snuck Hennacy a letter and a newspaper clipping telling him that his eighty-seven-pound mother was asked if she was frightened that her son was soon to be shot. As Hennacy recounts it, "Her reply was that the only thing she was afraid of was that they might scare me to give in." In an uncharacteristic understatement, he added, "This gave me added courage."[8] Added courage indeed, for the crusading young radical was quoted from prison in the local papers as saying, "If I have to take my choice between going to war and being shot at sunrise, I'll ask to be shot at sunrise. . . . Rather than make munitions for the government I want to be stood up against the wall and shot."[9] He was eventually sentenced to two years in the Atlanta federal penitentiary (a comparatively light sentence, relative to those men sentenced after the passage of the Espionage Act of 1917), and to an additional nine months in the county jail for refusing to register; this latter sentence was eventually dropped.

Put simply, Hennacy was an atheistic socialist who refused to dirty his hands in a capitalist war. But while in prison, he came to believe that all social institutions were evil, and therefore to be disregarded as possible vehicles for social change and reform. What was there in his prison experience that precipitated such a foundational change in his philosophy?

About midway through his prison term in the Atlanta federal penitentiary, the irrepressible radical organized a successful nonviolent protest against the rotten fish the prisoners were served every Friday. The result: he was put into solitary confinement for eight and a half months on the false charge of plotting to blow up the prison. It was during this time that the ideals and beliefs that would later guide his life were formed. He never deserted them, perhaps because of the manner in which they came into being: molded in the fiery aloneness and anguish of solitary confinement, where the flames of suicide and meaninglessness danced tempestuously about him.

The first ten days in solitary Hennacy spent in his underwear, lying about a small, three-cornered, very dark hole. A slice of cornbread and a cup of water were the day's fare. He was then transferred to "the light hole," illumined by a twenty-watt bulb hung fifteen feet from the cell floor. "The cell was exactly eight and a half steps from corner to corner," and six feet wide. After three months, the warden came in and presented him with a registration form for the second draft, warning Hennacy that he would receive another year in the hole for a second refusal to register. Hennacy's reply: "I told him that was O.K."[10] But that same night found Hennacy sharpening his spoon. He planned to relieve the endless despair by slashing his wrists. There was no longer any meaning to his struggle; he had taken all he could. But he put off the suicide one more day, as it was already evening, and he couldn't see to scribble a note to Selma and his mother with his contraband pencil.

When the long lonely night finally broke, however, the morning ushered in life and meaning, not death and purposelessness. The young radical managed to catch a glimpse of Alexander Berkman working in the prison's tailor shop. The famed anarchist had been an early hero of Hennacy's, ever since he read Berkman's *Memoirs* in Ohio in 1916. Before Hennacy was put in solitary, Berkman had passed him a note and had befriended him, showing the young convict the prison ropes. Seeing Berkman, Hennacy was immediately ashamed of his suicide temptation. Berkman had done fifteen years, three and a half of it in a dark hole in the Allegheny federal penitentiary for his attempted assassination of Henry Clay Frick, the manager of Carnegie Steel, the man who had ordered the Pinkertons as they killed hundreds of workers in the Homestead Massacre of 1892. "Here was Berkman who had passed through much more than I would ever have to endure if I stayed two more years in solitary. How was the world to know of the continued torture [of prisoners] if I gave up?" Hennacy asked himself.[11] He resolved to be finished with despair, to live through the solitary confinement, in order to make the world a better place.

It is perhaps best to allow Hennacy himself to recount his struggles and eventual conversion in prison, for as Dorothy Day said, "the story of his prison days will rank . . . with the great writings of the world about prisons."[12]

> I had passed through the idea of killing myself. This was an escape, not any solution to life. The remainder of my two years in solitary must result in a clear-cut plan whereby I could go forth and be a force in the world. I could not take any halfway measures. . . . I read of Jesus, who was confronted with a whole world empire of tyranny and chose not to overturn the tyrant and make Himself king, but to change the hatred in the hearts of people to love and understanding—to overcome evil with good will. . . . Gradually I came to gain a glimpse of what Jesus meant when He said, 'The Kingdom of God is Within You.' In my heart now after six months I could love everybody in the world but the warden, but if I did not love him then the Sermon on the Mount meant nothing at all. . . . The warden was never locked up in my cell and he never had a chance to know what Jesus meant. . . . So I must not blame him. I must love him. . . . The Kingdom of God must be in everyone: in the deputy, the warden, in the rat and the pervert—and now I come to know it—in myself. . . . The opposite of the Sermon on the Mount was what the whole world had been practicing, in prison and out of prison; and hate piled on hate had brought hate and revenge.[13]

It was this conversion experience that led Hennacy to describe himself upon his release from prison as a "nonchurch Christian." He had come to recognize Christ's Sermon on the Mount as the most revolutionary teaching in the world. The call for personal revolution that he discerned there was not only the most demanding one but was, in his final analysis, the only one worthwhile. He had already started this revolution by becoming a Christian; he was to complete it by becoming an anarchist.

A year and eight months after entering the Atlanta penitentiary, Hennacy was released. He was met at the gate and immediately arrested for refusing to register for the second draft while in prison. He spent seven weeks languishing in prison awaiting trial. However, the time was not lost, for he obtained a copy of Tolstoy's *The Kingdom of God Is Within You*. He felt the book must have been written especially for him, so pointedly did it answer the questions he had labored to figure out for himself while in solitary. Following Tolstoy, Hennacy came to believe that trying to change the world by bullets or ballots was useless. One system of oppression based on power and coercion would merely be exchanged for another. Studying the life of Jesus in the gospels, he gradually realized that Jesus knew exchanging a Roman despot for a Jewish despot was not worth dying for. Christ had found a better way—overcoming the enemy by love—a way that did not violate the essential dignity and free agency of the individual.[14]

Hennacy's adoption of anarchism should not be at all surprising. He was a Midwestern radical, born into and bred on the decentralized egalitarian radicalism that so marked the plains, prairies, and small towns of America's heartland in the later 1800s through to the Depression era. His was a radicalism informed and enlivened by a long litany of American rebels. His last book, *The One-Man Revolution in America*, published posthumously, consisted of seventeen chapters, each devoted to an examination of the life and beliefs of those who Hennacy thought had fought the good fight, displaying courage and integrity in living out their one-person revolution in a world of compromise. The chapters examine the famous and not so famous in U.S. social history. The book can be likened to a revisionist *Who's Who in the United States:* Thomas Paine, William Lloyd Garrison, John Woolman, Dorothy Day, Eugene Debs, Malcolm X, Mother Jones, Clarence Darrow, Albert Parsons, Yukeoma the Hopi. The dedication reads: "For All Young Radicals, in the hope that this book may inspire and guide them along The Road To Courage." It is no accident that thirteen of the seventeen profiled had spent time in prison for their radical ideas. When the final tallies came in, Hennacy had been imprisoned well over thirty times; he was not averse to wearing his arrest and prison record as a badge, a testament to the good fight.

Hennacy was one native rebel whose flavor and character was a direct result of the hot waters of American social dissent he was steeped in. He was very well read in U.S. social history—in this respect somewhat like Dorothy Day and unlike Peter Maurin. Day's emotional and intellectual roots drew heavily on the indigenous tradition, while Maurin was perhaps more formed by his European roots.[15] The niche Hennacy eventually carved for himself in U.S. society was reflected by the block headline run by the *Salt Lake City Tribune* upon his death in 1970: "An American Legend."

In adopting anarchism, Hennacy was aligning himself with the more radical proponents and early supporters of the U.S. revolution. As historian Staughton Lynd has described them, "American revolutionaries sought a society in which the state would wither away." This inborn aversion and distrust of centralized government has resulted in anarchism being defined as "undoubtedly the philosophy most native to the American temperament." It has also been interpreted by Norman Ware as "the only bona fide American radical tradition." David DeLeon has correctly noted that what is distinctively "American" about anarchism is its pervasive "suspicion— if not hostility—toward any centralized discipline."[16] Hennacy's own considerable hostility to centralized authority evidenced itself in the anticlericalism that so pained Dorothy Day when he lived at the New York Worker.

In the United States, anarchism has a double tradition: native and immigrant. The native, indigenous tradition is marked by individualism with an emphasis on individual freedom and personal sovereignty; the immigrant tradition is imitative and most often known by its fascination with Soviet communism. The indigenous movement is the more significant in U.S. social history, drawing as it does on the "basic beliefs of the general culture for meaning."[17] It includes in its surprisingly broad ranks such luminaries as Walt Whitman, W. L. Garrison, H. D. Thoreau, Benjamin Tucker, Dorothy Day, and Josiah Warren.

Hennacy crusaded for one great human value, freedom. At the end of freedom's rainbow was the classical anarchist paradise, where oppression, injustice, and institutional violence were done away with, where no state or church could divide people and plant seeds of discontent and oppression. It was, above all else, the reduction of the state that Hennacy worked for; he saw national government as the largest example of the organized return of evil for evil. He stood squarely in a long line of anarchists and libertarians who held that the one and only *modus operandi* of government is coercion and force. After reading Thoreau, Garrison, and Tolstoy, he understood all governments, even the best, to be founded upon the police officer's club—the very opposite of the teachings of Christ. And since he believed that government was created in humankind's own image, it was obvious to him that institutional reform had to begin with changing one's own motivations and actions.[18]

The bottom line of Hennacy's rather spare social philosophy was personal responsibility. One was decidedly not being responsible by choosing to participate in the government and looking toward it to cure social ills such as hunger, poverty, racism, and war. On the contrary, Hennacy felt that to do so was to short-circuit the compassionate current of the human heart, where complicity and individual responsibility for social injustices can take root and eventually make demands on one's life. To ignore this dynamic, or to refuse to foster it, was to live an unprincipled life. His prison experience had taught him the folly of such an existence.

At least one scholar of U.S. anarchism, William O. Reichert, has written approvingly of Hennacy's contributions to anarchism.

Reichert claims that "in many respects, Ammon Hennacy's auto-biography, *The Book of Ammon*, is one of the finest sorces of anarchist philosophy and theory available."[19] The book does contain diamonds of insight and wisdom, and is important in its own right for the rich detail it offers not only into Hennacy's life but into the history of the movements he was a part of. Unfortunately, many of these diamonds are buried under the weight of more than five hundred pages of discursive ramblings.

Hennacy had a glib manner of talking about anarchism, and his quick and easy definition of it was quoted often: "An anarchist is someone who doesn't need a cop to make them behave." But while his manner was glib, his thought on the subject was not. In *The Book of Ammon*, Hennacy revealed his thoughts on anarchism. "Anarchism, having faith in the innate goodness within everyone, seeks to establish the Golden Rule by working from within the consciousness of the individual while all other systems of society, working from without, depend upon human-made laws and violence of the state to compel people to act justly." Hennacy was not, of course, interested in reforming government. Rather, he preferred to tear it down, for he was against all government. He saw the function of the anarchists as essentially twofold. First, they help to tear down the present society by daily courageous resistance and noncooperation with the tyrannical forces of the state. Secondly, by daily cooperation with others in overcoming evil with good will and solidarity, they build toward the anarchist commonwealth, a commonwealth formed by voluntary action with the right of secession.[20]

He was personally more successful at the former. There have, in fact, been precious few radicals either before or after Ammon Hennacy who seem capable of carrying his picket sign when it comes to resisting state tyranny. That same pertinacity, however, coupled with the excessive self-confidence and doctrinaire spirit that so marked his persona, forever made the other half of his anarchistic formulation an elusive target in his personal life. Cooperation, which Robert Nisbet names as "the very heart of the anarchist prescription for society," did not come easily for one who had such singularity in vision.[21] Karl Meyer, a Chicago Catholic Worker in the 1950s and 1960s who was deeply influenced by Hennacy and has gone on to make his own considerable contribution to the peace movement, makes a similar point: "Ammon was impatient with meetings and seldom went to them. . . . He was unlike Gandhi and A. J. Muste who both made political compromises to build coalitions. . . . He didn't want to be limited. . . . He was not able to work in cooperation or coalition with other people."[22]

The positive dimension of Hennacy's anarchism was the acceptance of personal responsibility to approximate the highest ideal possible; in its negative aspect it meant the refusal to depend on politicians, pressure groups, or the police and military. He saw their power as transitory, and spiritual power as the greatest force in the world. Beside spiritual power's inherently unlimited possibilities, "all the two-penny political victories do not mean a thing." He believed that too many people with good intentions (liberals) foolishly dissipated their energies and therefore their efficacy by being "for all good causes," attending meetings, passing resolutions, and organizing petitions, all of which he saw as an effort to change others, when what that energy is really needed for is to change oneself. "We become tired radicals because we use our weakest weapon; the ballot box, where we are always outnumbered, and refuse to use our strongest weapon: spiritual power." He was deeply distressed by the tendency of many peace movement people to succumb to the allure of majority rule or numbers, so resolute was he in his behalf that "on any matter of importance the majority is always wrong." To this end, he was especially fond of quoting Thoreau: "A minority is powerless while it conforms to the majority . . . one on the side of God is a majority already."[23]

Along with Tolstoy, and later Dorothy Day, Hennacy believed Christian anarchism meant that those who had accepted and obeyed the laws of God were thereby freed from obeying the laws of humankind. He further believed they were, in fact, not in any need of them.[24] Day offered the clearest scriptural foundation for this position when she said, "Perhaps St. Paul defined the Catholic Worker's idea of anarchism, the positive word, by saying of the followers of Jesus, 'For such there is no law.' Those who have given up all ideas of domination and power and the manipulation of others are 'not under the law' (Galations 5). For those who live in Christ Jesus, for 'those who have put on Christ,' for those who have washed the feet of others, there is no law. They have the liberty of the children of God."[25]

In his characteristically cavalier manner, Hennacy dismissed all secular anarchism that was not anchored in a spiritual foundation, preferably that of the Christian gospel. "Anarchism without the ethical principles of Jesus and Gandhi is useless." Responsibility for the difficulty in welding the two lay with the church, however: "The very thing that keeps anarchists away from religion is the fact that religion has always been the handmaid of reaction and has stood for war and stands now for more war and more capitalism."[26]

The ethical basis of Christian anarchism is best explained, according to Hennacy, by Jesus's answer when asked what should happen to the woman caught in adultery:

> He said, 'He without sin cast the first stone at her!' He told us to love our enemy, to turn the other cheek and to return good for evil. . . . It means today that if you serve on a jury, if you vote for any candidate who makes a law . . . if you vote for a judge who pronounces the sentence, or if you vote for the best President or Governor possible who appoints the hangman and the jailor—these men are your servants: they are your arm to throw a stone, and then you deny Christ![27]

The myriad strains of anarchism—both secular and Christian—share an aversion to blueprint-making. In general, one finds little or no effort expended in drawing up a detailed or comprehensive portrait for some anarchistic society of the future. Emancipation of the individual human spirit and simple human cooperation are attended to. Ignored are reconstruction plans for social institutions and controls. Benjamin R. Tucker, editor of *Liberty*, who has been described as the chief formulator of indigenous anarchism, expressed this tendency in anarchism when he said that when people ask "what will replace the state? this is akin to such questions as: If you abolish slavery, what do you propose to do with your million ignorant 'niggers'? If you abolish popes, priests and organized religion, what do you propose to do with the rude and vicious masses? If you abolish marriage, what do you propose to do with the children? etc., etc." Anarchists generally believe these details will be adequately taken care of by popular ingenuity. It is presumed that the freed spirit will require little or no guidance and that natural patterns of decentralized organization will evolve, building on what Tucker calls "such crude step[s] in the direction of supplanting the state" as schools, commodity exchanges, cooperatives, labor unions, and day care centers.[28]

Hennacy was no anarchistic architect either. Far from it. Like Peter Maurin, who often responded to blueprint requests by simply stating that he only "enunciated the principles," Hennacy never bothered to develop a detailed picture of an anarchist society. But unlike Peter Maurin, for whom such a task may have been possible given his native ability to synthesize and think systematically, his keen sense of history, and his ability to see the larger picture, such a mandate would have been plainly beyond Hennacy's capabilities. Besides, he saw no earthly reason to complicate his already hard message in such a way. For the future belonged to the spirit, to the responses of the individual to the prompting of that still, small voice within: individual conscience. As his second wife, Joan Thomas, has said, "He knew in his heart there could never be an anarchistic society other than as it is embodied in an individual person."[29] Consequently, Ammon Hennacy's considerable energies were directed toward making an impression on individuals he came in contact with, whether through his writing, his daily street hawking of the *Catholic Worker*, or his often solitary picketing. Put simply, Hennacy would talk to any who would listen—whether one or one hundred—especially when the subject at hand was his favorite: his own one-person revolution.

It is important to note that although Hennacy's belief system hinged on the idea of personal conversion, he was frequently reluctant to color it in the dye of traditional Christian language. He was not a theologian in any sense of the word and his theological belief system was spare and simple purposefully—all the better to put it into practice. In his habitually judgmental and somewhat shortsighted way, he disdained much philosophy and most theology. He saw those disciplines as shackled by a tendency to abstraction, thereby letting the individual off the critical hook of responsibility. Refusing to take responsibility for personal complicity in social evil, either by commission or omission, was the mortal sin of his sparse theological system.

Not surprisingly, he decried the fundamentalist dogmas that emphasized the "sinner" need do little in order to be saved, where through faith one is saved forever without ever really struggling with any of the major evils of the world. He saw these fundamentalist dogmas as "a real opium of the people." This approach simply did not square with his emphasis on the one-person revolution consciously undertaken. Nor did it rest well on the foundation of his spirituality: his experience in solitary confinement where a conscious personal decision, arrived at with great turmoil and cost, eventually turned back the tide of sin and hatred for him. Speaking to a group of social workers at the Salvation Army, he was asked by a minister if he "rehabilitated derelicts" at Joe Hill House of Hospitality. In an effort to repel their Bible-thumping and shortcut conversion ideas, he replied shortly, "Hell, I haven't rehabilitated myself yet."[30]

But by the same radical token, and in consort with Day and Maurin, Hennacy rejected what he perceived to be a corresponding approach: theological liberalism. "The theology of the liberals is a milk and water sentimentalism which does not deal with the suffering necessary for spiritual growth."[31] In both instances, it was the requisite measure of suffering love which tipped his evaluative scales. In the language of Paul Tillich, if one's "ultimate concern" did not make serious demands on one's life, Hennacy felt it was simply not worth being concerned about. For him, it was clear that this meant that one's ultimate concern must be truly ultimate: it must be worth dying for. As he said in a forty-eight—page booklet the Worker published in 1959 entitled "Two Agitators: Peter Maurin— Ammon Hennacy," "You have to be ready to die or you are not ready to live." He adopted this stance in response to the physical attacks, public harassment, arrests, and imprisonment he was often subjected to because of his picketing, soapboxing, and street hawking of Catholic Worker papers.

Just as he refused to complicate his anarchistic vision with details, so he refused to engage in what he termed theological hair-splitting. Whenever he was in a Catholic church, Hennacy would pray for grace and wisdom; and upon converting to Catholicism in 1952 he found meaning in the Catholic doctrine of grace as it is found in traditional sacramental theology. But he only infrequently spoke or wrote about his understanding of grace, and never attempted to fit it coherently into his philosophy of the one-person revolution. This may have been a conscious "oversight" on his part, for he seemed to think he was much too engaged in the concretization of the demands of the Sermon on the Mount to complicate matters with orderly theological reflections. Yet the one-person revolution was not possible in his eyes without the gift of grace. "Anarchism will never come about until people are ready for it, until they are in a state of grace where they can live by the Sermon on the Mount instead of by human made laws with an eye for an eye." Similarly, he professed not to care about what happens in the afterlife, or to be concerned about why what happens does; the point is to live now, to act now, and to do it here in the world. "I am not at all interested in heaven. I feel that if I do what is right to the best of my knowledge and powers here that will take care of itself."[32]

Hennacy's philosophy of good and evil was also uncluttered with the fine distinctions of the academic; his was a life of prophetic activism whose springboard was, of necessity, a stance toward life that allowed for very few gray areas. As Dorothy Day recounted, "I talked to Ammon about not judging others . . . he doesn't see it . . . black is black and white, white." Catholic Worker historian William Miller has written that Hennacy's reference points in interpreting society were bipolar: those who perpetuated absolute evil and those who were the doers of good.[33]

Although Hennacy was not afraid to name the presence of evil in the world in the form of government, insurance, politicians, medicine, and war, he at the same time held that God (or "Good" as he often said he preferred to spell it) is the only true force that exists.

He believed power rested only in that which was eternal; evil is temporal and therefore defeats itself. Orthodox Christianity provided a key for Hennacy to unlock the problem of evil. He believed that Christianity's emphasis on free will was the proper starting point for any evaluation of good and evil. "[What] Orthodox Christianity has given is to say that humankind has free will to choose good or evil, that good is stronger than evil, it will prevail if we can work it out in our own lives." He judged harshly those who participated in the political system, for he thought the best it ever had to offer was the lesser of two evils. He would have nothing to do with choosing "to cast out devils by the prince of devils." Nevertheless, the presence of evil largely remained a mystery to him; he admitted to doubts about its eventual banishment, saying the best a person can do is be "aware of all detours and compromises with evil."[34]

Hennacy accepted the Tolstoian principle that truth is eternal. This meant for him that no sincere effort made on behalf of truth was ever lost. In other words, one need not entertain questions of political expediency or wordly effectiveness. It was precisely this belief in the ongoing power of truthful action that allowed him to maintain for fifty long years a life of extreme activism, a life that was frequently harsh. This belief succored him in his often solitary witness. He was further strengthened by the simple fact that he did not interpret reality objectively but rather subjectively (the one-person revolution). Consequently, he did not view history through the rose-colored glasses of landmark judicial decisions, sudden shifts in political power, or the abolition of existing and emergence of new social institutions. In Hennacy's simpler linguistics: the one-person revolution comes slowly.

Oftentimes a particular quote from a historical figure or a slogan raised up like a flag by a particular group will be used by social historians in an attempt to sum up that person or movement. While this practice has obvious limitations, it can also be put to good use. In the case of Ammon Hennacy, it was this question of stamina and consistency over the long haul that prompted his most oft-quoted statement. When asked while picketing if he really thought he could change the world, he replied, "No, but I am damn sure that it can't change me!"

Hennacy apprehended a simple yet profound human truth here, a truth that much of the church in the First World has yet to digest. The tentacles of the corporate capitalist consumer ethic, where the dollar supplants God and violence deserves more of the same, are omnipresent, thanks to the electronic age and its huge advertising budgets. Consequently, on both an individual and collective level, it is imperative for Christians to draw some clear lines across which they will not step. And when the state or society tries to compel them to step across, public resistance is often in order. In that resistance, a community of belief is created, which is able to nurture its members in living out their faith, and a much-needed prophetic witness is offered to the larger society as well. Hennacy's insight lies in the primacy of faithfulness over expediency: Acts of resistance to the false values of the world—acts of faith—build up faith. His genius was his willingness to draw clear lines and the unfailing vigilance with which he guarded them. His fault—and it is no small one, either—lies in not helping others to draw their own lines out of their own experiences, assuming rather that his were proper for others too.

Despite all that, Hennacy, like the rest of us, was surely plagued by doubts. Even with his firm belief in the transcendent nature of truthful action, he had his moments of questioning the ultimate meaningfulness of the hard path he had chosen. He may have been too full of his own image to admit them, but the doubts were present.

One way to explain his near-manic preoccupation with publicizing his peace witness is to recognize that he was reaching and striving for a meaning with staying power, one beyond his own volition. Meaning of that sort can never come exclusively from within. Nor can it come from the world, the media, or the attention of others, all of which offer only fleeting, transitory meaning. It flows out of the silence of the individual's graced faithfulness to the truth given by God. Ideally, this faithfulness is lived out behind closed doors where the left hand knows not what the right hand is up to. But Plato's best wishes aside, this is not an ideal world. Wracked with greed and deceit, it is a congenial home for evil, falsehood, and corrupted power, all of which are magnified by the unbridled technological forces that so mark our time. First-strike nuclear weapons, Reagan's Star Wars scheme, and the nuclear power industry's unsolvable problem of radioactive waste disposal are the tip of this dangerous iceberg. Consequently, prophetic witness fueled by compassion and evangelism for the power of love and truth are often in order. Individual trumpets do need occasional blowing in order to wake sleeping Christian consciences. Throughout his long life, Ammon Hennacy was ready to try to fill those orders, to blow the trumpet of his own considerable probity. When challenged on the highly public and visible nature of his fasts and civil disobedience, his response was straightforward and predictable:

> I do it [fast] to waken up the timid pacifists who know better and don't do better. Someone has to raise the ante of what

should be expected of a Christian and a Catholic. Talk is cheap and in this gluttonous world fasting can be a means of waking up some people. If anyone thinks the mainspring of my action is egotism I would ask by what measure they value their own actions. I am willing to be judged as a man, not as a mouse, by my fruits, both now and hereafter. My message is not meant for those unable to hear it.[35]

II

Peter Maurin . . . quoted Ibsen as saying that truth had to be restated every twenty years. I think that Ammon Hennacy in his life makes a restatement of Catholic Worker positions.

—Dorothy Day[36]

AMMON HENNACY WAS released from the Atlanta penitentiary on March 20, 1919. On Christmas Eve of that year, he and Selma Nelms, the daughter of the socialist sheriff of Milwaukee, sealed their common-law marriage with the pledge that they "would live together as long as they loved each other—for the Revolution." Then they hit the road.

For six years they traveled the country, occasionally stopping to do bread labor and at other times helping out local radical groups and communities. They logged 22,000 miles; 2,200 of them on foot. According to Hennacy, "We had needed this running around: Selma to counteract the staid, comfortable bourgeois Milwaukee outlook, and I to balance my confinement in solitary."[37]

On Ammon's birthday, July 24, 1925, they bought ten acres of woods near Waukesha, Wisconsin, with $100 down, and built a one-room home by hand. They later expanded it to five rooms. They named it Bisanakee, from the local Native American dialect; *Bisan* meant "quiet" and *akee* meant "place." They homesteaded there for six years, waging Tolstoy's Green Revolution. Ammon worked in a dairy, they gave each other two daughters, and they settled into what Hennacy described as a beautiful life. However, never able to sit passively by in the presence of what he perceived to be injustice, this indomitable crusader organized a strike by dairy workers in the midst of the Great Depression in 1931. Call it foolishness or fidelity, but color it Hennacy. He was fired from his job, they lost their house and farm, and they moved into the city of Milwaukee where Hennacy worked through the 1930s as a social worker.

In the late 1930s, as the war spirit increasingly gripped the nation, the lines of battle between Hennacy and the government once again emerged more clearly. Selma sensed that her husband might be imprisoned again for a long time, and generally tiring of the insecurities that apparently came with life with Ammon, she promptly packed up with their two young daughters and left. Predictably, in May 1942 Hennacy published in the *Catholic Worker* his statement of refusal to register for the draft, officially notified the government, and resigned his job. He fully expected to receive a five-year sentence, but probably because of age (he was forty-six), he was not arrested.

In his refusal to register he claimed to be honoring the principles of the Sermon on the Mount and following the example of the early Christians who refused to put even a pinch of incense on the altar of Caesar. He was particularly distressed with the response of the church leadership to the war; he consequently saw himself as speaking for the millions of Christians who had again been "sold out" by leaders who valued church property and power more than Christ. He also hoped that his refusal to register would be a prophetic witness to the millions of union women and men who succumbed to the glory of "time and a half" to become accessories to legal murder in the making of weapons of death, as well as to the thousands of radicals who had forgotten the ideals of Debs, Sacco, and Vanzetti. Finally, and perhaps most importantly, he saw his refusal to register as a statement on behalf of a just peace, one strong enough to break the endless cycle of violence likely to deliver World War III.[38]

Eventually he moved to the Southwest to be near his family. There, in 1943, he refused to pay income taxes for the previous year. It was his study of Tolstoy and the position of Dorothy Day and the Catholic Worker that led him to the belief that the payment of war-taxes was un-Christian. From then on, whenever he worked for a wage it was usually as a day laborer in agriculture, to avoid the newly instituted withholding tax and the possibility of the government garnishing his salary. He would never pay any federal income tax. In keeping with his anarchist principles, both of his books were self-published and not copyrighted. The exception was the first edition of his autobiography, published by Libertarian Press and then entitled *The Autobiography of a Catholic Anarchist*. His response to this apparent concession to the IRS was to tell the reader to note any sales tax and send it to the author: "I will refund any tax paid on this book."

At the age of fifty, he began what was to be a ten-year career as a migrant farmworker in Arizona and New Mexico. Hennacy chronicled this career in the pages of the *Catholic Worker* in a column entitled "Life at Hard Labor." Seemingly indefatigable, he genuinely enjoyed hard work and believed deeply in the value of manual labor. His anarchistic emphasis on personal responsibility was the root of his insistence that people be workers and not "parasites." Thus he would do away with advertising, banks, insurance, and much of the "parasitical work" that to him was the earmark of a failing society.[39] Following the examples of Jesus, Thoreau, Gandhi, and the Catholic Worker movement, he simplified his lifestyle to the point of living on $10 a month, sending the rest of his meager earnings to his daughters. It was during this period that he began in earnest the career of fasting, picketing, and committing acts of civil disobedience that would increase his already considerable notoriety.

Hennacy's anarchism was a practical one, and had both positive and negative dimensions. For him, just to be an anarchist by itself was negative. A Christian anarchist was called to pursue a dedicated life of poverty, service, labor, picketing, pacifism, and active love. This was the positive side. But his ideals were absolute. A dedicated life was free from complicity in the return of evil for evil inherent in the courts, prisons, and warfare. Anything less fell short of what Christ taught.[40] His views on pacifism grew not only out of his recognition that the reign of God was in everyone, but from his belief that anarchism and pacifism were really two sides of the same coin. One could not be a genuine pacifist and support the state; nor could one be a true anarchist and support war. A Christian anarchistic pacifism was the only real hope for Hennacy; all other roads led to tyranny, war, and death.

His interlocking approach to pacifism and anarchism was more the norm than the exception among U.S. anarchists. This, of course, stands in bold contradiction to the common misconception, entrenched in mass opinion since the Haymarket bombing of May 4, 1886, that violence and destruction are at the heart of anarchism. But as historian Staughton Lynd put it, "The ultimate goal of all anarchists was a society that would function nonviolently without need of the aggressive state." Some philosophers, like Robert Nisbet, even maintain that "the espousal of nonviolence . . . is the hallmark of the main tradition of anarchism."[41]

Similarly, there are some deeply ingrained yet false understandings in the popular mind about the nature of pacifism. For many, pacifism is equated with passivity: the refusal to become engaged in an issue to the extent of risking personal loss, usually defined as physical harm. But Hennacy's pacifism was of a piece with his anarchism. It did not, of course, mean that people should stand passively by when confronted with evil and violence. It meant rather the precise opposite: that they should act disarmingly, using the strongest weapon available, spiritual force, rather than the weaker one, violence. He was, perhaps surprisingly to some who met him picketing on the street, exceptionally well read. He had studied the Gandhian approach to nonviolence and found that it resonated with his own experience. He understood deeply that one cannot hope to use spiritual force unless one has it, and that there can be no shortcuts to obtaining it. Gandhi's spiritual weapon of *satyagraha* (truth-force) is the fruit of a steadfast clinging to the truth in one's daily life. Hennacy had abundant confidence in the power of nonviolence; as he saw it, it had seldom if ever failed him. In prison, in dangerous situations as a social worker during the Depression, through all his years of public fasting, picketing, and speaking on controversial peace issues (especially during the Red Scare of the 1940s and 1950s), he had effectively used the Gandhian method of moral jiu jitsu to defuse violent situations.

But in his experiments in nonviolence he had even more going for him than his own considerable soul-force. He had a quick and clever wit. He easily disarmed angry, threatening counterdemonstrators or hostile interviewers. In the 1950s in New York, Hennacy was on "Night Beat" more than once, a popular radio talk show "where they publicly tried to pick your brain and cause a laugh." He was asked, as an anarchist, if he believed in free love. His quick reply: "Sure; do you believe in bought love?"[42] When threatened with arrest for disturbing the peace by his picketing, his stock retort: "I'm not disturbing the peace, I'm disturbing the war."

Hennacy's brand of absolutist pacifism allowed for only the barest minimum of cooperation with the "war-mongering state" in order to get along in society. In 1955, the U.S. Quakers service arm, the American Friends Service Committee (AFSC), published a seminal booklet on nonviolence entitled "Speak Truth to Power." It was warmly and enthusiastically received throughout the peace movement, influencing more than one generation of pacifists on nonviolent strategies and dynamics vis-à-vis the state and society. (It became, in fact, a movement classic, and has recently been reprinted.)

In a review published in the *Catholic Worker*, Hennacy took AFSC to task for going only part way in disassociating itself from the power (government) to which it desired to speak truth. His position was that any temporizing with evil—state power—would make an otherwise clear message of noncooperation fall flat. He not only decried pacifists who made munitions, paid taxes for weapons, and bought government bonds, but suggested that creeping materialism and the acceptance of political maneuvering common among pacifist groups had swamped the idealism that had made noncooperation such a success for Gandhi. "We are too much wedded to prosperity. We will be pacifist but we will not give up our bourgeois way of life."[43] In his view, truth could be spoken to state power only when the truth-tellers had ceased to benefit from the violence of the state.

Hennacy insisted that one must not follow less than one knows. To one who knows the ultimate good, there cannot be the lesser of two evils. Pacifists are to refuse absolutely in matters of the draft, taxes, and loyalty oaths to the government. As for those who abandoned their pacifist ideals in World War II, he had a ready answer: "A pacifist between wars is like a vegetarian between meals." He understood pacifism to be strongest in its uncompromising witness; its appeal lies in the quality of its message. Both the United States and the Soviet Union were busy solidifying their respective spheres of influence. A bipolar approach to interpreting geopolitical reality was emerging. It was a period marked by a nationalism bordering on jingoism and an uncritical acceptance of the war and its results. A congenial home for peace activists it most certainly was not.

Nevertheless, Hennacy sounded the warning bell to the peace movement that it was selling out to the status quo. He felt pacifist groups were watering down their messages so as not to appear to be too radical and suffer a loss of followers. He believed the peace movement was itself suffering from western civilization's sacred love affair with quantity. He accused the Fellowship of Reconciliation (FOR) of falling into the same strangling quicksand of moral befuddlement as the churches and the labor unions had: the organization had become more important than the ideal it was supposed to stand for. While still being respectful of possible mitigating circumstances, Hennacy said, in effect, that those who pay taxes for war are second-class pacifists. For the FOR to maintain otherwise was "foolishness with God and humankind." He was of the belief that all people were sisters and brothers and would thus be, in time, capable of appreciating the absolutist pacifist message.[44] As he egotistically saw it, there was no need to grope about in the gray area, when with a little courage such as his, one could bask in the bright white light of righteousness.

Hennacy was a proverbial Pauline thorn in the side not only to the state. As he put it: "I love my enemies, but I'm hell on my friends."[45] Karl Meyer concurs, saying, "Ammon would never give a person a pass to be less than the perfect radical." No thorn in the side is pleasant, proverbially Pauline or not. What frequently made this thorn particularly unbearable was the fact that Hennacy's yardstick for the perfect radical was himself. T. S. Eliot once wrote that "the only wisdom we can hope to obtain is the wisdom of humility."[46] By this insightful measure, Hennacy must be reckoned a fool. But perhaps it is not quite that simple. Hennacy's one-person revolution turned humility on its head. He was humble in only one, somewhat backward sense: He expected others to be able to live the ideal as he did. "What I can do, everyone can do, if they would put fear from them."[47] Few in the peace movement beyond Dorothy Day and Dave Dellinger (he thought both were "the best he ever saw") escaped his sharp criticism. Karl Meyer believes Hennacy's fellow pacifists would in turn "tend to get back at Ammon by criticizing him for his egotism and attention-getting."[48] There were many who discounted his message, dismissing him as supercilious.

Though he surely would have never admitted to such a motivation, many of the barbs he directed at his movement colleagues probably had their root in his own fears. While he genuinely believed others were capable of the radical life, he was also threatened by that possibility. If others really began to sacrifice to live a principled and disciplined radical life through and through, he would no longer be the "unique American rebel" the newspapers proclaimed him to be. A prophet was Hennacy to be sure, but he was not of the demeanor of the great biblical prophets Amos or Jeremiah. They both dragged their feet, trying to throw off the call to prophetic witness; Amos because he saw himself as "just" a simple farmer, and Jeremiah because of his difficulties in speech. Reluctance and humility marked their prophetic vocation. Not so with Hennacy. We all need security blankets to wrap up in and protect ourselves from the fear of meaninglessness and mortality. It would seem Hennacy's blanket was his supreme radicalism and the accolades that came his way as a result. After all, not only was he touted as the *sui generis* radical, but he took it upon himself to proclaim his uniqueness to all who would listen. Fear of slipping through this safety net of meaning fueled Hennacy's proclivity to criticize others for making the compromises that are inevitable in human existence. Karl Meyer says Hennacy was wont to look "for the ways that people chickened out rather than the ways that they were [being radical]. And that was somewhat of a fault of Ammon's."[49]

While this fault may have been a negative influence among older activists, and did some harm in the building up of the radical movement, it was somewhat counterbalanced by the effect Hennacy's stance had on young people. With them he was even more demanding. But the young seem universally graced with large doses of idealism. What appears on the horizon to many as a treacherous mountain one had best detour, is embraced by young adults as a stairway— albeit steep and rocky—to a clear view of life. Hennacy's way of life promised them that view. His prophetic witness showed them it was possible to climb the mountain. This direct challenge to their idealism served to beckon them more deeply into the radical life. Both Dorothy Day and Karl Meyer agree on the tremendous influence Hennacy had on young people, even though, Meyer remembers, "he'd always call the young people pipsqueak and accuse them of chickening out . . . but he had such a charming way of doing [it] that he probably intimidated them less than most."[50]

Hennacy was a man who demanded a response. He was impossible to ignore. Many found his doctrinaire spirit unbearable; others recognized a strange, elusive sort of charm that traveled with his eccentricity. As Joan Thomas said, "You can't possibly conceive of what a humorous character he was, how he would be in perfect ecstasy after writing the most shocking diatribe of a letter to the bishop in Salt Lake City and yet, darn if he ever managed to make an enemy of that bishop, who was as fond of him as everyone else there."[51] One of the many entertaining vignettes in his autobiography recounts that the first time he spoke at a Lions Club meeting in 1937, he promptly announced, "The early Christians were thrown to the lions rather than put a pinch of incense on the altar to Caesar, while the modern ones join the Lions Club."[52] He neglected to tell his readers, however (perhaps purposefully?) whether he was ever invited back to speak at the Lions Club.

The truly profound effect Hennacy had on many is exemplified by the memorial article Jim Forest published in the Milwaukee Catholic Worker paper, the *Catholic Radical*. Forest, who wrote from the Waupan state prison where he was incarcerated for his participation in the Milwaukee Fourteen draft board raid of 1968, and who is now general secretary of the International Fellowship of Reconciliation, entitled his piece, "Men Acted Differently According to Whether They Had Met Him or Not." He wrote, "For myself, however, it is no pious funeral effort to suggest that he was a saint. And is. By which I mean he was not only one who rarely if ever failed to be responsive to the voice of conscience within himself—but that he was one of those raised up to show others how much is possible. He was the saint as prophet: the one who, with his life, widens the frontiers of imagination for others."[53]

Hennacy saw warfare, and militarism in general, as the greatest threat to humanity. He followed Randolph Bourne in seeing war as the health of the state, and therefore had no faith in any association of governments like the United Nations for preventing war. The only answer was to encourage individuals to oppose war. There are, he said, three ways to secure peace: getting 51 percent of the bullets, which is the approved way of all governments; obtaining 51 percent of the ballots, where the good candidate gets elected but soon turns out to be little different from the others; and changing ourselves— the most practical method. It was practical because those "who believe in bullets and ballots must gain a majority before they can begin to practice their beliefs and thus postpone indefinitely anything but conversation about their views. We do not need to wait on others for we have seceded about 90 percent from this exploitative system and are already practicing our ideals."[54]

Every year at tax time Hennacy would show up to picket at various IRS offices and federal buildings, openly declaring his refusal to pay taxes, revealing how much he owed the government in back taxes, and challenging all passersby with his vocal and well-orchestrated witness. He took the writing of his leaflets and the wording and construction of his signs with the utmost seriousness, often struggling and praying for days over them. He knew how to best utilize the press and the media, and through his extensive travels on frequent speaking tours he had a wide national network of media contacts. With nearly every picketing venture came an equally well-publicized fast. Some, like his 1958 fast at the Atomic Energy Commission office in Washington, D.C., lasted for forty days. He picketed four hours a day, and dropped thirty-one pounds from his already lithe, steel-straight frame. Forty-eight days marked the longest of his many liquid-only fasts.

Every year at the anniversary of the dropping of the atom bomb on Hiroshima, he would fast and picket one day for each year since the bomb was dropped. He also frequently picketed and fasted for people on Death Row, especially in Utah during the 1960s where he founded and directed the Joe Hill House of Hospitality in Salt Lake City.

Hennacy's fasting and picketing, and his acts of civil disobedience, were deeply imbued with his pacifist spirit. He was keenly aware that Gandhi fasted not to embarrass the British government, but to arouse the Indian people to sacrifice their comforts for the cause of Indian freedom. Just as the mainspring of Hennacy's Christian anarchism was for the most part positive and not negative, so was the focus of his fasting. When he fasted at the Internal Revenue Service, the Atomic Energy Commission, the White House, and other places, his emphasis was on waking up and encouraging "pacifists and half-pacifists" to the seriousness of living in the atomic world without challenging the powers that be. He wished to coerce no one; resistance must be the personal decision of each individual. But he did want to remind people that they must make daily decisions of acquiesence, or resistance, to the status quo of militarism.

His leaflets were clear and emphatic: he did not fast *against* the Atomic Energy Commission, but rather as a penance for his own sins of complicity in Hiroshima, atomic testing, and the arms race. He fasted not so much to change others—that was impossible given his understanding of human nature—but rather to deepen his own resistance and to offer a witness to the truth.[55] In this way, his fasting was an invitation to others to change. There were many who accepted the invitation.

Hennacy had an acute sensitivity to the relationship between theory and praxis. Words, values, and beliefs not concretized were meaningless. He was not an analytical thinker; he saw other points of view ideologically rather than analytically. As Ed Turner wrote in a memorial article on Hennacy, he was first and foremost interested in the answer to the question: what action would your thoughts produce?[56] It was for this reason that he studied and visited a wide range of peace and radical communities. He frequently wrote of these communities in the small pacifist, libertarian, and anarchist journals and periodicals to which he was a prolific contributor.[57]

He was intrigued by any religious thought that helped mold faith into action. While he helped introduce the Bruderhof, the Molokons, and the Christian anarchist and pacifist Doukhobors to the wider radical movement, it was the Hopi who enthralled him the most. During his many years in the Southwest, Hennacy had visited the Hopi often and was invited to participate in their Snake Dance, Bean Dance, and other religious rituals. In the bitter winter of 1949–1950, he accompanied Dan Katchongua, leader of the traditional Hopi and son of the legendary Hopi leader Yukeoma, to Washington, D.C., to lobby on the Hopis' behalf. At the age of fifty-six, Hennacy made the trip across the continent in typical style—bouncing in the back of a pickup truck! He counseled the many Hopi conscientious objectors both before and during the Korean War, and consumed reams of material about this pacifist community. Few white people knew more of the Hopi way of life than Hennacy; even fewer were held in higher esteem by the traditional Hopi. They counted him a brother. He, of course, viewed them through his radical glasses and championed the traditional Hopi because they were his living model of a pacifist, anarchist society.

In the summer of 1952, Hennacy commenced his annual fast and picket to commemorate the anniversary of Hiroshima/Nagasaki. He fasted for seven days, and distributed a leaflet that touted the Hopi as a thousand-year-old example of people living the good, anarchist life. Their keys were emphasizing the spiritual significance of life and recognizing the desire to get even when wronged as the major sin afflicting humanity. His leaflet said that these beliefs, coupled with their emphasis on each individual's complete acceptance of responsibility for personal actions, allowed them to live together harmoniously without need of courts, warfare, elections, or prisons.

Following the fast, Hennacy headed east for his first retreat: a five-day silent model with the Catholic Worker at Maryfarm. After the retreat he took his blue knees ("I got blue marks on my knees from kneeling so much on the hard floor") down to the New York Catholic Worker, where he stayed long enough to "be there for two mailings of the paper" and to speak at three of the Friday-night meetings. His last topic was the Hopi. When Tom Sullivan told him it was his best presentation, Hennacy's uncharacteristic reply revealed his deep respect for the Hopi: "That was because there was more Hopi and less Hennacy in the conversation." His respect ran deep enough to consider them "the spiritual conscience of America."[58]

He held Dorothy Day and her Catholic Worker movement in equally high esteem for their uncompromising radical pacifism. Hennacy was affiliated with the Worker to varying degrees for thirty-three years, beginning in 1937 with a loose association with Holy Family House in Milwaukee. In the 1940s he sold the New York paper all over the Southwest and contributed his "Life at Hard Labor" column. From 1952 to 1961 he moved his base of operations to the New York Worker house, and in 1961 he founded the Joe Hill House of Hospitality in Salt Lake City, remaining a regular contributor to the paper till he died in 1970.

In his valuable biography of Dorothy Day, William Miller focuses on Hennacy's love for and attraction to Day as the reason for his move to the New York Worker.[59] While that focus is certainly accurate, the picture is not complete without other considerations. Hennacy's keen interest in the relationship between theory and praxis also drew him to Day and the Worker. He disdained the self-proclaimed radicals who never moved beyond conversation and the propounding of theories. In Day and the Worker, he saw no dichotomy between talk and action. In addition, while a social worker in the Depression and later, he came to know all too well the tangled human wreckage lying at the bottom of the cliff of capitalist life. The Catholic Worker movement not only picked up those human wrecks and perhaps provided a graced space within which to restore them but had, as he saw it, the one method for ensuring that people didn't fall over the cliff in the first place—the one-person revolution in the heart of each individual.

A letter Hennacy wrote to the Milwaukee County Board of Trustees in January 1942 reveals how much the plight of his marginalized clients moved him. It is a typical example of his willingness to pursue the truth no matter where it led him. In the letter, he point-blank declined a $2.50 pay raise out of solidarity with his clients and the meager benefits allotted them. He requested the money be placed in a "conscience fund. I am a conscientious objector so far as accepting an increase in salary as long as the clients who I serve do not also have their budgets increased a like amount."[60]

Still, when he first arrived at the Worker, he was not at all sure he wanted to "major in feeding bums." Fifteen years later, at Joe Hill House, he was still calling the guests "my bums." But the term did not carry the pejorative connotations for him it did for others. Hennacy was too attuned to the reasons for his bums' marginalization in a corporate capitalist state. He served them quite literally, working and sacrificing on their behalf. His daily regimen at Joe Hill House included pushing a grocery store cart through the early morning light, and rummaging through the throw-away produce at grocery stores. Begging for his bums was not above him. He was vainglorious to be sure, but he knew the Beatitudes too well to be unwilling to gird himself and wash his sisters' feet. Indeed, Dorothy Day paid him what must have been the supreme compliment when she noted he was "the most ascetic, the most hard working, the most devoted to the poor and the oppressed of any we had met, and that his life and his articles put us on the spot. He was an inspiration and a reproach."[61]

The personalist philosophy of the Worker dovetailed nicely with Hennacy's one-person revolution. The radical personalism of the Worker movement uttered a resounding *no* to the reigning liberalism that caught and paralyzed so many others in its grasp. As William Miller has described it, that liberalism was marked by a deep faith in the processes of evolution. Social change "for the better" marched ever onward; all one needed to do was to hop on the bandwagon of institutional forms and perhaps offer just a little bit of guidance at the crucial turns. Social progress was perceived as inevitable, and was marked in quantitative and objectivized terms. The personalist philosophy offered by Day and Maurin did not expect change through and in social and political institutions, but rather looked for the creative changes in individuals as they elevated the Christian precept of active love to a place of practiced primacy in their daily lives. This stepping outside the tentacles of social progress was real precisely because it occurred in people's hearts. Hennacy understood better than most that its success was therefore not dependent upon the object world; the scope and purpose, like that of the crucifixion, was decidedly spiritual.[62]

Hennacy's thought clearly lacks the depth and breadth of both Peter Maurin's and the Catholic Worker movement; and the heavy Christological emphasis as well as the eschatological vision that stands as the victorious culmination of Worker philosophy is most assuredly absent in his discursive writings. But Ammon Hennacy understood the one-person revolution to be essentially an exercise in Christian love. In this sense his vision was the same as that of the Worker's. The myriad ways he endeavored to resist militarism and consumerism, returning good for evil, are examples of the Worker's ultimate goal: elevating the Christian precept of active love to that revered place of practiced primacy.

Though he would be averse, given his deep distrust of the institutional church, to use some of the terminology of Maurin and Day, while in prison he did "put on Christ," he did "carry the cross," and he discovered that the reign of God is within. Hennacy's life of self-sacrifice, his herculean pickets and fasts for death-row prisoners and for peace, his emphasis on personal transformation, and his repeated rejection of the objectivized world through his refusal to pay taxes, honor immoral laws, or take part in government, all make up the intricate designs on his blanket refusal to submit to the "progress" of evolutionary time.

Hennacy's disdain and distrust for social institutions extended to the Catholic church. It was on this point that he differed markedly from Worker philosophy as defined by Maurin and Day. Indeed, previous to having met up with them and their movement and paper, Hennacy shared the opinion expressed by Emma Goldman in a personal letter addressed to "Comrade Hennacy." After speaking appreciatively of their friendship, she writes, "I was rather surprised to find you have among your co-workers members of the Radical Catholic group [the Catholic Worker]. I confess that is a new one on me for I have never known of Catholics being radical." Goldman could hardly have been expected to know any differently, given the uniqueness of Catholic Worker radicalism in the church. But it wasn't just this uniqueness that contributed to her understandable ignorance. As Dorothy Day once complained, "Whenever the *New York Times* refers to me, it's as a 'social worker.' Pacifism and anarchism are just dismissed."[63]

Hennacy's official membership in Catholicism was to last only fifteen years (1952–1967). Even during that period, he was largely unable to overlook or forgive the church for what he perceived as its marriage to corruption and tyranny. For much of his life he had been simply unable to see a solid connection between Jesus and the churches, given their frequent blessings of economic exploitation and war.[64] The result: he defined himself a "nonchurch Christian." But over the years, during his long association and close work with Day and the Worker, the processes of spiritual osmosis began to break through Hennacy's anti-institutional armor. He admitted to weaknesses, to something missing in his life, namely to "a lack of spirituality." That same osmosis was partly responsible for his conclusion that he could best obtain this spiritual growth within the Catholic church itself.

The beginning of Hennacy's turn to the church occurred in the first week of August 1950, during his annual Hiroshima fast and picket. While at liturgy one morning (he was a somewhat regular mass attendee long before joining the church) he felt a deep affinity with the parishioners and wanted to be one of them, sharing their search for the true meaning of Jesus the Christ. He admitted to having known for some time that he was short on the "love which radiates from Dorothy and true CW's." He decided he would not allow the church's support of militarism to keep him "from God and from Jesus who was a true rebel."[65]

It would be another two years before his baptism. Immediately prior, he began a fairly rigorous study of Catholic doctrine and followed his baptism with a reexamination of his own religious beliefs.[66] Somewhat predictably, the veteran anarchist took refuge in the Catholic doctrine of the primacy of the individual conscience. It was as if the doctrine had been poured into a personalist mold and had come out custom made for this individualistic rebel. It gave Hennacy the green light of freedom to disagree with the church's conservative stand on a number of critical social issues, a freedom that was absolutely essential for his formal church membership.

The history of anarchism has been marked by an antithesis to organized religion. As Robert Nisbet puts it, anarchism has been "overwhelmingly secular and generally hostile to the Christian church."[67] But Hennacy had long been a tireless defender of the integrity of the Christian-anarchist formulation, writing rebuttals in secular radical periodicals and religious journals to articles that had questioned the possibility of a genuinely Christian anarchism. Frequently, it was Hennacy himself who was the focus of the original articles, as many considered him the contemporary paradigmatic expression of Christian anarchism. He developed a notion that it was up to him to show the world—both secular and religious—that one could be a Christian *and* an anarchist, indeed, that that was the only way to keep alive the ideals of the Sermon on the Mount. As he explained in a rebuttal to Bob Ludlow's disavowal of the term "Catholic anarchism" in the *Catholic Worker*, "I had been a Christian anarchist from 1919 until 1952 and received little sympathy from either Christians or anarchists."[68] He even wrote a 150,000-word manuscript on the subject, which was never published.

Once a member of the Catholic church, he set about vocally defending a formulation (*Catholic* anarchism) even fewer could understand, given the hierarchical/clerical nature of Catholicism.[69] He argued the two were compatible because the church was not the clergy or the hierarchical structure.

> The *real* Church consists of the Mystical Body of Christ in those who grasp the meaning of the Sermon on the Mount and who do not seek to change the world by ballots or bullets, but by changing themselves daily in that daily communion which the Catholic Church furnishes them. . . . The Catholic Church does offer in daily mass a method of spiritual growth and a world view of brotherhood [and sisterhood] entirely compatible in method and in ideal to the anarchist dream which envisions a world made different not by wholesale pushing around of crowds but by the individual revolution within the heart of each individual.[70]

With that, Hennacy came as close to the ecclesiology of Day and Maurin as he would ever get. He seems almost to have accepted the belief of those two fellow anarchists that the church was the one institution where meaningful change would happen. The church was for them the point where time was synthesized into eternity, the place where communal redemption finally occurs. It nearly appears that Hennacy has here agreed with Maurin and Day that the object church of the world was merely a symbol of its inner spirit.[71]

Nonetheless, Hennacy's radical life and his reading and admiration of the early American deists and anarchists like Thomas Paine and others had cultivated within him a hardy strain of anticlericalism the likes of which not even Dorothy Day could root out. It bloomed rather consistently, but out of deference to Day he refrained from watering it as often and putting it on display, as had long been his custom in writing and giving talks. He simply had no patience for those who did not live their ideals, and he saw precious few clergy living the gospel ideal as he understood it. That there may have been other viable interpretations of the gospel is a possibility that escaped him. He was too fixated on the plainly unviable interpretations of a Cardinal Spellman calling for total victory in Indochina, of the use of church yards to store scrap metal to be melted down to make weapons in World War II, of the church's failure to indict the consumeristic spirit running rampant in Catholic parishes in the 1950s and 1960s while the poor went without basic necessities.

Joining the church was in large part a marriage of convenience: he saw it as that rare institution that shared his ideals, thus a place in which he hoped to be better able to concretize those ideals. Becoming a Catholic was certainly one of those points in his life when he did in fact redirect his stance, making some personal concessions in the process. He was later to see it as something of a mistake, believing that he was baptized much too quickly. But he was grateful for

his fifteen-year membership in the Catholic church and the opportunities it offered him to spread his gospel of the one-person revolution. His Catholicism allowed him to speak in scores of Catholic
seminaries and colleges and hundreds of schools and churches that
might not otherwise have been open to him.

If the church was bound not to have a lasting impact on him, nor
he upon it, the same is not true for his influence on the Worker
movement. Day told long-time Catholic Worker Stanley Vishnewski
that there "were three men who had a great influence on my life,
and as a result, on the Catholic Worker." They were Reverend Paci-
fique Roy, Peter Maurin, and Ammon Hennacy.[72] When Hennacy
took up residence at the New York Worker in 1952, peace activism
was at a rather low ebb. He set about to lead the Catholic Worker
movement in particular, and the U.S. peace movement in general,
into another arena of activism, that of nonviolent resistance.[73]

Besides his tax resistance, Hiroshima fasts, and picketing of the
Atomic Energy Commission to stop nuclear testing, in 1955 he instituted a six-year resistance to New York City's annual air raid
drills, as required by the Civil Defense Act. The two years previous,
in 1953 and 1954, people were not actually required to seek "shelter" for ten minutes. Nevertheless, Hennacy characteristically took
the initiative and picketed, without being arrested. But in 1955,
when he realized it was compulsory, he organized a group of pacifists
that included Dorothy Day and twenty-eight others from various
pacifist organizations. They openly refused to take shelter when the
sirens sounded their warning and were promptly arrested. Media attention was broad. It was also relatively sympathetic. As Hennacy
saw it, the drills were a farce: a silly war game, based on fear, which
he refused to play. The religious leaflet for the action, written by
Dorothy Day and signed by her and Ammon, boldly stated that one
could not have faith in God and depend on the atom bomb at the
same time. Hennacy continued to play a leading role in these annual
acts of civil disobedience, and in the winter of 1960 he picketed the
Civil Defense office two hours daily for three long months, calling
for five thousand people to resist the compulsory air raid drill of
1961. Two thousand people joined the protest that year, with the
result that from 1962 onward there has been no compulsory drill.[74]

Hennacy worked tirelessly to move his adopted church closer to
the social demands of the gospel. He was forever writing letters to
individual bishops imploring them to be the prophetic pastors he
thought the gospel called them to be on matters of capital punishment and war. In 1958, he made a pilgrimage to Florida to protest the
nuclear missiles housed at Cape Canaveral. The plan was to picket
the Catholic churches in the area, attempting to prick the con-

sciences of the "faithful." One of the pastors angrily demanded that he remove the name "Catholic" from his sign because, as he saw it, Hennacy was giving Catholics a bad name and besides, he didn't have permission from either him or the bishop! Hennacy replied:

> We are laypeople and we don't need permission from the Bishop or from you to oppose missiles for murder. The Church has had a bad name long enough supporting wars. I like the name Catholic and I am trying to make it mean something like the early Christians meant it to be when Christians couldn't go to court or kill in war. I venture that in the years to come the Church will be proud that we Catholic Workers opposed missiles and war and that we gave the Church a good name.[75]

Hennacy was imprisoned well over thirty times for his uncompromising activism. Some arrests brought prison terms of considerable length, including a six-month stay at Sandstone Federal Penitentiary for going over the fence at the Strategic Air Command headquarters in Omaha in 1960. Dorothy Day wrote of the singular nature of his role in the movement during this time: "No one else I know . . . seems capable of putting forth the sustained effort, and of demonstrating the tenacity of purpose so needed in this time."[76]

Hennacy knew well the role and how to play it. The unwavering rebel believed that once truth, obtained in the fiery chambers of the one-person revolution and manifested in values, beliefs, and ideals, was concretized, it had a power to move the souls of women and men: "One person . . . with their witness in jail . . . is worth a dozen surveys or a score who pray and vigil. . . . There is that in even the most conservative person which reacts to courage rather than to timidity."[77] And react they did. Karl Meyer says, "Ammon had a tremendous influence. . . . If you're going to talk about the Vietnam war generation in the Catholic Worker movement . . . you're going to talk of people who were deeply influenced by Ammon because Ammon threw up that radical challenge."[78]

Although many have failed to recognize it, Hennacy was substantially more complex than he first appears. His own considerable courage was rooted not simply in his well-known inflated sense of self but in a deep and abiding faith. Hennacy summarized this faith in a letter to Dave Dellinger:

> The strength which builds up this moral and physical courage and Way of Life has to come from within ourselves through some deep trial which has proven to us that we work not alone but with God, the Absolute, Good, or what-

ever name by which we designate that which is greater than ourselves. We either choose to work in harmony with this great force or we are on our own. Thoreau has stated it by saying that "one on the side of God is a majority," and Jesus said, "Behold, the Kingdom of God is within you."[79]

AMMON HENNACY WAS, like both Peter Maurin and Dorothy Day, a member of that rare breed of people whose lives are a harmonious symphony, played out on the taut strings stretched between one's values and one's actions. The music occasioned by the lives of Maurin and Day may be more universally pleasing, to be sure, but every orchestra needs the occasionally shrill notes from its horn section to accompany and complement the refined chords of its violins. Many in the peace movement feel that Ammon Hennacy was a trumpet whose loud notes are still much needed in a troubled world. That is why they find it especially tragic that he has been so quickly passed over, less than twenty years after his death. The man who received the 1969 War Resisters League "Pacifist of the Year" award just one short year before he died has been little remembered. Of course, this is less surprising when one remembers that even during his life Hennacy's extreme radicalism and contentious spirit kept him somewhat marginalized within an already marginalized peace movement. But it is especially curious given the precipice of nuclear catastrophe on which the world teeters, and the basic human needs that go unmet around the world because of the institutionalized return of evil for evil that the arms race propagates and against which Hennacy stood steadfast. Whether or not Ammon Hennacy is important as a figure in the history of social thought remains problematic. Nevertheless, he still has a role to play in today's world where Libyan terrorism is met with more of the same: U.S. terror bombing of Libyan cities. Critics of society most often have insightful contributions to make toward understanding perduring social issues even though they may not happen to be, as in this case, especially good or comprehensive theorists.

The peace movement can learn much from Hennacy about personal courage. He was not afraid to wade upstream alone. Indeed, Joan Thomas has said she sees this as the "supreme truth about him." We should not be surprised at this; he himself often said that courage was the virtue he most prized, for without it one could not practice any of the others.[80]

In some ways he was to the peace movement of his time what the Berrigan brothers have been to the peace movement since the late 1960s. Their draft board raid at Catonsville in 1968 signaled a new departure in the active resistance to the Vietnam war.[81] In much the same way, their symbolic destruction of nuclear missile cones at the General Electric plant in King of Prussia, Pennsylvania, in September 1980 has given birth to a new genre of radical resistance to the nuclear arms race: the Plowshares movement.

Hennacy's decision to openly refuse to pay all income taxes, including the withholding tax, was a lonely and solitary one. He had written to all the leading pacifists and to various peace organizations asking them to either join with him or at least offer him their moral support. For many years he stood alone, except for the moral support of Dorothy Day. He was even occasionally censored at movement events, asked not to bring up his tax resistance. The frequently ignored yet widespread war-tax resistance movement once again present in this country can look to Hennacy as a sort of founding father. The numbers of military-tax resisters are growing rapidly, partly due to Catholic Archbishop Raymond Hunthausen's 1981 decision to publicly withhold 50 percent of his federal income taxes and partly due to public outrage over a military budget that presently consumes 64 cents of the tax dollar. This burgeoning resistance movement now has a national office serving as an umbrella and clearing house for a decentralized grassroots movement that boasts more than 125 war-tax resistance groups nationwide, serving anywhere from 10,000 to 20,000 individual war-tax resisters. Hennacy's life of noncooperation and total refusal to lay one penny upon the military tax altar still stands as a prophetic model.[82]

Similarly, Hennacy was one of the few to refuse to register in World War I and one of the very few in the United States to refuse to register for both world wars. The clarity of his prison witness for his World War I refusal and his willingness to repeat that risk in 1942 still rings true and clear for today's few nonregistrants who have gone public and risked prosecution.

Early in 1987, for the first time in U.S. history, Catholic bishops were arrested for committing acts of civil disobedience on behalf of peace. It happened in the desert at the Nevada nuclear test site, the site that was so familiar to Ammon Hennacy. The demonstration was organized by Pax Christi, an international Catholic movement for peace. Five years previously, Franciscans for Peace had begun an annual forty-day Lenten witness at the test site, and in November 1987 the Catholic Worker movement hosted a three-day international celebration of Dorothy Day's ninetieth birthday there as well. Attended by over 400 Catholic Workers and supporters, the celebration culminated with the arrest of over 200 people for committing civil disobedience. Through these and other actions coordinated by American Peace Test, the test site has become a pilgrimage point for peacemakers, with thousands attending demonstrations, fasts, and vigils there each year. Long before these actions became common-place at the test site, Ammon Hennacy had marked a trail for the peace movement, faithfully maintaining his solitary vigils and fasts both at the old Atomic Energy Commission offices in Las Vegas and on the wind-blown desert roads of the nuclear test site. Given his long struggle to move the bishops to active leadership on the peace issue, it is not hard to imagine the joy he would take in learning of this new level of activism.

If, on the world's terms, he was counted a failure—albeit a peculiar one—and quickly forgotten, that was all right with him. He actually expected much worse than that from a world where brutal violence is glorified and Christ's demanding message of suffering love is little understood. One of his stock statements, one that Joan Thomas says ran deep in his philosophy, conveys this idea: "Truth is forever on the scaffold; error on the throne." He found refuge and solace in the life of Christ for his own apparent failure on the violent world's terms. He understood that "if Jesus Christ couldn't change the world, how could he?"[83]

For Hennacy, the fate of Christ helped blunt the very real pain of his own life. That pain included a broken marriage, daughters and wife both lost because of his uncompromising, and somewhat personally insensitive, pacifism. It also included a resistance-based life that resulted in a truly ascetic lifestyle uniquely his own. Precious few embraced voluntary poverty as seriously and wholeheartedly as he. His was an austere life, one he welcomed and interpreted as the unavoidable result of being committed to truth. For Hennacy, there was no way out, no way to live a life of integrity and avoid the lion's den. He believed that whoever genuinely tried to follow the way of Christ would, in one way or another, end up crucified.

Ammon was a romantic Irishman. Maybe that is partly why he always said he wanted to die on the picket line. He thought, or perhaps hoped, that someone would one day shoot him down there.[84] This wasn't just idle romanticism either. He often said that the true test of a radical was whether or not he or she walked a picket line. To his mind, there existed no more honorable, or familiar, spot upon which this dyed-in-the-wool American rebel could stand when meeting his maker.

He was graced with his wish. More or less.

On January 5, 1970, at the ripe age of seventy-six, Hennacy trudged up the steep hill to the Utah state capitol in Salt Lake City. He was headed there to picket on behalf of Messrs. Lance and Kelback, two convicted murderers who were facing the death penalty on February 5. As was his custom, he had carefully laid out plans to carry on a daily, month-long picket in the middle of winter. He made this pil-grimage up the hill for three days without incident. On the fourth morning, January 8, he collapsed to the ground, struck by a heart attack. He was taken to the hospital, where after three days he made enough progress to be removed from intensive care. But three days later, on January 14, the walls of his heart, thin and weak from years of long fasts combined with hard labor, collapsed and sent him final-ly home.

Fighting for justice for others till the very end, Hennacy's last written words were dictated from his bed in the intensive care unit on January 11. It was a statement to be read to Lance and Kelbeck's pardons board hearing on January 14, the day he died. He argued that the death penalty and the Christian command of returning good for evil were simply incompatible, and closed with the remarks, "All that I'm trying to do is to go a bit farther like Christ did—that those without sin should first cast the stone. . . . I have been picketing and saying this for the last nine years in Salt Lake City and will continue to do so as long as I live."[85]

Ammon's body was cremated and, in keeping with his wishes, his ashes were scattered over the graves of the Haymarket anarchists in Waldheim Cemetery in Chicago. Cantankerous and stubborn as he was compassionate and humorous, Ammon Hennacy plowed a fur-row uniquely his own in the rich soil of American radicalism. As Michael Harrington put it, "I think that something of America died with Ammon Hennacy."[86]

> Love without courage and wisdom is sentimentality, as with the ordinary church member. Courage without love and wisdom is foolhardiness, as with the ordinary soldier. Wisdom without love and courage is cowardice, as with the ordinary intellectual. Therefore one who has love, courage and wisdom is one in a million who moves the world, as with Jesus, Buddha, and Gandhi.
>
> —Ammon Hennacy, *The Book of Ammon* (p. 136).

NOTES

Note: The *Catholic Worker* is here cited as *CW.*

1. Robert Frost, "Build Soil—A Political Pastoral," *Selected Poems of Robert Frost* (New York: Holt, Rinehart and Winston, 1968), 217.

2. Ammon Hennacy, *The Book of Ammon* (Salt Lake City: n.p., 1965). 1.

3. Ibid., 6; see also Ammon Hennacy, *The One-Man Revolution in America* (Salt Lake City: Ammon Hennacy Publications, 1970), 129.

4. Hennacy, *Book of Ammon*, 19, 7.

5. Ibid., p. 12.

6.   Quoted in Adolpho Perez Esquivel, *Christ in a Poncho* (Maryknoll, N.Y.: Orbis, 1983), 13.

7.   Hennacy, *Book of Ammon*, 10. Upon his arrest, Hennacy and his comrades were used to drum up nationalistic fervor. In the May 31, 1917 *Columbus Citizen*, Ohio governor Cox issued a statement saying that the investigations leading to Hennacy's arrest revealed that "Columbus was the nerve center of a widespread conspiracy treasonable in nature." Hennacy was labeled one of "the chief agents in a nationwide plot against enforcement of the selective service army bill." Dorothy Day–Catholic Worker Collection, Memorial Library Archives, Marquette University, Milwaukee (hereafter cited as "CW Papers"), W-11.1.

8.   Hennacy, *Book of Ammon*, 12.

9.   *Columbus Dispatch*, May 31, 1917, CW Papers, W-11.1.

10.   Hennacy, *Book of Ammon*, 19, 23.

11.   Ibid., 26.

12.   Ibid., from the foreword to the first edition. In this regard, see especially Hennacy's detailed and moving description "A Day in Solitary," 20–23. This account also appeared in a forty-eight page booklet the Worker published in October 1959 entitled "Two Agitators: Peter Maurin—Ammon Hennacy."

13.   Hennacy, *Book of Ammon*, 26–27.

14.   Tolstoy's influence on Hennacy was immense. He read all twenty-two volumes of Tolstoy's collected works, and took extensive notes, with commentary, under four headings: (1) Thou Shall Not Kill, (2) Christian Anarchism, (3) The Simple Life, and (4) Religion. He intended to publish all four topic areas in booklet form, but only the first was published.

15.   For material on Day, see Mel Piehl, *Breaking Bread: The Catholic Worker and the Origins of Catholic Radicalism In America* (Philadelphia: Temple University Press, 1982), 9, 22. For Maurin, see Anthony Novitsky, "The Ideological Development of Peter Maurin's Green Revolution," Ph.D. dissertation, State University of New York at Buffalo, 1976; and Marc H. Ellis, *Peter Maurin: Prophet in the Twentieth Century* (New York: Paulist, 1981).

16.   Staughton Lynd, *The Intellectual Origins of American Radicalism* (New York: Pantheon, 1968), 163, quoted in David DeLeon, *The American as Anarchist: Reflections on Indigenous Radicalism* (Baltimore: Johns Hopkins University Press, 1978), 41; Lillian Symes and Travers Clement, *Rebel America: The Story of Social Revolt in the United States* (Boston: Beacon, 1972, (1934), quoted in DeLeon, *American as Anarchist*, 41; Norman Ware, *The Labor Movement in the United States, 1860–1896: A Study in Democracy* (New York: Appleton, 1929), 304, quoted in DeLeon, *American as Anarchist*, 41; and DeLeon, *American as Anarchist*, 4. DeLeon's book is the best overall introduction to U.S. anarchism; it is well researched and provocatively insightful. His General Reference Bibliography is especially useful, and perhaps the best available. Two other studies deserve mention. One is William O. Reichert, *Partisans of Freedom: A Study in American Anarchism* (Bowling Green: Bowling Green University Popular Press, 1976); like DeLeon, Reichert is sympathetic to anarchism and focuses

his study on the U.S. experience; unlike DeLeon, his interpretive insights are less valuable, and the writing, while lively, is uneven. The second is Robert Nisbet, *The Social Philosophers: Community and Conflict in Western Thought* (New York: Thomas Crowel Co., 1976); Nisbet offers a very objective and scholarly treatment of anarchism.

17. DeLeon, *American as Anarchist*, 3.

18. Hennacy, *Book of Ammon*, 239.

19. Reichert, *Partisans of Freedom*, 504.

20. Hennacy, *Book of Ammon*, 183. This, Hennacy's functional definition of anarchism, originally appeared on page 8 of a booklet published by the bombastic anarchist monthly *MAN*, entitled, "Anarchism, A Solution to World Problems." Hennacy was a frequent contributor to *MAN*. See also Eunice Minette Schuster, *Native American Anarchism: A Study of Left-Wing American Individualism*, Smith College Studies in History, vol. 17, nos. 1–4 (October 1931–July 1932): 8, where she states "Anarchism . . . has both a positive and a negative aspect. Its positive character is revealed in its demand for liberty for the individual, its negative character in its demand that society destroy all authority."

21. Nisbet, *Social Philosophers*, 325. Nisbet also says that "overwhelmingly in anarchist philosophy is . . . reliance on simple, untrammeled cooperation and love among human beings rather than coercion in any of its manifestations" (321).

22. Karl Meyer, interview with author, Milwaukee, June 21, 1986.

23. Hennacy, *Book of Ammon*, 320, 230, 139; Hennacy, *One-Man Revolution*, 337. See also his "Christian Anarchism Defined," *CW*, December 1956: 7.

24. Hennacy, "Apostolate to the Left," *CW*, December 1956: 7; and Hennacy, *Book of Ammon*, p. 139.

25. Dorothy Day, *By Little and By Little: The Selected Writings of Dorothy Day*, ed. Robert Ellsberg (New York: Alfred A. Knopf, 1983), 343.

26. Letter from Ammon Hennacy to Mr. Krieg, September 30, 1951, CW Papers, W-11.1; Letter from Ammon Hennacy to "Jim," May 20, 1951, CW Papers, W-11.1.

27. Hennacy, "Apostolate to the Left," 7.

28. Benjamin R. Tucker, *Liberty*, October 1, 1882: 3., and June 10, 1881: 3, both quoted in DeLeon, *American as Anarchist*, 77.

29. Letter from Joan Thomas to Patrick Coy, July 10, 1981.

30. Ammon Hennacy, "Why I Am a Catholic Anarchist," *Individual Action*, January 25, 1955: 3, CW Papers W-11.1. Hennacy, "A Final Word from the Author," *Book of Ammon*, n.p.

31. Hennacy, "Why I Am a Catholic Anarchist," 3. For an interpretation of Day and Maurin in this regard, see William Miller, *A Harsh and Dreadful Love: Dorothy Day and the Catholic Worker Movement* (New York: Liveright, 1973), especially Miller's insightful introduction on pp. 3–16, entitled "The Radical Idea of the Catholic Worker Movement."

32. Hennacy, "Why I Am a Catholic Anarchist," 3; Hennacy, *Book of Ammon*, 265–78. Letter from Ammon Hennacy to "Jim," May 20, 1951, CW Papers W-11.1; Hennacy, *Book of Ammon*, 279.

33.   William D. Miller, *Dorothy Day: A Biography* (San Francisco: Harper & Row, 1982), 466; Day is quoted on pg. 467.

34.   Hennacy, *One-Man Revolution*, 83–84.

35.   Ammon Hennacy, "The One-Man Revolution," *CW*, February 1970: 12. This is a memorial issue of the *Catholic Worker*, completely dedicated to Hennacy and consisting of articles by those who lived and worked with him. It provides an excellent picture of the man.

36.   In introduction to booklet, "Two Agitators: Peter Maurin—Ammon Hennacy," 1.

37.   Hennacy, *Book of Ammon*, 41.

38.   Ibid., 57.

39.   Ammon Hennacy, "In the Market Place," *CW*, March 1985: 3.

40.   Hennacy, *Book of Ammon*, 34.

41.   Staughton Lynd, *Non-violence in America: A Documentary History*, (Indianapolis: Bobbs-Merrill, 1966), p. xxxi; Nisbet, *Social Philosophers*, 375.

42.   Hennacy, *One-Man Revolution*, 103.

43.   Ammon Hennacy, review of "Speak Truth to Power," *CW*, December 1955: 8.

44.   For Hennacy's views on the peace movement at this time see his "In the Market Place," *CW*, December 1957: 2; "Traveling," *CW*, November 1958: 6; "Quality vs. Quantity," *Catholic C.O.*, Fall 1947: 2; *Book of Ammon*, 205–6. Ammon Hennacy, "Hitting at Nothing," *Catholic C.O.*, Winter 1948: 14–16.

45.   Hennacy, *Book of Ammon*, 205.

46.   T. S. Eliot, *Four Quartets* (San Diego: Harcourt Brace Jovanovich, 1971), 27.

47.   Quoted in Dorothy Day's introduction to "Two Agitators," 2.

48.   Interview with author, Milwaukee, June 21, 1986.

49.   Ibid.

50.   Ibid.

51.   Letter from Joan Thomas to Patrick Coy, July 10, 1981. The historian of anarchism, George Woodcock, also commented on Hennacy's peculiarity: "Sprouting as much fire and brimstone anti-governmentalism as any two ordinary anarchists I know . . . as long as he continues to put up a good fight against the state, I personally don't feel like being self-righteous about the eccentricity of his banner" (review of *Book of Ammon* in *Freedom*, CW Papers W-11.1).

52.   Hennacy, *Book of Ammon*, 339.

53.   Jim Forest, "Men Acted Differently According to Whether They Had Met Him or Not," *Catholic Radical*, February 1970: 2.

54.   Ammon Hennacy, "In the Market Place," *CW*, April 1956: 2 and May 1956: 2.

55.   Ammon Hennacy, "In the Market Place," *CW*, June 1958: 2; *Book of Ammon*, 197, 241.

56.   Ed Turner, "In Memoriam," *CW*, February 1970: 6.

57.   Some of these included: *Freedom, MAN, Ark, Individual Action, Peacemaker, Catholic C.O.*, and Emma Goldman's *Mother Earth*.

58. Hennacy, *Book of Ammon*, 243, 247; Hennacy, *One-Man Revolution*, 196.

59. Miller, *Dorothy Day*, 423–26.

60. CW Papers, W-11.1.

61. Dorothy Day, "Ammon Hennacy—Non Church Christian," *CW*, February 1970: 2. For another, significantly different side of Day's opinion of Hennacy, see Miller, *Dorothy Day*, 466–69.

62. Miller, *A Harsh and Dreadful Love*, 3–6; Hennacy, *Book of Ammon*, 231.

63. July 24, 1939, CW Papers, W-11.1; Dorothy Day interview in *Protest: Pacifism and Politics*, ed. James Finn (New York: Random House, 1967), 382. For an excellent treatment of the uniqueness of Catholic Worker radicalism, see Piehl, *Breaking Bread*, esp. 25–55.

64. Hennacy, *Book of Ammon*, 476.

65. Ibid., 168, 161.

66. This reexamination can be found in Hennacy, *Book of Ammon*, 262–79.

67. Nisbet, *Social Philosophers*, 354.

68. Ammon Hennacy, "Christian Anarchism Defined," *CW*, July–August 1953: 3; see also his earlier "The Viewpoint of a Christian Anarchist," *Freedom*, May 1933, n.p.

69. Even scholars writing today struggle to understand Catholic anarchism. In a work as comprehensive in its treatment of U.S. anarchism as any, David DeLeon draws lines of classification to bring interpretive coherence to an unwieldy topic. But he throws up his arms at the Catholic Worker: "While my interpretive categories are elastic enough to encompass most groups, I confess that the Catholic Workers seem to be in another dimension . . . if it did not exist I would have thought it impossible" (*American as Anarchist*, 151).

70. Hennacy, "Why I am a Catholic Anarchist," 3.

71. Miller, *Harsh and Dreadful Love*, 340; see also Thomas B. Frary, "The Ecclesiology of Dorothy Day" (Ph.D. dissertation, Marquette University, 1971), p. 5, where he states that Day believed the "church must be understood as standing in eschatological tension between this world and the next." Frary's work is the most complete treatment of Worker ecclesiology, particularly valuable for understanding the way Day viewed the relationship of the church to the political and economic world.

72. Stanley Vishnewski, *Wings of the Dawn* (New York: Catholic Worker Press, n.d.), 209.

73. Patricia F. McNeal, *The American Catholic Peace Movement, 1928–1972* (New York: Arno Press, 1978), 184–85, 190; Piehl, *Breaking Bread*, 214–15; Miller, *Harsh and Dreadful Love*, 266, 283–99.

74. Hennacy, *Book of Ammon*, 286–95; see also the July–August 1955 issue of the *Catholic Worker*, which contains long articles by both Day and Hennacy describing the first civil disobedience. This issue of the paper is also indicative of Hennacy's strong influence in the Worker movement and paper during the 1950s. It contains three articles by him, plus his long, lead book review of a biography of William Lloyd Garrison.

75. Hennacy, *Book of Ammon*, 302.

76. Dorothy Day, *Loaves and Fishes* (New York: Curtis Books, 1963), 104.

77. Ammon Hennacy, "Traveling," *CW*, November 1958: 6.

78. Interview with author, Milwaukee, June 21, 1986.

79. N.d., CW Papers, W-11.1.

80. Letter from Joan Thomas to Patrick Coy, July 10, 1981. See for example Hennacy, *One-Man Revolution*, iii.

81. McNeal, *Catholic Peace Movement*, 84. See also Anne Klejment's essay in this anthology.

82. Hennacy, *Book of Ammon*, 63. The figure on the military portion of the tax dollar is from a fact sheet entitled "Your Income Tax Dollars at Work," published in 1986 by the War Resisters League, 339 Lafayette Street, New York, NY 10012. For more information on military tax resistance, contact National War Tax Resistance Coordinating Committee, P.O. Box 85810, Seattle, WA, 98145, (206) 522-4377.

83. Letter from Joan Thomas to Patrick Coy, July 10, 1981.

84. Joan Thomas, *The Years of Grief and Laughter* (Phoenix: Hennacy Press, 1974), 214.

85. For the full text of the statement, see Joan Thomas, "The Price of Courage," the final chapter in Hennacy, *Book of Ammon*, 490. For the text of the leaflet he used during his last picket, see Ernest Bromley, "Ammon Hennacy Dies After Heart Attack," *Peacemaker* 2, (1970); 1–2.

86. Michael Harrington, "Ammon Hennacy: Combined Pacifism, Moral Passion, Irish Humor," *CW* February 1970: 7.

II

Of Politics, Pacifism, and Spirituality

6. THE POLITICS OF FREE OBEDIENCE

Mel Piehl

IN HER GREAT essay on "holy obedience," Dorothy Day underscores a central paradox of Christian faith: that the believer freely chooses to submit individual free will to God and other people. Religious obedience, Day asserts, "is a matter of love, which makes it voluntary, not compelled by fear or force." But she further states that the demands on the self are no less compelling for being freely undertaken: "Even seeing through a glass darkly makes one want to obey, to do all the Beloved wishes, to follow Him to Siberia, to anatarctic [sic] wastes, to prison, to give up one's life for one's brothers since He said, 'Inasmuch as ye have done it unto one of the least of these My brethren, ye have done it unto Me.' "[1]

Day's description of this spiritual inversion of values, by which freedom becomes loving obedience, contains an important clue to the unique outlook of the Catholic Worker movement, an outlook that is often difficult to understand because it appears to violate some ordinary categories of thought. It has not been easy for many people to grasp the inner logic of a movement that is both deeply spiritual and deeply political; that radically challenges prevalent political values but embraces the religious authority of the Roman Catholic church; that endorses activism to effect social change but devotes much of its energy to personal service to the poorest members of society. Historian David DeLeon, for example, is frankly baffled by the Catholic Worker. "While my interpretive categories are elastic enough to encompass most groups," he says in his study of American anarchism, "I confess that the Catholic Worker seems to be in another dimension. . . . If it did not exist I would have thought it impossible."[2] Considering the Worker as an experiment in Christian "free obedience" may help explain some seeming peculiarities of its ideals and practice, and also suggest what has made it distinctive among various contemporary religious movements in modern society.

In particular, it may indicate why the voluntary practice of the works of mercy has been so central to the Worker's way of relating religion and politics, a way that attempts to link the inner and outer elements of human life, yet also tries to prevent politics from corrupting religion by maintaining "the primacy of the spiritual," in the phrase that Peter Maurin borrowed from Emmanuel Mounier. By holding up the perfectionist personal ethics of the Sermon on the Mount as the foundation of its vision of social transformation, the Catholic Worker has seemingly found a way to apply itself with equal vigor to the City of God and to St. Augustine's "third city" of the temporal social order, to uphold the transcendant mysteries of Christian faith while immersing itself in the mundane contemporary concerns of politics, economics, peace, and race relations.

To speak of the Catholic Worker's politics requires immediate clarification. The term *politics* can refer to the pursuit and exercise of power, to the general organization of society's public institutions, or to the fundamental values that underlie our common or public existence. The Catholic Worker has obviously had little interest in politics in the first sense. Peter Maurin stated that "the Catholic Worker Movement fosters Catholic social action and not Catholic political action."[3] And given the general distaste of many Catholic Workers for what Dorothy Day sarcastically called "Holy Mother the State"—an opposition that sometimes extended to participation in ordinary political processes such as voting—one might say that the Worker movement has practiced a kind of antipolitics, so far as the pursuit and exercise of state power are concerned.

But it is equally obvious that the Catholic Worker has been a political movement in the classical Greek sense of being concerned with the commonweal of society, and even more basically, that it has promoted a definite vision of the central values it believes should shape public life and institutions. Using this sense of the term, it is proper to ask what the Worker's political vision has been, and how its politics have been related to its spiritual outlook, including its practice of the works of mercy in the houses of hospitality.

At the level of political philosophy and values broadly conceived, it is possible to provide a fairly coherent account of the basic outlook of the Catholic Worker, and to locate it in relation to parallel movements in history, most of them just as small and politically marginal as the Catholic Worker.

Politically, the Worker represents a variety of styles of nonviolent communitarian pacifist anarchism, which has been a tiny but persistent strand of social theory and action going back centuries.[4] From ancient and medieval times until about 1700, most such political theories rested on explicit religious principles, as in the various forms of anarchism and pacifism that thrived during the Reformation and the English Revolution.[5] But after the eighteenth-century Enlightenment, many pacifist and anarchist movements also developed from secular theories of natural human goodness and perfectibility, which were contrasted to the supposedly corrupting influences of social and political institutions. Although all anarchists professed opposition to the large, coercive state, they differed tremendously in their views on such matters as individualism, community, property, sex, and violence.[6] Nineteenth- and twentieth-century European anarchism was generally of the radical working-class variety, emphasizing material production and ideals of equality and class struggle rooted in working-class or peasant experience. American anarchism was typically middle class and individualistic, and rooted in the ideals of liberty and personal autonomy widely valued in the whole of American culture.[7]

In the early twentieth century both European and American anarchism suffered a series of severe setbacks and gradually declined as serious social movements, while various forms of state-oriented liberalism and socialism gained ascendancy. Nevertheless, anarchist ideas remained alive in some radical circles, such as those Dorothy Day frequented during her youth in New York. Like many young radicals of the time, Day did not make fine distinctions among various social theories, but she did effectively assimilate a good deal of the anarchist sensibility that pervaded the free-form American radical movement in the World War I era.

Indeed, from the standpoint of the history of social thought, Day herself can best be seen as an old-time native American radical who reflected the strong but nondoctrinaire dissent against the corporate capitalist state that existed in the United States around the time of World War I, before the majority of American radicals were seduced into various forms of state-oriented Marxism in the 1920s and 1930s. During those decades secular anarchism retained few adherents in America, except for a few strays like Ammon Hennacy, until it was revived in the 1940s by intellectual radicals like Dwight Macdonald and Paul Goodman.[8] But meanwhile Dorothy Day had blended her free-style American anarchism with Peter Maurin's peasant communalism (which he preferred to call *personalism* rather than anarchism) to produce the basic stock of the Catholic Worker's hearty ideological stew.

But any strictly political assessment of the Catholic Worker's outlook is useless if it does not take into account the dominant feature of the Catholic Worker's social perspective: its attempt to link the spiritual values of the Christian gospel to the public or political sphere. Unlike secular social movements, which look to human action alone to improve the human condition, the Worker has practiced a "religious politics" that sees in the gospel itself the key to social betterment. Moreover, the Worker has strongly emphasized personal spiritual and ethical means, rather than political or institutional change, as the key method of bringing about a comprehensive social renewal. In the words of one editorial statement of Catholic Worker goals:

> [We advocate] a complete rejection of the present social order and a nonviolent revolution to establish an order more in accord with Christian values. This can only be done by direct action, since political means have failed as a method for bringing about this society. Therefore, we advocate a personalism which takes on ourselves responsibility for changing conditions to the extent we are able to do so.[9]

The Catholic Worker is thus primarily a religious and ethical rather than a simply social or political movement. In this respect it resembles all those social movements that have given primacy to inner or spiritual factors in the shaping of social life, rather than those that place economic, political, or institutional factors above inner or spiritual considerations. But such religious social movements, even those based on some kind of broadly Judeo-Christian belief, still differ greatly in character, methods, and goals—especially in the way they connect their religious, social, and political visions. Even apart from the differences in the content of their beliefs, religious social movements have the additional difficulty of establishing a proper and effective relationship between their spiritual commitments and their political ideas and actions. A key to understanding any religious social movement, therefore, lies in its handling of this fundamental relationship.

According to the way they make this connection, religious social movements might be categorized into "ethical-separatist" and "prophetic-transforming" types. Ethical-separatist movements, exemplified perhaps by much of Western cenobitic monasticism and

Tolstoyan pacifism, generally place primary emphasis on inner adherence to religiously based ethical norms by a committed minority within a whole society. Although they may advocate and work for social change, such movements do so primarily by trying to model the values they advocate in their own social relations. They tend to remain somewhat aloof from the harsher realities of worldly politics and power, and to avoid sustained contacts and alliances with other social and political groups that do not share their vision. They can be extremely firm in resisting political structures that contradict their ideals, but they tend over time to become more concerned with preserving their own vision than with transforming society at large, which usually comes to seem deeply corrupt. And depending on how particular religious or social beliefs are interpreted, such movements may eventually turn toward a purely intellectual assertion of their social ideal, toward communal withdrawal from the world, or toward sectarian religious innovation. Some of these tendencies may be seen in elements of medieval monasticism, in some forms of sixteenth-century Anabaptism, and in the Shaker and Oneida movements in nineteenth-century America.[10]

Prophetic-transforming religious social movements, on the other hand, while equally insistent on the religious roots of their social ideas, conceive their essential task as bringing the society at large closer to an ethically improved social condition. Such movements, of which some forms of Calvinism and Zwinglism, American abolitionism, and the Social Gospel may be considered representative, typically engage in direct political or social action designed to transform the dominant social structures and bring them closer to their understanding of religious ideals. In their determination to realize their religious-political goals, such movements sometimes form tactical alliances with other groups who may share some of their social goals but not their full religious or ethical outlook. Especially if they are at all successful, they often begin to confront the typical political dilemmas concerning coercion and the relations between ends and means. In some cases, the essential meaning of religion itself may come to be interpreted in strictly social or political terms—as a functional or idealistic ethic of social relations—rather than as a transcendant or spiritual vision founded on a relation with God that entails urgent ethical and social consequences.[11]

Such a categorization suggests why the Catholic Worker is quite unusual among religious social movements. It resembles the ethical-separatist movements in its uncompromising insistence on maintaining its own ethical vision of social life, and in refusing to countenance the use of politically coercive means to obtain desireable social ends, as in Maurin's distinction between "Catholic social action" and "Catholic political action." But unlike most movements that renounce the political methods of organization and coercion, the Catholic Worker has remained deeply engaged in the messy affairs of society, and has displayed relatively little tendency to withdraw into sheltered enclaves or abstract its ideal vision from the central issues of real political life. Indeed, its tendency toward activist social engagement suggests that it resembles more the prophetic-transforming religious social movements. Yet it differs from most such movements in putting personal spiritual transformation ahead of politics as a means of social reconstruction, in not compromising its ideals in order to achieve concrete social gains, and in making its ethical vision a corollary of religious faith, rather than redefining religion in purely ethical or social terms.

What, then, has undergirded the Catholic Worker's singular way of connecting the Christian gospel with politics? And how has the Worker been able to combine its spiritual outlook with its political witness in a way that testifies to the autonomy and priority of faith, yet remains fully engaged with the most difficult and controversial issues of actual public life in the United States and elsewhere?

The place to begin is surely with the Worker's religious orthodoxy. Almost from its beginnings, the movement's adherence to traditional Catholicism has been misunderstood or dismissed as a curious anomaly. Secular radicals and many Protestants have often considered it a baffling or irrelevant hindrance to the movement's admirable social views. The historian Lawrence Veysey, for example, is one of those who have considered the movement's churchly orthodoxy a strange, marginal quirk: the Catholic Worker, he declares, "insisted on maintaining a tenuous tie with the Catholic Church."[12]

Even many who recognize the centrality of religious tradition to the Worker's own outlook have considered such orthodoxy a weakness or limitation, especially to the extent it involves loyalty to the institutional church or the Roman Catholic hierarchy. People who think of Catholicism as a kind of military hierarchy, in which superiors hand out orders to inferiors on all subjects, tend to see the freewheeling Catholic Worker's commitment to the church as incomprehensible or contradictory. Even some Catholics, depending on their point of view, have seen the Worker's traditionalism as either a calculated ploy for infiltrating radicalism into the church, or a clever camouflage to deflect conservative criticism.[13]

Anyone who looks very closely at the history of the Catholic Worker must eventually recognize the inadequacy of such interpretations. It is abundantly evident that the Worker movement has drawn extensively on the central teachings of orthodox Catholicism

Dorothy Day leads picket line during New York Catholic Workers' August 6, 1955, commemoration of the atomic bombing of Hiroshima. Photo courtesy of Marquette University Archives.

Lanzo del Vasto ("Shantidas"), French pacifist and founder of the Ark community, visits Dorothy Day at St. Joseph's House in New York City in 1973, eight years after the Rome fast that del Vasto directed during Vatican II. Photo courtesy of Eileen Egan.

Dorothy Day, wearing UFW button, supporting the United Farm Workers and Cesar Chavez at California vineyards in 1973. Photo courtesy of Eileen Egan; © Bob Fitch.

Dorothy Day spinning wool with her grandchildren. Photo by Vivian Cherry.

Dorothy Day serving soup to visiting seminarians at St. Francis House in Detroit in 1945. Photo courtesy of Marquette University Archives.

Dorothy Day enjoying a summer afternoon with her daughter, Tamar, probably on Staten Island in 1929, the year of Dorothy's baptism. Photo courtesy of Marquette University Archives.

Daniel Berrigan, S.J., celebrating Mass with friends and his brother Phil-ip at New York's St. Joseph house on February 25, 1972, the day he was released from prison. Photo by Jon Erikson.

The daily breadline in front of the New York Catholic Worker at 115 Mott St. in the mid-1930s begins to move inside.

Many a like-minded couple who first met in a Catholic Worker house have eventually married. Here a wedding party poses in front of New York's Mott St. house in the mid-1930s. Peter Maurin is crouching, and Dorothy Day is second from right. Photo courtesy of Marquette University Archives.

Dorothy Day wearing prison uniform with signatures of fellow farm-worker prisoners grateful for her support in the 1973 UFW strike in California. Photo courtesy of Frank Donovan.

Students from St. Elizabeth's High School for blacks and St. Xavier's College in Chicago gather with Dorothy Day (fourth from right) at Catholic Worker headquarters on Chicago's Southside in 1936. Photo courtesy of Eileen Egan.

St. Louis Catholic Workers on a picnic with Dorothy Day during one of her visits in 1938 or 1939. Left to right: Skip, a CW guest; Reverend Leo Byrne, later bishop of St. Paul; unknown priest; Dave Dunne; Reverend Joe Huels, a CW supporter; Mr. Dooley, a CW guest; Cyril Echele; Margaret Echele; Josephine Brennan; and kneeling, left to right: Dorothy O'Brien; Evelyn Gilsinn; and Dorothy Day. Photo courtesy of Cyril Echele.

Peter Maurin on a visit to Agua Caliente, Mexico. Photo courtesy of Marquette University Archives.

Peter Maurin with an early edition of the Catholic Worker. Photo courtesy of Marquette University Archives.

Ammon Hennacy protesting seizure of Hopi land in Arizona in 1951. Photo courtesy of Marquette University Archives.

Ammon Hennacy at one of his most familiar and favorite activities: hawking the Catholic Worker *on the streets. Photo by Vivian Cherry.*

Ammon Hennacy and Dorothy Day working on the next issue of the Catholic Worker. *Photo courtesy of Marquette University Archives.*

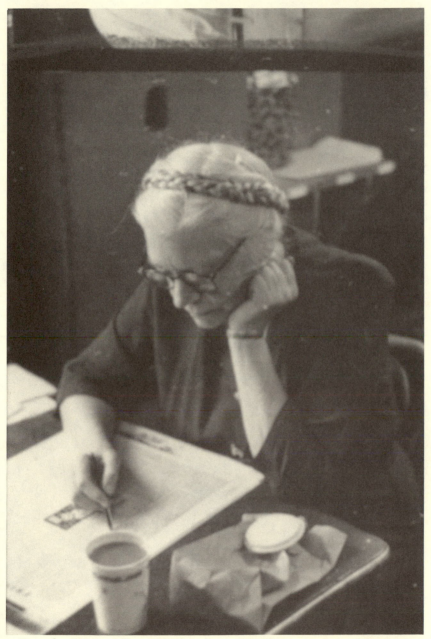

Dorothy Day proofing copy for the paper. Photo courtesy of Marquette University Archives.

Dorothy Day, Ammon Hennacy, and Deane Mowrer refuse to take shelter during air raid drill in 1960 at New York's City Hall Park. Photo courtesy of Marquette University Archives.

Mother Teresa on a visit to Dorothy Day at the New York Worker's Mary-house in 1978. Eileen Egan is at the far left. Photo courtesy of Eileen Egan.

Dorothy Day's portrait in 1942. Photo by Alda Jourdan.

for much of its social vision. What Peter Maurin conveyed to Dorothy Day, and what he personified in his own life, was the idea that the most traditional Catholicism was of supreme social relevance to modern humanity, and that it was only necessary to "blow the dynamite" of that ancient church to set the whole world afire. Maurin thus demonstrated to Day that there was not, as she had feared, a contradiction between her new-found Catholic faith and social radicalism, but rather that social transformation could come precisely by unlocking the power of traditional Catholicism.[14]

To the extent that the Catholic Worker *can* be described as simply an attempt to promote and apply the social teachings of the church, then, its loyalty to the institution ceases to be an anomaly. Over the years, the Worker has indeed drawn a great deal of its social vision directly from the central theological traditions of the church, as represented in scripture, the church fathers, the lives of the saints, papal encyclicals, bishops' statements, and so on. The emphasis on voluntary poverty, for instance (and the distinction between voluntary poverty and destitution), was drawn directly from the church fathers and other traditional orthodox sources. On many issues, such as racial discrimination, the Worker might be said to have turned passive and implicit Christian teachings into active and dynamic practices. In some cases this included pointing up contradictions between the church's official belief and its practice. The church always taught, for example, there should be no distinctions of race: the Workers "merely" applied that teaching in dramatically vivid fashion by treating blacks as equal sisters and brothers in the houses of hospitality, thereby shocking many people (including some Catholics) who were not exactly used to such forceful expressions of the church's ethical principles.

But if a recognition of the Catholic Worker's deep roots in traditional Catholic social teaching can explain much of its way of relating religion and politics, it is not quite the whole story. For as perceptive Catholic Worker critics of the 1930s like Father John LaFarge pointed out, not all the Worker's social stands could be presented as simply expressions of official Catholic teachings.[15] Early on, the movement took some social or political positions that departed from those taken by most church officials or from those commonly understood to be part of Catholic tradition. Peter Maurin, for example, thought that Pope Pius XI's encyclical *Quadragesimo Anno*, while valuable in stating some principles of social and economic life, constituted too great a compromise with secular capitalist economics on the issue of labor. Unlike the papal encyclicals, he advocated complete abolition of the entire wage system, which he considered part of the alienation of human beings from their labor.[16]

While some Workers attempted, through some ingenious interpretations, to reconcile the encyclicals' essentially corporatist social-economic theories with the Worker's communitarian anarchism or "personalism," it eventually became apparent that Day and Maurin were hostile to capitalism in a way that most Catholic churchmen, including the popes, were not—a fact that showed up in the 1940s debates between liberal reform-capitalist Workers and those who insisted that capitalism itself must go, root and branch.[17]

The case is similar, though more complicated, with issues of war and peace. When the Catholic Worker began in the 1930s, recognition of the rights of Christian conscience with respect to war was an almost unknown component of the Catholic church's traditional teaching. Over the course of the last half century, in part because of the witness of groups like the Catholic Worker, pacifism has come to be widely recognized as a legitimate form of personal Christian witness to the gospel. Yet despite the momentous changes in emphasis in the church's official teachings on war, it has never come close to endorsing the Catholic Worker's radical position that war itself is wrong under all conditions. Even the American bishops' pastoral letter "The Challenge of Peace"—the boldest pronouncement on these issues to date—falls considerably short of the kind of absolutist commitment to nonviolence promoted and practiced by the Catholic Worker.[18]

Some Catholic Workers over the years have argued with considerable effect that the church as a whole should and will eventually come to reject all war, just as it came to oppose slavery after tolerating it for centuries.[19] But in the meantime it appears difficult to say that the Catholic Worker's position is simply a product of official Catholic teaching. The Workers did not wait for the church to endorse pacifism before espousing it, and even if it were known for sure that the church would never condemn all wars before Judgment Day, one suspects the Catholic Worker would not alter its witness.

Since it seems, therefore, that in some instances the Catholic Worker has gone beyond official Catholic teaching, it is tempting to adopt what might be called a "crypto-Protestant" interpretation of the Worker's religious social vision. Such a view would suggest that, through their social witness, the Catholic Workers have been recovering the essential meaning of the whole Christian gospel, a meaning hidden or blurred by official theology and churchly compromise with the world. According to such a view, when the Workers have departed from official teachings on matters of capitalism, war, or the state, they have been practicing the full gospel, which other nominal Christians (and the official church) water down or violate altogether.

Such an interpretation would appear to explain some things about the Worker's social views. Like many previous Christian social movements, the Workers have derived inspiration and conviction from a direct appropriation of the apparent social ethic embedded in certain portions of the New Testament, especially the Gospels According to Matthew and Luke and the Acts of the Apostles. Certainly many Catholic Workers over the years have looked directly to the New Testament and the words of Christ for guidance in shaping their social outlook. And there is a strong family resemblance between many of the Worker's social perspectives and other historic attempts to follow a radical Christian social ethic, beginning with early monasticism and continuing through medieval movements like the Brethren of the Common Life, the Reformation-era "left-wing" Protestants, and some segments of the modern "social gospel."[20]

But if this explanation has a good deal to recommend it, it does not fully account for the most unique features of the Catholic Worker's way of relating religion and politics. Clearly, the Worker has attempted to recover and practice the full meaning of the Christian message for social life. But it has not generally claimed that the Christian faith as such makes a definitive set of political or social arrangements normative for Christian life, as many religious social movements do. While upholding the ethical ideals of the Sermon on the Mount—the "evangelical counsels of perfection," in Catholic terms—as real guides to social behavior, the Worker has tolerated considerable diversity on the question of how to apply those ideals to broad social issues and institutions.

Beginning in the 1930s, there have been numerous debates among the Workers themselves on many economic and political questions. Despite their fundamental agreement on the need for a religious reconstruction of the social order, for example, Dorothy Day and Peter Maurin disagreed almost immediately on the question of unions and strikes, and there have also been long-running Catholic Worker discussions on such matters as the necessity of going "back to the land," consumer cooperatives, the desired degree of private or communal living and property arrangements, the proper levels of technology, and so on.[21] And it is striking that, in contrast to many religious social movements that attempt to base themselves on scripture, the Worker did not feel compelled to establish a religious authority or ideology within the movement to definitively resolve such questions. Nor has it attempted to establish an internal rule to enforce its particular social vision of the gospel, as many such movements do.

The use of religious authority to define binding norms of thought or behavior—whether based on spiritual, ethical, social, or economic principles—is a characteristic of many religious social movements. To the extent any subgroup or authority claims to possess particular norms beyond those of the religious community at large, or tries to make such norms religiously *necessary* corollaries of true faith (and not simply voluntary options, as in Roman Catholic orders), it becomes implicitly sectarian. Especially when a movement departs drastically from dominant political or social values, the inclination to claim such religious authority for the group or its leaders can be almost overwhelming. Yet the Catholic Worker has apparently made no such assertions, nor has it ever claimed to possess a purer version of the Christian gospel than the one taught by Roman Catholic Christianity at large.

Neither has the Worker really attempted to introduce any genuine theological innovations of its own, based on dramatic new interpretations of the New Testament or other sources. Rather, it has spent most of its theological energy elaborating such thoroughly traditional doctrines as the eucharist and the mystical body of Christ.[22] While Day and her followers have of course strongly emphasized the social teachings of Christ and the early church, they have not attempted to portray Christianity itself as primarily a social or political movement aimed at improving the human condition through social change. In the Catholic Worker, it seems, the deep commitment to the social meaning of Christian faith has not in any way diluted other central doctrines of Christianity. The writings of Dorothy Day, for example, while especially concerned with the implications of the gospel for peace and social justice, are also profoundly attuned to such traditional Catholic doctrines as creation, personal sin and forgiveness, spiritual growth through suffering, and personal and corporate prayer and worship.[23]

The Catholic Worker's political departures from the church, therefore, rest on no claim of superior religious insight or authority, although many others have come to attribute insight and informal authority to it. But the movement's dissent does appear to rely on the way in which Day, Maurin, and many of their followers have interpreted the religious authority of Catholicism in relation to Christian liberty and action in society. For what seems to most people a restriction of liberty—submission to the spiritual authority of the Catholic church—has been understood by the Catholic Worker as the highest expression of human freedom. In her essay on "holy obedience," Day relates this spiritual obedience to both the post–Vatican II turmoil in the Catholic church and the special American dislike of any externally imposed authority, religious or otherwise:

Men and women have begun to exercise their freedom and are examining their own obedience, as to whether it was a matter of fear or of habit. . . . Someone said that Pope John had opened a window and let in great blasts of fresh air. With all his emphasis on obedience, I do not think he has been understood. What the American people—and I speak only of them, not knowing the condition of the Church in other countries—now feel free to do is to criticize, speak their minds. They have always been accused of a lack of diplomacy, or at least of bad manners, and they have felt it a virtue in themselves, the virtue of honesty, truthfulness. Freedom has meant searching and questioning. What do we really believe? It is as though man were realizing for the first time what is involved in this profession of Christianity. It is as though we were going through the Creed slowly, and saying to ourselves, "Do I believe this, and this, and this?"[24]

Day's contention, here and elsewhere, is that faith and obedience to the church is not a constraint but an expression of spiritual freedom—when, of course, it is freely entered into. And because the Catholic Workers have been embraced by the highest spiritual good of faith in God, Day asserts, they have been able to seek human good in more than earthly terms:

Faith is required when we speak of obedience. Faith in a God who created us, a God who is Father, Son, and Holy Spirit. Faith in a God to whom we owe obedience for the very reason that we have been endowed with freedom to obey or disobey. Love, Beauty, Truth, all the attributes of God which we see reflected about us in creatures, in the very works of man himself . . . fill our hearts with such wonder and gratitude that we cannot help but obey and worship. . . . My faith may be the size of a mustard seed but even so, even aside from its potential, it brings with it the beginning of love, an inkling of love, so intense that human love with all its heights and depths pales in comparison.[25]

Many such intensely spiritual visions of divine love result in a kind of interiorized piety that turns away from the evils and problems of the world and toward grateful religious contemplation of God. Especially when linked to religious institutions like the church, this often produces either an elevated but quietistic personal mysticism, or a commitment to Christian charity that focuses exclusively on individuals and overlooks social and political causes of suffering. The history of Roman Catholicism, and of some branches of Protestant-ism as well, contains abundant evidence of this tendency.[26] It is high-ly significant that the Catholic Worker has not repudiated or attacked either of these outlooks in themselves. Indeed, it has strongly af-firmed the value of both the purely contemplative vocation (as prac-ticed, for example, by many Catholic religious) and the individual practice of the works of mercy. But the Catholic Worker's own most distinctive emphasis has been the spilling over of the love of God into social action on behalf of humanity.[27]

But what kind of social action? What kind of politics? And above all, how has the Catholic Worker been able to keep social and politi-cal action subordinate to faith and Christian love, rather than letting faith become subordinate to the spirit and logic of politics?

The first part of the answer the Catholic Worker has evidently given is that the forms of Christian social and political action must be freely shaped by Christian believers themselves, and not simply dictated by the institutional church or the hierarchy. Obedience to the church as a spiritual institution, the Workers have claimed, does not imply obedience to all its political views. Individuals or groups of Christians are therefore free to explore the social implications of their faith on their own, seeking neither the official sanction nor even the approval of the whole church as such. Therefore, although some might interpret the Worker's religious obedience as an inher-ent limitation on its political or social views, Day and other Workers have insisted that as Christian laypeople they have been completely free to shape their politics according to their own Christian con-sciences:

> [Bishop O'Hara of Kansas City] meant that it was up to the laity to be the vanguard, to live in the midst of the battle, to live in the world which God so loved that he sent his only begotten Son for us to show us how to live and die, to meet the last great enemy, Death. We were to explore the paths of what was possible, to find concordances with our oppo-nents, to seek for the common good, to try to work with all men of goodwill, and to trust all men, too, and to believe in that goodwill, and to forgive our own failures and those of others seventy times seventy times. *We* could venture where priest and prelate could not or ought not, in political and economic fields. We could make mistakes without too great harm; we could retrace our steps, start over again in this attempt to build a new society within the shell of the old, as Peter and the old radicals used to say.[28]

The essential premise of the Catholic Worker's approach, therefore, is that the church's demand for spiritual and moral obedience— which the Workers have been willing to give—does not
require conformity on essentially political or economic questions.
And the ability to assert such a position is closely linked with the
Catholic Worker's status as a completely independent lay venture
within the church. This "structural" quality of the Worker movement has not received as much as attention as its more substantive
commitments to voluntary poverty, pacifism, and the like. Yet it is
especially by forging a strong commitment between status as lay
members of society and free commitment to the Christian "evangelical counsels of perfection" that the Worker has been able to spir-
itualize its politics without politicizing its spirituality.

From the beginning of the movement, Day and Maurin emphasized that they were acting on their own, as lay Christians, with no
official sanction or direction from the church. In contrast to most
Catholic social movements of this century and before, the Catholic
Worker was not instigated by clergy or by officially authorized
laypeople. As Peter Maurin said in an Easy Essay:

> The Catholic Worker
> is a free-lance movement,
> not a partisan movement.
> Some of the Bishops
> agree with our policies
> and some don't.[29]

The most the Workers have claimed is that their own views are
compatible with the teachings of the church, and that they themselves have been inspired to do their work by the gospel. But there has
been no attempt to claim—as there usually was in the various Catholic Action groups that flourished in Europe and Canada in the early
twentieth century, or as there has often been in the official social-
action agencies of the Protestant churches—that all the Worker's
stands were automatic or necessary extensions of true Christianity.
Maurin and Day acknowledged, for example, that there were good
Catholics who opposed their political views:

> We are criticized
> by many Catholics
> for some of our policies
> and especially
> our Spanish policy.

The Communist Party
has a party line. . . .
There is no party line
in the Catholic Church.[30]

This point also emerged, interestingly, in various conflicts over the name "Catholic Worker." Some Catholics, especially in the 1940s and 1950s, were shocked to find the name "Catholic" attached to a group (and paper) that opposed military service, defied civil defense drills, and cooperated with secular radicals. When they demanded that the New York chancery withdraw the name, Day successfully argued with Monsignor Edward Gaffney that the name "Catholic" was not a sign of official approval for everything the Worker did, but merely indicated the religious commitment of those undertaking the action. In this respect, she maintained, the Catholic Workers were no different from the Catholic Library Association, the Catholic War Veterans, or similar groups. As Day said in 1955, "We as a group . . . are not classed as a *religious* group, not even as a *Catholic* group, and so do not have the protection of that classification. We are individual Catholics, not Catholic Action."[31]

This basic distinction, which eludes some people only slightly acquainted with the Catholic Worker, has major consequences for the movement's way of connecting religion and politics. It has enabled the Workers to take religiously informed political stands without basing those stands on institutional religious authority as such. For as the religious sociologist Ernst Troeltsch points out, a social group that uses religious authority directly to shape its political existence introduces a sacred principle that tends either toward ecclesiastical control of politics or toward sectarianism.[32]

By maintaining a distinction between the sphere of religious authority, where the church acts through spiritual means on the believer's conscience, and the sphere of society, where no such authority rules, a religious movement can use spiritual principles as the basis of its politics without importing religious authority directly into the secular sphere, where it would run the danger of causing religious schism or being treated as simply another ordinary political force, thereby potentially weakening its spiritual character. By voluntarily acting and speaking as laypeople freely applying the gospel to the secular world of politics, economics, and international relations, the Catholic Worker has been able to maintain, more successfully than most religious social movements, a distinction between the core values of religion and the application of those values to society, without completely separating the two.

This distinction seems consistent with the principle of Catholic theology asserted by Vatican II concerning the proper relation between the church and the world. According to this teaching, the apostolic church is a special kind of community formed to witness God's love for the world. This community—the "people of God"—is not primarily concerned to order the world of public affairs, but to serve as the visible sign of God's transcendent presence among humanity. The Vatican Council declared the church always speaks to the historical condition of humanity in the world. But it does not itself seek to organize the political or economic orders along particular lines, beyond stating the essential religious principles that Christianity understands to affect all spheres of life. Bringing the world of politics and economics into closer conformity with Christian values is therefore primarily the task of the laity, who represent the church in the world:

> The laity must take on the renewal of the temporal order as their own special obligation. Led by the light of gospel and the mind of the Church, and motivated by Christian love, let them act directly and definitively in the temporal sphere. As citizens they must cooperate with other citizens, using their own particular skills and acting on their own responsibility. Everywhere and in all things they must seek the justice characteristic of God's kingdom. The temporal order must be renewed in such a way that, without the slightest detriment to its own proper laws, it can be brought into conformity with the highest principles of Christian life and adapted fully with the special circumstances of the world and the shifting circumstances of time, place, and person.[33]

This Catholic theological perspective, in which the sacred and the mundane are both distinguished yet intimately related through the lives of faithful Christian laity, provides a theoretical way, at least, for religion to shape politics without directly entering into the political arena as an institutional force. And as practiced by the Catholic Worker, it has enabled this thoroughly Christian social movement to remain loyal to the church without being bound by the political views of the church or its clerical leaders, or restricting its actions and alliances in the public world. This outlook has also distinguished the Catholic Worker from many modern "progressive" Catholic social movements, which have either tried to enlist the church's institutional authority directly on behalf of certain social policies, or directly attacked the church's perceived failures to carry out correct social principles. In either case, this approach runs the risk of heightening political conflict within the church, since political disagreements easily become entwined with issues of proper spiritual authority and action.

Of course many "progressive" religious movements have viewed such confrontations with the church as necessary, because they believe that only a transformed church can speak convincingly to the world on behalf of correct social principles. The weakness of a movement like the Catholic Worker, from such a point of view, is that it has not been aggressive enough in attacking the moral or social failings of the church itself. But such a criticism may overlook the way a movement like the Catholic Worker can change the church as well as society, though perhaps not as rapidly or directly as many would like. Dorothy Day was acutely aware of the failings of the church and its leaders, but she saw them in a different light:

> I loved the Church for Christ made visible. Not for itself, because it was so often a scandal to me. Romano Guardini said that the Church is the cross on which Christ was crucified. One could not separate Christ from his Cross, and one must live in a state of permanent dissatisfaction with the Church.[34]

In effect, the Catholic Worker attempted to change the church not by using the methods of politics but by holding up from within the Christian community a working model of what that community professes itself to be. By freely practicing values learned within the church itself, without committing the church to particular positions that might be mistaken, the Catholic Worker has tried to move the Christian community by inspiration and example rather than by direct confrontation.

Maurin and Day were both keenly aware of the distinction between their function as lay leaders of a social movement and the role of bishops as spiritual overseers of the whole church, and took care to maintain the essentially lay character of the Catholic Worker. While Day sought clerical backing and welcomed priests as confessors, advisors, retreat leaders, and writers for the *Catholic Worker*, she also made sure that their role was supportive, not directive. She was upset, for example, if too many articles by clergymen got into the *Catholic Worker*, which was supposed to be a "layperson's paper."[35] Where priests did assume roles, their primary task was to build up the laity to carry out "the work," not to take it over themselves.

One consequence of this approach is now a matter of considerable interest: the leadership of women in the Catholic Worker movement. Starting with Dorothy Day herself, women have occupied a considerably greater number of leadership roles within the Catholic Worker than in most mixed-sex Catholic groups, or in most secular groups for that matter. Dorothy Day's tremendous significance as a model of feminine spiritual and political leadership is only beginning to be explored.[36] The point here is that she plainly understood her role to be that of a layperson, and it was in that capacity that "familial" and "maternal" qualities were made integral to the Catholic Worker movement and its effort to radically transform all of society.

Although the Catholic Worker's lay status has made it possible for the movement both to distinguish and unite religion and politics, this structural factor alone does not explain its singular influence. For what has finally made the Catholic Worker's politics unique has been its attempt to bring the highest spiritual and ethical values of Christianity directly into public life. Unlike many Christian lay movements, which tend to see secular life as requiring a social ethic more compromised to worldly standards, the Catholic Worker has proclaimed the supreme social relevance of the morally heroic "evangelical counsels of perfection." If the Workers have not claimed that all Christians are required to adopt their own brand of pacifism, voluntary poverty, and communitarian anarchism as the only proper foundation of public life, they have demonstrated that Christianity can inspire politics of this sort, where the central spiritual and moral values derived from the faith are brought directly to bear on modern American society's fundamental values and institutions. It is this spiritual intention—to bring the undiluted *caritas Christi* directly into the public and economic arenas—that has given the Catholic Worker its distinctive ideology, its internal elan, and whatever small impact it has had on American politics.

Obviously, this is not a politics of organization or elections or laws, but a politics of religious commitment and moral integrity. It attempts to transform society not from without—by accumulating enough power to attack the existing power structures—but from within, by altering the fundamental assumptions and values that shape all of public existence. The basic appeal of this kind of social thought and action lies not primarily in the viability of its particular economic and political recommendations, provocative as those may be, but in its essentially spiritual vision of the human condition, a vision that it insists must be recognized in whatever economic or political arrangements are adopted. In this sense, then, the Catholic Worker's more particular political and economic prescriptions—anarchism, economic decentralism, and so on—seem less important than its gospel-based appeals to love, sacrifice, and service to the poor. The former are particular social judgments, derived from the

Worker's own convictions and experience of the best way to organize society, economy, and polity; but the latter are Christian ethical values central to the meaning and purpose of spiritually based human life.

Dorothy Day's way of defining her social beliefs suggests just such a set of priorities. Politically and economically, the Catholic Worker's prescriptions are simply one freely chosen option:

> I speak . . . to show the tremendous freedom there is in the Church, a freedom most cradle Catholics do not seem to know they possess. They do know that a man is free to be a Democrat or a Republican, but they do not know that he is also free to be a philosophical anarchist by conviction. They do believe in free enterprise, but they do not know that cooperative and communal ownership can live side by side with private ownership of property.[37]

Yet it turns out that the political theory of anarchism, for Day, is simply a means to an end, a way to realize in society the Christian ideal of love.

> Philosophical anarchism, decentralism, requires that we follow the Gospel precept to be obedient to every living thing: "Be subject therefore to every human creature for God's sake." It means washing the feet of others, as Jesus did at the Last Supper. "You call me Master and Lord," He said, "and rightly so, for that is what I am. Then if I, your Lord, have washed your feet, you also ought to wash one another's feet. I have set you an example; you are to do as I have done for you." To serve others, not to seek power over them. Not to dominate, not to judge others.[38]

Once again, the freedom—this time in relation to the whole social sphere—is defined by Day as an opportunity for obedient service, not to the church but to "every living creature." This is surely a political platform different from that of even the most radical conventional political movements. And the program for its practical implementation has been the personal practice of the works of mercy in the houses of hospitality. While the Workers have employed many means of nonviolent and noncoercive social agitation on behalf of their political views—a paper, speeches, demonstrations, labor agitation, and the like—the practice of personal service to the poor has undergirded all these activities.

Few other religious social movements, especially those attempting to effect basic social change, have made the practice of the works of mercy such a focus of activity and reflection. Most groups empha-

sizing charitable service eschew politics, especially of the unconventional variety, while those that seek fundamental social change
have typically seen such an emphasis as at best a distraction and at
worst a patching up of an indefensible social order. But for the Catholic Worker this dual emphasis has appeared to be central to its spiritually informed vision of public life.

The works of mercy have in effect erected a spiritual umbrella
over all the Catholic Worker's social and political activities, guaran-
teeing that religion would remain the basis of everything else. Day
frequently emphasized the importance of the works of mercy as a
kind of spiritual discipline, strengthening those who practice them
for more effective Christian social action in all areas of life: "The
Works of Mercy are a wonderful stimulus to our growth in faith as
well as love. Our faith is taxed to the utmost and so grows through
the strain put upon it. It is pruned again and again, and springs up
bearing much fruit."[39]

From this perspective, the unambiguously religious task of serving
the poor, directly inspired by the gospel itself, has guaranteed that
Christian faith and values would remain central to the Catholic
Worker outlook, and that it would not slip into the pursuit of mere
ordinary politics, however righteous or idealistic. The emphasis on
personal service to those at the bottom of society has also prevented
the Catholic Workers from abstracting, romanticizing, or depersonalizing social problems, because the personal "tax" that strengthens the Workers' Christian faith also tests their social theories in the
most intense and personal way. Day asserts:

> For anyone starting to live literally the words of the Fathers
> of the Church—"The bread you retain belongs to the hun-
> gry, the dress you lock up is the property of the naked";
> "What is superfluous for one's need is to be regarded as plun-
> der if one retains it for one's self"—there is always a trial
> ahead. "Our faith, more precious than gold, must be tried as
> though by fire. . . . This is expecting heroic charity, of
> course. But these things happen . . . for our testing.[40]

By freely choosing to put a difficult spiritual discipline at the heart
of their public activity, then, the Workers have been able to maintain
the transcendental quality of their public vision. But from a strictly
political standpoint, the practice of the works of mercy has also
served as a kind of test or model of what the Workers have meant by
their grand talk of building a society radically different from the present one. Because they have been so constantly forced to deal with
the injured members of the present social system, the Workers have
frequently been distracted from seemingly more effective activist

methods of transforming society. Over the years, schemes for farming communes or labor organizations or peace demonstrations have often been sidetracked by the demanding daily labor of serving the poor.

But that appears to be precisely the point. For Day and the Catholic Workers, putting religious service to others at the center of society is the very goal they seek, and it has therefore been the primary means as well. The forms of politics and society and economics thus become secondary means to the end—the care and nurture of "the least of these." A society where performing the works of mercy was central to the definition of all other economic or political tasks, as it has been in the Worker houses of hospitality, would be a very different sort of society. This is perhaps why Day always insisted that the works of mercy are neither paternalistic charity nor formal religious duty, but an opportunity for expressing the freely given love at the heart of Christian faith:

> For a total Christian, the goad of duty is not needed—always prodding one to perform this or that good deed. It is not a duty to help Christ, but a privilege. Is it likely that Martha and Mary sat back and considered that they had done all that was expected of them? Is it likely that Peter's mother-in-law grudgingly served the chicken she had meant to keep till Sunday because she thought it was her "duty"? She did it gladly; she would have served ten chickens if she had had them.[41]

It is through this approach of bringing spiritual values to the very center of public life that the Catholic Worker has made its distinctive imprint. No religious social movement, no matter how highly motivated, that talks about moral transformation but relies primarily on political methods could so directly appeal to the religious spirit. By "being obedient to every creature"—by losing power rather than gaining it—the Catholic Worker has kept in the forefront of its social vision a thoroughly religious sense of what all human life should be about.

But it must be stressed that this is not just a narrowly "religious" or moralistic approach to public life by "idealists" who fail to understand or confront the harsh realities of political life or human evil. The Catholic Worker is a spiritual movement, but it is also a serious political movement because it is deeply engaged in trying to transform the fundamental values of public life, the most basic political task of all. The fact that the Workers have not spoken in conventional political terms—and have usually steered clear of ordinary electoral or organizational politics—should not obscure the intensely political nature of their enterprise. Dorothy Day and Peter Maurin may have come to be considered saints by some, but theirs is a saintliness that challenges some of the most powerful economic institutions and political values of modern American society, which is why it is inherently, and legitimately, controversial. The Catholic Worker may be the Franciscanism of the twentieth century, but the depth of its "revolutionary" challenge to the whole social order means that it might take centuries for it to have the kind of pervasive influence that St. Francis's followers so rapidly achieved in the thirteenth century.

Whether the Catholic Worker's social vision could ever "succeed" in any ordinary sense is a difficult question. The ideal of a "Christian society" that pervaded the old civilization of medieval Europe contained elements of this vision, but the Christian church was so entangled with coercive and only nominally Christian political and economic structures that the notion of a religiously based society was deeply discredited in Western civilization. The idea that the functioning economic and political institutions of society could really be oriented around strong, freely chosen religious values is almost incomprehensible to most people in the modern world, since they tend to associate fervent public religious commitments with fanaticism and coercion. Given such attitudes, as well as the magnitude of the social crises of our time, it requires a considerable act of imagination to conceive of a social order in which spiritual values would occupy the same central place that commercial and individualistic ones do in our own.

Perhaps there is finally some paradox in any attempt to make values like those practiced by the Catholic Worker dominant in the mainstream of public life. Almost by definition the most perfect expressions of Christian values flourish not in the visible places of society but in the invisible, not among the conventionally powerful but among the powerless. The Catholic Worker itself has been remarkably indifferent to how "successful" it has been in conventional terms, preferring to focus on the question of how faithful it has been to the gospel and its ethical implications: "We believe that success, as the world determines it, is not the criterion by which a movement should be judged. We must be prepared and ready to face seeming failure."[42]

Perhaps in even the best of worlds there would be a difference between the ordinary politics of "natural virtue" and the heroic, spiritual social vision of a movement like the Catholic Worker. It is surely no accident that such a vision of "total Christianity" arose not among decent, faithful, ordinary Christians, nor among academic theologians or scholars, but among persons whose "extreme" religious commitment has inspired them to promote seemingly impractical social ideas as well as practice "the evangelical counsels of perfection." The mundane concern for the ordinary well-being of the polity that appears in the middle range of Christian thought, such as in St. Thomas and many of the papal encyclicals, may appear to be more "practical" for society at large, but it seems pale and uninspiring to those who feel the presence of Christ in the world as a burning spiritual and moral passion.

It is also surely no accident that Christianity itself arose at some distance from the centers of power and conventional thought, and that its greatest saints have often had an "irrational" or "extreme" quality that set them apart from the logic of ordinary society and ordinary politics. Although they have turned out to be far more relevant to modern American public concerns than anyone would have thought in 1933, Peter Maurin's and Dorothy Day's anarchist social ideals may never be fully implemented in any real society. But a wider acceptance of the Catholic Worker's spiritual vision would itself constitute a social transformation of the most profound kind.

NOTES

Note: The *Catholic Worker* is here cited as *CW*.

1. Dorothy Day, "Obedience: Reflections during Advent," *Ave Maria* 13 (December 17, 1966): 20–23.
2. David DeLeon, *The American as Anarchist: Reflections on Indigenous Radicalism* (Baltimore: Johns Hopkins University Press, 1978), 151.
3. Peter Maurin, *Catholic Radicalism* (New York: Catholic Worker Books, 1949), 38.
4. Mary C. Segers, "Equality and Christian Anarchism: The Political and Social Ideas of the Catholic Worker Movement," *Review of Politics* 40 (April 1978): 196–230.
5. Frank and Fritzie Manuel, *Utopian Thought in the Western World* (Cambridge, Mass.: Belknap-Harvard, 1979), 181–202, 332–66.
6. George Woodcock, *Anarchism* (Cleveland: Meridian Books, 1962); R. B. Fowler, "The Anarchist Tradition of Political Thought," *Western Political Quarterly* 25 (December 1972): 738–52.
7. DeLeon, *American as Anarchist*, 95–101, 150–51.
8. On anarchism and radicalism in early twentieth-century America, see John Diggins, *The American Left in the Twentieth Century* (New York: Harcourt Brace Jovanovich, 1973), and Daniel Aaron, *Writers on the Left* (New York: Farrar, Straus, and Giroux, 1974). On the revival of anarchism, see Dwight Macdonald, *Politics Past* (New York: Viking, 1957), and Paul Goodman, *Utopian Essays and Practical Proposals* (New York: Vintage, 1962). For Maurin's "personalist" anarchism, see Arthur Sheehan, *Peter Maurin: Gay Believer* (New York: Hanover, 1959), and Marc Ellis, *Peter Maurin: Prophet in the Twentieth Century* (New York: Paulist, 1981).

9.   "Catholic Worker Positions," *CW* 43 (May 1977): 6.

10.   C. H. Lawrence, *Medieval Monasticism: Forms of Religious Life in Western Europe in the Middle Ages* (London: Longman, 1984); Peter Brock, *Pacifism in Europe to 1914* (Princeton, N.J.: Princeton University Press, 1972), 453–68; Cornelius J. Dyck, "Anabaptism and the Social Order," in *The Impact of the Church Upon Its Culture,* ed. Jerald C. Brauer (Chicago: University of Chicago Press, 1968), 207–29; Lawrence Foster, *Religion and Sexuality: Three Communal Experiments of the Nineteenth Century* (New York: Oxford University Press, 1981).

11.   G. L. Hunt, *Calvinism and the Political Drder* (Philadelphia: Westminster Press, 1965); Robert C. Walton, *Zwingli's Theocracy* (Toronto: University of Toronto Press, 1967); Ronald C. White, *The Social Gospel: Religion and Reform in Changing America* (Philadelphia: Temple University Press, 1976); Lewis Perry, *Radical Abolitionism: Anarchy and the Government of God in Antislavery Thought* (Ithaca, N.Y.: Cornell University Press, 1973).

12.   Lawrence Veysey, *The Communal Experience: Anarchist and Mystical Communities in Twentieth Century America* (Chicago: University of Chicago Press, 1978), 38.

13.   As one example of many opinions of this sort, see Daniel Lyons, S.J., "Dorothy Day and the Catholic Worker—It Could Have Been So Different," *Our Sunday Visitor,* January 16, 1966: 10.

14.   Maurin, *Catholic Radicalism,* 3; William D. Miller, *Dorothy Day: A Biography* (San Francisco: Harper & Row, 1982), 247–48; Ellis, *Peter Maurin,* 41–44.

15.   John LaFarge, "Some Reflections on the Catholic Worker," *America* 57 (June 26, 1937): 275.

16.   Peter Maurin, "A Question and an Answer on Labor Guilds," *CW* 1 (February 1934): 8. Anthony Novitsky, "Peter Maurin's Green Revolution: The Radical Implications of Reactionary Social Catholicism," *Review of Politics* 37 (January 1975): 83–103.

17.   John C. Cort, "The Catholic Worker and the Workers," *Commonweal* 55 (1952): 635–37; Frank Sicius, "The Chicago Catholic Worker Movement, 1936 to the Present," Ph.D. dissertation, Loyola University, 1979.

18.   Philip Murnion, ed., *Catholics and Nuclear War: A Commentary on "The Challenge of Peace," The U.S. Catholic Bishops' Pastoral Letter on War and Peace* (New York: Crossroad, 1983), 272–85.

19.   Robert Ludlow, "Pacifism and Natural Morality," *CW* 17 (March 1951): 1. Ludlow, "A Reply to Three Critics," *CW* 18 (July–August 1951): 1.

20.   Lawrence, *Medieval Monasticism;* T. P. Van Zijl, *Gerard Groote, Ascetic and Reformer* (Washington, D.C.: Catholic University of America, 1963); George H. Williams, *The Radical Reformation* (Philadelphia: Westminster Press, 1962); Lowell P. Zuck, *Christianity and Revolution: Radical Christian Testimonies, 1520–1650* (Philadelphia: Temple University Press, 1975); Jo Ann Ooiman Robinson, *Abraham Went Out: A Biography of A. J. Muste* (Philadelphia: Temple University Press, 1981), 19–31.

21.   Miller, *Dorothy Day,* 304–7.

22. See, for example, "Liturgy and Sociology," *CW* 3 (December 1935): 4.

23. Dorothy Day, "Adventures in Prayer," *The Third Hour* 9 (1970): 39–45.

24. Day, "Obedience," 21–22.

25. Ibid., 22.

26. Ernst Troeltsch, *The Social Teachings of the Christian Churches*, vol. 1 (London: George Allen and Unwin, 1931), 237–45; Martin Marty, *Protestantism* (New York: Holt, Rinehart, and Winston, 1972), 129–41.

27. Dorothy Day, "Holy Fools," in *By Little and By Little*, ed. Robert Ellsberg (New York: Knopf, 1983), 351–53.

28. Day, "Obedience," 21.

29. Maurin, *Catholic Radicalism*, 126.

30. Ibid.

31. Dorothy Day, "Our Fall Appeal," *CW* 22 (November 1955): 2. James Forest, *Love Is the Measure: A Biography of Dorothy Day* (New York: Paulist Press, 1986), 130–33.

32. Troeltsch, *Social Teachings*, 378–81.

33. Walter M. Abbott, ed., *The Documents of Vatican II* (New York: New Century, 1966), 498.

34. Dorothy Day, *The Long Loneliness* (San Francisco: Harper & Row, 1981), 149–50.

35. Nancy Roberts, *Dorothy Day and the Catholic Worker* (Albany: State University of New York Press, 1984), 100–1.

36. Debra Campbell, "The Catholic Earth Mother: Dorothy Day and Woman's Power in the Church," *Cross Currents* 34 (Fall 1984): 270–82; Sally Cunneen, "Dorothy Day: The Storyteller as Human Model," *Cross Currents* 34 (Fall 1984): 291–93.

37. Day, "Obedience," 21.

38. Ibid., 22–23.

39. Dorothy Day, "The Scandal of the Works of Mercy," *Commonweal* 51 (1949): 99–102.

40. Ibid.

41. Dorothy Day, "Notes by the Way," *CW* 12 (December 1945): 7.

42. "Catholic Worker Positions," 6.

7. THE PROPHETIC SPIRITUALITY OF THE CATHOLIC WORKER

Daniel DiDomizio

PAUL'S ADMISSION TO the Corinthians that they had become a spectacle unto the world captures the essential characteristic of the prophetic experience. Every prophet by reason of loyalty to the Word of God stands exposed to the glare of public critique. To fully grasp a prophetic message we need to attend to both poles: the prophet's words and deeds, and the reigning values of the prophet's world. For what the prophet has to say will be directed to the deepest assumptions of the culture in question. The prophetic challenge will generally call into question the reigning world view. "The task of prophetic ministry," according to Walter Brueggemann, "is to nurture and evoke a consciousness and perception alternative to the consciousness and perception of the dominant culture around us." The Catholic Worker movement has become a true spectacle unto the world, as Robert Coles's book calls the movement, because the Worker has consistently raised questions about the very basic values that make our world go around.[1] Our society's orientation toward self-interest and competition, for example, comes into the spotlight for us when we are faced with the display of disinterested love on the part of those Catholic Workers who offer hospitality to the poor day after day.

When the prophetic experience in question, moreover, is termed a spirituality, the event becomes more difficult to articulate. A spirituality can never be confined to individual texts and sayings, but is encompassed only in the unfolding story of people's lives as they go about the ordinary task of growing and loving, experiencing joy and sorrow, success and failure. A spirituality can be revealed only through patterned actions, attitudes, and values over a period of time. A spirituality can only be lived, rarely if ever described in the reasoned syllables of theological discourse. As a total style of life, a spirituality includes external deeds as well as inner awareness and motives. The effort of expressing a spirituality, helpful as the task may be, will always result in an approximation, an attempt to grapple with the mystery of God's ineffable presence to human lives in the flow of history.

The person who would venture to articulate a prophetic spirituality faces additional hurdles. Who can most accurately describe a prophetic spirituality—those immersed in the prophetic or alternative community, or those on the outside of this body, who shape their lives according to the traditional wisdom? Who best presents the truth about a prophetic experience—the protectors of the status quo, or the prophet whose lips and deeds proclaim a different vision of life? If possible, the observer ought to hear both sides. The prophetic vision, which slices through the layers of accepted wisdom, can portray its truth only to the extent that this vision effectively challenges the mind set of the representatives of the established consciousness; each party shapes the message in some fashion. To whom does the observer choose to listen? The option selected reveals as much about the observer as it does about the spirituality under consideration.

The Prophetic Spirituality of the Catholic Worker

In presenting the Catholic Worker movement as embodying a prophetic spirituality, therefore, a writer faces a twofold challenge. First, a spirituality exists in the realm of concrete lives and deeds. How have the lives of Catholic Workers through more than fifty years measured up to the radical gospel lifestyle envisioned and expressed by Dorothy Day and Peter Maurin beginning in the early 1930s? Do written sources, articles in the *Catholic Worker* and elsewhere, for example, adequately describe a spirituality that can be termed Catholic Worker? Though the focus of this chapter is the spirituality shaped by Dorothy Day, Peter Maurin, and Workers of the early period, the contention is that the underlying attitudes of this early spirituality provide a firm foundation for grasping a broader Catholic Worker spirituality.

Second, if this spirituality is aptly called prophetic, then do we find the prophetic flavor expressed almost exclusively in the radical vision of Dorothy Day, Peter Maurin, and other Catholic Workers? Or must we not pay heed also to the commentary of others who have viewed the Catholic Worker movement from the outside, whether they have judged it as admirers or as critics? From the very beginning until the present, the *Catholic Worker* has thrust the movement's vision into constant dialogue with the world. Indeed, like any authentic Christian spirituality, the core of the Catholic Worker message is essentially the basic gospel proclamation that Jesus is Lord. Because this proclamation must vary as times and issues change, the Catholic Worker movement has found numerous ways to announce the same basic theme. The work and actions of Dorothy Day and other Workers, for instance, have voiced prophetic cries whether they faced the Depression of the 1930s, World War II, or the air raid drills of the 1950s. Many voices, therefore, are needed to sound the depth of a prophetic witness.

This chapter will bring to bear on the topic of the prophetic spirituality of the Catholic Worker not only the writings and deeds of Dorothy Day, Peter Maurin, and other well-known Catholic Workers, but also the reactions of those on the fringe or outside the movement. The body of literature from this latter source has become quite extensive in scope, and its analysis of the Worker has grown more mature in insight. We are beginning to see evidence that the Catholic Worker movement has had a hand in shaping the American Catholic church in general and the evolution of contemporary Catholic spirituality in particular. The focus of this chapter, therefore, is to examine how Catholic Worker spirituality has exercised a prophetic role on U.S. Catholic culture and spirituality.

Among the factors influencing U.S. Catholic culture and spirituality, two seem dominant: the Catholicism of its early immigrant forebears and its very existence within the matrix of U.S. society. It is inevitable, therefore, that the prophetic spirituality of the Catholic Worker has had to confront American Catholic culture precisely in its adaptation to the American way of life.[2] While the colonial American sense of mission and the early settlers' spirit of group self-reliance seemed in some way congenial to the Catholic Worker vision, other later American values were seen as less, if at all acceptable. Specifically, the spirit of competition spawned by the industrial revolution and the rise of the United States to political and military domination had, in the eyes of many Catholic Workers, created a seedbed of national values that had taken root even in the lives of immigrant Catholics.

Which vision of life most shaped the social psychology of American Catholics—the social encyclicals of Popes Leo XIII and Pius XI, or the lure of success represented by the so-called self-made industrialists and entrepreneurs? The Catholic Worker movement appeared clearly in opposition to the latter mind set. Yet some Workers often seemed ambivalent even about the reform-minded approach of the church's social teaching. At issue for Catholic Workers was a single-minded focus on a radical gospel way of life, a focus that did not necessarily address the everyday issues of the bulk of U.S. Catholics. Perhaps Catholic Worker spirituality has at times not only espoused a prophetic critique, but also betrayed an undertone of self-righteousness to which alienated prophets remain liable.

Certainly the spirituality of the Catholic Worker after fifty years has attained an identifiable character; this unified thrust, however, is composed of a number of elements, no one of which can be isolated from the others. Nevertheless, for the sake of this chapter, the following aspects of Catholic Worker life will be distinguished and treated separately. The spirituality of the Catholic Worker is found in their life of *voluntary poverty* and *hospitality*; it is further marked by a strong *sense of community* on the one hand, and a *spirit of personal autonomy and responsibility* on the other hand. All these facets of Catholic Worker life, furthermore, stand in stark contrast to values and attitudes that have been integral parts of the collective U.S. culture during the past fifty years, and continue to be. The chapter will contend that the spirituality of the Catholic Worker has exercised and continues to exercise a truly prophetic role on the U.S. religious scene.

VOLUNTARY POVERTY AND HOSPITALITY

Voluntary poverty is utterly incomprehensible to most contemporary Americans. Few concepts are more antithetical to U.S. culture, even to religion. When the early Catholic Workers adopted voluntary poverty as a component of their way of life, the only model they could call upon was the vow of poverty in religious life; yet, given the Worker style of life, there was little real similarity between the two experiences. Describing both the content and the purpose of voluntary poverty among Catholic Workers, Wayne Labue commented, "members of the Catholic Worker community lived a voluntary poverty, by which they meant not destitution but a dignified, simple, even obscure condition, in order to share with others their interpretation of the good society."[3]

Catholic Workers know better than most people that destitution is not a legitimate human choice, if indeed it could be a choice at all. Destitution bespeaks not only material poverty, the lack of adequate food and housing, but also the emotional and spiritual devastation caused by lack of opportunity to assume any significant control over one's life. Powerlessness and humiliation frequently characterize the destitute. No one deliberately chooses such spiritual, moral, and material deprivation. Yet in espousing voluntary poverty as a life-style, the Catholic Worker recognizes that to freely choose to live without abundance and in radical insecurity can be a worthy, digni-fied human option, indeed a profound act of faith.

Such a stance, moreover, speaks volumes about what is termed the good society. Seen in the light of a life of renunciation and com-passion, the so-called good society is essentially parasitic; it con-forms neither to a vision of human goodness nor to the basic social nature of the human person. Pursuit of the good society leaves countless victims in its wake. To Dorothy Day and Peter Maurin in the midst of the Great Depression of the early 1930s, achievement in the good society was seen as the reward for successfully competing in the marketplace, an engagement in total opposition to the love of neighbor dictated by the gospel. "Modern society," wrote Peter Maurin, "has made the bank account the standard of values. . . . When the banker has the power, we have an acquisitive, not a func-tional society."[4]

A constant refrain in the writings of Catholic Workers has been the link between the dynamic of the good society and the lives of men, women, and children waiting in line for food and clothing out-side the Houses of Hospitality. "The involuntary poverty of any age," wrote Tom Frary, "is the theological source for understanding voluntary poverty. . . . For the community it [voluntary poverty] de-mands a continual renewal of its identification with the real poor in keeping with Christ's identification with the poor and suffering."[5] The Catholic Worker has never become a traditional social service agency. Voluntary poverty has been a key factor. Catholic Workers have not only distributed food and clothing and provided housing, but they have stood with society's castoffs on picket lines and at City Hall whenever human dignity has been at stake.

To choose to stand with the poor as one who shares their plight is a unique act of solidarity. These activities of advocacy have frequently brought the Catholic Worker community into conflict with the de-fenders of the good society, often even with supporters of their corpo-ral works of mercy. As James Douglass has written:

> The condescending tone of the term "charity" can be avoided
> only if we sink to poverty ourselves and continue to give from
> our poverty. . . . The Catholic Worker counteracts these pres-
> sures [of the affluent society] by the protest of the poor giving
> to the poor, shattering the illusion of the billfold apostolate.[6]

The voluntary poverty of the Catholic Worker, therefore, has lent a ring of authenticity to its hospitality. The act of hospitality posits vulnerability, allowing others access to one's life space. When one is tied to possessions, even the most meager, one can readily become anxious for their safety. The coveted item may be an insignificant article of clothing or a keepsake. Dorothy Day occasionally wrote of this temptation to grow attached to such objects, objects that regularly enough vanished into the pocket or bag of a guest at the House of Hospitality. Hospitality means vulnerability embraced and accepted day after day.

Most difficult of all, however, is the relinquishment of other more subtle, even spiritual possessions. Dorothy Day told of an elderly guest, a former newspaperman, whose conversation was punctuated with words like "kikes," "dingos," and "dagoes"; his "greatest affliction was having to share the hospitality of the city with Negroes."[7] Yet he too was Christ-among-us for the Catholic Workers. The vulnerability of hospitality becomes especially painful when one must accept with gentle grace those who trample upon one's most treasured values and principles. The poor, for example, are not always grateful according to middle-class standards. Love in action, Dorothy Day often remarked, is a harsh and dreadful thing. Traditional spiritual masters teach that the last and most wrenching act of detachment is to have one's spiritual possessions and satisfactions disappear into the dark night of the spirit.

For Peter Maurin, voluntary poverty and hospitality were to have a twofold effect: the sanctification of the Catholic Worker and the transformation of the church's attitude toward the poor. Former Catholic Worker Ed Willock describes, in Maurin's words to a guest, the Catholic Worker approach to "serving" the poor: "I can give you bread and meat and coffee. Yes, I can give you these—but you, you can give me the chance to practice Christian charity. You are an ambassador of God. Thank you." Willock continues, "Contrary to prevailing norms of social service is this notion that the worker, the volunteer, is the object of reform rather than the poor."[8]

Behind Maurin's simple, blunt statements lies a profound theological truth. Christian conversion takes place when one ventures into the uncharted shores of radical gospel living. Face to face with the flesh and blood, sometimes disagreeable poor, Catholic Workers lose their spiritual and cultural bearings. The warm feelings of self-satisfaction and the spiritual elation quickly vanish. Calling nothing their own, tossed into an unusual mix of human personalities, the Workers survive only by letting go of expectations, previous stereotypes, and unchangeable truths about serving others. Cynicism becomes an ever-present temptation; self-righteousness hovers over the Workers on the other side of the spectrum. In this spiritual waste-land, people of faith can live only in blind faith and submit them-selves to the transforming power of God's mysterious presence in the poor. "It becomes inevitable," comments Willock, "that rather than winning, they themselves [volunteers] will be won over."[9] Though the context is vastly different, the dynamic of conversion remains the same as that described by the ancient spiritual guides. Withdrawing into the desert, the monastery, or the retreat center, believers must face and do battle with their own demons in order to be transformed into the likeness of Jesus Christ.

Peter Maurin saw Catholic Worker hospitality as effecting another sort of transformation. Drawing on his knowledge of church history, Maurin was aware that hospitality had been an important value and practice in the early centuries among Christians. He therefore hoped that the witness of Catholic Worker hospitality would move the church toward a renewal of this ancient spiritual practice. In one of his Easy Essays Maurin wrote:

> We need Houses of Hospitality to give to the rich the
> opportunity to serve the poor.
> . . . to bring the Bishops to the people and the people to the
> Bishops.
> . . . to show what idealism looks like when it is practiced.
> People with homes should have a room of hospitality so as
> to give shelter to the needy members of the parish.
> The remaining needy members of the parish should be
> given shelter in a Parish house.[10]

Along with a back-to-the-land movement and his project of edu-cating Catholics in the church's social teachings, hospitality was the third pillar in Maurin's utopian vision of a new Christian society. According to his plan, poor urban workers would come to be edu-cated spiritually, professionally, and esthetically. City and country would interact creatively for the benefit of everyone. Each aspect of this new lifestyle would find its underpinning in simple, evangelical values. "It is they [Catholic Workers]," commented a German visitor in 1938, "who fight for the installment of the poor in the place of honor in the Church. . . . Peter is a jealous prophet; the slightest deviation from their original evangelical simplicity arouses him to fits of anger."[11]

How describe the role of voluntary poverty and hospitality in Catholic Worker spirituality? If we focus on the details of voluntary poverty and the mechanics of hospitality, we would miss their true place in Catholic Worker life. It is significant that the Catholic

Worker houses of hospitality have no constitutions, as do religious communities, spelling out how poverty is to be lived. In fact, the actual work of hospitality differs from one Worker community to the other. Even the composition of the communities varies.

The role of voluntary poverty and hospitality in Catholic Worker spirituality, therefore, is found not in patented individual actions, but in the overall atmosphere created by the struggle to be faithful to these primitive gospel vocations. They create a certain spiritual style, a certain presence that has come to be distinguished over these fifty years as the Catholic Worker way of being in the world, of standing in the presence of God. Neophytes receive no intensive formation in the rarefied atmosphere of a rustic novitiate. Rather they enter into this presence and begins their initiation by accepting the vulnerability of sharing the lot of the poor, by feeding, clothing, and housing society's outcasts. They become thereby a Catholic Worker. They take on a characteristic spirituality, whose contours, however, are daily shaped by the people and tasks encountered.

The comparison of Catholic Worker spirituality with the format of religious life is not merely coincidental. Except for movements such as the Young Christian Workers and the Young Christian Students, the model for American Catholic spirituality in the 1930s, 1940s, and 1950s was the religious life. The literature of spirituality generally came from the pens of religious priests. To pursue a spiritual life, the layperson was frequently exhorted to structure daily life, whenever possible, in a fashion reminiscent of the flow of religious life. Retreats were almost always pursued in religious houses, under the direction of a retreat master. Indeed, when Dorothy Day and other Catholic Workers of the early period write of retreats, they usually refer to an actual monastic setting, or at least to an atmosphere that simulates a religious house, for example, the Catholic Worker farm, silence, and orarium of prayer and worship. In fact, within the Catholic Worker movement that espoused a harmonious blend of prayer, study, manual labor, and community, the Benedictine vision was especially appealing.

Was the early Catholic Worker spirituality, then, only a laicized version of the spirituality of the Order of St. Benedict? The answer, despite the similarities, would have to be *no*. As this chapter intimates, though the process of the Catholic Worker "way of holiness" seems to reflect the traditional spiritual way, the setting, the less ordered reliance on the church's sacramental life, indeed the very inner dynamic of the spiritual process of the Catholic Worker trace a uniquely lay spirituality. Theologically Catholic Worker spirituality is situated in the biblical conviction of the poor being a profound, redeeming revelation of God's presence and grace. No religious garb, no vows or rule of life, no set of prayers or daily regimen are necessary to establish the Catholic Worker spiritual identity. The desert in which the spiritual pilgrim confronts the awesome spirit of God is no longer populated by shifting sands or green fields, but by extended, cut, and dirty hands, human hunger and desperation, and the ever-present threat of violence. This ambiance and the Worker's presence and commitment therein outline a pursuit of the gospel Jesus that has few precedents in the history of Catholic spirituality.

THE STRUGGLE FOR COMMUNITY

Community becomes the first achievement of Catholic Worker commitment to voluntary poverty and hospitality. Regardless of the actual living situation, people who allow themselves the vulnerability of stepping aside from the pursuit of material betterment and of performing the works of mercy form community as if instinctively. Even living under the same roof is not an absolute requirement for membership in this community. In *Loaves and Fishes* Dorothy Day describes the beginning of the first Catholic Worker house of hospitality. People came for food and clothing, the unemployed and other distressed people. Others wandered in to cook, to serve, to discuss the vision of Peter Maurin. All were drawn not by a carefully formulated program, but by a vaguely articulated vision of a simple gospel life of voluntary poverty and care for others. According to Maurin's vision, "People who are in need and are not afraid to beg give to people not in need the occasion to do good for goodness' sake."[12]

The community of Catholic Workers was not a self-conscious creation of well-meaning people filled with clear-cut ideals. Rather, community happened as unlikely people—itinerants, pregnant women, self-educated philosophers, priests, and the curious—gathered to find understanding and healing, to share their good will and meager resources. Dorothy Day remembered:

> Characters of every description and from every corner of life turned up—and we welcomed them all. They "joined" the Catholic Worker in many ways. Some came with their suitcases, intending to stay with us for a year, and, shocked by our poverty, lingered only for the night. Others came for a weekend and remained for years. Someone visiting us simply to challenge some "point" made in an article in the paper would become a permanent member of the community.[13]

In time houses of hospitality arose in many cities. Some continued for decades; others were open for shorter periods until the Worker staff members moved on. No two houses have ever been the same; each has responded to different social and economic situations. Personalities of the staff have varied; the needs of guests differed. Each house, however, has witnessed to a unique spirit of community and mutual aid. "In general," wrote Dorothy Day, "every house has a resemblance to a large and disorderly, but loving family."[14]

Despite the diversity and haphazard evolution of each house of hospitality, Catholic Worker communities all have reflected the broad, utopian ideal of Peter Maurin:

> Catholic Houses of Hospitality should be more than
> free guest houses for the Catholic unemployed . . .
> They could be vocational training schools . . .
> They could be Catholic reading rooms . . .
> They could be Catholic Instruction Schools . . .
> In a word, they could be Catholic Action Houses,
> where Catholic thought is combined with Catholic
> Action.[15]

This vision was infused, moreover, with the personalist views of Maurin, which he found in the French philosopher Emmanuel Mounier. The Catholic Worker was not to be a social service agency, but a community of free individuals, whose lives would be spent in exchange with each other in a personal, caring fashion.

> The training of social workers enables them to help people
> to adjust themselves to the existing environment. . . . In
> houses of hospitality social workers can acquire that art of
> human contacts and that socialmindedness or understand-
> ing of social forces which will make them critical of the ex-
> isting environment and the free creative agents of a new
> environment.

Against Marxism and other secular philosophers, Maurin insisted that the human person was destined for a transcendent fulfillment, yet this goal would be reached not as an isolated individual, but as one bonded together in community with others. "The Commu-nitarian Revolution," he wrote, "is basically a personal revolution. It starts with I, not with They. One I plus one I makes two I's and two I's make We. We is a community, while 'they' is a crowd."[16]

Catholic Worker houses were to be not only communities that refined this vision of a new social order, but also centers of action. In addition to direct, personal service of the poor, Catholic Workers were to support Workers' in their struggles and to generally live out the values of a new social order as leaven in society. Though this revolution was geared to Workers in an urban setting, Maurin also urged a return to the land, where Workers would experience the humanizing effect of tilling the soil. The sociopolitical benefits of this exposure to the land did not escape Maurin. "The escape from industrialism is not in Socialism nor in Sovietism. The answer lies in a return to a society where agriculture is practiced by most of the people. It is in fact impossible for any culture to be sound and healthy without a proper respect and proper regard for the soil."[17]

The spirit of community was, and remains, therefore, the underlying assumption of the Catholic Worker vision of social change. "The only answer in this life," wrote Dorothy Day, "to the loneliness we are all bound to feel is community. The living together, working together, sharing together, loving God and loving our brother, and living close to him in community so we can show our love for Him."[18] Hence Catholic Worker spirituality is profoundly communitarian.

In a Catholic setting, the sense of community of necessity implies a liturgical, eucharistic dimension. Indeed the eucharistic liturgy completes the cycle of free individuals interacting with mutual love and thereby experiencing God's incarnate love. Though the Catholic Worker movement did not exercise leadership in the updating of Catholic ritual life, the sense of community it brought to worship was to be a major contribution to the liturgical renewal of the 1960s. The theology of Vatican II later substantiated the faith instincts of the early Catholic Workers as they sought to connect liturgy and life. Wayne Labue sums up this insight well:

> Sensitive to the necessary tension between individuality and a sharing community, Maurin understood that liturgical experience encouraged both needs and that the life of the spirit involved open-handed gestures of hospitality as well as isolated moments of quiet thought. Liturgical celebrations produced temporary models of the shared life, a unity, without imposed conformity, between the One and the many, the self and others.[19]

This portrait of Christian community had an integrity that was appealing to intellectuals steeped in the Catholic humanism of the 1930s and 1940s. Radical though it was, the communal vision of the Catholic Worker found a certain popular response at a time when people had to depend on one another to survive the hard times of the Depression. When people frequently shared living quarters and meager financial resources, when the extended family was still the common experience of many, and cities were still networks of strong ethnic communities, the presence of community life among Catholic Workers was not seen as too unusual.

The phenomenon of urban flight of the late 1940s and 1950s, however, changed both the geography and outlook of most Americans, including American Catholics. The exodus to the suburbs separated suburban dwellers from those whose racial makeup and economic condition relegated them to urban slums. With this isolation came the reluctance to effectively touch the lives of the poor in a manner other than the monetary donation. Moreover, suburban life fostered an individualism among families. The nuclear family became a distinguishable sociological reality. Former familial, ethnic, or neighborhood ties were rarely renewed.

The surge of anticommunism of the 1950s was accompanied by a strident apologia for the American way of life. Many American Catholics were troubled by the specter of a radical community living among the poor espousing a new social order. Given the Catholic Worker public stance about war and the arms race, it is hardly surprising that the movement was frequently the target of attacks by militant anticommunists, especially within the Catholic church itself. Former supporters of the movement, even among the episcopacy, grew lukewarm, and subscriptions to the *Catholic Worker* declined.

As the decades wore on, therefore, the Catholic Worker community came to represent an even greater contrast to the prevailing American culture. "The Catholic Worker is laboring to solve the problem of Mott Street," commented the editor of *Today* in 1949, "and paradoxically enough, perhaps it is on Mott Street that Main Street will find the solution to its own problem, if, through God's grace, it can even be made aware that it has a problem."[20]

Yet another facet of the communal dimension of Catholic Worker spirituality finds subtle expression in the reflections of Workers, namely the constant tendency of community to fail. While she accepted people's admiration for the idealism of the Catholic Worker and the heroic efforts to attain it, Dorothy Day was quick to present this other side of Catholic Worker life. Reflecting in 1966 on Peter Maurin's vision of a new social order, she noted that people frequently came to the Catholic Worker with the expectation that the community had taken great strides toward building the good society. Then with her usual bluntness she added:

> It is a wonder with all their expectations and disappointments, they do not go away, but bad as we are, it is worse outside, some said. . . . And so we are really not a true communal farm, a true agronomic university, but a community of need, a community of "wounded ones," as one girl who came to us from a state hospital, expressed it. I myself have often thought of our communities as concentration camps

of displaced people, all of whom want community, but at the same time want privacy . . . to seek for sanctity in their own way. This kind of sanctity of course has for most of us as little validity as the sense of well-being of the drug addict.[21]

Here and there in her writings Dorothy Day gave candid descriptions of both the generous and the ungenerous residents of Catholic Worker communities. Reflecting on forgiveness, she added, "but it was harder to forgive each other—those of us who worked together." She wrote about the fallings-out, the tensions that characterize community life. "Committed as they are to non-violence in thought, word and deed," she commented with loving irony, "they accept the hard saying 'Love your enemies,' many of whom are of their own household." Stanley Vishnewski, a long-time Catholic Worker, once coined the phrase "house of hostility" to describe the atmosphere of the community at times. "Sometimes we did feel sad, indeed," wrote Dorothy another time, "when our houses seemed to be filled more with hate and angry words than with the love we were seeking."[22]

The communal dimension of Catholic Worker spirituality, then, presents a paradoxical challenge to U.S. Catholics. To the individualist, the Catholic Worker insists that love, to be authentic, forms community. To the overly romantic enthusiast, it reveals that communal life in the concrete, even among Catholic Workers, is often a flawed reality. The words of two contemporary Workers capture this paradox with profound insight.

> That ingrained, structural sin is most visible in the dirt and disorder of the houses and the brokenness of all who live there. The closer we get to a Worker community, the more glaring that sin becomes. We celebrate the values of community in contrast to the egoism of bourgeois society. Can we ignore the daily evidence that broken people living together are as likely to deepen wounds as to heal them? . . . It seems that it is in the moments of our failure that God finds room to touch us . . . but while we are confident that the Catholic Worker movement looks towards the reign of God, we cannot postulate a relation of cause and effect, but only one of cross and resurrection.[23]

Perhaps, then, the witness of Catholic Worker community life lies not so much in the elevated ideal espoused, as in the imperfect, halting yet faithful effort at community amid frequent failures. God is indeed found when two or three gather in Jesus's name, but that God may well be the crucified Jesus.

PACIFISM: A COMMITMENT TO COMMUNITY

According to the logic of the gospel, nonviolence and the pacifist stance flow out of Catholic Worker hospitality and commitment to community. Less than a decade after its beginning, the Catholic Worker movement was embroiled in major public controversies. While siding with those who hunger for justice, Dorothy Day and other Workers refused to accept the use of violence in its pursuit. The Worker's neutral position in the Spanish Civil War brought the movement into sharp conflict with many Catholics who saw the forces of General Franco as a bulwark against communism. Referring to the ancient Christian martyrs, Dorothy Day remarked, "And did they not rather pray, when the light of Christ burst upon them, that love would overcome hatred, that men *dying* for faith, rather than *killing* for their faith, would save the world?" Yet she was sympathetic toward those who felt the need to take up arms in what they saw as a just cause. Perhaps, she mused, only a radical commitment to martyrdom could overcome our human willingness to exert violence. "Of all at the *Catholic Worker* how many would not instinctively defend himself with any forceful means in his power? We must prepare. We must prepare now. There must be a disarmament of the heart."[24]

The outbreak of World War II brought increasing tension into the Catholic Worker movement. Many Catholic Workers felt called to take up arms to defend the innocent against Hitler's armies. Others maintained their status as conscientious objectors, some of whom were imprisoned for their refusal to serve. Subscriptions to the *Catholic Worker* fell off, and the movement found itself in disagreement with many U.S. bishops who supported the war effort as morally justified. Writing in January 1942, Dorothy reflected the pain of the division in the Worker movement. "We are at war, a declared war, with Japan, Germany and Italy. But still we can repeat Christ's words, each day, holding them close in our hearts, each month printing them in the paper. . . . We are still pacifists. Our manifesto is the Sermon on the Mount, which means that we will try to be peacemakers." Recalling the Worker commitment to hospitality, she wrote, "Our works of mercy may take us into the midst of war. As editor of the *Catholic Worker*, I would urge our friends and associates to care for the sick and the wounded, to the growing of food for the hungry, to the continuance of all our works of mercy in our houses and on our farms."[25]

Wars have come and gone. Yet the Catholic Worker commitment to nonviolence and pacifism remains. Celebrating fifty-two years of publication by renewing its statement of aims and purposes, the editors of the *Catholic Worker* wrote in May 1984: "To achieve a just society we advocate a complete rejection of the present system and a nonviolent revolution to establish a social order in accord with Christian truth. . . . We believe that the revolution to be pursued in ourselves and in society must be nonviolent and cannot be imposed from above."[26]

The mention of a nonviolent revolution in oneself, moreover, removes any possibility that nonviolence be seen as a tactical maneuver to be used or discarded as circumstances dictate. Rather, for the Catholic Worker the ongoing process of becoming nonviolent suggests an attitude at the very core of Catholic Worker spirituality. The open embrace of true hospitality cannot coexist alongside the concept of enemy. Hospitality that would discriminate between friend and enemy, worthy and unworthy person, would cease to be hospitality. For the Catholic Worker, therefore, one's community cannot have national, racial, or religious boundaries. This communitarian spirituality must find concrete, flesh and blood expression. Nonviolence and pacifism have been among the most tangible and demanding incarnations of Catholic Worker spirituality.

THE PERSONALIST REVOLUTION

What distinguished Peter Maurin's visionary speeches to his listeners from those of other theorists was Maurin's orientation to action. One was to do the works of mercy, not just organize others to perform them. People were to touch others, sharing with each other not only food and clothing but human warmth, presence, and pain as well. According to Maurin, if people began to live out these gospel precepts, they would eliminate those agencies that tend to make the poor into clients. The effect of individuals inspired by the same vision was inestimable for Maurin. "Everybody would be rich if nobody tried to become richer. And Nobody would be poor if everybody tried to be the poorest." A compulsive teacher, Maurin was seldom able to organize others. Hence he rarely spoke to more than a handful of people. "The impact Peter made on us all, from one end of the country to the other," remarked Dorothy Day in 1953, "was because he personally lived a life of poverty and work."[27]

Both Peter Maurin and Dorothy Day had an innate distrust of the state's ability to serve people in a human manner. The need for a personal touch rather than elaborate organization characterized their work. The first house of hospitality, for example, began in a haphazard way, as Dorothy Day described in *Loaves and Fishes*. An unemployed, pregnant young woman arrived and began to prepare meals for those who wandered in; people needed a place to stay, and they were taken in. When the rooms were filled, an apartment was rented. Soon they moved to a larger house. The house of hospitality was born. Structure remained minimal. Finances were always precarious; somehow money was there when needed, though often no one knew when and how the miracle would happen. What was essential was that men and women struggled to live together as if the gospel were an outline for their lives. Instead of waiting for society to act, editorialized an observer, "each person must take upon himself the moral responsibility of combatting evil and correcting what is wrong in the world as far as he is able."[28]

Echoing the attitude and trials of the early Catholic Worker Houses, two contemporary Catholic workers wrote of a Worker House of the 1980s: "Our communities are rarely accountable to an independent governing board, and we usually have a rather informal bookkeeping system. The sole guarantee of our financial probity is our personal integrity. Dare we claim that that integrity is always irreproachable?"[29]

This personalist, almost anarchist style has bestowed on the Catholic Worker an identity and a spirituality similar to that of a sect. Just as members of sectarian groups, Catholic Workers tend to define themselves against the surrounding society. They claim a vision and espouse a behavior rarely found in the culture. In this regard, what amazed an English visitor in the late 1930s was the phenomenon of the Catholic Worker as a successful lay movement in the U.S. Catholic church, a church largely dominated by the clergy.

> It is a bold and naive simplicity, which is its distinguishing mark, a simplicity difficult to find in more traditional and conservative surroundings. . . . But I think that even if the present Catholic Worker collapses or proves to be incapable of rebuilding American Catholicism, through some human shortcomings of its members, the spirit which animates it is the only one which can save the Church in America.[30]

The Catholic Worker was indeed a spectacle, even to the U.S. Catholic community. In a society and church that frequently looked for results, the Catholic Worker disdain for signs of success was both unusual and disconcerting for some. Personal autonomy and a collective neglect of structure were and are more than incidental to the Catholic Worker spirit. The unconventional lives of Catholic Workers and characteristic bluntness of the *Catholic Worker* complete the portrait of an alternative community.

Like other alternative communities, the Catholic Worker habors within itself many contradictions. Throughout the decades, many

Catholic Workers have maintained a deep suspicion of official, especially government-sponsored, efforts toward labor reform, disarmament, and other ventures to build the kingdom of God. Yet from the very outset Catholic Workers have supported workers' strikes and other structured actions to obtain a just society. From the brewery workers' strike of the early years to the farmworkers' strikes and boycotts of the 1970s and 1980s, the Catholic Worker has stood with workers, even on the picket lines. Several former Catholic Workers, including John Cort and Ed Marciniak, later made significant contributions to the labor movement. Yet a favorite saying of Peter Maurin was "Strikes don't strike me." He saw organized labor as attempting to merely reshuffle the wage system, rather than promote a totally new way to see labor and its creative impact on the evolution of a new social order. "A personalist," he wrote, "is a go-giver not a go-getter. He tries to give what he has and does not try to get what the other fellow has."[31] The personalist, in other words, brings about the new social order by freely contributing his or her efforts to the common good. Organized attempts at labor reform impose a strategy and vision often remarkably similar to the way things presently are.

The Catholic Worker contribution to the religious peace movement in the United States has been both constant and courageous. One finds, however, the same sense of paradox. From the Worker opposition to World War II to the noncooperation with the mock air raid drills of the 1950s to the Plowshares type actions of the 1980s, Catholic Workers have been prominent in opposing war and warmaking. The statement of the aims and purposes in the May 1984 *Catholic Worker* clearly describes this commitment.

> We condemn all war and the nuclear arms race, and we see oppression in any form as blasphemy against God who created all in his image . . . when we fight tyranny and injustice, we must do so in humility and compassion using the spiritual means of fasting and non-cooperation with evil. Refusing to pay taxes, . . . and withdrawal from the system are methods that can be employed in the struggle for justice.

The concluding sentences of this statement then highlight the radical, religious personalist stance characteristic of the Catholic Worker:

> We believe that success as the world determines it is not a fit criterion for judgment. We must be prepared and ready to face seeming failure. The most important thing is that we adhere to these beliefs which transcend time, and for which

we will be asked a personal accounting, not as to whether they succeeded (thought we hope that they do) but as to whether we remained true to them.[32]

While they would support efforts toward disarmament, for example, one would scarcely find Catholic Workers involved in the technicalities of disarmament negotiations, where absolute principles are frequently compromised amid the give and take of arriving at only relatively acceptable solutions.

Similar to other aspects of Catholic Worker spirituality, this personalism and spirit of autonomy are both rooted in a visionary ideal and expressed in concrete deeds and commitments. The Catholic Worker has provoked deep antagonism as well as profound admiration. Some observers of the movement have been led to reexamine their social and political stances. Others have found their view of the church expanded. Very few, however, who have encountered the movement have failed to experience the sometimes abrupt challenge to personal, spiritual conversion, to examine and redirect their deepest personal goals and commitments. Activist theologian James Douglass captured the force of the Catholic Worker witness well:

> The encouragement to community, voluntary poverty and agrarianism will often make a middle-class apartment dweller uneasy without moving him to denounce them as un-American. Anarchism and pacifism are less palatable and are usually spit out at the first taste. Yet each of these proposals is an attempt to counteract an evil in our society, and it is forwarded with a zeal that derives its strength and apparent recklessness from a desire to refer every action to God.[33]

CONCLUSION

At the core of the Catholic Worker way of life is the gospel of Jesus Christ. Like countless Christians before them, Dorothy Day and Peter Maurin launched a movement whose tenets emerged from a simple reading of the gospel; they lived with the conviction that this gospel is livable in twentieth-century America. There is much about this way of life and its accompanying spirituality that is paradoxical and even questionable, yet, when one moves beyond certain details and expressions of the Catholic Worker, one uncovers a vision that has the ring of authenticity. Amid the varied interpretations of the gospel Jesus, the portrait traced by the Catholic Worker for more than fifty years contains the outlines of a human life pursued in intimate contact with the God of justice and compassion. Virtually no one denies that the Catholic Worker encompasses what is most unique, challenging, and radical about the Christian gospel life.

How has this vision fared over five decades? What success can the Catholic Worker movement claim? These questions can be raised on various levels. Clearly the eschatological age is not at hand after fifty some years of Catholic Worker life. The Catholic Worker strongly supported the labor movement, and Peter Maurin had definite views about the direction of this movement. In fact, however, to this day the labor movement has never evolved in a fashion desired by Maurin. For the most part, the U.S. laborer does not appreciate the dignity and humanizing potential of labor. Labor and management continue in an adversarial relationship. Rarely do laborers have a stake in the enterprise, other than the salary and benefits the job can provide. Such options as shared management and shared ownership remain uncommon in U.S. industrial life.

Passionately devoted to peacemaking, the Catholic Worker movement finds the world closer to a nuclear confrontation than ever before. With thousands of weapons poised on either side of the globe, the world, as some suggest, is beyond the eleventh hour, moving ever closer to an unimaginable catastrophe. Catholic Worker noncooperation with war-making and its advocacy of civil disobedience have not uprooted the nation's tendencies toward violence in general and war in particular.

As Catholics, Maurin and Day and their followers ardently looked for the church to become more compassionate, more sensitive to deep-seated racism, more willing to stand for justice in every sphere. Herein one can point to evidence of modest success, from official episcopal pastoral statements to organized efforts to make justice an integral dimension of Catholic life. But, for all that, the church still largely reflects the value system of the culture, the priority of institutional concerns over those involving risk taking. The sense of community, so integral to the Catholic Worker spirit, has yet to become a vital ingredient in the life of the church, despite the theological rhetoric since Vatican II. On the whole, the general profile of U.S. Catholics presents a picture of a people uninvolved in issues other than those of personal and family morality.

At this level, then, the transformation of society and the church according to the Catholic Worker gospel vision, one would have to declare the Catholic Worker efforts a failure. Judged from the perspective of structural change in politics and society, the Catholic Worker witness seems to have been either unheard or relegated to the fringe where it is readily ignored. In spite of this apparent ineffectiveness, however, the Catholic Worker has continued to flourish. Men and women, young and old, are drawn to this harsh life in order to express an active love for society's dropouts.

This paradox has great significance. The tension between eschatological vision and practical, political failure forms the familiar world of prophetic witness. The prophetic figure is driven to proclaim the word of God, despite the imperfection of his or her articulation. But from the political perspective, the word of God simply does not work; it cannot. "The prophetic person," wrote Tom Frary, "addresses a possible future that demands action in the present for which the present offers little credibility."[34] The word of God is always a call for radical transformation. This does not happen through political structures. In the Jewish and Christian scriptures, God's word brings creation out of chaos, freedom out of slavery, indeed life out of death itself. The word is addressed to people's hearts, where such conversions take place.

Personal transformation begins when people face the futility of the present ways of the world. Once they realize that the "system" does not work and accept their helplessness under the present conditions, they learn the paradox of failure: only in uncertainty and the chaos of futility are the transforming energies of the spirit released and the future opened up again. People can begin again to pursue the vision because they rely not on human resources but on the power of the God of history. "The Catholic Worker was radical," wrote Wayne Labue, "because it would have history submit to it and would not itself submit to history."[35] Immediate success or failure becomes unimportant as long as one is willing to remain rooted in the power of the word of God.

The spirituality of the Catholic Worker is prophetic, therefore, not because the movement has radically altered society, but because it has led people through the confrontation with the chaos of poverty, violence, and alienation into the new life proclaimed by the gospel vision. Among those so formed—names like John Cogley, John Cort, Ed Marciniak, Michael Harrington—can be noted among many others, writers, labor and political leaders, community organizers. The peace movement in the United States has been blessed by the witness of countless Catholic Workers, such as Eileen Egan, James Forest, Thomas Cornell, James Douglass, Michael and Nettie Cullen, and others. Hundreds of men and women in many walks of life trace their religious and social convictions to their days of feeding the hungry, housing the destitute, and standing against war and injustice as members of Catholic Worker communities.

But the prophetic witness of the Catholic Worker way of life has not been confined to those within the movement. Indeed, contemporary American life, especially among U.S. Catholics, bears evidence of the Catholic Worker presence. U.S. Catholics, like their compatriots, are in the main a generous, caring, and at times naive people. Caught up in the quest for affluence, few even recognize the price such well-being exacts from the poor. Few are conscious that their economic and social status requires an underclass. The fact that this national affluence of necessity calls for an elaborate political and military infrastructure becomes even more difficult to face. The Catholic Worker presence, whether directly or indirectly, radically challenges the American way of life.

By the simple actions of housing and feeding the poor, the Catholic Worker reminds U.S. Catholics of the lie that hides embedded in the American myth of the good life. By refusing to cooperate in warmaking, the Catholic Worker holds before Catholics the contradiction between their weekly celebration of human oneness in the eucharist and their willingness to cooperate in the destruction of countless brothers and sisters around the world. U.S. Catholics are therefore collectively invited to acknowledge the present system and its accompanying values as death-dealing and to mourn its necessary demise. The ultimate prophetic challenge of the Catholic Worker movement is to call people to let go of this specter of death and to be thereby transformed into life-givers.

In terms of the accepted norms of success, the Catholic Worker effort can only fail. Judged, however, by the criterion of radical faith, hope, and love, the Catholic Worker way of life promises and celebrates true success, albeit the success of the cross.

NOTES

Note: The *Catholic Worker* is here cited as *CW*.

1. Walter Brueggemann, *The Prophetic Imagination* (Philadelphia: Fortress Press, 1978), 13; Robert Coles, *A Spectacle unto the World* (New York: Viking Press, 1973).

2. Dorothy Day's roots in the American, socialist, revolutionary tradition need no further elaboration here. Peter Maurin saw himself as a Christian anarchist. His early formation in the Sillon movement in France may well have been influential. The movement was founded toward the end of the nineteenth century by Marc Sangnier, a charismatic lay Catholic with both mystical and activist tendencies. Trying to balance lay political autonomy with loyalty to the church, Sangnier and the movement came into conflict with the conservative leanings of the papacy of Pius X. In 1910 Pius X censured the movement. Perhaps this early experience in France accounts for Maurin's populist tendencies and the tensions in his life between loyalty to the church and Christian lay autonomy.

3. Wayne Labue, "Public Theology and the Catholic Worker," *Cross Currents* 26 (Fall 1976): 282.

4. Peter Maurin, *The Green Revolution, Easy Essays on Catholic Radicalism* (Fresno, Academic Guild Press, 1961), 63–64.

5. Tom Frary, "Thy Kingdom Come—The Theory of Dorothy Day," *Commonweal* 127 (November 11, 1972): 387.

6. James Douglass, "Dorothy Day and the City of God," *Social Justice Review* 54 (May 1961): 42.

7. Dorothy Day, *Loaves and Fishes* (New York: Curtis Books, 1963), 35–38.

8. Ed Willock, "Catholic Radicalism," *Commonweal* 58 (October 2, 1953): 631.

9. Ibid.

10. Maurin, *Green Revolution*, 9–11.

11. H. A. Reinhold, "The Catholic Worker Movement in America," *Blackfriars* 19 (September 1938): 640, 648.

12. Maurin, *Green Revolution*, 8.

13. Day, *Loaves and Fishes*, 35.

14. Dorothy Day, *On Pilgrimage: The Sixties* (New York: Curtis Books, 1972), 14.

15. Maurin, *Green Revolution*, 11.

16. Ibid., 94, 105.

17. Ibid., 100.

18. Dorothy Day, *The Long Loneliness* (New York: Harper & Row, 1952), 243.

19. Labue, "Public Theology," 276.

20. "Summer on Mott St.," *Today* (October 1949): 11.

21. Day, *On Pilgrimage*, 171.

22. Day, *Loaves and Fishes*, 97, *On Pilgrimage*, 14; *Loaves and Fishes*, 38.

23. M. McIntyre and V. Druhe, "The Worker: A Tradition in Contradiction," *The Round Table* (Summer 1984): 11.

24. Dorothy Day, "Catholic Worker Stand on the Use of Force," *CW*, September 1938: 37.

25. Dorothy Day, "Our Country Passes from Undeclared War to Declared War: We Continue Our Christian Pacifist Stand," *CW*, January 1942: 54.

26. "Aims and Purposes," *CW* 51 (May 1984): 3, 5.

27. Maurin, *Green Revolution*, 37; Dennis Howard, "Interview with Dorothy Day on the Twentieth Anniversary of the Catholic Worker," *Advocate*, May 9, 1953.

28. Danny O'Neil, editorial, *Manhattan Quadrangle*, November 13, 1957, n.p.

29. McIntyre and Druhe, "The Worker."

30. Reinhold, "The Catholic Worker Movement in America," 642.

31. Maurin, *Green Revolution*, 116–17.

32. "Aims and Purposes," *CW*, May 1984.

33. Douglass, "Dorothy Day and the City of God," 42.

34. Frary, "Thy Kingdom Come," 387.

35. Labue, "Public Theology," 283.

8.   HOUSES OF HOSPITALITY
A Pilgrimage into Nonviolence

Angie O'Gorman and Patrick G. Coy

THE MYRIAD CONTRIBUTIONS of the Catholic Worker movement to the cause of peace are significant, and well known. Sociologist Gordon Zahn has said that "the Catholic Worker, with its founding in 1933, was the beginning of the U.S. Catholic peace movement." On the pacifist front, Zahn concurs with other historians in maintaining that "the Catholic Worker was the sole example of Catholic pacifism during the 1940s and 1950s."[1] The distinctive role the Worker has played within the church and within the peace movement has been ably examined, with important new studies appearing in this anthology. However, among the Worker's distinctive contributions is one that has received far too little attention: the daily praxis of nonviolence in the hospitality houses.

It was Jean Paul Sartre who said that the greatest sin lies in making abstract that which is concrete.[2] At Catholic Worker houses there is little danger of that. The hard human reality of soup lines and houses filled with society's often angry castoffs keeps the movement rooted in the concrete. Indeed, dealing with the effects of human brokenness and blockage resulting from a variety of personal and social sources are part of the daily experience in a Worker house. Situations of verbal abuse stemming from frustration, anger, psycho-

239

sis, or the effects of alcohol and drugs, as well as physical abuse with or without a weapon, make up the heart of the Worker experience, day in and day out. This is the real world writ large.

Though Workers are often an intellectual lot, there has never seemed to be time for them to construct any ivory towers amidst the chaos of life at the houses. Contributions the Catholic Worker has made to the development of nonviolence in the United States have been born of the elusive dialectic between theory and praxis. As such, the weight of their significance is increased. Gandhi's insistence on daily praxis and experiments with nonviolence notwithstanding, it is a rare and distinctive event to have such interplay between the theory and the practice, the ideal and the real. As Sister of Loretto Ann Manganaro, one of the founders of the St. Louis Worker ten years ago, points out:

> The theoretical commitment to nonviolence is tested in very practical ways by living together—community and guests together. It's real easy to be committed to nonviolence when you like people and have no conflicts. But when with people who are very different, and conflicts of emotion and principle arise consistently, that tests nonviolent commitment. One of the things that's valuable about the Workers' long term commitment to living and being with poor people is that it puts the theoretical commitment in such a radical place—where it must be tested by very mundane practicalities, by raw, real-life human situations, by all the failings and frailities and marvelous strengths of people who are very different in background.[3]

The Catholic Worker has long maintained that if a value is subscribed to and is, in fact, to be truly enlivening, then an attempt to live it out through the grace of God must be made. Religious values worth their salt need to be lived out even when the going gets tough, maybe especially then. Proclamations and theorizing not rooted in the real world are readily dismissed at the Worker, for Catholic Workers are forever having to cross the chasm between the principle and the particular. Yet it is with considerable tenacity that the Worker movement continues to cling to its belief in the ultimate power of love and nonviolence. The attempt to practice nonviolence in the Houses, and not only on the picket lines, has not been at all naive. Struggles and failures have been accepted as part of the nonviolent script. The Worker is a training ground, with all the strengths and weaknesses that implies. Workers have learned as they went. A pilgrimage into nonviolence resulted.

It is these very struggles, failures, and successes, and the reflections and clarifications of thought they have occasioned, that are of singular significance in the history of nonviolence in the United States. Before the opening of Catholic Worker houses across the land, there had been no large-scale daily experiment with nonviolence. In particular, little had been written about nonviolence in the face of violent, interpersonal confrontation. Other pacifist groups had employed nonviolence as a tactic for social and political change, occasionally experimenting with nonviolence on the picket line and proposing it as a lifestyle. But fidelity to voluntary poverty, solidarity with the poor, and a commitment to nonviolence, have consistently placed members of the Catholic Worker movement in conflict situations, some quite violent, others less so. Ann Manganaro reflects on this dimension of life at the Worker: "We sometimes forget how much conflict there is here—everyday, even on a low-grade level, there are a whole lot of altercations, a lot of difficult and demanding people at the door whom we try and respond to, take care of lovingly. We may not think anything of it, forgetting that, in fact, those are all training sessions for adopting an attitude of nonviolence as a part of one's life."[4]

These situations, along with encounters with outright violence, have become the context for a new generation of "experiments in truth," much as Gandhi used his own precarious situations during the struggle for Indian independence to better learn the ways of nonviolence. The Catholic Worker gives those who want to learn an opportunity to engage in a resocialization process, one leading away from a culture that resolves conflict and threat by destroying that which is threatening.

Although the Catholic Worker has traditionally stressed the need for individual change in order that societal change might become possible, the truth of the situation is that many members first come to the movement emphasizing different sides of this two-edged revolution. Some stress the need for change within the self, others stress outward, social change. But the majority learn, soon after arriving at a house of hospitality, that it is easier to organize against nuclear war than to reorganize the self against the violence within. It is one thing to speak of nuclear disarmament between world powers and another to actively disarm one's heart when the missiles of anger and revenge are ready to fire. The Catholic Worker provides a context in which a different kind of "preparedness" is learned: one can begin to understand that self-preservation requires reconciliation rather than defense, and that security, whether personal or national, is impossible until it is available to all. Life at the Worker reveals that people can be firm in their personal need for security without jeopardizing the security of another—a lesson still far from our national consciousness. The Catholic Worker creates a graced space in which nonviolence can be learned from the inside out.

Some workers, like Mary Ann McGivern, S.L., come to the movement after being introduced to nonviolence elsewhere. "I first learned nonviolence on the farmworkers' picket line over a couple of years, and then by the daily practice of it. . . . I only came to understand the gospel, and the hard sayings of the Sermon on the Mount, after having some experience with nonviolence." More frequently, however, Workers come to the houses without much grounding in nonviolence. As Ann Manganaro says, "I'd never had any real training, but after spending a summer at the New York house, before we opened Karen House in St. Louis, I began to understand a little about it. Just by observing others intervene nonviolently somehow made me realize that nonviolence was possible in this violent setting."[5]

Others already know the words about nonviolence; now they begin to learn their meaning. The Worker provides the context; the gospels supply the ethic. The integrity at the core of the Worker vision holds them in its grasp and will not loosen its grip until their faith has taken action. They are invited to live out the belief that the God whom Jesus revealed loved humanity without regard for a person's "worthiness." As St. Matthew phrased it, God's love reigns on the just and the unjust alike (Matt. 5:45).

Throughout U.S. social history, many pacifists and pacifist groups have been criticized for not paying attention to "the real world." Pacifists in love with the lofty ideal have frequently stubbed their toes on the rocky road of everyday human reality. Former *Catholic Worker* editor Robert Ellsberg illustrates this point in reflecting on his experience at the New York house. "One of the things that impressed me a lot was the ability to practice nonviolence in a day-to-day kind of way. I and a lot of other pacifists talk about nonviolence as a way of life . . . not just as a tactic. And yet we have so little contact with real violence, which I think really is making yourself kind of vulnerable."[6]

Conflict and violence are synonomous with the human condition. Anyone who adopts and promotes nonviolence as a tactic and as a way of life must quickly face the ever-present conflicts in the world, and themselves. Precious few have realized this as profoundly as Dorothy Day. It is, in fact, the insight contained in the saying from Dostoyevsky's Father Zossima, which she was so fond of repeating: "Love in action is a harsh and dreadful thing compared to love in dreams." In the select company of Adolpho Perez Esquivel and Dom Helder Camara, she was a proponent and theoretician of nonviolence who had no illusions about the difficulty of living out the nonviolent ethic of Jesus. She knew all too well the inevitable failures, the frequently feeble attempts to answer hate with love; the meltdown of theory in the furnace of action. Yet it was precisely these daily experiments with nonviolence that emboldened her to maintain a pacifist stance in international affairs. For instance, she once wrote a rather impassioned reply to a charge that her pacifist stance was sentimental, revealing at the same time her understanding of the interconnectedness between nonviolence and economic justice:

> Let those who talk of softness, of sentimentality, come to live with us in cold unheated houses in the slums. Let them come to live with the criminal, the unbalanced, the drunken, the degraded, the perverted. . . . Let their flesh be mortified by cold, by dirt, by vermin. . . . Let their noses be mortified by the smells of sewage, decay, and rotten flesh. Yes, and by the smell of blood, sweat and tears spoken of by Mr. Churchill, and so widely and bravely quoted by comfortable people.[7]

Put simply, the Catholic Worker's commitment to nonviolence is not lived out in a vacuum, divorced from the forces that often compel and control our daily behavior. On the contrary. As Day so passionately related, the hospitality houses are right on the front lines of the battle for a peaceful world. The spiritual weapons brandished are the works of mercy. Day maintained that the hospitality work is not superfluous, but rather an essential exercise in Christian love, which she understood to be the linchpin in the dynamic of nonviolence.

Even within the peace movement, the value of the Catholic Worker's hospitality work was readily called into question. Although Peter Maurin often referred to the houses and farms as "schools"—learning centers where theory was tested in praxis—there were many in the peace movement and beyond who failed to recognize the practical importance of these "experiments in truth." As a letter from another Worker house conveyed to Day in 1969, "The past year has been difficult, particularly in dealing with the problems of relevancy. To many in the peace resistance movement, feeding and sheltering the poor is looked upon as non-revolutionary and a mere band-aid applied to a cancerous world. To many, only when the American giant is confronted at its jugular vein is it worthwhile. So our involvement and work has really been put into question."[8]

Perhaps the attitude referred to in that letter is one reason why the contributions of the Catholic Worker experience to the development of nonviolent theory in this country have frequently been overlooked. The jugular vein sought in the revolutionary struggle is most often understood to be the Pentagon or some other institutional manifestation of the military-industrial complex. It may be that scholars and historians have been as guilty of this tendency as peace movement people; thus the dearth of written or oral material on nonviolence in the Catholic Worker houses. For Day and Maurin, however, it was the violence in the individual's own heart that most needs to be rooted out. They saw that institutional and social violence are inextricably linked to personal violence, to the failure to love.

The genius of the Catholic Worker's contribution is to place a new slide under the microscope, replacing the institutional with the individual. The real struggle to be examined and learned from is the individual's attempt to live the revolutionary gospel of Jesus, the ethic of nonviolence revealed in the Sermon on the Mount. This personal struggle yields insights into the intricate dynamics of nonviolence, insights that may also be useful on the corporate level, in the attempt to win over Goliath—the corporate capitalist system and its supporters, which Peter Maurin saw as the bane of human freedom. But first, Goliath must be named and understood in the individual, in the violence and selfishness of one's own actions. This is the personalist revolution of Peter Maurin, and the spiritual foundation of Dorothy Day.

The Catholic Worker has always taken the Sermon on the Mount as the heart of the Good News. Indeed, the Sermon on the Mount has frequently been referred to as "the manifesto of the movement."[9] This approach to the Christian scriptures is not uncommon in groups or individuals with pacifist and anarchist learnings. Leo Tolstoy, Mohandas Gandhi, and Ammon Hennacy before he joined the Worker, all embraced the Sermon on the Mount as a compelling distillation of the gospel message. Not surprisingly, it also became the beginning point for Catholic Workers in understanding the principles of nonviolence and how they are fleshed out in a hospitality house. "You have learnt how it was said: 'Eye for eye and tooth for tooth.' But I say this to you: offer the wicked person no resistance. On the contrary, if anyone hits you on the right cheek, offer them the other as well; if a person takes you to law and would have your tunic, let them have your cloak as well. And if anyone orders you to go one mile, go two miles with them. . . . You have learned how it was said: 'You must love your neighbor and hate your enemy.' But I say this to you: love your enemies and pray for those who persecute you" (Matt. 5:38–45).

The gospel's invitation to vulnerability and loving service is at the center of the Catholic Worker ethic. Houses of hospitality are, by design, places where vulnerability and openness to the other—specifically to the guests—are highly valued. There is even a sense in which they are *required* by the communal living arrangements. Living with the poor, sharing living, eating, and working space, demands a certain openness from the start. And when the Worker vision of an active, compassionate love is thrown into the mixture, the end product is sure to include the bittersweet taste of vulnerability. It is the victory of the cross of Christ that makes it possible for Workers to accept the inevitable risks in the Catholic Worker experiment. Christ's own posture of vulnerability and forgiveness informs the work of the houses, and is the matrix within which the movement reflects on and interprets the experience. The following reflection from the Ammon Hennacy House of Hospitality in Los Angeles is not atypical in this regard. The incident was reported in a letter to supporters of the house.

Occasionally the existential reality of the men whom we serve comes home to us in the only way that it can, through violence and brutality. . . . The blasphemy that we know as Skid Row is a modern day Golgotha wherein greed and oppression have daily erected a new cross, and the tortured body of Christ comes to us under the appearance of so-called "winos" and "bums." Here on a daily basis is the reenactment of that ancient tragedy on Calvary. . . . On the fringes of society where Christ lives a marginal existence with his poor brothers and sisters, suffering and brutality is the price one pays for walking the streets. Lives are lost over an extra piece of meat or bread. A stolen pair of shoes makes the difference between surviving and not. And, alcohol is the only anesthetic to dull the sharp, cutting edge of reality.

Over the past four years we have been witnesses to much violence in our kitchen. Knives have flashed, fists have clenched. We have been in the midst of it attempting to bind up wounds and ease pain. . . . Friday, July 26, the day was tense, not enough people to do the work, a large crowd waiting to be served, some impatiently. The action is quick, a bit confused, carrying pots of steaming food, mixing salad, stumbling over empty produce cartons, making the transition from preparing food to serving it. Tempers are short. Some of the men are required to help with the serving, things are not going smoothly. One of the men has been drinking. He stumbles when trying to get more salad. Jim Sullivan moves quickly, taking over the job. The man is insulted at Jim's sudden intervention.

It was over before anyone knew what had happened. The

guy swung at Jim from the side, punching him in the eye, breaking his glasses. The doctor said the eye cannot be saved. A piece of glass has severed the optic nerve, it must be removed immediately.

From his tragedy we are able to see more clearly our participation in the redemption as suffering witnesses. Jim joins with us in the realization that the violence visited upon him is not the sole responsibility of one individual but of a whole system of organized injustice. With this realization Jim's suffering becomes receptive in so far as it shares in Christ's continuous crucifixion on Skid Row. . . . The work continues at the Kitchen.

This incident shows the wider context in which Catholic Workers have come to perceive violence, the men and women who become violent, and the role of nonviolence as participation in something larger than the moment at hand. But it also says something about the willingness needed to disarm one's own heart. The letter continued: "The work goes on at the Kitchen, not without increased trepidation, I might add, but also with a renewed sense of the reality of our work. We have begun to realize that serving the poor involves risk—pray that we might meet the challenge." The challenge spoken of here is not only the risk of attack, but the risk of wanting revenge, of accepting hatred, of acting out the anger one naturally experiences when under attack. Patrick Jordan, a member of the New York Worker during the 1960s and 1970s, remembers Dorothy Day speaking on nonviolence at the house one night. "She said that we have to turn the violence back on *ourselves*, take it into ourselves as Jesus did, rather than turn it on the other." Jordan says it was this attitude "coupled with the forgiveness of one's enemies that Jesus calls for, which gave me a sense of the nature of nonviolence."[10]

Catholic Workers believe that with his recitation of the Beatitudes, and through his passion, death, and resurrection, Christ turned the world upside down, offering not just a new perspective on reality but a new reality itself. It is difficult for the world to hear and understand Christ's command to "love our enemies," and equally difficult for the world to believe that nonviolence is stronger than violence, that love conquers hate, and that the poor should be honored, in Peter Maurin's words, as "the ambassadors of God." Yet it is precisely these principles—so hard to hear without a heart softened by grace—that inform the Catholic Worker approach to nonviolence and hospitality. The Worker generally believes moral behavior should be based on the maximum standards of Christ: the extra mile, the freely offered

246

cloak, the willingly turned left cheek, should be the norm and not the exception. Maurin spelled out this approach in one of his Easy Essays.

To give and not to take,
> That is what makes a person human.

To serve and not to rule,
> That is what makes a person human.

To help and not to crush,
> That is what makes a person human.

To nourish and not to devour,
> That is what makes a person human.

And if need be, to die and not to live,
> That is what makes a person human.[11]

Such an approach is not merely difficult to live out; it is hard to subscribe to in the first place. But the Catholic Worker's emphasis on the mystical body of Christ doctrine makes such an approach to relationships seem possible, and even desirable. Day often said that the truth of the mystical body of Christ was the foundation that undergirded the entire Worker movement. She frequently quoted Clement of Alexandria: "Why do the members of Christ fear one another? Why do we rise up against our own body?"[12] When the mystical body of Christ doctrine is fused with the personalist revolution so that each moment is the revolution and each individual the locus of liberation, the end result is a radical call to live the nonviolent gospel ethic in every moment, in each human encounter. Fritz Eichenberg's 1939 woodcut, "The Christ of the Breadlines," where Christ is shown as a street person standing in a breadline, is a symbol for the entire movement.[13] It plainly and boldly suggests that the one with whom we eat at the soupline tonight is Christ himself.

The practical effect of all this is the attempt to recognize the person of Christ in all who come, transcending traditional categories of adversary and ally. The preferred principle, therefore, is service and suffering love, modeled on the servanthood and humanity of Christ himself. As Day said, "It is because we love Christ in His humanity that we can love our brothers and sisters."[14]

The daily practice of nonviolence follows quite naturally upon this theological lead. At the heart of nonviolence is a similarly deep concern for the well-being of the other. The adversary is not an object to be defeated and vanquished, but a person of inestimable value. As Zack Davisson (a seven-year veteran at Cass House in St.

Louis) observed, "It is important to respect each person's individuality, no matter how bizarre and violent he or she may be."[15] It is the nature of human encounters, especially violent ones, that the health of the adversary is tied to one's own health, physical as well as spiritual. Nonviolence strives for a resolution that will not only maintain the relationship but build it up. A distinctively Christian ethic of nonviolence, like the Catholic Worker's, takes the same encounter and invests it with divine meaning. It becomes a sacramental moment: we meet God, and we are received by God.

The movement's nonviolent posture has been strengthened further by Dorothy Day's incarnational spirituality. Day had an uncommon ability to perceive the extraordinary in the most ordinary everyday activities and encounters.[16] Her keen sense of the sacramental knew no bounds; it included the most violent of experiences. It was liberally sprinkled through most everything she wrote, and this theme became (due to sheer weight of repetition in the New York paper, as well as to Day's rather plain yet compelling theological musings) a dominant interpretive category which those who come to join in the work quickly pick up and adopt. When one approaches each human encounter—whether violent or not so—with the expectation of finding transcendent meaning and food for personal growth, the terms of the encounter are already redefined in a profoundly radical way. Violence no longer need be answered with kneejerk reciprocal violence. Rather, the call to human fulfillment in active love is issued, and a new way is opened up.

The Catholic Worker possesses an added resource in its attempt to live nonviolently with the urban poor: community life. Workers generally live in the same house with guests, and a certain sharing of lives naturally results. In addition, many Worker houses are intentional communities. That is, efforts are made to attend to and nurture life *within* the Worker community itself. Although long-term commitment requirements are usually fluid (given the anarchistic roots of the movement), many communities have expectations of their members in terms of pooling economic resources, emotional sharing, and a common spiritual life. Living in community, with its emphasis on vulnerability in relationship, is understood to be itself an act of resistance to the status quo of violence and rugged individualism that so marks U.S. society. In a fundamental sense, Worker communities are thereby engaged in Maurin's ever-present challenge: to build a new society within the shell of the old.

In keeping with the personalist philosophy, today many Worker houses don't rely on a "leader," or a governing board. These houses eschew majority or one-person rule, and operate instead on consensus decision-making models that depend on principles of nonviolence. Persuasion replaces pressure, discussion supplants voting, and attention to feelings and process avoids adversarial relationships and helps to ensure individual ownership of group decisions. All these various dynamics in community life affect the nonviolent experiment with the guests at these houses: a nonviolent milieu is created within which the larger experiment is nurtured. One Worker noted the dialetical nature of this relationship. "I'm sure the commitment to work together to solve community problems respectfully, carefully, and lovingly influences how we interact with our guests. And hopefully our commitment to treat the guests respectfully, lovingly, and as full human persons also affects the way we deal with one another in the community. I think it is a real reciprocal kind of commitment."[17]

When the Catholic Worker's tenacious commitment to nonviolence is viewed from a purely pragmatic perspective, the results are decidedly mixed. Nonviolence has both worked and not worked, succeeded and failed. It is also worth noting that the Catholic Worker is never overly concerned with the pragmatic results of the experiment. The sacramental nature of human encounters—the ever-present grace mysteriously working in the silence of the human heart—is trusted to redeem even the most miserable of failures on the world's terms. Adolpho Perez Esquivel, the Argentinian who won the Nobel Peace Prize for his practice of nonviolence, refers to this dynamic as "the effectiveness of the ineffective." It is, after all, a world marked by violence that insists on the evaluative categories of winner and loser, victor and vanquished. No such interpretive framework exists within the Catholic Worker, where the nonviolent ethic of Christ is a call to be "perfect as your heavenly Creator is perfect," and where the violent encounter is received as an opportunity to grow in love.[18] Dorothy Day addressed this question repeatedly over the years. Most often her answer went along these lines: "Day after day we accept our failure, but we accept because of our knowledge of the victory of the cross."

A related perspective is offered by former Catholic Worker Ann Marie Fraser, who worked in the New York house in the 1960s. "Does nonviolence *work*? I'm not sure it does and I'm not sure we can be motivated by that question. The *apparent* failures could so demoralize us. But is it *true*? Is it one of the hard teachings of Jesus? If it is, then we can only pray for the grace to try."[19]

Trying has been costly. The history of the Worker movement is full of instances when individual Workers were scarred deeply by their experiences, when their communities failed them, when their support was not enough to stand against the violent tide of society and soupline.[20] As one Worker, a veteran of nine years at the St. Louis house, puts it:

> There have been maybe the most serious failures within the community . . . Workers who came with huge needs and the philosophy of nonviolence couldn't meet them. In fact, they were hurt themselves by trying to take on this philosophy which is so demanding. And sometimes we allowed that, and used them. . . . There is an erroneous idea of nonviolence which says we can take on other people's burdens *but* that ours somehow don't need to be borne. This mistake is magnified at the Worker. By absorbing so much violence, and by taking on the burdens of the guests who are so very needy, our own needs suddenly seem very slight and not worth attending to. So if people come to the Worker without any support system, without knowing who they are, if they have no life outside the Worker and they then want to use the Worker to become perfect, it doesn't work; it is a failure.[21]

Two other Workers wrote: "Can we ignore the daily evidence that broken people living together are as likely to deepen wounds as to heal them?"[22] Similarly, the pages of the *Catholic Agitator*, the monthly tabloid of the Los Angeles house, were marked in 1985 and 1986 with very introspective articles reflecting on the pain *within* the community. Much of it seems to have resulted from an uncommonly hectic pace of life: the crush and crunch of doing the daily works of mercy on a large scale within the violent settings of Los Angeles's Skid Row, without a corresponding degree of attention to the inner spiritual needs of the Workers.

It seems especially important to attend to failures of this sort since so much has been written in praise of the Catholic Worker. The Worker experiment in nonviolence with the victims of institutionalized violence is indeed significant and historic. Much has been learned, and the pacifist witness has been sustained and furthered. But triumphalism must be avoided, for there have been failures all around, in both method and practice. At times, and in certain houses, there has been little more than a groping in the dark. Such is the nature of experiments, especially one as human as this.

Often the failures can be traced to specific causes such as a general lack of preparation of the Workers and volunteers in nonviolent principles and practice, or Workers' attempts to use nonviolence beyond their skills or experience. In addition, trying to serve too many hungry, homeless people at one time in one place creates a critical mass factor that breeds violence. This can be an especially unresponsive

250

situation for nonviolent intervention. In searching for reasons, one can also ask how open members of the movement are to the empowering work of grace in their lives. Responsibility for the failures does not belong to God and cannot be blamed on any unavailability of grace. Foundational Catholic theology has always maintained that grace doesn't work in a vacuum; individuals must be open and willing recipients to the gift of grace, ready to cooperate in faith. It is clear Workers have failed here too.

Whatever the particular reasons behind the failures, the sad result is that people have been hurt, and not only physically. Emotional and psychological wounds have run deep. Some Workers leave angry and embittered, feeling the demands of the experiment are unrealistic. Frequently changes are made as a result. There are numberous examples of communities recommitting themselves to nurturing the spiritual life through retreats and shared prayer, reducing the numbers of guests housed or served on the soupline, or taking some training in nonviolence. But while the failures need attending to, so do the successes and the considerable amount that has been learned about nonviolence through the Catholic Worker experiment.

The Catholic Worker has learned that nonviolence must be rooted primarily in one's own desires, rather than in the knowledge of theories or techniques. Many Workers have experienced firsthand that when they wanted to dominate, to win out over the hostile guest, or to look good, they acted in ways that increased the hostility, whether they intended to do so or not. When they wanted victory, their actions, tone of voice, and general mannerisms tended to make the other person feel like a loser. When their personal defense became the priority, the other felt threatened, even though he or she had initiated the hostility. On the other hand, when their desire was for the safety of the threatening guest—not out of pity or paternalism, but out of an experience of real concern for the person who confronted them—something changed in their own behavior that in turn affected the dynamics of the confrontation. They became more human and less threatening. Often, as Workers felt themselves allowing the threatening person to become human to them, they also experienced the other person's decreased ability to objectify them. The Worker was becoming human to the other. The dynamic was reciprocal.

In these situations Workers began to see how strongly their own desires, as well as their own anger and violence in the form of revenge and the desire for power, can effect the outcome of a hostile encounter. When they armed themselves in attitude or action, they played into the fundamental thrust of violence toward escalation because they increased the possibility of the other person perceiving them as a threat to selfhood. They unintentionally set off the same dynamic that Thomas C. Schelling speaks of in *The Strategy of Conflict.* He uses the example of an armed person confronting a burglar:

> If I go downstairs to investigate a noise at night with a gun in my hand, and find myself face to face with a burglar who has a gun in his hand, there is danger of an outcome that neither of us desires. Even if he prefers just to leave quietly, and I wish him to, there is danger that he may *think* I want to shoot, and shoot first. Worse, there is danger that he may think that I think *he* wants to shoot. And so on. Self-defense is ambiguous when one is only trying to preclude being shot in self-defense.[23]

Rarely in Worker houses is the question one of shooting, but the same dynamic holds true with lesser forms of violence. Our defensiveness heightens the other person's sense of threat. Workers learn how to act in more positive ways that do not press on the assaultive person the need for "self-defense." The experience of a Worker at Holy Family House in Kansas City, Missouri, shows the power of the "victim" to effect the outcome of a hostile encounter.

Late one summer evening in August 1980, Angie O'Gorman was asleep on the third floor of an otherwise empty Catholic Worker house. The house was temporarily closed so repairs could be made and the staff would have time off. Suddenly Angie's bedroom door was kicked open by a man demanding to know who she was and if she lived in the house. She felt totally vulnerable and deeply afraid. There were few alternatives open to her. Screaming would have been useless. The man was not about to let her get up and make a phone call. None of the "usual" reactions seemed viable. Perhaps that is what stimulated her "unusual" reaction—that, and the grace of insight. Angie realized that either she and the man would make it through the encounter safely together, or both of them would be hurt. Whatever the intentions the man might act on, he too would be violated physically or emotionally should his actions lead him to prison. The desire for their mutual safety was a pivotal grace. Angie found herself asking the man, "What time is it?" Her tone was not fearful, not threatening, but her voice conveyed the message that she needed his help, this small piece of information about the time. His response meant that conversation was possible. Another question followed, the conversation continued. Minute by minute, word by word, the hostility of the original encounter was modified. The man spent the night in a room on the second floor of the house and ate breakfast with Angie the next morning. She attributes the positive outcome of this meeting to the fact that she was graced with a sincere concern for the welfare of this man as well as for her own safety. Experiences like this have taught Workers a central truth in nonviolence: what one desires affects how the other person acts.

Through such experiences, Workers come to understand how the dynamic of nonviolence can halt the escalation inherent in violence. They learn that when they react to hostility with further hostility, fear, or paternalism, the violence tends to increase. But when time and skill allow, a new dynamic can be introduced which is geared to the broader personhood of the hostile guest. This new dynamic must be rooted in a firmness edged with compassion; it requires mutual respect and shared responsibility. Workers in threatening situations find they can give the hostile persons new options until they no longer find their initial intent necessary or desirable. An escalation of one disarming action building on another is possible—not inevitable, but possible. That is enough. Something had been learned about the elusive grace we call nonviolence. Such a delicate grace. A grace of immense sensitivity to the relational moment. What works in one situation may cause disaster in the next. It is like a dance; the rhythm is the thing. The steps change according to the partners. Workers learn to be sensitive, light on their toes. They learn to look for the right moment to introduce the next creative step; the proper use of eye contact, the use of touch, body language, tone of voice, gentle humor, respect for personal space, making clear and definite requests of the person, behaving like "neither victims nor executioners."[24]

But the right moment and the right action are not always easily identified. The use of touch, for example, is a very sensitive thing. It is perhaps the one action most likely to be perceived as a potential threat. When to touch, and how firmly, depend on the relational moment. Mary Ann McGivern states, "In times when people are psychotic and threatening, touch helps a whole lot. Not if you reach out and touch them. But if they will reach out and touch you. If they take your hand."[25] She found that when touch seemed appropriate, it was often more calming if she asked the distraught person to hold her hand rather than taking theirs. The step of asking is a clear act of deference to a person's freedom to accept or reject the offer. It gives them a bit more control of the situation without making it necessary to escalate their own violence. It is an active request for more humanity in the exchange. It is also an invitation to trust, predicated on the vulnerability inherent in the asking and in the possible rejection. Several other women have commented on their experiences with hostile guests and the effects of a well-timed, strong handshake, which begins with the Worker extending her hand as an invitation, leaving the guest free to extend a hand or not. There is an element of mutual respect here that is hard for the guest to overlook.

Touching brings into play another critical issue—personal space. Moving uninvited into someone else's space often causes hostility to increase. It can be experienced as an infringement on personal privacy and frequently feels threatening. These feelings seem to be intensified at hospitality houses where so many people have so little that they can call their own. What little they do have—their bodies and the space immediately around them—is often guarded with a keen eye and a short fuse.

Worker Zack Davisson described an incident in which a guest pulled out a knife, was loud and disruptive, and eventually was asked to leave. "What I remember most, is that in order to approach this nonviolently, I couldn't invade his space, I couldn't touch him. I knew if I touched him at all he would have real reason to fight and resist me. I couldn't usher him to the door by taking him by the hand; I knew it wouldn't work, that he would fight back. So I stood my ground and asked him to leave. He slapped the glasses off my face, but I didn't react at all, just tried to stay calm, and eventually he left. . . . A lot of fights and escalations occur when personal space has been violated." Perhaps one of the worst combinations is to shake one's finger in a guest's face; this not only violates their personal space, but challenges their self-respect. Peter Maurin's propensity to make his case with a pronounced pointing of his finger notwithstanding, Zack Davisson relates that the first time he pointed a finger in someone's face he realized the person had lost respect for him immediately. "People will become even more hostile or violent; they won't even listen to you. It is a question of respect."[26]

Respect and the issue of personal space are often difficult to handle when the person involved is disruptive and potentially violent. Some years ago we had a guest at Karen House in St. Louis who happened to be about five months pregnant.[27] She also happened to be loud, angry, and prone to arguments. We repeatedly explained to her that violence was not allowed in the house, and that if problems arose with other guests, please ask a community member to help mediate the dispute.

One Friday afternoon while Pat Coy was on house duty Susan was in the dining room in the middle of a loud three-way argument with two other guests. It was escalating quickly. When Pat arrived on the scene, Susan and another guest were yelling obscenities and flailing at each other with punches, slaps, and scratching. He pushed himself between them, trying to keep them out of striking distance of each other. But each time they calmed down and stopped trying to rush at each other through his outstretched arms, Susan would fly off on the attack again and the predictable cycle of violence readily resumed. Finally, another community member arrived and the two of them kept backing Susan up until they had her out the door and in the hallway. They told her that she would have to leave . . . now. Susan's response: a loud, theatrical refusal which she carried throughout the first floor. But they were equally insistent. She finally headed upstairs toward her room, no longer either openly refusing or agreeing to leave.

Pat eventually followed her upstairs, and in her bedroom doorway he continued to insist on her departure. She warned him not to touch her, which he told her he had no intention of doing at the moment. But when he told her again that she had no choice and would have to leave, she coiled up her short and pregnant body, making ready to deliver her response to his ill-timed ultimatum. Before he knew it, her clinched fist landed directly under his left eye, and she immediately disappeared behind her bedroom door.

What went wrong? When we move uninvited into someone's space by standing too closely or, as Pat did, by pursuing Susan to her bedroom door, hostility is often increased. The question of invitation is especially crucial since it ultimately has to do with mutual respect and control over one's destiny. Perhaps if Pat had asked Susan if he could help her gather her things, her reaction would have been different. The point of her leaving would have been reinforced, but she would have been given a choice, and retained some personal control over her leaving.

There may have been another dynamic present here as well: sexual politics. Would it have made a difference if the Worker dealing with Susan was a woman rather than a man? The question is often asked if the dynamics of nonviolence are affected by the sex, race, or ethnic group of those involved. Does it matter if the guest is a woman and the Worker a man, or vice versa? If one is black and the other white? Workers have learned that these social factors can complicate the dynamics of any interchange if not taken into account when a confrontation is developing. They can be used effectively and made to work for a nonviolent resolution, or, if ignored, an unnecessary escalation of violence may result.

Guests come to Worker houses with the same firmly held, deeply ingrained beliefs that are present in the larger society about what is proper and acceptable behavior for the two sexes. The frustration of economic injustice, of no hope of finding meaningful work, for example, often results in men turning more easily to violence. But even among the most violent-prone and victimized male segments of society, physical force directed at a woman is frequently held in great disdain (the glaring exception here is what is popularly called "domestic" violence, where a man often has a sense of ownership over "his woman"). It is also widely assumed that women will not be violent, or the purveyors of physical force; thus women are generally experienced by men as less physically threatening. Because of these factors, women on Catholic Worker staffs are frequently more effective in dealing with violent situations involving male guests. The women have more freedom and more resources at their disposal. A gentle touch from a woman, intended to make human contact, is most often interpreted in a violent situation as just that. But while the sexual politics of our society have gifted women with touch as a disarming mechanism, touch is less likely to disarm when the volatile interaction is between two men. Indeed, physical touching between men can be quite threatening under the best of circumstances. When a violently charged situation exists, involving a man used to the impersonal norms of life on the streets, any touching, including one man simply placing his hand on another man's arm, can be perceived as a challenge and a threat. What works in one situation may well cause havoc in another.

In Worker houses where community members are of different racial or ethnic groups than the guests, dynamics are added to the sexual politics that also must be taken into consideration. One white male Worker reflected on his experience at a house that served primarily black male guests: "As a man working on the soupline on the men's side [of the house], I don't receive nearly the respect the men give to the women community members. Over the years, I've come to understant it as part of the black culture, part of the fallout from the disintegration of the black family. Many of these men were raised by mothers in single-parent families. The role model of women is much stronger and demands more respect from them. As a man, I'm seen as just one of the guys."[28] Workers come to realize that a variety of racial, ethnic, and cultural considerations must be used in their approaches to intervention.

All these issues—sexual politics, race, and cultural background—relate to the issue of power; what is perceived as power, what is perceived as weakness, and who is perceived as being powerful. Over the years, as part of the fruit of committed experience, Workers have learned that power resides elsewhere than in the barrel of a gun or a steroid-inflated bicep. As Workers speak of their pilgrimage into nonviolence, one senses that the power that is constructive, that builds up rather than tears down, lives primarily in the human heart, in the will, and in a creative, imaginatively engaged mind. It resides in those higher human faculties that have been graciously bestowed on all humanity, occurring and evolving over the millenia. Nonviolence has taught this new, less constricting notion of the nature of power. The truth of the matter may be that women not only have access to such power, they may possess unequal access. As Ann Manganaro puts it, "We have learned that when really belligerent street people come in the house, the women community members are perceived to be less threatening. Our very vulnerability as women makes us more nonthreatening, especially to men, who more easily perceive the male workers as a threat, a rival, a potential adversary. Also, there is a way in which women have a sort of practical training, upbringing, and experience in peacemaking and mediation. That role has most often been the responsibility of women in family situations. . . . Maybe women take it on more naturally, maybe it's because women are more likely to enter a conflict situation without an effort to win."[29]

It may well be that this greater freedom from the desire to win gives women the edge in facilitating disarmament in violent situations. The more liberated a person can become from the need to win, to dominate, the freer she is to base her responses in a desire for the well-being of everyone involved in a crisis situation, to root her actions in the love that the Christian gospel calls for, even of one's enemies. At the same time, however, the effects of these actions are partially dependent on the distraught guest's choice to accept or reject the opportunity not to do harm. In truth, this is a highly vulnerable exchange with consequences for both the Worker and the guest.

No Worker would deny the risk, but neither do Workers want to deny the gospels and such scenes as the arrest of Jesus in the garden of Gethsemane when he let his disciples, his "protection," flee (Mt. 26:36–56). Certainly he could have commanded their immediate return—using guilt if nothing else. But he let them go, leaving himself alone and vulnerable, knowing that each would return only when and if he freely chose to do so. A coerced choice is no choice at all. Sooner or later it will backfire.

In a similar vein, both Peter Maurin and Dorothy Day shared a deep distrust, if not hatred, for coercion. On the positive side, the personalist philosophy of the movement entails a corresponding love for freedom. Human freedom, the graced ability to choose the often harder, more costly path because it is the path of love and reconciliation, is understood to be not only the higher road, but the only road to God and fulfillment. It is no mere coincidence that an aversion to coercion, and a rejection of force that completely cuts off the individual's ability to choose between competing options, mark Christian nonviolence. As Day frequently said, "We try always to love, rather than coerce."[30]

The long-term commitment of the Catholic Worker to live amidst the disenfranchised has cast a particular color on its nonviolent experiment. It is difficult to postulate the effect this solidarity has had in particular encounters with violence. While instances abound where prior personal relationships with guests and a resulting modicum of trust have clearly given Workers an edge in defusing anger and the spiraling cycle of violence, in other cases it has also seemed to make little or no difference. Where the long-term commitment to solidarity with the poor has more clearly mattered is in the Workers themselves. The relationships with the poor are real and not easily dismissed when the Workers know they will wake up in the morning still sharing the house with the same guests, or have to encounter them again tomorrow night, and the night after, on the soupline. For some, this reality has significant effects.

Patrick Jordan, after discussing an incident when a guest held a knife to his throat, and another where he was being strangled, says, "A truth I learned at the Catholic Worker was that I knew I was going to have to keep living with these folks. What a profound effect that has! If I visit violence on them, then they will surely return that violence on the community later on, and probably to an even greater extent. By taking some of that violence, I may prevent future violence . . . these are people God has put us with. We've got to work it out together. If God puts me here, it must be possible. In other words, [we had] a sense of family. In fact, both of these people came back at another time, and in each his own way pardoned himself."[31]

Perhaps more frequent is the experience of guests threatening other guests. Arguments that begin on the street are carried into the house and disrupt the entire community. Verbal fights over missing clothing, a lost place in the soupline, an antagonistic glance from another guest, or just the need to blow off steam, are frequent occurrences. Workers have learned to gauge these situations and sense when they will escalate or simply run their course and die down. Sometimes intervention is needed, and knowing when and how to intervene requires a keen sensitivity. Knowing when not to intervene is as important, and as respectful, as learning when to intervene. The art of intervention, especially when physical blows are being exchanged, is a hard-won skill. There is a range of possibility between the usually held extremes of standing back and allowing someone to be hurt, or rushing headlong into a situation shoving and swinging while verbally threatening the troublemaker. Stories of such encounters in soup kitchens have provided some valuable lessons, and yielded important insights into a theology of intervention.

Tom Lumpkin from Day House in Detroit describes an intervention he made between two men in the soup kitchen. One man, phys-

ically well developed but mentally disturbed, suddenly began screaming at a man next to him, someone he perceived had affronted him. As
he yelled threats of bodily harm and jabbed his finger at the man, Tom
moved between them and tried to maintain a calm and quiet tone of
voice and body posture. Eventually the man threw his bowl of hot
soup across the table and stalked out. This experience caused Tom to
wonder whether his behavior would have changed if the man had
been holding a weapon. The issue is reminiscent of the question
many of us have been asked: "What would you do if an armed person
was attacking your mother?" The assumption in the question is that a
nonviolent response is a nondefensive response, equivalent to no
response at all: a choice to ignore the person being attacked. But
Tom's reflection led him to make a biblical analogy.

> It's not often realized that at one point Jesus was in a com-
> parable situation to the one posed above. Remember the sto-
> ry of the woman caught in adultery? Here's a defenseless
> woman faced with attackers. If they don't actually have
> stones in their hands, they are at least poised and ready to
> carry out that cruel and bloody manner of killing. And what
> does Jesus do? Well, he doesn't refuse to become involved.
> But neither does he pick up his own rocks or organize his
> disciples to attack the attackers. His way is different from
> both cowardly passivity and violent defense. He directly but
> nonviolently intervenes. He places himself, as it were, be-
> tween the defenseless woman and her attackers: "Let the
> one among you without sin cast the first stone." His active
> nonviolence "works" on this occasion: the attackers are dis-
> armed, the woman's life is spared, and Jesus himself escapes
> unharmed.[32]

This story bears more than a symbolic relationship to the dynamics of successful intervention as experienced over the years at a variety of Catholic Worker houses. First of all, it speaks of a willingness
to involve oneself in a personally threatening situation. And the
threat is not solely physical. What if, even after the intervention, the
attacker continues the violence toward the other person and the intervenor is seen as a failure? Worse yet, perhaps nonviolence itself will
be seen as a failure. Or the violence may be turned against the intervenor. Noble efforts do not always receive noble rewards. As one
Worker put it, "There are times when you are going to get burnt."[33]
The choice is difficult and life at the Catholic Worker confronts many
with the risk of this type of involvement. For those who take it, a
wealth of experiential insight is gained.
  In the biblical story about the adulterous woman, some of the

same lessons are echoed. Whatever Jesus actually wrote in the sand, and whatever his actual words were, he introduced a new element into the confrontation between the woman and her attackers. He introduced something new for the attackers to deal with, something that distracted their attention away from the woman. This dissipated, however briefly, the rush of their violent behavior. Why? Simply because they became distracted. It is difficult to maintain one's anger in a focused way when something else is calling for our attention. Psychologically it is difficult for people to maintain cruelty and experience wonder at the same time.

This aspect of distracting the anger seems to arise time and time again in the stories of successful interventions at Worker houses. Sometimes this is done by simply creating distractions through a surprising gesture or statement which redirects a guest's attention away from the object of their anger. Other times this means that a Worker must absorb some of the violent energy which was originally directed elsewhere, hoping it will dissipate through expression. Often as not, this violent energy is expressed verbally, but sometimes physically as well. In describing such a situation in the St. Louis house involving a woman who periodically drew a knife on guests and staff, Ann Manganaro defined her role as "drawing Audrey's attention away from the object of her anger."[34] It had the effect of breaking the rush of the moment's emotions and gave Ann an entry point to defuse the situation.

The anger unleashed in a violent interchange, whether physical or verbal, can often require a more assertive presence. Many Workers have felt it necessary to physically intervene between two guests. Again, in Ann Manganaro's words, "You have to interpose something between their violence toward each other and very often all you have to interpose is yourself." Clearly, great sensitivity is needed. Mary Ann McGivern comments, "The bottom line is placing your body in such a way that another person does not get hurt, but it's how you do it, what you say, what you ask for—and everything is affected by your attitude, your style. I know this much, sometimes it must be done. And it can be done effectively."[35]

Many would question the advisability of physically interpositioning in such situations. Certainly the physical risk to the intervener is increased. There is always the chance that the antagonists will turn on the intervener; a common enemy can unify people who were hostile toward each other only minutes ago. As noted earlier, Workers often enter these types of situations with a past relationship with the people involved. Their immersion in the context of the poor is a type of preparation for such crises. In addition, violence in the house is frequently sufficient cause for a community to put a guest out of the house. Guests know this and are reluctant to risk being put back on the street. The mixture of these factors reduces the Workers' risk of being turned against physically.

Workers have learned how to intervene so that their presence is felt, but not felt as an added threat that must be defended against. They have learned how to get the attention of guests who are fighting. This is the first, and often most difficult, task. When people are angrily fighting with one another it can take some patience and gently assertive insistence before the intervenor's presence is felt and must be reckoned with. At this point it can be hostily rejected, challenged, questioned, or accepted as a relief in an otherwise threatening situation.

What have Workers learned to watch out for while intervening? Not to take sides, not even with one's body. In an intervention this means standing in an objective position, no matter how close to the fight the intervenor has had to move. It means not taking up one person's arguments against the other, but acting with calmness and control: talking and listening to each side without judgment.

Frequently, the best one can hope for in an intervention is that the cycle of violence is broken long enough for those involved to regain some control. An intervention is not a long-term solution, and Workers have learned not to expect too much from their momentary successes. Intervention is a response to the effects of human brokenness, but usually does not affect the brokenness itself. It is simply a chance for people to catch their breath, to regain personal control, and Workers have tried to use this pause as creatively as possible to prevent a further flare-up of the hostility.

An interesting example of this took place at Holy Family House in Kansas City. Late one evening, close to midnight, Angie O'Gorman looked out her third-floor window to see one man holding another down on his knees while slamming his head into the bumper of a parked car. It was clear that the man would be killed if someone did not intervene. Angie went down to the street, noisily approached the two men in order to get their attention and not surprise them, and blocked the next attempt to beat the man's head down onto the bumper of the car. When the man doing the slamming began to turn his anger toward her, she called his attention to the house from which she had come and commented, "I have kids in that house and you are scaring them. They can't get to sleep. Besides, don't you think you have already made your point?" The man agreed that he had, but what really affected him was the knowledge that he had been scaring the children so much. He began talking about the children's fear. In the meantime the other man crawled away and Angie continued talking with the attacker until he calmed down. During their conversation afterward, he explained why he had beaten the other man. "He has been mistreating a prostitute and someone had to teach him a lesson."

There is a lesson wrapped in the lesson. Though Catholic Workers may not agree with the manner in which this man chose to make his point, it was a clear attempt on his part to defend someone else. His goal was admirable even if his means were unacceptable. The lesson takes us back to the biblical story in which Jesus refrained from passing judgment on the individuals confronting the woman; there was no accusing, no taking sides in the sense of one over the other. Apparently, there was a clear message about behavior, but the persons themselves were not discredited. In case after case, Workers have learned that to intervene does not mean to take sides, to judge, to pronounce right or wrong. Perhaps later, after the tensions are calmed and people are more free to be objective, there will come a time to evaluate responsibility with those involved. But in the heat of the moment, accusation, taking sides, and blaming only fan the flames and force the persons being blamed into a more defensive position, blocking their ability to disarm. Comments one Worker, "It's crucial to listen to their reason for their behavior; don't close them out, don't move to a judgment decision."[36]

The implications of this are not to be taken lightly. Workers learn that they must be able to put aside not only their personal anger in such situations, but also their own fear. There is not always the willingness or ability to do this. "Sometimes," states a Worker from the St. Louis house, "we lose it, give in to our anger and begin accusing, when what is really needed is a commitment to listening to the frustration on all sides, to understanding and helping the persons know they are heard. That can help to defuse a situation. But it is hard to keep cool in the middle of other people's anger. I don't think I've ever been able to do it except as a kind of grace."[37]

If it is a grace to put one's anger aside for the good of someone else, it is an especially precious grace to do the same with one's fear. And yet, this too seems to be a requirement for successful interventions within the Catholic Worker houses, souplines, and daily dealings with the people of the street. Perhaps the most vivid statement of this dimension of intervening was described by Ann Manganaro. "A lot of it is laying aside your own fear. If you bring your own fear into the situation you may add fuel to the fire. But if you can lay aside your own fear then there is a physical peace which you can bring into a situation that is felt just as a person's anger is felt. If what you bring is fear or anger, you may be stirring the waters instead of calming them. You may be complicating the situation."[38]

Where does this ability to stay calm come from? Two responses prevail. The first is simply the belief that it is possible. It has been done before and the experience has been told and retold, as oral history, throughout Worker houses in a way that bolsters belief and strengthens the ability to risk. The second source is grace. The grace of the moment. The grace of spontaneous prayer. The grace of living with the poor, of coming to know one's own self in the midst of human brokenness and violence. The grace of learning to disarm the self and thus gain insight into disarming others. Workers learn that if they make themselves available and vulnerable to this grace, it is there to be used. Jeff Dietrich, writing from the Los Angeles house on Skid Row, offers an illustration.

> Ron is standing next to me, an empty green wine bottle clenched in his fist like a hand grenade ready to explode into a million shards of glass shrapnel. Adrenaline surges through my body like a narcotic, reducing arms and legs to the consistency of overcooked pasta. Terror grips me as Ron's enormous six-foot-two-inch bulk looms overhead. His neck muscles tighten like knotted steel and great gobs of saliva fly from his mouth as he hurls obscenities at me. It is at those moments of terror that I have learned the power of prayer, quick and furtive and repetitious: "Lord, deliver us from evil; Lord, deliver us from evil; Lord, deliver us from evil"; anesthesizing the brain, lowering the pulse rate, stiffening the rubbery limbs—prayer under fire, prayer in the trenches, practical prayer that reaches down to a place of strength that is beyond the fear. Pretend that no one can hear the pounding of your heart or smell the stink of your sweat. Get your voice under control, slowly reach out your hand. Now I hear my voice speaking calmly with all the bluff and bravado of an animal trainer, pretending a calm that I do not feel, knowing that any hint of fear on my part will surely invite disaster.
>
> "Ron, give me the bottle and I'll bring you a tray of food. Now go on outside and eat. You're too agitated to eat in here today."
>
> "O.K., punk, but be quick about it," he says, handing me the bottle.

The value and profundity of these lessons is more easily understood when one compares the Catholic Worker's successful experiences of disarming and calming with the history of the standard approach to similar situations. Only more recently have law enforcement officers and others realized that while "tough is fun," more human qualities yield better results. Dietrich continues his reflection:

> This is not the first time that Ron has terrorized us, and once after an epic struggle, we banned him for an entire year. I used to think that our method of dealing with terrorism— prayer and nonviolence—was hopelessly idealistic and impractical. Until I heard that a security guard in a similar Skid Row institution was murdered with his own gun after a struggle with an irate client. So much for the use of force.[39]

In many ways the skills of intervening and the skills of working one to one with a violent person overlap a great deal. Different skills are emphasized in different situations, but there is a clear continuum from being in touch with our own desires, anger, and fear to knowing what voice tone and what eye contact is most helpful, to basic good communication and negotiating skills. All require the tender sensitivity that produces the right timing, the correct choice of word and action, and the appropriate balance of firmness and flexibility. It is a quality of awareness that seems to be a byproduct of life at a Catholic Worker house. Is this a form of spiritual hype? Not if one goes by the lived experience of nonviolence meeting violence at Worker houses. There is a dynamic at work in some of these encounters that brings many a Worker to a far greater understanding and ability to implement a disarming exchange than either the police or our national security advisers have yet to realize.

Despite Workers' best intentions, however, their actions can be mistaken or misperceived by a distraught guest as threatening or demeaning, as in the case of Jim Sullivan of the Los Angeles house mentioned earlier. In Jim's situation there was no time to alter his offending action of intervening and getting the guest's food for him. In other situations, when time has allowed, Workers have found rather common-sense ways to recover ground lost because of an inopportune word or action. One woman, realizing that placing her hand on a guest's shoulder had triggered strong hostilities, recovered by simply apologizing, without defending herself. The honest apology derailed the hostility that had built up in seconds within the guest. On other occasions, it seems that nothing the Worker did could lessen the movement toward violence or altered the guest's intention to disrupt.

The genuinely feared situation of hostile guests refusing to leave a hospitality house has presented some of the most difficult encounters between staff and guests. It has at times caused Workers to seek outside help. There exists a much-repeated myth in the secondary literature on the movement: the notion that the Catholic Worker *never* calls the police for help with unruly guests. It simply is, not true at most houses, and in the Day era in New York there were occasions, albeit rare ones, when the police were called. In general, it is true that calling on the police is avoided if at all possible; it is nearly universally seen as the court of last resort.[40]

A good example of Catholic Workers turning reluctantly to this court of last resort occurred at Karen House in St. Louis. Two young black women, twins, both suffering from emotional problems and deeply angry with the costs of racism, had been an ongoing source of trouble in the house. After one of them pushed an elderly member of the community, they were asked to leave by 3:00 P.M. that same day. Pat Coy was on house duty as the hour drew near and found himself in the small nine-by-twelve office with the two very angry, agitated women. At first they confined their violent reactions to the decision by hurling loud, incessant, racial slurs at Pat, who responded in large part with silence and internal prayer. But they gradually escalated to tearing things off the walls, throwing them out into the hallway, and sweeping other items off the desktop and onto the floor. All this was accompanied by very personal verbal threats to Pat's safety and promises of arson. His attempts to acknowledge their anger while still holding firm to the decision that they would have to leave were shouted down with violent, racial epithets. At that point he told them that 3:00 P.M. was too far off and they would have to leave immediately. One responded by setting fire to the wastebasket to "show you honkies we mean business." A few minutes later the other sister held her lighted cigarette to Pat's ankle as he reached to open a drawer. No matter what approach he tried, he was unable to pierce through their armor of anger. They steadfastly refused to leave, insisting that Pat could not make them go and daring him to touch them, to try to physically force them out. Feeling exasperated, with no hope of resolution as neither patience nor silence nor reason nor prayer had helped to defuse the situation, he reached for the desk phone to call the police. One of the twins grabbed the wall cord and yanked the phone out of his reach. This cat-and-mouse game was replayed a number of times with the twins insisting that "no black cop would force them to leave anyway," and daring Pat to try again for the phone, "so we can strangle your white bastard neck with the cord."

Another community member, Ann, walked into the office and Pat explained the situation to her. As they talked, the twins moved away from the phone, so Pat slowly but deliberately began to dial again. One of the twins grabbed for the phone. Ann, not fully aware of the level of violence in the room, put her hand on the guest's arm to stop her. That was all that was needed to trigger more violence. The twin imbedded her fingernails in Ann's forearm and tore upward to her elbow. Sensing the potential for an even greater escalation, Ann left to call the police from the community's phone line upstairs while Pat stayed with the two women. He was finally able to convince them that their departure was inevitable, and imminent, and they had best start gathering their belongings before they lost them as well. When the police arrived the twins were ready to leave and there was no further disruption.

In this instance, the court of last resort was the only court. All means of persuasion, reason, and patience had failed in moving the twins on. Those tactics had kept the violence on a manageable scale, but were unsuccessful in hastening the departure of the twins. Pat had even tried to defuse the situation by absorbing considerable amounts of verbal, emotional, and physical violence, hoping it would simply run itself out after not encountering the hoped-for and more natural resistance. That too failed to bring the desired result. When Ann reached for the arm of the twin, the response she received demonstrated that physical force was a poor option as well. It beget more force, more violence. However inevitable, the decision to call in the police is quite problematical for those trying to be true to their belief in the ultimate power of love and nonviolence.

The recourse to armed coercion violates the word and spirit of the Catholic Worker ethic in a way that only outright violence by a Worker could equal. If you don't allow weapons in a house, how can you invite an armed police officer in? If you don't believe in coercion, how can you insist that guests leave by force? For that matter, how can you insist they leave at all? These are blatant contradictions. They are also dilemmas for which there are no easy answers. Perhaps Workers do not yet have the depth or breadth of skills in nonviolence to match many of the hostile scenarios that confront them in Houses of Hospitality. Is the answer to give up the ethic? No, it is to live in the dilemma until further insight breaks through. Workers grope along in daily experiments, fully aware that the insights—like the reign of God—are here, but not yet. In the meantime, Workers struggle to face the dilemmas with as much faithfulness as possible. Thus, at one house, after an incident in which police were called and abused a guest in the process of removing him from the house, a Worker now escorts police whenever police presence is needed. In some houses, when the police become too physical, they are asked to leave. These are steps, however imperfect, toward living faithfully within a dilemma until nonviolence can develop a greater capacity to alter violent situations, or protect bystanders should violence occur. In this way Workers give witness, often in front of the guests, that they are trying to be consistent, asking nothing more of the guest than they would ask of themselves, or even of the police. Guests learn that a Worker will step in to protect a guest, an important experience for people who have often been told by our society that they are worthless.

All in all, when one considers the vast numbers of guests who go in and out of the doors of hospitality houses, the incidents of violence are remarkably limited. That in itself is a credit to the women and men who put nonviolence to work in a preventive way. While the often chaotic nature of Catholic Worker living can create a volatile atmosphere, other dynamics inherent in the commitment to nonviolence tend to create an infrastructure of safety and support for the people who come to the houses. The lack of competitiveness in the houses, for example, seems to have a calming, reassuring effect on many guests used to competing for survival on the streets. The need for cooperation in order to survive tends to bring out a cooperative spirit in people, even though a periodic rebellion may occur.

The reliance on guests to contribute their talents to the house, whether it be in the form of cooking or giving an opinion as to what color the wall should be painted, or how best to approach a new guest, tends to remind guests of a long-forgotten truth—they have something of value to contribute that others need. All of us like to be needed. For the desolate and alone, it can be the difference between hope and despair. One house newsletter relates a comment by a guest who now works in the soupline: "One Sunday morning Gary told me, 'You have to work in here.' I said, 'Nope, you've got to be kidding! . . .' But then one Thursday, Bill said, 'Ron, I can't handle this mess no more,' so I said, 'O.K., I'll come.' There were six hundred people that day. Been here ever since."[41] For all of us the sense of being needed and valued, the sense of belonging, of being a part of something larger than ourselves, bolsters our self-image and reduces hostility. It is no different for the women and men who come seeking sustenance at a Worker house. By channeling these normal needs toward situations of fulfillment, the Worker environment has defused much of the pent-up anger in the guests.

IN THE HISTORY of the United States, no other nonviolent group, movement, or organization has experimented with the daily living out of the nonviolent ideal to the extent the Catholic Worker movement has in its hospitality houses. While organizations like the War Resisters League, the Fellowship of Reconciliation, and the American Friends Service Committee have maintained a commitment to nonviolence over time, their experiments have been largely confined to direct-action tactics as a means for social and political change. But every day for fifty-four years, in hospitality houses around the country, Catholic Workers have carried the light of nonviolence into the dark, violent inner cities of the United States.

Often the flame has flickered, threatened by the rushing wind of street violence. But for these nonviolent followers of Jesus Christ, the resurrection and the rising sun bring a new day. The works of mercy must go on: the same soupline that erupted in violence yesterday must be served again today. A new experiment calls, and to it, the individual Worker brings not merely the theoretical knowlege often so highly prized in other parts of the peace movement, but the concrete wisdom gained in the throes of yesterday's eruption. Nonviolence has often illuminated violent situations, providing a means of resolution, revealing a doorway leading away from violence and harm. All this, the successes and the failures in houses far and wide, becomes the collected wisdom of the Catholic Worker movement in matters nonviolent.

The pilgrimage into nonviolence, Catholic Worker style, is really nothing more or less than the gospel of Christ applied to the human reality of poverty, anger, and human brokenness. Through this pilgrimage Workers learn that nonviolence is not simply a technique but a relational dynamic based on gospel love. In the Catholic Worker movement, that dynamic is the gospel applied in every human encounter. Gospel nonviolence is not merely a desire for harmony but a new way of perceiving the meaning behind hostility and violence, whether the source of threat be a guest or a co-worker. It is a relationship in which one can offer to others who want to harm the chance to change their mind. It is possible to create, through word and action, a relational bond that allows a person to choose differently, knowing all the while that to force the choice is impossible. Catholic Workers learn to remain present and vulnerable until the choice is made—one way or another. Disarmament occurs when the will to harm has been disarmed; this change of heart cannot be forced, but only nurtured. Such is the nature of conversion. This disarmament is something violence can never achieve, either on a personal or international level. Violence tends to arm. Even when it causes defeat, violence arms.

Nonviolence *can* disarm, but that does not mean it always will. Freedom to choose is present and thus a choice to harm is possible.

People do not always choose as we wish them to (the same dilemma God faces with each of us), and so Workers learn that nonviolence also calls for personal sacrifice. It calls for a willingness to place oneself physically between a victim and an assailant, for discipline, hard work, plain common sense, compassion, humor, and always an intense openness to be surprised. For fifty-four years, the pilgrimage into nonviolence has called Workers to immerse themselves in the struggle to forgive, the struggle to exchange the possibilities of revenge for the hope of gospel reconciliation.

This chapter offers a brief and limited view of a much wider range of material. The Catholic Worker would do a great service to the study of nonviolence if it would gather the invaluable oral history of the practice of nonviolence that has accumulated from living with the disenfranchised of our society since 1933. While the peace movement and the larger society may have failed to recognize the fruits of this Catholic Worker experiment, it may be that the Worker has also failed to see the treasure it holds in its collective memory. Countless stories remain unrecorded, their lessons hidden from a world apparently convinced that there are few, if any, alternatives to violence.

A great debt is owed to the Catholic Worker movement, not only because of what it has taught us about justice and peace, but because it provided a context for a living dialogue between violence and nonviolence. The dialogue continues and if we are smart, we will keep on listening. Fifty-four years may have given us only the first few words.

NOTES

Note: The *Catholic Worker* is here cited as *CW*.

1. In an address entitled "Conscience and Catholic Pacifism," delivered at Saint Louis University, October 9, 1984.
2. Quoted in Daniel Maguire, *The Moral Choice* (New York: Winston, 1978), 119 n. 126.
3. Interview by Patrick Coy, St. Louis, April 8, 1985.
4. Ibid.
5. Interviews by Patrick Coy, St. Louis, April 29 and 8, 1985.
6. Interview of Robert Ellsberg by Deane Mowrer, New York, September 9, 1980. Dorothy Day–Catholic Worker Collection, Memorial Library Archives, Marquette University, Milwaukee (hereafter cited as "CW Papers").
7. Dorothy Day, *By Little and by Little: The Selected Writings of Dorothy Day*, ed. Robert Ellsberg (New York: Alfred A. Knopf, 1983), 263–64.
8. Quoted in "Occasional Letter" No. 4, September 1969, Dorothy Day to Nina Polcyn, CW Papers.
9. "Our Country Passes from Undeclared to Declared War," *CW*, January 1942: 1. See also "Fools for Christ's Sake," *CW*, October 1939: 4.

10.   Letter from Ammon Hennacy House of Hospitality (Los Angeles) to Supporters, September 1972, p. 2, CW Papers; Letter from Patrick Jordan, New York, to Angie O'Gorman, March 7, 1984.

11.   Reprinted in *The Round Table,* Fall 1980: 1. In the reprint, the language has been made inclusive.

12.   Quoted in Mel Piehl, *Breaking Bread: The Catholic Worker and the Origins of Catholic Radicalism in America* (Philadelphia: Temple University Press, 1982), 87.

13.   Letter from Peggy Scherrer, New York, to Patrick Coy, February 15, 1985. Scherrer, a former managing editor of the *Catholic Worker,* argues that this woodcut is closer to being "the symbol of the movement" than any other.

14.   Dorothy Day, "The Humanity of Christ," *CW,* June 1935: 4.

15.   Interview by Patrick Coy, St. Louis, April 18, 1985.

16.   Day, *By Little and By Little,* XXV; see also Patrick Coy, "The Incarnational Spirituality of Dorothy Day," *Spirituality Today,* Summer 1987.

17.   Interview with Ann Manganaro by Patrick Coy, St. Louis, April 8, 1985. For the most complete discussion of consensus decision-making and its role in nonviolent movements for social change, see Virginia Coover et al., *Resource Manual for a Living Revolution,* (Philadelphia: New Society Publishers, 1977).

18.   Adolpho Perez Esquivel, *Christ in a Poncho,* ed. Charles Antoine (Maryknoll, N.Y.: Orbis, 1983). Tom Lumpkin, "Nonviolent Intervention," *On The Edge,* Spring 1984: 3 (*On The Edge* is the quarterly newspaper of the Detroit Catholic Worker); see also "Security," *CW,* July–August 1935: 4.

19.   Letter from Ann Marie Fraser, New York, to Angie O'Gorman, March 17, 1984.

20.   Letter from Patrick Jordan, New York, to Angie O'Gorman, March 17, 1984.

21.   Interview with Mary Ann McGivern by Patrick Coy, St. Louis, April 8, 1985.

22.   Virginia Druhe and Michael McIntyre, "The Worker: A Tradition in Contradiction," *The Round Table,* Summer 1984: 10. (*The Round Table* is the journal of Catholic Worker life and thought in St. Louis. Published in 8½ × 11 inch format, this 24-page quarterly journal is available free by writing to Karen Catholic Worker House, 1840 Hogan, St. Louis, MO 63106).

23.   Quoted in John G. Stoessinger, *The Might of Nations* (New York: Random House, 1982), 205, 206.

24.   The phrase is from the title of Albert Camus's classic essay on nonviolence, recently reprinted; Camus, *Neither Victims nor Executioners* (Philadelphia: New Society Publishers, 1986).

25.   Interview by Patrick Coy, St. Louis, April 29, 1985.

26.   Interview of Zack Davisson by Patrick Coy, St. Louis, April 18, 1985.

27.   Incident reported by Patrick Coy in "A Nonviolent Pilgrimage," *The Round Table,* Autumn 1986: 8–9.

28.   Interview of Zack Davisson.

29.   Interview by Patrick Coy, St. Louis, April 8, 1985. For more material on male/female differences in personality and moral development, see the

seminal work by Carol Gilligan, *In a Different Voice* (Cambridge: Harvard University Press, 1982), 30–49 especially.

30. Dorothy Day, "Fall Appeal," *CW*, November 1957: 2. William Miller, *A Harsh and Dreadful Love: Dorothy Day and the Catholic Worker Movement*, (New York: Liveright, 1973), 10–11; Piehl, *Breaking Bread*, 97–98. For a particularly insightful treatment of the role of coercion in Christian nonviolence, see William Robert Miller, *Nonviolence: A Christian Interpretation* (New York: Schocken, 1966), 37–40.

31. Letter from Patrick Jordan, New York, to Angie O'Gorman, March 7, 1984.

32. Tom Lumpkin, "Nonviolent Intervention", 3.

33. Interview of Zack Davisson.

34. Interview by Patrick Coy, St. Louis, April 8, 1985.

35. Interviews, April 8 and 29, 1985.

36. Interview of Zack Davisson.

37. Interview of Ann Manganaro.

38. Ibid.

39. Jeff Dietrich, "The Roots of Terrorism," *Catholic Agitator*, May 1986: 5.

40. Ammon Hennacy, *The Book of Ammon* (n.p., 1965), 317. This view was the consensus of about twenty-five Catholic Workers from the United States and Canada who attended Patrick Coy's workshop on "Houses of Hospitality and Nonviolence" at the International Catholic Worker Gathering in Milwaukee in June 1986. Tape of workshop at CW Papers.

41. Ron Moriconi, quoted by Marianne Arbogast, "An Abundance of Gifts," *On The Edge*, Spring 1984: 4.

9. War Resistance and Property Destruction

The Catonsville Nine Draft Board Raid and Catholic Worker Pacifism

Anne Klejment

In October 1968, veteran peace activist Dorothy Day traveled from her home at the Catholic Worker in New York City to Baltimore. Seventy years old and frail, she journeyed there to support a group of Catholic war resisters, the Catonsville Nine, who had five months earlier seized and burned draft files from a Selective Service office in a suburb of Baltimore.

Her support for the nine grew out of her lifelong work for Christian social revolution by nonviolent means. For many years the co-founder of the Catholic Worker movement had suffered the rebukes of powerful bishops and common laborers for her uncompromising pacifism. As one of a few American Catholic pacifists, she often aided Catholics who were defying draft laws or simply seeking conscientious objector status. During the 1930s her movement had been the cradle of Catholic pacifism in the United States, and since then the most significant new Catholic peace groups developed from

272

it.[1] Some of the Catonsville raiders traced their antiwar sensibilities back to the Catholic Worker's pioneering pacifism.

For the most part, the pacifism of the Catholic Worker movement and the groups it inspired developed on an ad hoc basis, meeting new needs as they arose. The movement, of course, adhered to the gospel command to love God, neighbor, and self, and it interpreted Christ's message literally as an endorsement of absolute nonviolence. At the Catholic Worker, individual conversion rather than group coercion nurtured a communitarian commitment to love God and one's neighbor. "We can only show our love for God by our love for our fellows," Dorothy Day insisted.[2] Without love of neighbor, Christianity merely institutionalized hypocrisy. Love for others, a central belief at the Catholic Worker, was well illustrated by the movement's opposition to war.

After her conversion to Catholicism, Day, who once espoused secular radicalism, rejected class conflict and the use of violent means to promote social change. During the 1930s, in response to fascism, imperialism, and industrial capitalism, Day began to recommend the exclusive use of powerful nonviolent tools, such as prayer, fasting, picketing, and noncooperation with evil. She judged protest actions in part by how they addressed opponents. Her opponents were neighbors, "poor and oppressed," and she considered them protected by the commandment of love. A Christian radical tinged with progressivism, Day even wished to educate the oppressors—"but not by clubs," which compromised absolute gospel nonviolence.[3] Furthermore, her version of the Christian revolution would change structures rather than dole out piecemeal protection for the needy. Her refusal of violence was not acquiescence in the status quo, for she believed that nonviolence, voluntarily embraced and rooted in Christian spirituality, would lead to a new order.

History had taught her that conflicts resolved by force begat force. This painful lesson also proved to her that when Christians abandoned their spiritual shields to adopt the enemy's choice of arms, they automatically suffered moral death. By using violence, they behaved like pagans, thus limiting their access to grace. She believed that the Christian code of behavior, found in the law of love, required moral purity, not victory.[4] And her Christian faith prepared her for the reality that the just cause might not triumph on earth.

By the time the administration of Franklin D. Roosevelt plunged into preparations for World War II in 1939, the Catholic Worker had already begun to define and justify its pacifist position, a weighty task given the American Catholic church's usual wartime chauvinism. The Worker also initiated a modest program of resistance and developed the scriptural and theological foundations for its pacifism during this time of national peril. Even the horrors of the Holocaust, with which Dorothy Day was familiar, did not draw her from non-violence. She supported neutrality toward all nations—*not* neutrality on moral issues—and openly urged and practiced non-cooperation with the national military defense effort.[5]

Emerging from this period of testing, the Catholic Worker movement began to regain supporters lost during the 1940s, and houses of hospitality were built in many cities to replace those that had closed.[6] Vigilance against potential nuclear holocaust, unwittingly promoted by government civil defense drills, catalyzed radical pacifists of the cold war era, including many at the Catholic Worker. Dorothy Day and her colleagues received jail sentences several times for their acts of civil disobedience each year. Overall, however, the Catholic Worker exerted a limited influence on the larger Catholic population during the 1950s, especially on the peace issue.

Throughout the 1960s, the pages of the *Catholic Worker* were filled with reports on nonviolence, theological discussions about pacifism, news from the Vatican Council on the church's attitudes toward modern warfare, and accounts of opposition to the Vietnam war.[7] Many Catholic war resisters took their inspiration from the Catholic Worker movement. These individuals used direct action tactics like draft refusal, war-tax resistance, and draft card destruction to express their outrage over the Vietnam war. As radicals in search of a new social and political order, they committed acts of civil disobedience to emphasize their refusal to cooperate with the liberal capitalist order. Thomas C. Cornell and James H. Forest, who staffed the Catholic Peace Fellowship, had close ties to the movement, as did Christopher Kearns and David Miller, who were at the Catholic Worker in 1965. As the draft resistance against Vietnam accelerated, Kearns and Miller received national media coverage when they burned their draft cards. Kearns's act, captured in a *Life* magazine photograph, enraged Representative L. Mendel Rivers, who sponsored an amendment to the Selective Service Act to punish those who damaged their cards. Miller was the first young man to receive a jail term for his open violation of this act.

The appeal of Catholic Worker pacifism expanded with the Vietnam war. During the 1960s the chance convergence of demography, social mobility, and theological renewal in the American Catholic community—and the controversial war—encouraged greater Catholic participation in antiwar protests.[8] But while the Catholic Worker's significance to and acceptance by American Catholics increased, only a few Catholic peace seekers adopted Dorothy Day's radical Christian pacifism.

The Catholic Worker and the Berrigans

Among those who had never lived at the Catholic Worker but who were nonetheless influenced by its resistance to war were the two priest-brothers in the Catonsville Nine raid, Daniel and Philip Berrigan. Born into a working-class family on the rugged Iron Range of northern Minnesota during the early 1920s, the two youngest of Thomas and Frida Fromhart Berrigan's six sons showed no signs of pacifism in their youth. Most of their family experiences shaped them into fairly conventional pious Catholics.[9] Yet, though the family appeared to be typically Catholic, they nevertheless subscribed to Dorothy Day's radical monthly, the *Catholic Worker*.

The family was attracted to the paper by its position on unionism, not pacifism. When World War II broke out, the four draft-eligible sons, including the youngest, Philip, marched away to fight for God and country.[10] Daniel Berrigan, then sequestered in seminary, prayed, studied, published his poetry, and feted the surrender of Japan after the bombing of Hiroshima and Nagasaki. He had been exposed to the writings of John C. Ford, S.J., an early critic of obliteration bombing during World War II, but initially the young Jesuit showed little concern with pacifism. In fact, during the cold war, he worked temporarily as a military chaplain while in Germany. For a time Philip Berrigan accepted the cold war as inevitable. Like many other American Catholics of the 1950s, he deplored the atheism and materialism reputedly exported by the Soviet Union.

Their reading of the *Catholic Worker* eventually enabled Daniel and Philip Berrigan to reexamine their conventional assumptions about the cold war. Although they were already familiar with Thomas Merton's spirituality, they now read his more controversial writings on peace in the *Catholic Worker*, one of the few places where Catholics could challenge the conventional wisdom of the nuclear age. Merton, in an article published in 1961, shattered the idealistic pretensions of America's cold warriors. He convinced Philip Berrigan, a Josephite priest who ministered to southern blacks, of the systemic nature of violence in the United States and of the symbiotic relationship between the cold war and domestic racism. Merton's writing suggested that one could eradicate racism only by challenging cold war assumptions. The Berrigan brothers used Merton's ideas to justify their plunge into peace activism.[11]

The extent to which the Catholic Worker influenced the Berrigans is not clear. However, during the 1960s the brothers' activities complemented the ideals of the movement. Advocate of Catholic Workers–style voluntary poverty, Philip Berrigan relished the spartan existence of the Josephite missionaries in the South. His brother

Daniel practiced and recommended poverty and communal living to students at his experimental International House on the campus of LeMoyne College in Syracuse, New York. Daniel's poetry showed a clear appreciation of Catholic Worker spiritual values. *The World for Wedding Ring* honored three Catholic Worker friends: Dorothy Day, Tony Walsh, founder of a house of hospitality in Montreal, and Karl Meyer, a young convert who founded a Catholic Worker house in Chicago and who had corresponded with him about peace issues. A unifying theme of the poems, the presence of Christ in all people, echoed the Catholic Worker's similar concern for the members of the mystical body of Christ. When Daniel Berrigan received a transfer to New York City in 1964 to help edit *Jesuit Missions*, he naturally gravitated to the Catholic Worker, where he offered occasional services as an unofficial chaplain.[12] Increasingly, he became identified with the visible Catholic protest against the Vietnam war. By 1965, Philip Berrigan, too, devoted much of his energy to the peace movement, despite the open displeasure of his religious superiors.

Thus, the Berrigans had well-established connections to the Catholic Worker and to the Catholic peace movement. Throughout the decade the Berrigans had written feature articles in Dorothy Day's paper. Both priests had condemned the war in the pages of the *Catholic Worker*, and their analysis of American involvement abroad reflected a radical Christian perspective similar to the Worker's.[13] And Daniel Berrigan had grown close to some of those active in the Catholic Worker peace witness.

A turning point for the brothers came in 1968, when Philip Berrigan recruited Daniel Berrigan into the ultraresistance, a new tendency within the antiwar coalition that advocated the destruction of war-related property largely by persons ineligible for the draft. The priests felt that they had personally exhausted liberal means of protest. They had spoken, marched, picketed, petitioned, organized, prayed, trespassed, and been arrested on behalf of peace in Vietnam. When they realized that their efforts were not stopping the war, they turned toward more radical means of protest. This shift from respectable protest to antiestablishment resistance drew them closer to the direct action radicalism advocated by Catholic Worker pacifists.

On May 17, 1968, Daniel Berrigan joined his brother and seven others in an act of ultraresistance: the Catonsville Nine draft board raid. First, they liberated about four hundred folders from a Selective Service office, drenched them with homemade napalm in an adjoining parking lot, then set them on fire. While the papers crackled, the protesters joined in prayer. They aimed to awaken other Americans to the immorality of the Vietnam war.

This action was probably more successful in generating publicity, focusing attention on Christian social conscience, and mobilizing concern than the fifty similar ones that followed it. Rallies, speeches, interviews, a rock festival, theatre, film, and art works, and an outpouring of poems, articles, and books addressed the issues raised by the nine. Neither by force nor by ballots, but rather by appeals to conscience and culture did the Catonsville raiders intend to foment revolution.[14] For Philip Berrigan, who convinced the group of its value, property destruction was hardly an innovative tactic. Harkening back to the example of the Boston Tea Party, he viewed the raid as another action in the American revolutionary tradition. The Catonsville Nine believed that they were acting nonviolently when they burned government records. They had not physically harmed anyone. It was a justifiable protest because by damaging the files they detained and prevented eligible men from a rendezvous with military destiny in Vietnam. The raiders therefore thought they were protecting Asian and American lives. The war did not end and American soldiers and Vietnamese people still were dying, but the protest served nonviolent ends and was accomplished by nonviolent means. It spoke of a heightened moral outrage over the contribution of the United States to death and destruction throughout Southeast Asia.

The controversial Catonsville Nine raid won mixed reviews. Traditionalists were troubled because the raid shattered their image of the church as a haven for law-abiding and respectable citizens. Liberal Catholics, often sympathetic to wider social awareness on the church's part, did not always agree that under extraordinary conditions government property might be destroyed to serve the common good. Even radical Catholics occasionally criticized the raiders' definitions of nonviolence or civil disobedience, their male leadership, or the apparent ineffectiveness of the raids. Admirers praised the prophetic message of the Berrigans. These priests, they felt, lived according to their words. They reached those alienated by complacent bourgeois Christianity and they tried to redeem a sin-ridden society. Their peace witness inspired others to repeat it.

Given the severe penalties that could be incurred for this type of civil disobedience, a surprising number of protesters committed similar actions. According to the most detailed study of the Catholic Left or ultraresistance, more than fifty protests were modeled on the Baltimore and Catonsville raids between 1967 and 1972. But not all those who followed the Berrigans were practicing Catholics or practicing Christians.[15] Thus, the Catholic nature of this movement remains debatable, even though the Berrigans were motivated by religious belief. In the 1980s, however, the Berrigan-inspired Plowshares actions, with their damage to nuclear weapons and facilities, has largely attracted radical Christian participants.

The Catholic Worker and the Catonsville Draft Board Raid

As the preeminent and senior Catholic pacifist in America, Dorothy Day sometimes was blamed unfairly for inspiring excess zeal in Catholic peacemakers during the 1960s. In 1965 the tragic immolation of Roger LaPorte, a young man tenuously associated with the Catholic Worker, was a case in point.[16] Then, as the eclectic antiwar coalition experimented with new tactics during the late 1960s, Dorothy Day needed to carefully define her pacifist principles, for the antiwar movement opposed the Vietnam war without necessarily accepting Christian nonviolent values.

On the surface, the draft board raiders seemed to emulate the Catholic Worker's peace ideals. Historical precedent sided with them; Dorothy Day resisted war and went to jail for protesting civil defense drills during the 1950s. Some remembered her suggestion that young men fill the jails in this country to stop war. At the age of sixty-seven in 1964, she signed and later published an antiwar complicity statement that could have resulted in her imprisonment. She herself favored an interpretation of the New Testament passage on "rendering to Caesar" that unequivocally sided with the primacy of divine order over the state. The voluntary poverty of the Catholic Worker, with her wry observation that "poverty is lice," hardly glorified the protection of property.[17]

During the late 1960s, the draft board raids seemed at the time a natural evolution of Catholic Worker pacifism. Jim Forest, whose connections bridged the Catholic Worker and the new ultraresistance, claimed that the Berrigan movement advanced beyond Catholic Worker pacifism.[18] Besides the testimonies of participants, other evidence suggested that the raids were compatible with the Catholic Worker's philosophy. Both the Worker and the ultraresistance readily accepted the failure of liberal reform. The antiwar experience provided abundant evidence of the impoverished state of liberal politics. Consciousness raising, petitions, marches, and balloting had not ended the war. Liberals seemed capable only of moral compromise. Thus, radical means of change clearly were needed. The Berrigans settled on direct action protest. Like many Catholic Workers before them, they agreed that they must resist evil laws. They risked jail for their beliefs and considered their activities a religious sacrifice. Finally, both the Catholic Worker and the ultraresistance emphasized their Christian concern for all victims of war, including the soldiers sent overseas. To express their concern, they chose to burn papers in the belief that they would say *no* to war without harming any person.

The draft board raids, however, were not initiated by those closest

278

to Dorothy Day and the Catholic Worker. The Berrigans operated on the periphery of her movement. Not until September 1968, nearly one year after the first raid, by the Baltimore Four, did Catholic Workers Mike Cullen and Larry Rosebaugh from Milwaukee join in a raid. With them was Jim Forest, who had edited the paper in New York City during the early 1960s, but these men could hardly be considered Day's closest associates.

Normally, Catholic Workers had resisted war in ways that fell short of property destruction. They chose other alternatives. The *Catholic Worker* printed articles on the roots of war, the ethical issues involved in modern warfare, and news of the peace movement. The Catholic Worker community supported its pacifist friends. During the Vietnam war, Workers risked imprisonment when they signed complicity statements, refused to pay federal taxes, burned their own draft cards, or refused to respond to their Selective Service summons. While some avoided the unhappy prospect of military service or jail by filing for conscientious objector status, to which every religious pacifist was entitled in theory, other Catholic Workers spent months in prisons throughout the United States.

The Catholic Worker responded to the draft board raid movement on an ad hoc basis. Tom Cornell, selected by Day in the early 1960s to edit the paper, immediately decided to write a piece on Catonsville for the *Catholic Worker*. The paper's feature article on the draft board raids came from Cornell, whom Dorothy trusted and who already was recognized as a leading Catholic peace activist. Cornell and Catholic Worker colleague Chris Kearns had organized the first anti-Vietnam war protest in 1963, and by 1965, when public protests against the war were beginning, Cornell had already destroyed his draft card several times. During the late 1960s, he held an executive position at the Catholic Peace Fellowship, which he helped found in 1964. Thoughtful and articulate, Cornell contributed a lengthy description and evaluation of the Catonsville action. His article suggested that the nine had carried out the raid according to the general principle of nonviolence: the preservation of human life. Nonetheless, Cornell realized that the raiders challenged traditional Christian and Gandhian teachings on nonviolence. Therefore, he cautiously analyzed some of the controversial innovations of the ultraresistance.[19]

Heinous war crimes committed in the name of U.S. citizens, Cornell believed, demanded a creative and "vigorous" kind of nonviolent action and the Berrigans "have given an example, an ingenious act of *nonviolent* revolution [emphasis added]. If nothing short of such revolutionary acts will accomplish the goal of the overthrow of the institutions of death and oppression, then let it be!" As a radical Christian, Cornell could accept revolution, but only if it remained bloodless. Separating himself from the political and religious mainstream, he castigated those who mindlessly supported the violence of the status quo while they opposed both the violence of the oppressed and the "escalating nonviolence" of the draft board raids. He also rejected the theory, sometimes espoused by the New Left, that nonviolence was the tool of the status quo and that it inescapably curtailed the potential for radical change. Nor did he agree that nonviolence worked less effectively than brute force.

Tom Cornell, as an observer of and participant in the antiwar movement, had witnessed the escalation of militant protest in recent years. While the anti-Vietnam protests had begun with the nonviolent resistance of radical pacifists like himself, pacifists had lost control of the antiwar coalition when the growing unpopularity of the war swelled the antiwar movement. Not everyone in the antiwar movement shared the pacifists' nonviolent orientation. Without such a consensus, frustration and revolutionary terrorism could inflame destructive passions in others. He pragmatically believed that violent revolution could not overthrow a modern industrial society. Some secular radicals, noting that the established order possessed a monopoly on "conventional force," justified violence because they believed that violence could be fought only with violence. However, Cornell, with his anarchistic vision, predicted that in such a confrontation fascism rather than the revolution would triumph.

Cornell was also troubled by the essential despair that lurked beneath the secular radicals' challenge to established order. Their use of violence denied the spiritual revolution, a change in heart, that would bloodlessly create an altered social system. Secular revolutionaries denied the Christian message of love. Instead, they relied on force, the defective weapon of the old order. For him, revolutionary violence and official violence amounted to the same thing: the taking of human life.

Like the secular radical approach, the political mainstream mishandled the peace issue. A good part of the problem was the nature of the electoral system. In Cornell's opinion, liberals, often lacking a mandate from the majority, jostled for power and bargained timidly for social justice when compared to the direct action nonviolent tradition. Furthermore, during the spring and summer of 1968 evidence mounted that the liberal order, if not the electoral system itself, had collapsed. Doom pervaded the carnival-like atmosphere of national politics. Martin Luther King, Jr., civil rights activist and antiwar critic, lay dead. The emergence of black power, white backlash, the grinding war, not to speak of the unfulfilled promises of the Great Society reforms, eroded any hope for resolving America's domestic crisis by consensus. The antiwar elements in the Democratic party were upset by Robert Kennedy's murder, Eugene McCarthy's frizzled Children's Crusade, and the ominous show of police force at the national convention in Chicago. Tainted by his position in Lyndon Johnson's administration, the unfortunate Hubert Humphrey proclaimed "the politics of joy" while his opponents, Richard Nixon and George Wallace, capitalizing on popular discontent, ran law-and-order campaigns that showed as much contempt for antiwar protesters as for the enemy Viet Cong. At such a time, Cornell's attitude that electoral politics was futile—and the Catonsville Nine's similar observation—seemed to justify the building of a creative, nonpartisan war resistance movement. Religious radicals, not politicians, could provide the leadership to create a new order.

Thus the emergence of the ultraresistance made sense in a highly charged political atmosphere where traditional structures were crumbling. But Cornell did have reservations about the nature of the ultraresistance's positions on life and liberty. In an otherwise favorable account of the Catonsville raid, he worried that individual conscience might be violated by the tactics adopted by the raiders. "When an individual takes his own draft cards and burns them," Cornell wrote, "he makes a decision for himself: I will no longer be a part of the war system." According to Cornell, such individuals separate themselves from what they believe to be evil, but they do not impose upon others the same choice. The draft board raids operated on a different set of assumptions. While they entailed the refusal of certain individuals to consent to the war, they also indirectly involved the young men whose records were housed in a Selective Service office. The destruction of nearly four hundred files at Catonsville in effect delayed or attempted to preclude military service for men who had not asked the Catonsville Nine to favor them with this act of exemption by destruction. Ineligible for the draft due to age, sex, or clerical status, the Catonsville Nine did not alter their own personal draft status; instead they protested war in a way that affected those most likely to be called to serve. Thus, Cornell questioned whether or not the raid violated the right of individual choice.

The real issue raised by the Catonsville raid involved the government's right to conscript citizens. Like earlier generations of anarchists, Cornell understood that the military draft was a form of involuntary servitude. Few young men were socialized to question the government's right to enslave them by drafting them into the military. Potential draftees never consciously consented to permit the government to draft them. Cornell eventually concluded that the raiders were restoring individual liberties to deprived citizens.

While the ends of the raid satisfied him, Cornell was disturbed by the possibly impure means used by the raiders. As a Catholic Worker pacifist, Cornell could find no justification for the use of violence, even if it were limited and the cause was just. He subscribed to a moral absolutism that cautioned, "The means inevitably determine the ends." By examining the specific case rather than a theoretical problem, he concluded that the Catonsville raid had been well planned and he applauded the conspirators' care in choosing a site that "was logistically well situated and relatively vulnerable." He dismissed the potential for violence in the seizure of the files and noted that the papers burning in the parking lot posed "no danger to any person or any other property." Yet he was still uneasy and suggested that the nine consider how narrowly they had escaped an ends-justifies-the-means mentality. Pure intentions and dangerous means could contaminate nonviolence, reshaping it into conventional force.

Hesitant about approving the purity of their means, Cornell scrutinized the nine's handling of social responsibility. This he found satisfactory. Almost glossing over his earlier reservations, he felt that human rights took moral precedence over property rights in life-or-death matters. In his argument he anticipated a major point in the legal defense of the nine. All agreed that immoral property, which destroys human life, does not enjoy an absolute guarantee of protection. Only human life, created in God's image, is dignified by that right.

On the balance, Cornell presented a fairly positive analysis of this new form of resistance. He agreed with the raiders' assumptions about war and conscription. When he probed into the moral implications of their means, he found nothing to condemn. True to Christian anarchism, he left these weighty issues for his readers to ponder. He did not intend to have the final word.

Cornell's mixed review confused some of his readers. John Leo LeBrun, a scholar of the Worker's pacifism, for example, concluded that Cornell "rejected" the draft board raid as an expression of nonviolence. Stressing the Catholic Worker movement's conciliatory ways, LeBrun was convinced that Cornell refrained from an outright condemnation only to prevent a debilitating rift in the peace movement.[20] While LeBrun could be right about Cornell's reluctance to split the movement, Cornell's overall assessment of the raid, at least in print, was quite positive. In any event, to the credit of Cornell, his position on the raids could be attributed to inner strength, rather than cowardice. His hesitant support for the Nine expressed moral questions rather than a reluctance to make sacrifices for the cause of peace. In fact, Cornell served time for one of his Vietnam-era draft violations. His only regret was caused by scruples: in 1965 he briefly had convinced himself that his own resistance to war might have been a model for Roger LaPorte's grisly immolation.[21]

Tom Cornell's nuanced viewpoint disappointed some at the Worker, and they aired their disagreement with him in the paper, a direct approach unusual at the Catholic Worker. If his reservations seemed disloyal to the Christian resisters at Catonsville, his sympathetic understanding of their protest provoked substantive criticism from three Catholic Workers. Two of the younger volunteers at the New York house, Michael Ketchum and Jack Cook, and long-time anarchist Ammon Hennacy rejected the moral and political implications of collective property destruction. Dorothy Day's role in printing these alternative positions is unknown, although she later echoed Hennacy's position.

Ammon Hennacy, the colorful one-person revolution, had influenced the direction of Catholic Worker pacifism especially in the 1950s. An anarchist since World War I, Hennacy had converted to Catholicism after coming to the Worker, but he cultivated connections with anarchists and radical pacifists that inspired the Worker's bold campaign of civil disobedience against civil defense during the cold war. He unabashedly attacked the raid as "less than the ideal form of protest." By nature more of an anarchist than a doctrinal Catholic, Hennacy singled out for criticism the courtroom defense of the nine. The old radical, who resisted war taxes by holding low-paying jobs, implied that the defendants compromised their radicalism. Hiring lawyers and preparing a legal defense meant that the raiders were operating according to rules set by the establishment. They were in effect seduced back into the system by attempting to exonerate themselves and condemn the war in a federal court. Hennacy's preference was a simple individual protest, an art that he had developed over decades by noncooperating with the draft, fasting, picketing, and resisting tax. None of these approaches obstructed his freedom to think and act in accordance with the moral dictates of his conscience by burdening him with unwanted "lawyers and legal techniques." Furthermore, he believed that his preference for the one-person revolution also freed him from the taint of compromise that could arise when one was dependent upon a retinue of donors to pay for the legal defense.[22]

Jack Cook, an unassuming college instructor who was drawn to the Catholic Worker because of its antiwar stand, also rejected Cornell's relatively benign view of the ultraresistance. A disciple of Ammon Hennacy, he countered Cornell with three original points. He criticized Cornell's understanding of nonviolent revolution, deplored his apparent support for "guerilla tactics," and quibbled with his laudatory interpretation of the place of the raid in the history of the nonviolent peace movement.[23]

Michael Ketchum, like Cook, had arrived recently at the Worker. Unsure of his moral credibility with others, he added weight to his views by claiming that he had arrived at his conclusions after discussion with other Catholic Workers and pacifists. Like Cornell, Ketchum feared that the raids could lead toward political polarization. But beyond this shared premonition, Ketchum worried that the ultraresistance had unintentionally subverted pacifism's traditional aim of "reconcil[ing] . . . men." "Nonviolent sabotage," as he called the raid, might lead not to peace but rather to an undesirable escalation of violence in the burgeoning antiwar movement. Imitators of the Catonsville Nine, he feared, would not distinguish between the destruction of property and the reckless endangering of human life. The raid seemed only a step away from the fire bombing of ROTC buildings, draft boards, and factories, a tactic that surely compromised pacifist values and the sacredness of human life. So strong was Ketchum's distress over the "blur[ring] [of] the once clear distinction between pacifism and violence" that he found nothing positive to say about the raid.[24]

Without the direct involvement of Dorothy Day in the early stages of the debate over the means used by the ultraresistance, the *Catholic Worker* initiated a series of articles about the Catonsville raid shortly after it occurred in May 1968. The paper's reaction to the new form of protest ranged from Tom Cornell's mixed but sympathetic assessment, to the primarily negative evaluations of anarchists Ammon Hennacy and Jack Cook, and that of the pacifistically inclined Michael Ketchum. Many of the standard reservations about these raids were first printed in the *Catholic Worker*. Three issues clearly dominated the debate: the degree of potential violence inherent in the raid, the safeguarding of its moral authority from political bartering, and the level of coercion involved in the destruction of Selective Service files. What would ultimately distinguish Dorothy Day's evolving response from those of her followers was the depth of her spiritual reservations about ultraresistance. While she did share some of the more practical considerations raised by the first Catholic Workers who commented on Catonsville, she alone attempted to analyze the spirituality of such protests.

THE EVOLUTION OF DOROTHY DAY'S VIEWS ON PROPERTY DESTRUCTION

Dorothy Day set precedents for Vietnam-era peace activists. By participating in the protests against the civil defense air raid drills, she endorsed the practice of civil disobedience for other Catholic peace seekers. Her defiance of the law led to four arrests and jail sentences. But in spite of her higher regard for human life over property rights, she stopped short of actually damaging or destroying government or corporate property in her peace witness. She never considered destroying property to be an antiwar tactic. Daniel Berrigan's participation in the Catonsville raid with his brother probably took Day by surprise. The Berrigans were relative newcomers to nonviolent war resistance and they hardly seemed bound by its traditions.

At first, Day expressed to Daniel Berrigan unreserved enthusiasm for the Catonsville raid and his brother's earlier act of resistance as one of the Baltimore Four. Writing to the Jesuit a couple of weeks after the second event, she praised their "very strong and imaginative witness against conscription." She recognized that the raid's symbolic destruction created controversy about its value as a means toward peace. The damage to these draft files, however, had not "in any way injured any individual." Apparently satisfied that the action qualified as a nonviolent protest, she next considered whether it violated the freedom of conscience of any persons. Again, the raid passed muster. She wrote, perhaps more for her own peace of mind than Daniel Berrigan's, that although the nine had destroyed some 1-A files, "those who wished to be drafted can enlist."[25] Therefore, even young supporters of the war still had the personal freedom to remind their draft boards of their availibility.

Three months elapsed before Dorothy Day mentioned the Catonsville raid in public. Invited to address the Liturgical Conference on August 19, she called the raid "an act of prayer," which certainly indicated that she felt no qualms about its authenticity as a Christian nonviolent response to an intolerable war. Jim Forest, a peace activist and former *Catholic Worker* editor, who traveled to Washington to hear her speak, soon began to prepare himself to recreate the Catonsville act in Milwaukee.[26] On September 24 the Milwaukee Fourteen, with Forest and two others close to the Catholic Worker—Larry Rosebaugh and Michael Cullen—damaged thousands of draft files. Soon it would be clear to observers that the Catonsville action was not an isolated event, but the beginning of a movement, the ultraresistance.

By early September Philip Berrigan sensed that Day's private attitude toward the Catonsville raid was changing. Obviously disappointed that the founder of American Catholic pacifism was having second thoughts, he confided to his brother that he detected signs of her displeasure with the raid.[27] Unfortunately, he did not disclose the source or substance of the information that led to his observation, and available sources, including interviews, provide few clues about the timing and reasons for her apparent shift in thought.

Weakness from a chronic heart condition and her own reservations notwithstanding, Dorothy Day traveled to Baltimore to be present when the federal trial of the Catonsville Nine convened on October 7, 1968. She spoke there to a gathering of supporters of the nine, a group with impeccable antiwar proclivities (FBI agents on duty excepted). Dorothy began her statement with the observation that the raid sent two prophetic messages. To the U.S. government, the Catonsville action meant the opposition of responsible middle-class, middle-aged Christians to the Vietnam war. More profoundly, the raid signified a vital new attempt to enlarge the role of the church in the United States and to purify Christian teaching of compromise. The nine condemned the shameless alliance of church and state in America. She concluded that "only actions such as these [Baltimore Four, Catonsville Nine, Milwaukee Fourteen] will force the Church to speak out when the state has become a murderer."[28] The prophetic voice of Christianity, as she heard it, was directed to all believers, clergy and laity, and to those who were scandalized by the modern church's failings on social issues. Her remarks about church and state reflected her traditional concerns with the preservation of the prophetic purity of Christianity.

On the issue of the moral responsibilities of the church and the individual, Day and the Berrigans were in complete accord. The power and technology available to the modern state, they agreed, usurped moral prerogatives that once belonged to the church. This reality posed a challenge to the survival of the modern Christian church. They shared a belief that people of faith should face the systemic evil of U.S. capitalism. "Whether we like it or not," she had written a year and a half earlier, "we are Americans. It is indeed our country, right or wrong, as the Cardinal [Francis Spellman] said in another context." Vietnam was perhaps the most visible problem of the times, but it was only one of the effects of the American system on the Third World. To emphasize her point that wealth contradicts the gospel, she deftly summarized the story of Dives and Lazarus, reminding her readers that "we [Americans] are the rich." Therefore Christians had to challenge the system.[29]

After she praised these nonviolent Christian war resisters, Day spoke to the audience of her greatest fear: that antiwar activists might turn to violence. Before a plea to the young audience to reject violence, she reminded them that she had earned credentials as a radical pacifist long before the Vietnam war. After mentioning ("arrogantly," according to Francine du Plessix Gray, or "authoritatively," according to Tom Cornell) her many jail sentences, she urged absolute pacifism "in the face of all violence."[30] Without explaining why she feared an upswing in antiwar violence, she suggested that the young antiwar activists lacked religious faith, the essential ingredient for preserving the nonviolent legacy of Gandhi, King, and Chicano labor organizer Cesar Chavez. Pacifism, she thought, was "the most difficult thing in the world" to practice. Oddly, she omitted an evaluation of the extent to which the Berrigans and the other raiders shared this pacifist pedigree.

In private Day voiced the opinion that the Catholic Worker and the ultraresistance had their differences. "Dan isn't a Catholic Worker," Dorothy confided to a young nun who was attending the trial while researching the Catholic peace movement. "He came to us and stole our young men away into the peace movement." Jealousy was an unlikely explanation of her sharp response, according to her close associate Tom Cornell.[31] Rather, she was probably suggesting that the ultraresistance did not necessarily subscribe to the Catholic Worker approach to social change. At this early stage in its development, the ultraresistance seemed to share the same radical interpretation of the roots of violence in U.S. society as did the Worker. But one major difference was the Berrigans' concentration on one issue: peace. Dorothy Day believed that peace was a primary issue, but it was for her only one part of a larger nonviolent Christian revolution.

To achieve the nonviolent revolution, Dorothy Day believed that Christians must first undergo a conversion to honor the law of love literally. Her movement supported a variety of progressive causes also, including pacifism, which she regarded as especially significant. However, the Catholic Worker was not simply another peace group. The immediate care of the poor and sick formed the core of the daily work at Catholic Worker houses of hospitality. Peace activity was one way of bringing about the nonviolent revolution, but she found other concerns to address and other tasks to perform besides war resistance. Jim Forest, who had lived at the Catholic Worker in the early 1960s and who moved into full-time work in the peace movement, recently recalled that Day admonished peace people to "remember the poor."[32] The law of love, as it pertained to distant nations and long-range plans, would mean little, she thought, if Christians neglected their daily duty toward those among them requiring immediate relief from their suffering. Furthermore her movement, with its voluntary poverty, farming communes, paper, and shelters for the poor, attempted to withdraw from the established political, economic, and social structures that contributed so generously to the oppression of the poor at home and abroad.

When Day returned to New York and devoted part of her column "On Pilgrimage" to the Berrigans, she reached a larger audience than had gathered in Baltimore to hear her speak. The spiritual depth of the Berrigans' protest pleased her. They had boldly chosen to use sacrifice as a metaphor and as a means of self-purification. To a traditional Catholic like Day, Christ's sacrifice and its reenactment at the mass were at the center of Catholic belief and liturgy. Modeled on the life of Christ and rooted in the law of love proclaimed by Jesus, the Catonsville raid was built around the theme of sacrifice. When the nine napalmed nearly four hundred 1-A files and prayed the Lord's Prayer, they offered a sacrifice, albeit an unconventional one. Their sacrifice prevented or delayed a sacrilegious sacrifice of human life by the state. Day, however, was most impessed by their offering of personal freedom, a gift of great cost in a society that so values self and wealth. By renouncing their freedom, the "most precious possession," they embraced the highest Christian virtues.[33] She also complimented them for their prayer and fasting, which they directed to the needs of others.

Dorothy Day wrote of the raiders' traditional spirituality, but her praise for their politics uncovered a contradiction in their approach to social change and hers: their goals were the same, they believed in nonviolence, but they found different means to express their concerns and forward their cause. All were radicals. And their Christian beliefs shaped the direction of their protest. Day approved of their targeting of Selective Service, a government agency. A long-time opponent of both war and conscription, she explained that the destroyed files concerned "our criminal drafting and enslavement of young men for our immoral wars." And she added that in foreign wars where soldiers were not sent, our government substituted "weapons, planes, [and] bombs."[34] Yet she worried about young recruits to this resistance movement and suggested alternative ways of practicing nonviolence.

On a personal level, she wrote that she considered the Berrigan brothers "great men" and she carefully observed that they had attracted a large following. This new, vibrant movement, with its charismatic leaders' potential for brilliant publicity and its emphasis on personal risk, would probably attract some persons unprepared for it. She was not worried about the Berrigans' spirituality, but she feared for some of their young followers. These impressionable young people, "in and out of the Church," as she put it, lacked the spiritual maturity required of nonviolent revolutionaries.[35] In this amorphous movement of activists and their admirers, in which the young, the unchurched, and the insecure could participate, they might all too easily compromise Christian nonviolence. They risked hurting themselves, others, and their cause.

Dorothy Day still supported the Berrigans, but she worried that their prayerful action had suddenly become a mass movement and that it could easily go out of control. She questioned the readiness of raw recruits to sustain the peace cause without the proper emotional maturity and spiritual discipline. She also refused to endorse their approach as the best way to resist war. Other ways of opposing the Vietnam war that she suggested included "refusal to work in any industry pertaining to war or to pay taxes for war."[36] These were acts of individual witness with considerably less flair for drama than a raid. Furthermore, their potential for dangerous confrontation with authorities or right-wingers was minimal. These were traditional means used by the radical pacifists of the postwar era. These, too, challenged the structure for war in the U.S.: the military-industrial complex.

Dorothy Day's position on ultraresistance evolved over the course of a few years, from 1968 through 1972.[37] After Catonsville, Day revised her assessments of the raids by focusing on the potential violence of the new movement. Having apparently expressed her thoughts privately to the Berrigans before the trial and to their followers at the rally, Day refrained from preoccupation with the differences between herself and these other Catholic war resisters. She naturally stated her misgivings more candidly in private than in public, and did so only when circumstances required it. Interestingly, her opinion on ultraresistance rarely appeared in her own paper. Her cautious approach prevented her from sowing discord in the vulnerable Catholic peace community. By avoiding a complete rupture with the ultraresistance, Day established a relationship in which each movement was free to influence the other.

Day kept silent about the reasons for her critical but minimalist approach to the issues raised by the Berrigans' innovations. However, she often handled internal differences at the Worker with tact and generosity despite her formidable temper. This nonconfrontational approach enabled the Catholic Worker to endure. As a matter of principle and survival, then, she avoided intramural disputes whenever possible. Hence, even the closest readers of the paper rarely grasped the depth of Catholic Worker conflicts, even though Day's writing acquainted them with charming and personal details of life at St. Joseph's House or at the farm.

Day's conception of radical Christian journalism, which evolved with her spirituality, likewise discouraged overzealous correction of those whose concepts of the Worker, social justice, or Catholicism strayed from her ideas. While she taught Christian perfectionism, or a literal interpretation of the law of love, Day ably tempered her prophetic message with responsible criticism. For example, she once earned compliments from Thomas Merton for such balance. Her "soft-toned and restrained" manner in an article discussing Cardinal Spellman's public bellicosity on the issue of the Vietnam war reminded him "of love more than of reproof." Merton endorsed Day's approach as "the way a Christian should speak up."[38]

The potential for harsh criticism within a prophetic, perfectionistic movement was further modulated by Day's approach to nonviolent revolution. Because she believed that the revolution began in each person's heart as soon as that person embraced the law of love, converts could trust that the efficacy of grace working within themselves could transform friends, enemies, and even social structures. Total concentration on any one social issue missed the point of the nonviolent revolution and, in fact, slighted the revolutionary possibilities of Christianity. Therefore, as searing as her criticism of the Vietnam war was, war-related issues never became the sole focus of the paper even during the height of the antiwar movement. In fact, the Vietnam war occupied a fraction of her diminishing energies. Consequently, she skillfully balanced spiritual, social, and peace concerns in the paper.[39]

Day's desire to live in solidarity with the oppressed also checked any possible impulse to dwell on her differences with the Berrigans' new tactics. She genuinely appreciated the sacrifices of those who forfeited their freedom to live by their convictions, for they voluntarily shed their privilege, they experienced poverty, and they followed the example of Christ in laying down their lives for others. She could soothe the pain of the Berrigans and their followers created by her changing position by reminding her readers that they and other war resisters were in prison.

The nonviolent revolution of the Catholic Worker accentuated harmony, and thus tempered Day's criticisms of others. Clearly, the path to a new heaven and a new earth was paved with practicality. Day's avoidance of dissension enabled her radical Catholic movement to survive against strong odds. This same practicality was at work when Day chose to give her views on the raids a minor place in her paper. The *Catholic Worker*'s readership reached into the Catholic and political mainstream. Not all of its readers agreed with the paper's advocacy of pacifism, for example. Therefore, involved discussions of nonviolent resistance tactics were irrelevant to those drawn to Dorothy Day's solid and traditional piety or her unreserved charity to the poor. These readers needed no warnings about the dangers of ultraresistance because they had not yet been won over to pacifism. Furthermore, the Berrigan movement was relatively small and amounted to a minority of her paper's readership. Because Day had no intention of setting herself up as a rival to the Berrigans, she wisely limited the amount of energy she would devote to questioning the tactics of ultraresistance. The paper, therefore, was not an appropriate forum for extended discussions of the issues raised by the ultraresistance.

Nonetheless, after the Catonsville trial in October 1968 there were pressing reasons that accounted for her distress over the direction of the antiwar movement and her occasional attempts to address the tactics of the ultraresistance. From 1968 to 1972 the Catonsville action sparked a whole movement of similar raids on government and corporate headquarters.[40] In some instances the raiders deviated from the Berrigans' innovations, for example, by hit-and-run actions that evaded the police. The Berrigans themselves decided to delay their impending prison terms by going underground. These rapid changes in the tradition of nonviolent resistance challenged Day's beliefs and practices; in particular, she questioned the new trend for the excessive physical risks they demanded.

Well before the Berrigans embarked on their new path, destructive tendencies began to surface in the antiwar movement. During this period, angry counterdemonstrators created threatening scenes at large antiwar rallies. A remarkably high degree of social turmoil manifested itself during the late 1960s and early 1970s in many other situations, thus adding to Day's uneasiness about the status of nonviolence in the antiwar movement. And, of course, she was deeply troubled by Roger LaPorte's immolation.

Liberal and radical pacifists certainly grounded the peace movement in traditional nonviolent practice. Individual protests like tax resistance, draft card destruction, and petitions, and group activities like the massive peace marches in many cities operated within the nonviolent tradition. As the war became more unpopular and protest against it swelled, many joined the antiwar movement without a commitment to absolute nonviolence. Antiwar protesters and counterdemonstrators mirrored the attitudes of American society. They felt that under certain conditions one could justify the use of force. During the Vietnam war, pacifist opponents of U.S. involvement in Southeast Asia eventually were outnumbered by those who protested against the war but who never wished for a nonviolent revolution. Day was therefore cruelly reminded that the strength of the antiwar movement was also its major weakness. The large numbers of people who dissented against the war represented a wide range of the social, economic, and political spectrum. This loose coalition opposed the war, but did not agree on the basic issues of how to end the war and the direction of future U.S. policy.⁴¹

Throughout the late 1960s and early 1970s, much evidence supported the interpretation that political process could not solve the problems of the time. A police riot, aimed at quelling dissent during the 1968 Democratic convention in Chicago, showed how official violence could batter bystanders, provoke retaliation, and mock electoral politics. In April and May 1969 Dorothy Day's friends at War Resisters League headquarters in New York City experienced the theft of their mail and a mailing list and the trashing of their office.⁴² Later that summer the Weather faction of Students for a Democratic Society (SDS), the best-known student radical group, planned a rampage in Chicago. During the academic year 1969–70, with the government's escalation of the air war in Southeast Asia, campus violence further fueled the widely held view that antiwar protest was moving out of control. Old Left and New Left groups were hardly immune from attacks by the fringe of the New Left whose different vision of reality tended toward terrorism. Even in western Europe, these same trends toward violence surfaced in a variety of protest groups, including the British and French Catholic Left.

After reviewing this great expanse of destructiveness, Dorothy Day defended pacifism. She found that "a great many of the protest movements are not peace groups at all." It was true that some of their concerns converged with those of the pacifists, but the other protesters identified themselves as "revolutionary groups, opposing the present war, but working with the expectation of inevitable conflict."Day rejected class conflict when she turned away from secular radicalism and converted to Catholicism in 1927. Day liked class war no better than any other kind of war. As a radical pacifist and Christian, she painfully recognized that "war . . . means far more than war in Viet Nam." The attitudes and practices of war could be uncovered "in the whole turning toward violence of the Catholic Left."⁴³ So sobering and senseless was indulgence in official and revolutionary terrorism that Day distanced herself further from any act falling short of the traditional definition of nonviolence. The Berrigans were hardly to blame for this violence—and she never suggested that they were—but she began to propose alternatives to the draft board raids.

The slightest hint of potential violence in the Catholic peace movement disturbed Dorothy Day. Physical and emotional harm to humans always affected her, but, above all else, the spiritual hazards of hatred, violence, and war inspired her shift to a more critical understanding of ultraresistance. According to her spirituality, violence implied a loss of Christian faith and a profound despair in the efficacy of grace to remake individuals and society. To illustrate her point, she explained that she deplored the "unholy Trinity" of unchecked emotion: anger, hatred, and violence. She associated this regrettable pagan triumvirate in part with the "violent spirit of . . . Catholics" who crusaded, drank, and brawled their way through history. She confessed to Dwight Macdonald that the destruction of "inanimate objects . . . could lead to the real thing." She meant that property destruction could lead to murder, although the Baltimore and Catonsville raid contributed no evidence to substantiate her anxieties.[44]

For the moment, however, the important matter is not the extent to which the ultraresistance dabbled in violence. The fundamental issue separating the ultraresistance from the Catholic Worker was the world view of each movement, not mere tactics. The Catholic Worker considered itself a Christian anarchist movement. All authority came from God; and the state, having by choice distanced itself from Christian perfectionism, forfeited its ultimate authority over the citizen. The workings of grace would, of course, ensure the final victory of good over evil, and each Christian could begin the process of turning self and society toward God.

The ultraresistance, however, was still in transition from a progressive to a radical mentality. Daniel Berrigan at the time of Catonsville had not yet broken with Teilhardian theological optimism. That mentality, based on the concept of the incarnation, viewed human development in glowingly positive terms and was therefore inadequate in explaining the desire of modern people to manufacture their own holocaust. Initially the ultraresistance remained faithful to the increasingly untenable Teilhardian vision.

The movement's evolving perceptions of human nature sometimes led to inconsistencies in its view of human governance. Occasionally the ultraresistance sought to reform the state; at other times, aware of the primacy of God's law over Caesar's, it rejected state authority. Lacking at this time a commitment to holistic nonviolent revolution, the ultraresistance concentrated on one issue: ending the war. The ultraresistance was pulled toward both liberalism and radicalism and therefore it operated on mixed assumptions. Its liberal tendencies fostered the belief that peace, by freeing the economy from massive military spending, would enable society to devote its human and material resources to solving the perplexing problems that wracked the modern world. On the other hand, having already exhausted the possibilities of liberal protest, the ultraresistance began to understand the systemic roots of war in modern American society: the military-industrial complex ensured its own survival by promoting military solutions to hotly contested civil issues.

Deeply Christian, the Catholic Worker and the ultraresistance relied on charismatic leadership and conversion to spark their social movements. At the Worker, however, a predilection for communitarian anarchism offered the advantages of an intentional community to those who chose life at the Worker. Day's followers shunned the modern state and tried to create a "new society within the shell of the old" one. They believed that by living in a supportive community of like-minded people, they could increase the likelihood of a nonviolent revolution. But in the ultraresistance, without the clear commitment to either radicalism or community life, friendships or the temporary intimacy of religious retreats or prison rarely bonded individuals to one another and to a goal of nonviolent revolution over the long haul.

Intentional communities like the Catholic Worker resolved the issue of authority within the group for survival's sake. In theory, each Catholic Worker member was free to follow conscience while the community defined its practices and goals. Yet the Worker was hardly a democratic movement. While Day did not oversee all details of the movement, she sometimes chose to exert leadership vigorously and some of her followers subsequently thought that she violated their freedom of conscience. Ideally, a Christian anarchist offered moral guidance without violating the conscience of others. Day therefore preferred to teach by example. Catholic Worker anarchism followed Christ as a model of nonviolent revolutionary behavior. Day noted that "Jesus . . . came to serve rather than to be served and . . . [he] never coerced."[45] He respected individual conscience. But he also preached a prophetic message, difficult for many of his contemporaries to embrace.

Dorothy Day could work within the church on some issues, but, because of modern mainstream Christianity's accommodation to war, she found nonreligious peace groups especially congenial to her Christian approach to peace. She identified herself with the "philosophical-anarchist tradition" of War Resisters League and Peacemakers, whose advocacy of "the long enduring, patient suffering struggle to change the hearts and minds of men so they will refuse to fight" was in accord with her own goals.[46] Nonetheless, in her attempt to convert others to peace seeking, Day worked within a tradition of persuasion, conversion, and perfectionism that in the United States marked the rise of radical evangelicalism in the abolitionist movement more than a century earlier.

As odious as she found violent revolution with its un-Christian disregard for the dignity of the oppressor, she believed that for those unconverted to nonviolence it bested inactivity as a solution to the world's problems. "Better than do nothing, it is better to fight," she mused. "I think the violent crowd see it in that sense, but I would say that they are stunted in their development, by not going any further than that." Day treated the secular radicals like Fidel Castro and Camilo Torres, a former priest, with some understanding because their spiritual atrophy developed from the church's failure to live the prophetic, perfectionist teachings of Christ, a failing of the institution rather than of the alienated radical. As she wrote in *The Long Loneliness*, "I loved the Church for Christ made visible. Not for itself, because it was so often a scandal to me. . . . There was plenty of charity but too little justice."[47]

Day believed that the Berrigans were nurtured by a Christian spirituality, but she was not so sure about their young followers, whom she saw as similar to those at the Catholic Worker during the late 1960s. A common problem the Catholic Worker and the ultraresistance faced was young antiwar activists unconverted to a nonviolent Christian view of life and who could easily succumb to the appeal of terrorism. Day was tempted to call the raids "gentle sabotage," but quickly curbed her impulse.[48] Day referred to the acts of ultraresistance as sabotage, separated from the all-inclusive love required in the gospel message. Therefore, she suggested alternatives to the raids. The "indispensible means" for nonviolent revolution that she suggested involved no conflict or coercion. She favored prayer and austerity, prayer and self-sacrifice, prayer and fasting, prayer vigils, and prayer and marches, traditional means of nonviolence with a visible spiritual component "animated by love."

The love that Day advocated could meet practical needs. When sabotage was aimed at peace groups, Day could not contain her frustration with the ultraresistance. The Golden Rule, she thought, embodied a message of great wisdom for resisters. They should do only what they would wish to endure if it were inflicted upon them. Her main concern, however, was preventing the spiraling of violence within the peace movement. "We ourselves have suffered violence," she said, identifying with the larger radical pacifist community. She was objecting to the means used "by hostile right-wing groups," such as "the beating of individuals, the destruction of mailing lists and records, the burning of houses and barns, etc."[49] Unenthusiastic about experiencing more of this trouble, she simply recommended that the peace movement refrain from such provocative actions, even if property, rather than human life, were the object of destruction.

Dorothy Day justified her interpretation of nonviolence on the basis of her participation in the civil defense protests of the 1950s. In order to challenge war-making, the arms race, and the legitimization of nuclear war, radical pacifists like Day jointly defied civil defense instructions. They committed civil disobedience by breaking a law that instructed citizens to take cover during air raid drills.

These cold war–era protests, although she reluctantly participated in them, seemed to her more in accord with classical nonviolence than the newer raids. "For one thing," Day said, Ammon Hennacy, who inspired Catholic Worker direct-action civil disobedience in the 1950s, "tried openly to always follow Gandhi. In that when you have a demonstration to notify the authorities to get the necessary permit, to let them know what you are doing, and to submit to arrest, and to accept the normal treatment, etc."[50] By following Gandhian openness, Day felt confident that she was indeed challenging the system and not playing into its rules. Yet, in spite of her negative view of the establishment, as a Christian she wanted to show respect for officials who worked for this evil system. She therefore applauded openness in protest, an attitude that required full disclosure of one's plans to the appropriate authorities. The clandestine plans of the ultraresistance, which in the case of the Baltimore and Catonsville raids involved the participants awaiting police after their deed was done, perhaps violated the rule of openness less than did other acts of ultraresistance, in which the protesters surfaced later or raided and ran. Truth, however, required openness; so the raids were flawed in their nonviolent logic.

Part of Dorothy Day's defense of traditional nonviolent direct action relied on her scruples about violating the examples of Christ and Gandhi. But other spiritual and personal preferences made small-scale protests especially appealing to her. In all of Dorothy Day's work, "the little way" of St. Thérèse of Lisieux guided her activities. Thérèse's practice of humility seems excruciatingly perfect and unattainable to many modern Christians, but Day admired the freedom inherent in Thérèse's unassuming approach to life. The saint was unconcerned with such burdensome cares as the efficiency or success of her deeds, or the adulation she could expect for them.

Day applied insights from Thérèse to her Skid Row ministry and to her peace activism. Thérèse's principles led Day even further from the ultraresistance, whose hubris during this period seemed to be its preoccupation with measurable results. Hence, when she wrote to Michael Cullen, who had become disillusioned by the discrepancies between the theory and reality of the Milwaukee Fourteen raid in which he acted, she recommended "the little way." Day comforted him and suggested that he would not be regressing spiritually if he were to choose an alternative to the raids in the future. She admired the faith exacted in living "the little way": "It is hoping against hope, and believing, in spite of 'unbelief,' crying out by prayer and by sacrifice, daily, small, constant sacrificing of one's own comfort and cravings—these are the things that count."[51]

Personal considerations also entered into Day's preference for small-scale protests. First, from previous experience with provocative protest and unruly counterprotesters during World War I, Day had come to fear "massive demonstrations." In a highly charged atmosphere, she felt, large numbers of people could smash planned nonviolent direct action. Quality of leadership had little to do with the potential for mob violence, because even someone of Martin Luther King, Jr.'s stature was not omnipotent over unruly protesters, especially if they were untrained in nonviolent tactics and subjected to provocation. The few who underwent conversion to radical Christian nonviolence, however, apparently could face hostility with a greater chance of responding nonviolently. Thus Day's nonviolent revolution suffered from a trace of spiritual elitism. Furthermore, in old age Day suffered from vertigo, a condition that contributed to the horror that permeated her while in a crowd. Thus, Dorothy Day preferred picketing to other forms of protest. Requiring few persons and cheap signs and pamphlets, picketing met Day's criteria of simplicity, openness, and nonconfrontation. She explained that "it is sometimes the only way you have of meeting people" who might respond positively to the highly disciplined nonviolent revolutionary.[52] It was, therefore, a sound pedagogical way of reaching others.

Many of Dorothy Day's qualms about ultraresistance were rooted in the actual or potential results of the raids and the trials of the new movement. These concerns naturally emerged over the course of a few years. Day had not faulted the Catonsville Nine defense at the time of the trial, although Ammon Hennacy did, but her views started to change after the Milwaukee Fourteen trial in the spring of 1969. Dorothy Day eventually rejected the idea of costly legal defenses. But no evidence except that she certainly read Hennacy's article in her paper establishes his influence on her change of mind. Day's criticism of the trials actually applied more to Catholic Workers who participated in the raids or thought of doing so than to the Berrigans. She simply could not justify spending Worker money or squandering time raising defense funds when the poor needed care. Structured on a foundation of voluntary poverty, the Catholic Worker depended on the largesse of many small supporters, many of whom did not share the movement's social radicalism.

While Day continued to publicize and work toward the nonviolent revolution, she also deliberately refused to alienate the movement's benefactors. For example, during the 1950s, when the Catholic

Worker engaged in direct-action nonviolence against the forced civil defense drills, Day refused to open the movement's modest coffers to pay for elaborate defenses for Catholic Worker dissidents, herself included. Uncompromising in her vision of a socially just world, Day nonetheless refused to retract her social radicalism to please those who opposed it, but she did tailor her protests to actions that would not threaten the continued survival of her movement. Furthermore, out of a sense of solidarity with the jailed poor, she considered it unthinkable to seek funds for her defense when the whole purpose of her movement was to live like the poor, that is, without adequate legal defense.[53]

Growing from their different conception of civil disobedience, the ultraresistance defendants actually appeared to want not-guilty verdicts and to challenge policy in the government's own court system by creating elaborate defenses and employing celebrity lawyers. In her own acts of resistance, Day and other Workers felt little need to vindicate themselves before the law. They expected harsh punishment from a system that institutionalized injustice. Therefore, they represented themselves in court, presented simple defenses, and took the rap. Each group challenged the status quo by breaking the law. In a sense, however, both groups compromised with the system: the ultraresistance for trying to seek justice within it and the Catholic Worker for acquiescing in this miscarriage of justice.

Other implications of the raids disturbed Day. Sensitive to institutional tendencies toward paternalism, which she naturally deplored, she had long championed freedom of conscience, criticizing both church and state for transgressing on this essential right for all persons. Now she thought that the raids limited the right of young men to make their own choice about Vietnam. If they wanted to choose the American dream from the marketplace of ideas, she wished them well, for military service could mean opportunity for ghetto blacks. In any case, she defended freedom of choice from the interference of a few middle-class radicals bent on maintaining their own purity.[54] "Conscience is supreme," she explained once. "I go along with [Cardinal John Henry] Newman in that. If you drink a toast, he said, to the pope, he would say, to conscience first, and to the pope second. That was in relation to war."[55]

Day's criticisms of the ultraresistance were growing, but she praised some aspects of its protests. By destroying property, the raiders increased the likelihood of serving time in prison—and the length of their sentences. Day supported these resisters for "sharing the utter misery of the poor." She nearly repeated her own words from a year earlier when she asserted that "the noblest aspect" of the ultraresistance was "not [to be] the rebuking [of] the sinner but

the willingness . . . to give up one's dearest possession, 'freedom.' "
By enduring the same treatment as the poor, Day believed that resisters could find inner peace, open themselves to grace, and share
their lives with the poor. When she thought of the Catonsville Nine,
she loved them because by going to prison they were imitating
Christ's laying down his life for others. Prison sentences took many
members of the ultraresistance out of circulation temporarily. Day
believed that the loss of leaders of the resistance need not debilitate
the movement, for through prayer God would raise new leaders.[56]

Still another innovation of the Berrigans, however, gave Day cause
for concern about her admiration for the ultraresistance. In April
1970 Daniel and Philip Berrigan and a few other members of their
movement went underground. By evading prison temporarily, they
broke again with the traditional understanding of Gandhi. Day dis-
liked the legal defense of the raiders because she believed in accepting even unjust punishment, presumably for its redemptive value.
Going underground strongly suggested that the Berrigans still felt
that meek acceptance of unjust punishment was intolerable. Their
approach to war resistance maintained the necessity for continuing
resistance to evil. Thus, their practice illustrated another implica-
tion of radical Christianity's anarchist tendencies.[57] The Berrigan
underground added considerable physical risk to which the fugitives
subjected themselves. But it also permitted Daniel Berrigan to exercise his right of conscience. During periodic surfacings, he pub-
licized the immorality of war and the need for resistance. Except
perhaps for the added physical risk, this seemed perfectly consistent
with the spirit of Dorothy Day's teachings.

Dorothy Day, however, apparently did not agree that the Berrigan
underground had been a wise decision. In fact, the period shortly
after Daniel Berrigan went to prison formed the backdrop of some
unusually caustic remarks by Day about the Jesuit. In the late summer or fall of 1970, the *Catonsville Roadrunner*, a Left publication
with ties to the Student Christian Movement, published a brief interview she gave while visiting England. The main point of her interview was a reaffirmation of her commitment to traditional nonviolence. Indulging her alarm over the violence of the western
European Left, Day oddly berated the priest, her "old friend," with
whom she "sure [didn't] go along," for being "out for a good time"
and acting like "a romantic adolescent," likely indirect references to
his four-month stint underground, which ended that August. She
also mentioned that the prison mystique, which she associated with
radical priests, perturbed her.[58] By this time Dorothy would have
realized that some resisters, most of them not even associated with
the ultraresistance, would suffer greatly from their prison experi-

ences, some to the point of loss of faith, mental anguish, or a broken marriage.[59] She could hardly blame the Berrigans for their encouragement to resisters in all of these cases, but she seemed to be urging more caution on their part, and perhaps on hers as well. In addition, traditional Catholic though she was, Day exhibited a well-defined streak of anticlericalism throughout her adult life. More than once at the Worker she had reminded people that hers was a movement of the laity. She refused to idolize priests and their heroic actions, although she always respected the priesthood. On another occasion, she exclaimed with reference to the antiwar movement, "Those priests and sisters! I admire their courage and dedication but not their arrogance."[60]

Discussion of the draft board raid issue ended, as far as Day was concerned, in 1972 with her publication of an open letter to Daniel Berrigan upon his release from prison. By this time, the ultraresistance, like the broader antiwar movement, had wound down, keeping pace with withdrawals of U.S. troops from Vietnam. There was little point in writing about an apparently fading movement. Without presenting much detail, Day emphasized some standard themes. She repeated that she could understand the appeal of his "violence" but that nonresistance, or a less confrontational form of protest, seemed morally more correct to her. She added that she considered Cesar Chavez's farmworker movement to be a part of the larger peace movement "because they resist and fight for their lives."[61] In that remark, she simply reiterated her conviction that the Catholic Worker should avoid concentrating on one issue. Love of neighbor included peace activism but did not preclude work on behalf of farmworkers, prisoners, the mentally ill, and other groups for whom social justice was only a dream. Peace activists especially needed to experience the reality of how the system exploited the poor at the very moment that it prepared for and waged war. And of course the United Farm Workers' traditional civil disobedience, with its picket lines, appealed to her. Day's last arrest occurred in California in 1973 while she was visiting with Cesar Chavez.

ULTRARESISTANCE REVISED: THE PLOWSHARES ACTIONS AND THE CATHOLIC WORKER LEGACY

The decline of U.S. involvement in Indochina ended one phase of the antiwar movement that had directed its attention to the situation in Southeast Asia. By the time the war in Indochina actually ended, with the capture of Saigon in April 1975, the strength of the nuclear power industry and the amount of government expenditures for nuclear missiles led to a resurgence of the antinuclear movement. A new era of Catholic war resistance was dawning, directed almost exclusively to the nuclear arms race. Built from the remains of the ultraresistance and fueled by an unequivocal radicalism, the new movement benefited especially from the organizational efforts of Philip Berrigan and Elizabeth McAlister and the prophetic voice of Daniel Berrigan. It now concentrated on resisting the production and deployment of sophisticated weaponry capable of destroying the world many times over. By the 1980s the rehabilitated movement would have a new name, the Plowshares, a biblical spirituality, greater self-assurance, and proven tenacity.

The movement appealed to a few, mostly radical, Christians, many of whom had connections to the Catholic Worker, either as volunteers at one of the houses or simply as social activists rooted in the Worker's teachings or in similar radical Christian or pacifist traditions. During the 1980s, the Plowshares movement proved its commitment to human life and its ability to sustain community, although the 1984 Silo Pruning Hooks, by using a jackhammer, disturbed some nonviolent activists who preferred symbolic destruction with hammers, blood, and paint to instruments of actual power. No misfits flocked to the movement.

The test of time has defended the Berrigans' commitment to property destruction as a form of civil disobedience. In the first place, the somnambulant political climate of the 1980s has isolated radical Christians from the circus atmosphere of the Vietnam-era antiwar movement. Public awareness of this peace witness has undoubtedly declined in part because the media has easily tired of the endless litany of resistance: trespass, property destruction, and prison terms. Weak public awareness of Plowshares is paradoxically a source of its strength. Unlike the more visible peace movement of the 1960s, Plowshares cannot be dismissed by critics as a mere radical-chic reflection of the times, for the 1980s generation values economic stability and individual survival over social conscience. Furthermore, the lack of fanfare that accompanied peace activism in this period could calm fears—such as those of Dorothy Day during the Vietnam war—that undisciplined and unchurched youth would be tempted to commit terrorism in order to end the greater evil of total war. The more conservative political climate of the 1980s, then, contributed to an image of greater stability, seriousness, and commitment in the peace movement.

Paul Magno, Jr. and Marcia Timmel were Catholic Workers who beat swords into plowshares during the early 1980s. Both residents of the Dorothy Day House of Hospitality in Washington, D.C., they participated in separate Plowshares actions. Magno and Timmel, like Dorothy Day and the Berrigans, believed that "genocidal weapons" do not serve the common good. Therefore, those arms were not protected by moral law. Closely following the reasoning behind the ultraresistance's raids, Magno and Timmel agreed that "the assembly of resources into deadly nuclear weapons is itself a violence against creation. To render them unusable, to restore them to a harmless state is not destruction of property, but rather is a creative act; the act of a steward protecting all creation from destruction."[62]

At the same time, others connected to the Catholic Worker who initially supported or participated in the ultraresistance now prefer alternative means of peacemaking. A couple of years after his trial, Michael Cullen, who eventually paid the heavy cost of deportation back to his native Ireland for joining the Milwaukee Fourteen, thought that he would never partake in such an action again. He could accept property destruction "for that time in history," but he preferred "Gandhian-type, peaceful and lawful demonstrations" at which he could gently confront others. Cullen specifically deplored his "arrogant" stand and added that the action put a person's family and marriage at great risk.[63]

Dorothy Day was still alive when the Berrigans breathed life into the Plowshares movement with their destruction of nuclear-missile nosecones at a General Electric plant near Philadelphia on September 9, 1980. Her precarious health, however, prevented her from addressing any serious issues during the remaining months of her life. "On Pilgrimage," her column, a *Catholic Worker* parallel to the *New Yorker*'s "Talk of the Town" feature, was reduced to a fragmented journal of her diminishing activities. Day's example inspired the Berrigans, however, and the new directions taken by the Plowshares movement appeared to pay silent homage to her earlier criticisms.[64] But at the time of her death in November 1980 Day still had not rescinded her reservations about participating in an act of symbolic property destruction.

Since 1980 nearly twenty Plowshares actions have taken place, a testimony to the renewed vigor of war resistance. In those actions, nonviolent values have outweighed secular solutions, for only property has been destroyed, not human life. Some Plowshares activists have defended and nurtured human life from "prebirth to last gasp." Espousing "an integrated conscience," Daniel Berrigan has criticized the church and the Left for their unintegrated and hypocritical positions on abortion and war, the church preferring war to abortion and the Left advocating abortion while condemning imperialist wars.[65] During the late 1970s and 1980s, he volunteered his services at St. Rose's Hospital for the Cancerous Poor in New York. Berrigan of course noted the link between increased cancer in today's society and the risks and expense of keeping a nuclear arsenal ready. More recently he has assisted with the care of AIDS patients, whose treatment has been a minor priority for the military-minded Reagan administration.

Following the example of the Catholic Worker, the Plowshares movement has built a network of resistance communities, offering mutual support, subsistence living, and an opportunity to deepen one's spirituality. At Jonah House in Baltimore, where Elizabeth McAlister and Philip Berrigan have lived with their three children, community members rotate resistance and subsistence duties, giving continuity to the young and adults there and offering outreach to those struggling with decisions about their role in resisting the arms race.

Ironically, the political climate of the 1980s, chilling for radicals and liberals alike, and the leaders of the ultraresistance, forgotten or disdained when the antiwar movement eclipsed, created the seedtime for a new resistance movement. The Plowshares movement shares the basic values of the Catholic Worker: love, anarchism, pacifism, resistance to evil, and the sharing of wealth, all rooted in Christian perfectionism. Likewise, Plowshares evolved from the ultraresistance. Consciously or not, it adapted property destruction to the teachings of Dorothy Day by building resistance communities based on a radical biblical spirituality and geared to the long haul.

What Dorothy Day once said about the Catholic Worker surely applies to the Plowshares movement:

> Who knows . . . how much influence a thing has. I think we have to follow our consciences and to do the work we have set ourselves out to do. And to accept it sometimes as small. And yet, I have a great confidence that it has affected people's thinking and their interests tremendously.[66]

In their own small way the Catholic Worker and the Plowshares resisters disarmed the country.

NOTES

For Nina Polcyn Moore and Anita Morreale. The author wishes to acknowledge the help of Lois Dament, Nancy Giguere, David W. Smith, and Mary Swanson of the College of St. Thomas, Sarah Elbert of SUNY Binghamton, David J. O'Brien of the College of the Holy Cross, Nancy L. Roberts of the University of Minnesota, and Phil Runkel of the Catholic Worker Archives at Marquette University. Part of the research and writing of this paper was funded through the faculty development program of the College of St. Thomas. Earlier versions of this chapter were presented at the 1985 meeting of the Organization of American Historians and as a part of the Sister Muriel Ford lecture series at Briar Cliff College in 1986. Permission to quote from papers in the Daniel and Philip Berrigan Collection, Department of Rare Books, Cornell University, courtesy of Cornell University Library. Thanks to Cornell University and to Rosemary S. Bannan for use of her interview materials. Thanks as well to Marquette University for permission to quote from letters in the Catholic Worker archives.

Note: The *Catholic Worker* is here cited as *CW.*

1. A solid, brief history of Catholic Worker pacifism can be found in Mel Piehl, *Breaking Bread: The Catholic Worker and the Origin of Catholic Radicalism in America* (Philadelphia: Temple University Press, 1982), 189–239. Since the 1930s, when the Catholic Worker movement was founded, new Catholic peace groups emanated from the Catholic Worker movement. Before World War II, Joseph Zarrella and William Callahan started Pax, a Catholic Worker front. The Association of Catholic Conscientious Objectors, which met the needs of the war-torn 1940s, likewise was created by Catholic Workers and supported by meager Catholic Worker resources. During the 1960s and 1970s, somewhat more independently of the Catholic Worker but still drawing from its human resources and intellectual legacy, Pax Christi and the Catholic Peace Fellowship mobilized a new generation of liberal Catholics into peace activism.

2. Dorothy Day, *From Union Square to Rome* (1938: reprinted New York: Arno Press, 1978), 148.

3. Ibid.

4. One of Day's most powerful arguments on behalf of practicing the law of love is her "Editorial—CW Stand on the Use of Force" (September 1938), reprinted in Thomas C. Cornell and James H. Forest, eds., *A Penny a Copy: Readings from "The Catholic Worker"* (New York: Macmillan, 1968), 35–38.

5. John J. Hugo, G. Barry O'Toole, and Dorothy Day contributed the most substantial articles on peace during the period 1939–1945. A convenient guide to Father Hugo's pacifist thought is *The Gospel of Peace* (privately printed, 1944). For G. Barry O'Toole, see specific citations for 1939–1940 issues of the *Catholic Worker* in Anne Klejment and Alice Klejment, *Dorothy Day and "The Catholic Worker": A Bibliography and Index* (New York: Garland, 1986), 110ff. Dorothy Day's views on war and peace are sprinkled throughout her writings, but see especially her classic statement in "Explains CW Stand on Use of Force," *CW* 6 (September 1938): 1, 4, 7. On Day's knowledge of the Holocaust, see her "Where Is Sanctuary?" *CW* 10 (June 1943): 1, 9.

6. Piehl, *Breaking Bread,* 209, 215, 231.

7. Klejment and Klejment, *Bibliography* (233–85) lists *CW* articles from the 1960s. Some specific examples are James W. Douglass, "The Council and the Bomb," *CW* 31 (July–August 1965): 1, 8, and Herve Chaigne, O.F.M., "The Council and Nuclear War," *CW* 32 (July–August 1966): 4–5, 7.

8. As more Catholics completed a higher education and entered into the middle class after World War II, there was a new constituency for the peace movement. Papal pronouncements against modern warfare and the Second Vatican Council's reevaluation of traditional teachings on war and peace

inspired mass Catholic participation in the antiwar movement of the later 1960s. And, of course, there was the Vietnam war. The tensions in modern U.S. Catholic social history have been explored in David J. O'Brien, *The Renewal of American Catholicism* (1972; New York: Paulist Press, n.d.), 80–108, 138–62, and Jay P. Dolan, *The American Catholic Experience* (Garden City, N.Y.: Doubleday, 1985), 384–459.

9. Anne Klejment, "The Berrigans: Revolutionary Christian Nonviolence" in *Peace Heroes in Twentieth-Century America*, ed. Charles DeBenedetti (Bloomington: Indiana University Press, 1986), 228–31.

10. Ibid., 230. Also Anne Klejment, "In the Lions' Den: The Social Catholicism of Daniel and Philip Berrigan, 1955–1965" (Ph.D. dissertation, State University of New York at Binghamton, 1980), 96, 104–9.

11. Thomas Merton, "The Root of War," *CW* 28 (October 1961): 1, 7–8. The most accessible account of Merton's influence can be found in Daniel Berrigan, *Portraits of Those I Love* (New York: Crossroad, 1982), 13–31.

12. Daniel Berrigan, *The World for Wedding Ring* (New York: Macmillan, 1962), see for example, "The Face of Christ," 47. Robert Gilliam, interview by author, May 1985.

13. See especially Daniel Berrigan, "In Peaceable Conflict," *CW* 31 (March 1965): 1, 7, and Philip Berrigan, "Vietnam and America's Conscience," *CW* 32 (October 1965): 2,6.

14. Catonsville Nine, "Press Statement," reprinted in Philip Berrigan, S.S.J., *A Punishment for Peace* (New York: Macmillan, 1969), 173, and Tom Lewis's illustrations in Daniel Berrigan's *Trial Poems* (Boston: Beacon Press, 1970); "America Is Hard to Find," poetry by Daniel Berrigan and a rock mass by John Hostettler, Alan Sorvall (?), David Turner (Multi-Trax, [1970]); and the Hollywood version, "The Trial of the Catonsville Nine."

15. Some thoughtful evaluations of the Catonsville Nine were collected in two anthologies: William VanEtten Casey, S.J., and Philip Nobile, eds., *The Berrigans* (New York: Avon Books, 1977), and Stephen Halpert and Tom Murray, *Witness of the Berrigans* (Garden City, N.Y.: Doubleday, 1972). On the issue of a Catholic core in the ultraresistance, see Charles A. Meconis, *With Clumsy Grace: The American Catholic Left, 1961–1975* (New York: Seabury, 1979), 169 (table 4).

16. Piehl, *Breaking Bread*, 232–33.

17. See Dorothy Day, "'Sanctuary,'" *CW* 35 (February 1969): 1–2, 8; Raymond Hohlfeld, M. M., "Rendering to Caesar," *CW* 35 (June 1969): 7; Daniel Berrigan, "Tape 15" (5 January 1973), Berrigan Collection, Olin Library, Cornell University (hereafter cited as CU). The "lice" phrase, quoted in *Meditations: Dorothy Day*, ed. Stanley Vishnewski (New York: Newman Press, 1970), 48, is actually a heading added by Vishnewski and adapted from one of Day's 1939 articles.

18. James H. Forest quoted in John Leo LeBrun, "The Role of the Catholic Worker Movement in American Pacifism, 1933–1972" (Ph.D. dissertation, Case Western Reserve University, 1973), 315.

19. Tom Cornell, "Nonviolent Napalm in Catonsville," *CW* 34 (June 1968): 1–2, 8; All further quotations of Cornell on Catonsville are from this

article unless otherwise noted. According to Cornell, the decision to write the Catonsville article was his; interview by author, June 1985.

20.   LeBrun, "Role of the CW," 298.

21.   Cornell, interview by author, June 1985.

22.   Ammon Hennacy, "The One-Man Revolution," *CW* 34 (November 1968): 6.

23.   Jack Cook, "36 East First," *CW* 34 (December 1968): 7.

24.   Michael Ketchum, "Baltimore," *CW* 34 (October 1968): 1–2.

25.   Dorothy Day to Daniel Berrigan, May 31 [1968], CU.

26.   James H. Forest quoting Dorothy Day in John Deedy, *"Apologies, Good Friends . . .": An Interim Biography of Daniel Berrigan, S.J.* (Chicago: Fides/Claretian, 1981), 86. The Liturgical Conference did not have a tape or transcript of Day's talk. Virginia Sloyan to author, July 21 and 29, 1986; Robert W. Hovda to author, August 13, 1986.

27.   Philip Berrigan to Daniel Berrigan [9 September 1968?], CU.

28.   Day quoted in Francine du Plessix Gray, *Divine Disobedience: Profiles in Catholic Radicalism* (New York: Alfred A. Knopf, 1970), 162. Also see William D. Miller, *Dorothy Day: A Biography* (San Francisco: Harper & Row, 1982), 456.

29.   Dorothy Day, "In Peace Is my Bitterness Most Bitter," *CW* 33 (January 1967): 1. Gray, *Divine Disobedience*, 162; Dorothy Day, interview [transcript] by Rosemary Bannan, September 1969, 26, CU.

30.   Day quoted in Gray, *Divine Disobedience*, 163; Cornell, interview with author, June 1985.

31.   Day quoted in Patricia McNeal, *The American Catholic Peace Movement, 1928–1972* (New York: Arno, 1978), 2. Cornell, interview with author, June 1985.

32.   Jim Forest, interview with author, July 1985.

33.   Dorothy Day, *On Pilgrimage: The Sixties* (New York: Curtis Books, 1972): 344.

34.   Ibid.

35.   Ibid., 354.

36.   Ibid., 344.

37.   My sources for this period include an unpublished interview, a letter to a follower, comments sprinkled through her *CW* articles, a story by Dwight Macdonald, an interview in a British antiwar newsletter, and some recent interviews.

38.   Thomas Merton, *The Hidden Ground of Love: The Letters of Thomas Merton on Religious Experience and Social Concerns*, ed. William H. Shannon (New York: Farrar, Straus, Giroux, 1985), 152.

39.   During the late 1960s and early 1970s, the *CW* thorough coverage of Cesar Chavez's UFW union suggests that one alternative that Day presented to the ultraresistance was the more traditional nonviolent direct action of this union, a point that could be missed if nonviolence is compartmentalized into separate categories for the peace movement, the labor movement, the civil rights movement, and so forth.

40.   The scope of this movement is covered in two works by Charles Meconis. See "Religion and Radicalism: The American 'Catholic Left' as a

Social Movement, 1961–1975" (Ph.D. dissertation, Columbia University, 1977), and *With Clumsy Grace.*

41. The most readable and best conceptualized account of the antiwar movement is "The Deferred Reform" in Charles DeBenedetti, *The Peace Reform in American History* (Bloomington: Indiana University Press, 1980), 165–96.

42. Thanks to Ralph DiGia of the WRL for a photocopy of the May–June 1969 issue of *WRL News,* documenting the theft and attack.

43. Day, interview by Bannan, 5, 14, CU.

44. Dorothy Day to Michael Cullen, ca. February 1970, Dorothy Day–Catholic Worker Collection, Memorial Library Archives, Marquette University, Milwaukee (hereafter cited as "CW Papers"). Dwight Macdonald, "Revisiting Dorothy Day," *New York Review of Books,* 28 January 1971: 18. Tom Cornell explained that Macdonald's interview of Day annoyed her, for it had been conducted by telephone; Cornell, interview by author, June 1985.

45. Day, interview by Bannan, 1, 9–10, CU. John Cort, a Catholic Worker member during the 1930s and a self-proclaimed realist, viewed Dorothy Day as a sort of abbess. See "My Life at the Catholic Worker," *Commonweal* 107 (20 June 1980): 361–67. Also see James Forest, "Dorothy Day and the Sermon on the Mount," *The Other Side* 119 (August 1981): 18, who says that "there wasn't a democratic bone in her body," and Tom Cornell, "Dorothy Day Recalled: Worker Leader 'Didn't Want Any Sugar Coating,'" *National Catholic Reporter* (27 November 1981): 16, who remembered that "if she was an anarchist it was only if she could be the anarch."

46. Day to Cullen, ca. February 1970, CW Papers. She tacked an unidentified quote on her letter, explaining to Cullen that "wars will cease when men refuse to fight."

47. Day, interview by Bannan, 45, CU. Dorothy Day, *The Long Loneliness* (1952; San Francisco: Harper & Row, 1981), 149–50.

48. Day to Cullen, ca. February 1970, CW Papers. She drew a line through the "gentle" that preceded "sabotage" in this handwritten letter.

49. Dorothy Day, "Dan Berrigan in Rochester," *CW* 36 (December 1970): 1, 6; Day, interview by Bannan, 58, CU.

50. Day, interview by Bannan, 25–26, CU. In the same interview (6, 28), Day briefly mentioned her initial lack of enthusiasm for the protests of the 1950s. Day did not specifically examine the historical evidence of property destruction by Gandhi and his disciples. On Gandhi and the destruction of property, Richard McSorley questioned an English disciple of Gandhi, Donald Groom. "He remarked," according to McSorley, "that though Gandhi was involved in the burning of cloth, the cloth burnt always belonged to those who did the burning." See McSorley's *Peace Eyes* (Washington: Center for Peace Studies, 1978), 4.

51. Day to Cullen, ca. February 1970, MU. In 1960 Day had published a popular biography of this saint, her only nonautobiographical book. A reprint edition of *Thérèse* is published by Templegate.

52. Day, interview by Bannan, 17, 20, 59, CU. Cornell, "Dorothy Day Recalled," 17. One SDS student who attended Day's talk at the Catonsville

rally recalled: "It was very obvious that time in Baltimore that she was almost ill at having to walk through the mass of people." Sarah Elbert to Anne Klejment, March 30, 1987.

53. Day, interview by Bannan, 30, CU.

54. Macdonald, "Revisiting," 19. Eric Hennessy, one of Day's grandsons, served in Vietnam.

55. Day, interview by Bannan, 41, CU. Within her movement, however, Day hardly subscribed to a laissez-faire attitude toward the behavior of Catholic Worker volunteers. During the 1940s she reminded Workers who supported the war of the limits on their right to dissent. Twenty years later, she accused a few young Catholic Workers of obscenity and fornication and threw them out, an episode that is remembered by insiders as "the Dorothy Day stomp."

56. Day to Cullen, ca. February 1970, CW Papers Day, interview by Bannan, 36, 59, 42, CU.

57. Daniel Berrigan, *America Is Hard to Find: Notes from the Underground and Letters from Danbury Prison* (Garden City, N.Y.: Doubleday, 1972), 35. Philip Berrigan was captured by the FBI shortly after he disappeared underground. Daniel Berrigan eluded the FBI from April through early August and thus had more opportunities to engage in consciousness raising with the public.

58. "Dorothy Day Talks to Roadrunner," *Catonsville Roadrunner #20?* (1970): unpaginated. Once Day complained about the prison mystique of the ultraresistance. In fact, this mystique alienated some feminists from the larger resistance movement, according to Barrie Thorne. They fleshed out their objections to machismo, criticizing female subordination, elitism, and the apotheosis of risk, which called into question the genuineness of the revolution. Machismo probably served a practical purpose in the antiwar movement by countering the stereotype of effeminate resisters. The New Left spoke freely of "putting one's balls on the line," as in Jesse Lemisch's commentary "Who Will Write a Left History of Art While We Are All Putting Our Balls on the Line?" (Boston: New England Free Press, 1968). Barrie Thorne has studied sex roles in "Women in the Draft Resistance Movement: A Case Study of Sex Roles and Social Movements," *Sex Roles* 1 (1975): 179–95. With reference to the Catholic Left, see Meconis, *With Clumsy Grace,* 104–5.

59. Day was underscoring the need for spiritual, mental, and physical preparation of oneself and one's family for the prison experience. The author wishes to acknowledge the help of Tom Cornell in documenting this sensitive point.

60. Day quoted in Macdonald, "Revisiting," 18. Day's anticlericalism noted by Cornell, interview by author, June 1985; Forest, interview by author, July 1985; Robert Gilliam, interview by author, May 1985.

61. Dorothy Day, "On Pilgrimage," *CW* (December 1972): 2, 8.

62. Paul Magno and Marcia Timmel, "But Why This?" in *Violence Ends Where Love Begins,* ed. Karl Welsher (Plowshares Press, n.d.), 33–35. An indispensable source on the Plowshares movement is Arthur J. Laffin and

Anne Montgomery, eds., *Swords into Plowshares: Nonviolent Direct Action for Disarmament* (San Francisco: Harper & Row, 1987).

63. "Wouldn't Raid Draft Today: Cullen," *Catholic Messenger* [Davenport, Iowa] September 9, 1971: 1, 3.

64. For a recent assessment of Day's influence on war resisters, see "The Woman" in Daniel Berrigan, *Portraits Of Those I Love* (New York: Crossroad, 1982), 88.

65. Daniel Berrigan, *Ten Commandments for the Long Haul* (Nashville: Abingdon, 1980), 149.

66. Day, interview by Bannan, 63, CU.

III

Catholic Worker Communities

Two Case Histories

10. EXPERIMENTS IN TRUTH

An Oral History of the St. Louis Catholic Worker, 1935–1942

Janice Brandon-Falcone

THE WORST SNOWSTORM St. Louis had seen in sixty years had occurred the previous day. Main streets were mostly open but side streets were questionable. Homeowners carved out parking spots from snow drifts, then guarded the empty spaces from squatters like myself. I peered down the street where Evelyn Gilsinn lived and wondered aloud if Catholic Worker scholarship always entailed the risk of one's life and the health of one's auto. On a snow-packed, one-lane street lived Ms. Gilsinn, a retired schoolteacher who had been a mainstay of the group around the St. Louis Catholic Worker in the Depression years. Having made a date to meet on this particular morning, and with a deadline hovering on the horizon, I was too foolish to cancel because of a snowstorm.

I was expecting Emma Goldman, or someone almost as radical, but the door opened to reveal a thin gray schoolteacher. Wiping my feet without a reminder, I introduced myself and was ushered into Evelyn Gilsinn's apartment. It was neat and spare like herself; crocheted doilies protected the backs and arms of chairs, but reading material was piled everywhere in small stacks, awaiting her commands. I almost addressed her as "Aunt Evelyn" as we settled in with coffee and tape recorder to talk. Speaking was difficult for Evelyn Gilsinn; she had a chronic hoarseness that sounded painful, but she assured me that it was not. Hoarseness aside, her eyes began to dance ever so slightly as she thought back to the early days when she first had met

Dorothy Day. "Once I heard Dorothy speak," she remembered, "I could never feel the same way about self-indulgence again."[1] She indulged me all morning with cups of coffee and stories that were fifty years old. From time to time, Evelyn Gilsinn pulled me into her present-day activities. Before the morning was over, she had induced me to sign a petition against a special nuclear bomb, introduced me to social justice organizations with a battery of pamphlets and newspapers, and talked me into joining Bread for the World. Evelyn Gilsinn was no typical maiden-aunt schoolteacher.

Neither was she Emma Goldman. She described herself as an "ordinary person" who had listened to someone extraordinary, Dorothy Day. It had changed her life, though she insisted she was not one of the central people in the St. Louis Catholic Worker movement. But then, most of those whose memories formed the following story of the St. Louis Catholic Worker said much the same self-deprecating things. They were ordinary people but their lives had been transformed by the personalist vision of the Catholic Worker movement. Like Evelyn Gilsinn, the St. Louis Catholic Workers shared with Dorothy Day and Peter Maurin the vision of a world that conjoined physical and spiritual realities. It was a vision of anomalies and paradoxes, antonyms and contradictions; but mostly it was a sacramental vision that transformed the everyday elements of these ordinary lives into something beyond politics, social theory, or formal religion.

The fluid nature of the Catholic Worker gave rise to as many failures as successes, but also redefined the terms of success. The Catholic Worker became a movement as a result of individual, often eccentric, and personal responses to the visions of Day and Maurin. This oral history of the group in St. Louis that responded to the Catholic Worker idea is more than a collection of individual stories. The ordinary/extraordinary lives of Evelyn Gilsinn and her comrades reveal something of the nature of the Catholic Worker movement. I have come to understand them as experimenters with truth, a metaphor borrowed from Gandhi's autobiography. It is an apt metaphor to describe the diversity and personality found in the thousands of stories that comprise Catholic Worker history. Though the St. Louisans with whom I spoke would hesitate to compare themselves to Gandhi, his own call to pacifism and resistance would be echoed in the writings of Dorothy Day. Friends of Day's in St. Louis created their own response to the Catholic Worker and their own experiment with Catholic radicalism.

The stories that Evelyn Gilsinn wove for me on that snowy February day have been rewoven with the stories of other old St. Louis

Catholic Workers to produce another sort of experiment—my own. Mostly, however, it is the story of ordinary people in St. Louis during the 1930s translating the Catholic Worker vision into their own experiments.

THE FEW WHO put out the fledgling *Catholic Worker* in the early 1930s began to receive requests to address audiences at Catholic colleges and civic and women's groups.[2] Most of the invitations were for Dorothy Day and Peter Maurin; most were accepted if bus fare was included. In St. Louis and other cities, small groups of people heard about the paper, its call for hospitality and the practice of the works of mercy. As early as 1935, a few in St. Louis set about to imitate this radical version of Christianity.

Dorothy and Peter never offered a centralized office or organizational plan. "Begin where you are," Dorothy Day told her audiences. "You can start a Catholic Worker house and call it a Catholic Worker house without any confirmation from New York," said Bolen Carter, recalling his Worker association in the 1930s.[3] Most of the subsequent houses of hospitality, soup kitchens, or farming communes did not ask for confirmation, but they did receive encouragement in the form of visits from Dorothy Day, Peter Maurin, or associates, comments or articles in the paper, and unofficial membership in a network that sprang up across the country.

St. Louis developed its own Catholic Worker house in response to the immediate needs of the Depression and the charismatic influence of Dorothy Day. The St. Louisans involved in the Catholic Worker were ordinary people, "conventional" by their own account, whose lives were never the same again.[4]

In the spring of 1935, Saint Louis University took official note of the Catholic Worker. Father Husslein, of the newly formed department of social studies, invited Dorothy Day to address the university in the spring of that year. On May 7, 1935, Dorothy spoke to a group of eight hundred in the university's Law Auditorium. She received front-page coverage in an article by Bolen J. Carter, then a student, in the next issue of *The University News*. The young reporter must have listened with more than passing interest when Dorothy offered the following suggestion:

A group of students in Boston have rented a store for the distribution of literature, for giving lectures, and a general headquarters for Catholic Action of a vital nature. There is no reason why a similar group could not be started at Saint

Louis University. Groups in Cleveland, Boston or Chicago . . . did as you did on May Day—distributed copies of the *Catholic Worker* at Communist meetings.[5]

In response to Dorothy Day's lecture, a recent graduate of the university, Cyril Echele, wrote to New York to obtain a list of subscribers in the St. Louis area. From this list of about forty, Echele proposed a meeting of anyone interested in forming a local Catholic Worker group. In July, six or seven interested people met to discuss the ideas of social action proposed by the Catholic Worker. They continued to meet at intervals throughout the year. In early February 1936, Dorothy had a speaking engagement in Kansas, which enabled her to stop over in St. Louis for a day. Her visit gave the group encouragement and renewed zeal. They felt they must get a place of their own for meetings. By March, the group had acquired an address, a name, and stationery, but little else. Using the address of one of their members, Donald Gallagher, a graduate student at the university, they called themselves the Campion Propaganda Committee. According to Gallagher, the Campions were "discussion groups formed . . . under the inspirations of the Catholic Worker."[6]

The year 1936 proved a full and exciting one for the St. Louis group. Cy Echele had by then lost his job and was devoting much of his time to the Catholic Worker both in New York and St. Louis. In the spring the New York Catholic Worker obtained its first farm at Easton, Pennsylvania, and began to set up the farming commune envisioned by Peter Maurin.

The agenda that Peter Maurin carried in his head was categorical rather than chronological. He saw a Christian community, which he characterized in his alliterative fashion as cult, culture, and cultivation. By this he meant a community of worker/scholars, infused with Christian spirituality, living together on or near communal farms. In actuality, his vision most closely paralleled village life in the Middle Ages: a self-supporting community living off the surrounding lands and simple handicrafts, with the church at the center of the village and its life.[7]

In reality, Catholic Worker farming communes never approached the model that Peter Maurin dreamed and spoke about. The actual nature of the farming experiments demonstrated something of Catholic Worker limitations. The Christian anarchism that worked in the city did not translate well to the country. The urban soupline and clothes room could sustain some disorganization, the transiency of cooks, servers, and house organizers, for example. In contrast, the farming communes that worked best operated under the authority of one skilled and stable personality; yet this pattern of centralism was not often realized in the farming experiments.[8]

The history of the Catholic Worker experiment, especially in its regional expressions, can be retrieved through the memories of the participants. Cy Echele went to Easton, Pennsylvania, in the spring of 1936 to help develop the farming commune, but became embroiled in one of the many Worker altercations there and returned to St. Louis. Meanwhile, the St. Louis Catholic Worker received its own offer of a farm. John Dreisoerner, a diocesan seminarian, offered the St. Louis group the use of a tract of land in the St. Francois Mountains south of St. Louis. Don Gallagher wrote an excited letter to New York in March telling of the offer:

> There are some 250 acres, about 10 acres of fruit trees. The granite cottage is furnished. The terms: "someone live there and take care of the orchard from which we [the owners, three religious] would receive half the crop to pay the taxes. Outside of that your actions would be as free as if the property were yours."[9]

A note of potential difficulty was sounded when he added, "There are some disadvantages to the place, chiefly its distance from St. Louis and the fact that the soil is not very rich." Another letter a few weeks later informed Dorothy that "we have taken over the farm to the extent of putting a man on it."[10] The man was Echele, who had some farming background as well as the few weeks' experience at Easton. Neither prepared him for that summer.

In the June issue of the *Catholic Worker*, Echele reported on his activities at the farm. Under the promising headline of "Catholic Worker Farming Commune NO. 2" Echele described the farm and the weather: "As soon as it rains, and we need it badly, we will have the neighbor plow a piece of land." Privately, he wrote to his friends in New York, "I have been just as discouraged and sad as I have been quiet . . . the terrific heat is burning up the garden . . . it has not rained for two months."[11] Forty-five years later he remembered the farming experiment as "a glorious failure!" The summer had been so dry that he "almost starved to death and even my chickens died!"[12] A September letter to Dorothy informed her that "it has been a hard summer in more ways than one . . . the Catholic Worker Embryonic Agronomic University is being 'closed' for the season."[13]

Thus ended the St. Louis attempt at a farming commune. Perhaps it would have met with more success if it had not been a summer of record drought and if the land had not been a "godforsaken tract down in the Ozarks."[14] In the best of summers a harvest is wrested from Ozark land in a most unyielding fashion.

Fortunately, there were other aspects of the Catholic Worker vision to which the St. Louis group could turn their attention. In the fall of 1936 they rented two front rooms at 3526 Franklin Avenue, a few blocks north of Saint Louis University. The first month's rent was paid by Father Martin Hellreigel, a friend of the Catholic Worker group who shared his interest in the liturgy as well as the $25 rent. They named their small center the Campion Book Shop and continued to refer to themselves as the Campion Propaganda Committee.[15]

Why "propaganda" committee? They regarded propaganda in a different light than simply as uncritical support of an issue; propaganda reflected their enthusiastic support, not uncritical, of what they called Catholic Action. Propaganda included not only issues of the *Catholic Worker*, but the philosophic literature of Mounier and the works of Kropotkin, Dostoyevsky, Georges Bernanos, religious pamphlets, Virgil Michel's early works on liturgy and, later, social reconstruction. Also, since the communist bookstore was only a few doors away, there might have been less literary reasons for calling themselves a propaganda committee.

Don Gallagher lived in the two back rooms of the bookshop, while the front room sheltered the small library of pamphlets and material on social justice, personalist philosophy, and Catholic Action. The young people who visited to read and argue philosophy or social action might have felt that one of Peter Maurin's Easy Essays was directed at them as part of a propaganda committee.

> In St. Louis University
> you turn out Masters of Arts,
> but as Diego Rivera says:
> "All art is propaganda."
> And as all propaganda is agitation,
> it behooves St. Louis University,
> to turn out Masters of Agitation.
> So *The Catholic Worker* suggests
> that you, our Master Catholic Agitator,
> start in St. Louis University
> a school of Catholic Agitation
> for the popularization of Catholic Action.[16]

Weekly meetings were held so that the small group could discuss matters of mutual interest: an increasing involvement with the liturgical concerns of Father Hellreigel; discussions on the philosophy of personalism; their concern for the current social crisis of unemployment—their own and others'.

A few doors away stood The Vanguard, the local communist bookshop; with its proprietors they maintained the relationship of "respectful adversaries." The two groups borrowed chairs from each other for their respective meetings, argued their particular positions without hope of conversion, and tried to offer alternatives to each other's cause. For the most part, the Catholic Workers were less sophisticated than the communists. "It was a very informal and slightly starry-eyed group" that opened the storefront on Franklin Avenue, "but serious about things that the Worker represented."[17] It is easy to catch the enthusiasm, even fifty years later, in the memories of those early meetings. "Personalism inspired me," recalled Cyril Echele. "Oh, we had a tremendous vision of what this was going to do."[18]

Most young people enjoy a time of idealism and enthusiasm, but this particular group found itself in the midst of the Depression; hard times cast shadows of failure into the most spirited enthusiasms and kept a serious note in the weekly meetings. The Campion Book Shop and Propaganda Committee was intent on developing the exchange of ideas proposed by Peter Maurin, but there was little else in progress except their weekly meetings. Other cities had houses of hospitality, but the storefront on Franklin Avenue was too small to provide any sort of shelter. Gradually, they began to focus some energy on the works of mercy, specifically feeding the hungry. That fall they began a coffee line at the bookshop on Franklin Avenue. "We started that when somebody came in one night and said, 'Yes, you have all these *ideas*, but what are you *doing*? You ought to be serving food.' Well, we did not have facilities for serving food but we started a little line . . . with a big pot of coffee . . . we got day-old (or more than day-old) bread from some bakeries."[19]

Anne Loftus and Evelyn Gilsinn were friends who taught together at a North Side Elementary school. They also became interested in the Catholic Worker group and the meetings at the propaganda center. In the fall and winter of 1936–37, Anne and Evelyn rose early each morning to brew several pots of coffee. On their way to work they dropped off the coffee to be distributed with day-old bread. Religious orders heard of the group's efforts toward a soupline and donated bread, butter, and leftover coffee grounds to be reboiled by the young women. So began the group's modest attempt to provide the rudiments of a soupline in a personalist fashion.

This was not a well-organized, smoothly operating committee with the support of a federal agency. Nor did the St. Louis Catholic Worker enjoy the patronage of Archbishop Glennon as an official arm of diocesan charity. It was, in effect, a loosely organized group held together only by a shared admiration for Worker ideas and a desire to respond socially (and also liturgically) to the issues of the day. Members had jobs all over the city. Don Gallagher continued his graduate studies at Saint Louis University. Bolen Carter, Luke Lanwermeyer, and Dave Dunne were working, but also began to write and publish a small paper, the *Catholic Alliance.*

Without any organizational backing, the St. Louis Catholic Worker had only the New York house to use as a model. New York had more organization because of the leadership and personality of Dorothy Day. The more one learns of regional expressions of the movement, the more one comes to see Day's charismatic personality as integral to the success of the New York Worker community. Day's visits to outlying communities such as St. Louis encouraged their success, but hardly ensured it. New York also had a house of hospitality occupied by those who were able to live there and run it. Despite the enthusiasm generated by Catholic Worker ideas and periodic visits from New York Workers, the St. Louis group "had difficulty harnessing ideals to work."[20] Still, they continued their meetings and a variety of projects that, in retrospect, suggest a great deal of energy and time devoted to the Worker despite heavy demands of school and jobs.

In the spring of 1937 a new technique of striking was employed at Emerson Electric in St. Louis. The sitdown strike, first developed by the United Auto Workers a few years before, made its appearance in St. Louis that April. In a letter to the *Catholic Worker,* Cy Echele referred to the strike at Emerson Electric and the sympathetic involvement of the St. Louis Worker community. There was some concern among the Catholic strikers that they would not be able to leave the plant for mass. "With the permission of the union organizer, three of the members of our St. Louis Catholic Worker unit visited the sitdowners to talk over the matter (i.e. mass) and to distribute the paper." In addition, Echele reported, "we continue to have round table discussions on modern problems at the 'Catholic Worker' center. We make an appeal for men and women who are interested in social action to come to our meeting." A few months later the Workers would announce, "We have set aside Wednesday night especially for labor meetings. We are attempting to formulate a program whereby the teaching of the Church on labor can be effectively spread among the workers. Eventually, we may form a local of the ACTU here."[21]

The Association of Catholic Trade Unionists was yet another group that grew out of the Catholic Worker. Formed in 1937 in the New York house of hospitality by Catholic Worker John Cort and others, the ACTU represented not only Catholic laborers but also Catholic social thought. It separated from the New York Catholic Worker to begin an independent life of its own in 1938.

The Catholic Worker supported strikes and especially sitdown strikes as an attempt at nonviolent social change, but the Worker, despite its name, was not a labor movement. Mel Piehl, in his excellent study of the movement, notes that the Catholic Worker was "unwilling to subordinate its own social ideals to the aims of the unions" and thus would "continue to discuss the labor question in the language of religious idealism." Dorothy Day's support of labor issues must be understood as growing out of the central role of liturgy and sacrament (especially the eucharist) in the movement she cofounded. The spearhead of the American liturgical movement, Father Virgil Michel, an early and strong supporter of the Catholic Worker, also put great emphasis on social action.[22] The connection is essential to understanding the Catholic Worker position on strikes, labor and social change. Father Martin Hellreigel, the St. Louis equivalent of Michel, shared rent money with the St. Louis Worker but also provided a like-minded understanding of labor, liturgy, and the resulting social action.

The St. Louis Catholic Workers grasped this understanding of the essential connection between the social activism of a strike and the central role of religion. Meetings held with Fathers Hellreigel and Michel mean nothing until seen in the context of these attempts to "harness ideals to work." Likewise, the visits of the St. Louis Workers to the locked-in strikers appear nothing more than pietistic or pompous until seen in the context of a social activism latent within liturgical ideas. The support of the strikers represented the application of a liturgy/labor paradigm.

Peter Maurin was always interested in laborers but seldom in labor issues, especially strikes. "Strikes don't strike me," he told anyone who would listen, a play on words that suggests the aversion of a gentle man to confrontation. Nevertheless, his version of Catholic Action called for a synthesis of work and liturgy. Worker involvement in the Emerson Electric strike was an expression of their commitment to such a synthesis. This synergistic ideal would emerge again and again.

Strikes and labor problems were not the only items of concern for the St. Louis group. In July, Don Gallagher provided a fuller summary of their activities. "We have indeed done more than before in regard to paper distribution, interracial activity, labor, works of mercy, spreading of ideas and prayer."[23] Their commitment to the synthesis of work and liturgy led them to experiments in several areas.

Their interracial concerns were somewhat premature for St. Louis and Saint Louis University. "We were kind of a thorn in the side of Saint Louis University," remembered one Worker, "because we were agitating for the admittance of blacks. At that time, it was not yet done."[24] At that time in St. Louis, there was also a separate "colored" parish, and the St. Louis Catholic Worker offered doctrine classes for children from this parish.

An early and abiding concern for the Workers was liturgy, and they had maintained a fruitful relationship with Martin Hellreigel because of their mutual interest in the liturgical movement. "Monsignor Hellreigel was heart and soul with the Catholic Worker," recalled Father Joe Huels, a young and unofficial chaplain to the St. Louis Worker. They went as a group to various parishes around the city "where the liturgy was good." They traveled the forty miles to Father Hellreigel's Mass in O'Fallon. (One needs to put their understanding of "good liturgy" into the perspective of that time. "If the priest would turn around to say '*Dominus vobiscum*' and we could get the people to say '*Et cum spiritu tuo*' that was real participation.")[25]

Their meetings opened with prayer and ended with the recitation of Compline together. Their involvement with Worker ideas and action was closely tied to this liturgical concern. Interest in the liturgy was part of their attempt to translate an abiding spiritual life into the real world. One Worker reflected on this attempt: "In the past there was too much division. You were a Christian on Sunday and you never had anything to do with that big bad world out there. That big bad world was going to hell and you had to let it alone because you might go to hell with it."[26]

Perhaps the most distinctive feature of the Worker movement, both locally and nationally, was this sense of the material infused with the spiritual, a healthy antidote to latent Jansenism. For modern secular analysts, it is not only the most distinguishing feature but the most puzzling. Workers possessed and nourished a deep sacramental understanding of their relation to society, church, and God. The St. Louis Logos Study Group, formed in 1943 to "implement the word of God into action in the secular world," continues to this day to meet on a monthly basis for prayer and study.[27] Cyril and Margaret Echele and Evelyn Gilsinn are three members whose involvement in the study circle stretches back to their Catholic Worker days.

What is remarkable about the Catholic Worker is that it is not one more movement of social reform. Nor is it one more religious group that gets together to pray. "All the way through," remembered Joe Huels, "the Catholic Worker was both an intellectual movement and down-to-earth charity, feeding the hungry . . . and [other] works of mercy."[28]

Their interest in liturgy and daily devotions was not merely a coincidental corollary to their social activities. A primary goal of the movement has always been to infuse the spiritual into the physical world, and not the reverse, which sometimes attempts to politicize spirituality. This is an important distinction. Peter Maurin, speculative father of the Worker movement, regarded this understanding of the dialectic between spirit and matter as central to their work. Such was the stuff of salvation.[29] They were equally familiar with such traditionally Catholic concepts as the mystical body of Christ as they were with social questions. Their sense of kinship and social responsibility often found expression in this idea of the mystical body. "Employer and employee, white and black, sinner and saint are not separate entities with conflicting purpose, but are united in common bonds of brotherhood in the Mystical Body of Christ. What happens to one happens to all."[30]

A short-lived newsletter, "The Catholic Alliance," served as a forum for many of these ideas. Among them was the insight that liturgy was an essential aspect of the church's social teachings. An article entitled "The Liturgy and Social Action" addressed this very idea.

> The word *liturgy* . . . means a public service performed by a group for a common purpose. In its specific sense it includes all acts of homage . . . given by man to his creator. . . . The liturgy, above all, implies social responsibility, and in the Mass, man's individualism becomes merged with that of his fellows . . . . Priest and laity pray together so that service becomes a social rather than an individual act.[31]

Their mutual interest in liturgy and social action was hardly coincidental; it was rather an essential and logical corollary. Certainly they were opposed to defining liturgy as "an antiquarian interest in the ritual or decorative element of the Church quite apart from her real mission." A few years later, another St. Louis Worker would write, "The main point of this program is the renewal of Christian life, public and private, especially by participation in the liturgical and sacramental life of the Church."[32]

On one hand, the devotional life of the church served as a source of nourishment and energy for the social aspirations of the group. Their commitment to the spiritual life served as a sort of fuel, providing momentum for the social aims. On the other hand, this devotional life was more than the means to another end. It could hardly be divided. The liturgical and sacramental interest was central to the movement's social aims. Without this spirituality, there was not only no impetus, no motivation for social concerns, but there was no end to work toward either. The Workers aspired not only to alleviate suffering amongst the poor and promote justice, but to live the Christian life as well. Thus it could be said with equal accuracy that the works of mercy, the social activism of the Worker, was the means to this other end, a life devoted to the spirit, the imitation of Christ. The means and the ends of one's life became as inseparable as the double helix of a DNA molecule.

Again and again, the dialectic between the works of mercy and the spiritual, devotional life would present itself. Many times this ideal created tensions in the individual and in the movement as a whole. Often there arose a sense of tension between one's personal lifestyle and the aspirations of the movement. This was aggravated as individuals grew older and took on the responsibilities of raising a family. It proved to be easier to discuss voluntary poverty when one lived as a single student or was unemployed. Perhaps because "we didn't have much money ourselves then," the notion of a poverty that was voluntary did not appeal to the St. Louis Workers as anything more than a temporary condition.[33] Perhaps they were too close to an involuntary poverty to be attracted to one freely chosen.

The year 1937 ended on such a note, as the St. Louis Catholic Workers struggled with their own material concerns. "How very difficult it is to leave our material nets and take up the spiritual," they wrote to New York. "Thanksgiving morning we started giving out coffee, bread, and apple butter to a small number of our . . . ambassadors."[34]

Sometime in the winter of that year a new arrival appeared on the scene. Herb Welsh was acquainted with the New York Catholic Worker as both guest and worker and had made friends with Cy Echele and Don Gallagher. Young and antibourgeois, he was full of enthusiasm for the movement. His experiences in New York proved valuable for opening a genuine house of hospitality in St. Louis. Thus it was that in April of 1938, the Catholic Worker of St. Louis had a new address. The dilapidated three-story house was located across the street from Saint Louis University's College Church. The Workers were proud of this house; it enabled them to continue their soupline and also provide shelter on a limited basis. They began to circulate a small newsletter from what they called the St. Louis Hospice.

The hospice at 3526 Pine Street served as the St. Louis headquarters during its most active period, from 1938 to 1941. The house was large enough for meeting rooms, a dining room for the soupline, and shelter for a number of men. Like all Catholic Worker houses, it was subject to outbursts of temper among guests and residents and a certain fluctuation among those who came and went; it depended heavily on a strong personality who could cope with daily crises. For an interim, Herb Welsh provided that personality.

Their activities were many and varied. Every morning the Workers who lived at the hospice faced a line of 150 people waiting for breakfast. In the summer, a Confraternity of Christian Doctrine class was held in rooms of the hospice for "about thirty colored children" from St. Elizabeth's Parish. Several of the women made hospital visits with a priest friendly toward their aims. They continued their programs of social service along with weekly meetings that included guest speakers. They lost Don Gallagher as an active participant when he moved to Easton, Pennsylvania, near the Catholic Worker farm there, in order to write his thesis.

Their interest in the liturgy grew with the soupline and was reflected in the list of speakers that fall. One week Father Hellreigel spoke on liturgy. The next week Dr. Franz Mueller spoke on liturgy and family life; then Emil Frei (stained-glass artisan responsible for several windows in the College Church) talked on liturgy and art. Lastly, Dom Virgil Michel, O.S.B., spoke on liturgy and social life—a favorite theme of both Michel and the Catholic Worker.

The end of the year saw the departure of the house director, Herb Welsh, who left St. Louis to start another house in New Orleans. Perhaps the urge to move on overwhelmed him. Running a house of hospitality caused emotional exhaustion for many. One of the hoped-for occurrences in a house was that a guest would turn into a Catholic Worker capable of beginning his own hospitality program. (At that time, shelter was provided only for men.) So running the house was handed over to one of the guests. His problems with alcohol, apparently overcome, surfaced once again when he faced the pressures of running the hospice. It proved to be a difficult time for the group.

In February 1939, a cheerful letter to New York boasted of feeding three hundred men a day, painting and wallpapering the house, meetings, and CCD classes every night of the week. By the middle of April, another letter revealed that a new man, Bill Camp, had taken on responsibility for the house. Another month passed and in May, Dorothy Day received a letter asking for a visit.

We need a renewal of spirit that we might have the courage to go on to be better Catholic Workers. . . . We have many problems that you may be able to help us with . . . our chief problem is that there is none of us except Bill Camp who sleeps, eats and breathes Catholic Worker day and night. . . . Then the complexion of the group has changed somewhat . . . I think there is considerable wondering among members as to whether we should go on with the House at all. Then we lack leadership. . . . Do come and help us.[35]

Such crises were not uncommon to the Catholic Worker, and Dorothy Day was accustomed to being arbiter and counselor. The June bulletin of the St. Louis Hospice referred to some problems that prevented writing the bulletin for two months. It also made the happy announcement that Dorothy Day would be arriving in St. Louis on June 18. Dorothy's visit did not solve any problems, but rather encouraged the various factions to continue their work together. In their July newsletter they reported, "Dorothy Day's visit last month inspired us anew to grapple with our problems and keep on striving."[36] Don Gallagher also visited St. Louis that June to receive his degree and gave a talk on his year at Easton.

Dorothy must have gotten in touch with Herb Welsh about the troubles in St. Louis, for he returned to take the house again in early November. "Have been working like a fool 'trying to right the sinking ship,'" he wrote to Dorothy. "Do believe things are better here now. . . . Some of the clergy are getting over their jitters (God knows they had ample justification for them) . . . regarding conditions in the past year. . . . The group here is away down in the dumps and it's a bitterly difficult job to get them in the right state of mind."[37]

If 1939 was a difficult year for the St. Louis Catholic Worker, it was even more so for the rest of the world. Before that pivotal year, the prime concern of the Catholic Worker was the same as the rest of the nation: coping with the economic disaster of the Depression. Feeding the hungry and clothing the naked were very real concerns, not only for the religious or select Catholics but for the compassionate of all persuasions. The Catholic Worker did not necessarily support the New Deal. "We were against it," Dorothy Day would tell Studs Terkel thirty-five years later. "On the other hand we had to go ahead. . . . So we did try to get people on welfare. . . . But if it could be done by a smaller group, it would be better. There must be decentralization. . . . What do *I* do?"[38]

In August 1939, Germany and Russia signed a pact of nonaggression that dismayed the rest of Europe. In September, Nazi forces invaded Poland, and Europe was at war. Catholic Worker concerns were no longer limited to conditions of the unemployed and laborers. Their position of neutrality during the Spanish Civil War a few years before began to develop more clearly into one of pacifism. This was especially true for Dorothy Day and the New York house. The Christian anarchists and gentle personalists in various Catholic

Worker groups across the country were less convinced about pacifism. On this issue, they became disturbingly individual and some were openly contentious. During the summer, Dorothy Day, Joe Zarella, and Monsignor Barry O'Toole went to Washington to register opposition to the Selective Service bill then before Congress, the Burke-Wadsworth Compulsory Military Training Law. Questions of war, neutrality, peace, defense appropriations, and aid to the Allied forces became as compelling as the works of mercy, and the various Catholic Worker houses addressed these questions in their own way.

St. Louis Catholic Workers were divided over the growing spirit of pacifism in the movement. "We never took up that cause," remembered one. "We weren't impressed with it at the time." Others talked peace but found it difficult to actively oppose conscription that summer. "Re the peace business, must plead for time," Herb Welsh wrote in noncommital fashion to Dorothy in August 1940; "I am certainly opposed to . . . compulsory conscription, but whether the law to be enacted will be the same thing that I oppose is impossible to determine until the law is written and put into the books." Don Gallagher expressed a more conciliatory opinion after the war, "I do not agree with its [the Catholic Worker] particular interpretation of the Church's teachings upon peace and war, but I feel that its critics . . . have failed to see the profound insights . . . expressed by Dorothy Day."[39] The son of Alice and Emil Frei sought and obtained conscientious objector status, in part as a result of Catholic Worker influences. Still others became active in the America First Committee, which, though not pacifist, was certainly noninterventionist and isolationist.

Though sympathetic to Dorothy Day's pacifism, some found the growing war effort economically tempting, especially newly married and unemployed Cy Echele. "I worked in the war industry, which hurt me. I didn't want to. I didn't want to build those damn tanks. But I had to make a living for my family, so I worked in the war industry in St. Charles." One St. Louisan found Catholic Worker pacifism too embarrassing to handle while serving as a chaplain in the Navy. "In fact, I finally, in order to be over the embarrassment, had her quit sending me the *Catholic Worker*."[40]

As the war continued, the pacifism of the Worker movement became more articulate, more personalist, and more clearly Christian. At first they discussed in good Thomistic fashion the traditional view of a just war, doubting all the while that such a war was possible with modern technology. There were hints that the war was a capitalist conspiracy. As the Workers became more practiced in their pacifism, they turned more to the biblical sources of the historic peace churches and less to political and scholastic arguments.

Dorothy Day continued to uphold her stance of Christian pacifism after the United States entered the war in 1941. Her pacifism
was consistent with the notion that the ends and means of one's life
were inextricable. The call to "turn the other cheek" came to be
regarded more and more seriously, whether it was in one's relation
to a disturbed guest or another country. In later years, peacemaking
would become one of the primary activities of the Worker movement and the initial center for Catholic pacifism.

Sometime late in 1940 the group in St. Louis prepared to move
from Pine Street to a duplex at 312 South Duchouquette Street. Herb
Welsh planned to marry a woman from New York and move to one
of the flats. He proposed to run the soupline and hospice from the
flat next door. But when he went to New York for his wedding, he did
not return.[41] Another man took over the new house, and the St.
Louis Worker continued in the tenuous style it had always enjoyed.
Donations came from a variety of sources, most often in the form of
food rather than money. Several high schools sent leftover cafeteria
food each day, or unconsumed food from suppers or social gatherings. Some restaurants consistently donated leftover food. With an
old car or donated truck, the Workers made the rounds. At times
they were without a vehicle and donations were sparse, appearing
only in what seemed the nick of time. Joe Huels remembers a house
cook telling him, " 'That thin soup I just served, that's everything we
got, we're out!' and while I was thinking about what we were going
to do, somebody came in and said, 'I got a couple sacks of potatoes
out in back of my car.' This is the way that thing operated; it was
amazing."[42]

The house on Duchouquette Street continued to operate throughout 1941 and 1942. A letter to the paper in May 1941 reported that
they were still feeding about "three hundred men a day" and had
twenty-two men as residents. Their new location brought them
closer to the poor than the old midtown location. The same letter
spoke of increased donations and enclosed $5 "which you can use as
you think best in your good work."[43]

In August, Bill Camp wrote again to say he would be attending the
retreat at Maryfarm in Pennsylvania that same month. By February
1942, another letter announced that Mr. Camp had found a job and
another man, Skip, had taken over the house. By 1942 jobs were
more available than ever; the United States was in the thick of a
wartime economy.

The *Catholic Worker* lost many subscribers and supporters during
the war years; more than 100,000 dropped their subscriptions. It also
lost many of its houses of hospitality. By 1941, at least thirty-two
houses had been established throughout the country; by the end of

1942 only half that number remained in operation. By 1945, there were only ten houses left. World War II brought on the availability of jobs and a changing economic picture. The controversial pacifism of Dorothy Day produced disagreement in St. Louis and elsewhere, but the St. Louisans' love for Dorothy might have overcome these differences had it not been for the increasing pull of other responsibilities. "We had no one capable of running the house," remembered one long-term supporter. "You had to have a certain ability to handle the situations there."[44]

The St. Louis Catholic Worker had also grown up. Two members married and moved to East St. Louis. Another's marriage took him back home to St. Charles. Herb Welsh went to New York; Don Gallagher had moved to Milwaukee much earlier. House residents who had become Workers and house managers found jobs or moved on, their temporary personal crises resolved. Several were drafted or enlisted after Pearl Harbor.

The individuals who were drawn to the Catholic Worker took a variety of directions, yet shared a common spirituality. Their involvement with the intellectual, cultural, and social justice activities surrounding the Worker represented an expression of their faith. In their attempt to translate an active spiritual life into the real world, they returned again and again to the source of that life. This religious commitment is evident both in their reminiscences of that period and their lifestyles today. "The Worker had a well-grounded spirituality that kept it balanced . . . it always had that dedication to prayer."[45] Another emphasized the spiritual underpinning of her social activism:

> If you stayed . . . without . . . getting yourself involved in the everyday thing, the things that called forth your own love and charity, then you're unbalanced. . . . It's true the other way too. There are loads of people who are in justice movements today who are not filled with love and justice; they're filled with anger.[46]

Though primarily a lay movement, the St. Louis Worker was encouraged for the most part by the church hierarchy. More than one cleric, even a bishop, paid the rent on houses of hospitality.

From family and friends the Workers received a sideways glance and benign criticism. "You had this funny little kind of persecution, more so than now; most of our friends, even our family, thought we were slightly nutty, and they would excuse us . . . because we were dear and innocent and stupid." Most of the Workers were fervent Catholics who did not view themselves as part of the mainstream. "I was part of the lunatic fringe [of Catholicism] at that time," announced one.[47] Their activities flowed out of an intense faith that evoked unconventional responses.

The influence of Dorothy Day and the Catholic Worker continued to exert itself on the lives of these individuals. "I don't think there's been a stronger influence in our lives," asserted Anne and Bolen Carter. "If I hadn't found the Catholic Worker, it's hard telling what I would have done," reflected Cy Echele. They were, in effect, waiting for the movement to come along. Luke Lanwermeyer: "I was never the same again. It filled a void socially, philosophically, liturgically." The center of this influence was found in the person of Dorothy Day. Evelyn Gilsinn: "Once I heard Dorothy speak, I could never again feel the same about self-indulgence." Luke Lanwermeyer: "She was an incredible human being." Joe Huels: "She really put into practice the beatitudes more than anybody that I ever met." Anne Carter: "Once you waken to an appreciation of Dorothy, she gets under your skin . . . it's a rare and beautiful thing."[48]

Some of the first Workers, now in their late seventies, still hand out literature on the nuclear freeze, Bread for the World, and liturgical renewal. Some still write newsletters combining political issues, organic food, and religious topics; others make talking books for the blind. Though the St. Louis Worker closed its doors in 1942, the members' lives were transformed by their activities, a transformation that did not end in 1942. Seeds were planted that, while lying dormant for years, would yet bear life.

Forty years after the first St. Louis Catholic Worker community was formed, another "informal and slightly starry-eyed" few opened yet another Catholic Worker house in St. Louis. When they began their investigations preliminary to the opening of today's Karen House, they sought out two members of the original group for input and suggestions. Today, St. Louis has a Catholic Worker community comprising two houses, a quarterly newsletter and a strong support group.

WHAT CAN fiNALLY be adduced from such a history? "To talk in retrospect is to do so coldly and, in a sense, to falsify what people experienced in the Thirties," the historian Christopher Lasch has correctly observed. The very manner in which history is written can imbue the story with more organization than may have actually existed, at least in the memories of experience. If this is not true for any other movement or group, it is certainly true of the Catholic Worker. "Sounds a lot more organized than the Catholic Worker actually was," wrote Evelyn Gilsinn, after reading a first draft of this chapter. "It was just a bungling effort of a half-committed group of people . . . to meet serious needs of the time." Remembers another Worker just as ruefully, "We muddled around trying to accomplish something until we ran out of steam." [49]

Any history of the Catholic Worker is compelled to address themes and personalities more than institutions and organization. The success of the St. Louis Worker may have been qualified by its share of bungling efforts and muddling around, yet in the end this is not a story of success or failure. Instead, certain general themes, as opposed to clearly drawn conclusions, may emerge from the stories of the Catholic Worker. These themes could be perhaps too neatly categorized under such headings as Spiritual and Material. There is a sense of dualism in the movement, the spiral image of a dialectic, the interplay of devotion to concerns both other-worldly and this-worldly. One Worker's recollection identified divisions in the St. Louis Worker as being composed of those who engaged more specifically in the corporal works of mercy and those who engaged in the spiritual works. Always there was the tension and difficulty resulting from trying to "harness ideals to works."[50]

There were the political concerns of wars and strikes: the Spanish Civil War, the seamen's strike in 1936, World War II, and later, Korea, Cuba, Vietnam. There were more specific material concerns: two hundred people lined up outside the door on a daily basis, coal-eating furnaces, interpersonal disputes, overdue rent, broken-down autos, and other living things. There were spiritual concerns: mass with Fathers Hellriegel or Huels; lectures on prayer, family life, art; discussions about prayer and personalism; recitation of the evening office. To many, these political, material, social, and spiritual concerns did not necessarily belong together; but for Catholic Workers they did. There were other groups in the 1930s and 1940s whose allegiance was claimed by one type of activity, social reform perhaps, but who had no interest in religion. What is most intriguing, and ultimately most confusing for contemporary analysts, is the Worker balance of theological orthodoxy and political progressivism.[51]

To think in terms of such double categories is a modern habit. It is such a habit that it is difficult to imagine a resolution. One is inclined to regard the material and spiritual as mutually exclusive or, at best, unrelated. When the life of an individual or movement appears to have effected a resolution of that dualism, one encounters the difficult job of explaining that resolution. After publishing a review of William Miller's biography, *Dorothy Day*, the editors of *Time* take Miller to task for his failure to "offer . . . a hypothesis which might help to understand the area where Dorothy Day's right and left joined."[52] "How did this ardent puritan reconcile her contradictions?" the reviewer asks.[53] One of the most appealing, and apparently puzzling, aspects of the Worker is its ability to balance the individual and the group, the spiritual and the material, the left and the right, the liturgy and the soupline. Its concerns have always been both timely and timeless. "Is the Kingdom a present day reality or only a future hope? For Dorothy, the Kingdom is a very present reality, and not purely other-worldly living."[54]

William Miller has suggested that the radical idea of the Catholic Worker is rooted in the life of the spirit, which seeks to end time, "and it will be ended when Christ, in an active and selfless love, is taken into every aspect of creation."[55] To be sure, this attempt to end time took shape with some very timely activities: support of strikes, an unpopular position on neutrality during the Spanish Civil War, a pacifist position during World War II. For all their primacy of the spirit, Workers were not afraid to mingle with the masses or besmirch their reputations by supporting unpopular causes. On a more mundane level, Workers drank the same reboiled coffee they offered their guests. They lived lives of intentional simplicity if not voluntary poverty.

It would be better to say that the Worker movement pursued not so much the end of time but sought instead to end the tyranny of time as the inevitable, inexorable tread over the life of the spirit. Time as an utterly material activity is regarded as moving with the immutable grind of a glacier across the face of history, leaving in its wake the altered topography of gutted economic systems, impotent religions, passé politics, and new visions of society where old problems become redefined in terms of supply and distribution. Such an understanding of time was challenged by the essentially sacramental nature of the Catholic Worker.

"The central fact of existence should not be process, with man holding on in whatever spot he found most tolerable," Miller explains. "Love should redeem process itself. This redemption began with man, for in the human person was the final, indivisible entity that stood above process." Miller quotes Day: "When one loves, there is at that time a correlation between the spiritual and the material. Even the flesh is energized, the human spirit is made strong. All sacrifice, all suffering is easy for the sake of love. . . . This is the foundation of the Catholic Worker movement."[56]

Both Dorothy Day and William Miller understood this love as essentially sacramental, the consumation of a life with Christ that saved the world from consuming itself. A love that is essentially incarnational redeems time and humankind from being defined as an exclusively material activity. This sense of sacrament is found not only in Worker speculations on love, process, or bourgeois life, but also in devotion to liturgical practices and its parallel social engagements. This communion with the life of the church runs throughout Worker history, granting continuity to the movement.[57] The Catholic Worker was neither another social reform group nor a group of religious who got together to pray.

This sacramentalism should come as no surprise to latter-day analysts. After all, this is the Catholic Worker under examination, springing from that most sacramental of churches. Because of this perspective, the Worker movement has translated its radical political position through the prism of a stained-glass orthodoxy. Workers entered into a life of active, radical love that welcomed suffering as a sign of kinship, a relationship defined in terms of the mystical body. They saw themselves as family, perhaps a "rather large and quarrelsome family" as Dorothy Day described them, but family nonetheless.

Embracing the least comfortable of positions and people has given an enduring credibility to their church affiliation, even creating precedents for less radical Catholics to follow. Likewise, their devotion to liturgy, mass, and sacraments was the hinge upon which turned their life of hospitality, simplicity, and peacemaking. The best that the Worker movement called forth anticipated the call to make one's life into sacrament. "There was no need for a theological plastic overlay of the image of Christ," wrote Tom Frary in a discussion of Dorothy Day's theology. "No matter how the other person appeared, no matter what he apparently had done of his own free will, no matter what labels the Church or society places on him, the very least of men is in fact Christ's brother and ours, and our salvation turns around our concrete response to that brother."[58]

If one accepts the theme of sacrament as appearing throughout Worker history, the need to think in terms such as "spirit" and "matter" begins to disappear. Labels such as "conservative" and "liberal" become irrelevant. It becomes important that men and women should have enough bread to eat, but not only as a matter of material preoccupation. The sharing of bread takes on the importance of a survival that is both physical and spiritual. One enters this salvific activity with a willingness to renounce. Peter Maurin regarded this renunciation as the act of taking less so someone else could have more. This sharing of bread and spirit is effected through sacrifice and, not by coincidence, what Workers saw as the imitation of Christ.

To affirm the life of the spirit in the world as central and essential rather than optional and possible, is to confirm the sacramental tradition. To commit oneself bodily to this notion is to consent to being broken from the start. Success is redefined. One is broken for another, and it is seldom what is known as a "deserving" other. To choose voluntary poverty is to claim a security in relation rather than possession. It is to stand in contradiction to Western, bourgeois material tradition.

The lives of Catholic Workers were indeed, as the old catechism defined sacrament, the outward sign of an inward grace. Workers understood this grace to be, like the God for whom they looked, both transcendent and imminent. Here are people who reconciled a life of the spirit in the world. These are people who did not regard the spirit as a form of antimatter, nor did they reject life in the world as one of automatic depravity. For the twentieth century they were indeed a puzzle, but also the best to which it could aspire.

NOTES

Note: The *Catholic Worker* is here cited as *CW.*

1. Evelyn Gilsinn, interview with author, St. Louis, February 11, 1982, Oral History Collection, Saint Louis University (hereafter cited as SLU).

2. Two excellent and varied examinations of the movement in the 1930s are William Miller, *A Harsh and Dreadful Love, Dorothy Day and the Catholic Worker Movement* (New York: Liveright, 1972), and Mel Piehl, *Breaking Bread: The Catholic Worker and the Origin of Catholic Radicalism in America* (Philadelphia: Temple University Press, 1982).

3. Anne and Bolen Carter, interview with author, St. Louis, September 22, 1981, SLU.

4. Luke Lanwermeyer and Alice Frei Lanwermeyer, interview with author, Kirkwood, Missouri, October 7, 1981, SLU.

5. *The University News of Saint Louis University,* May 10, 1935.

6. Donald Gallagher, "The Personalist Mission of the Catholic Worker," *The Historical Bulletin* (of Saint Louis University), May 1947: 76. Other cities had Campion Propaganda Committees also; the first was formed in New York by an early Catholic Worker, Tom Coddington. See Miller, *Harsh and Dreadful Love,* 69, and Piehl, *Breaking Bread,* 124ff. for a discussion of this splinter group within the New York Catholic Worker. St. Louis apparently was not affected by this schism.

7. Marc H. Ellis, *Peter Maurin: Prophet in the Twentieth Century* (New York: Paulist Press, 1981).

8. For example, Larry and Ruth Ann Heaney successfully operated a farming commune on Catholic Worker principles in central Missouri after World War II. See also Stanley Vishnewski's account of the first farming experiments at Easton, Pennsylvania, with its attending conflicts and personalities in *Wings of the Dawn* (Catholic Worker, New York, 1984, privately printed).

9. Don Gallagher to Dorothy Day, March 17, 1936, Dorothy Day–Catholic Worker Collection, Memorial Library Archives, Marquette University, Milwaukee (hereafter cited as "CW Papers"), W-4.

10. Lee Carter to Dorothy Day, April 3, 1936, CW Papers, W-4.

11. *CW,* June 1936: 3. Cyril Echele to Joe Zarella, June 21, 1936, CW Papers, W-4.

12. Cyril Echele, interview with author, St. Charles, Missouri, October 20, 1981, SLU.

13. Luke Lanwermeyer to Dorothy Day, September 10, 1936, CW Papers, W-4.

14. Lanwermeyer interview, SLU.

15. There is conflicting evidence concerning the time of year when they began to look on this address as their headquarters. Stationary using this address and the name of Campions was used to send a letter to Dorothy Day in the spring of 1936. Yet memories and articles pertaining to the St. Louis Catholic Worker in later years refer to the fall of 1936 as the beginning of their own place.

16. Peter Maurin, *Easy Essays* (reprinted, Chicago: Franciscan Herald Press, 1984), 13.

17. Lanwermeyer interview, SLU.

18. Echele interview, SLU.

19. Gilsinn interview, SLU.

20. Lanwermeyer interview, SLU.

21. *CW*, April and July, 1937.

22. Piehl, *Breaking Bread*, 126. Virgil Michel, *Christian Social Reconstruction* (Milwaukee: Bruce Publishing Company, 1937).

23. *CW*, July 1937.

24. Lanwermeyer interview, SLU. See also Donald J. Kemper, "Catholic Integration in St. Louis, 1935–47," *Missouri Historical Review*, October 1978.

25. Reverend Monsignor Joseph Huels, interview with author, Cape Girardeau, Missouri, November 5, 1981, SLU. Anne and Bolen Carter, interview 2 with author, St. Louis, May 25, 1982, SLU.

26. Echele interview, SLU.

27. Gilsinn interview, SLU.

28. Huels interview, SLU.

29. See especially the last chapter of Ellis, *Peter Maurin* for an exposition of Maurin's understanding of salvation. "He took so seriously the question of salvation that he thought personal and social life had to be oriented around it. To give up what was superfluous, to honor the least by becoming the servant of all, to live personal and community life centered on the spiritual, was to enter into the message of salvation" (170).

30. "The Catholic Alliance," April 1939, Saint Louis University Archives, SLU.

31. Ibid.

32. Ibid. Gallagher, "Personalist Mission," 84.

33. Carter interview 1, SLU.

34. *CW*, December 1937.

35. Evelyn Gilsinn to Dorothy Day, May 22, 1939, CW Papers, W-4. A telegram sent a few weeks later reiterated the same worries. "We need you badly as we are divided on the wisdom of carrying on the house. We'll send bus fare from Cleveland." June 9, 1939, CW Papers, W-4.

36. "St. Louis Hospice Bulletin," July 1939, Saint Louis University Archives, SLU.

37. Herb Welsh to Dorothy Day, August 1940, CW Papers, W-4.

38. Studs Terkel, *Hard Times: An Oral History of the Great Depression* (New York: Pantheon Books, 1970), 343–44.

39. Carter interview 1, SLU. Herb Welsh to Dorothy Day, August 1940, CW Papers, W-4. Gallagher, "Personalist Mission," note 5.

40. Echele interview, SLU. Huels interview, SLU.

41. Evelyn Gilsinn to author, January 1982, Saint Louis University Archives, SLU.

42. Huels interview, SLU.

43. *CW,* May 1941.

44. Gilsinn interview, SLU. See also Piehl, *Breaking Bread,* 197.

45. Huels interview, SLU.

46. Carter interview 2, SLU.

47. Carter interview 1, SLU. Lanwermeyer interview, SLU.

48. Carter interview 1, Echele interview, Lanwermeyer interview, Gilsinn interview, Huels interview, SLU.

49. Christopher Lasch in Terkel, *Hard Times,* 383. Evelyn Gilsinn to author, February 1982, Saint Louis University Archives, SLU. Lanwermeyer interview, SLU.

50. Lanwermeyer interview, OHC-SLU.

51. This confusion is perhaps the real reason why so many are fond of Dwight Macdonald's quote of Dorothy Day's 1952 remark: "If the Chancery ordered me to stop publishing the *Catholic Worker* tomorrow, I would." Such obedience to hierarchy is intriguing when it comes from one who was consistently jailed for civil disobedience to state laws, but it is not inconsistent for Dorothy Day.

52. Elizabeth L. Wilson, for the editors of *Time,* to the author, August 1982, Saint Louis University Archives, SLU.

53. "Secular Saint," *Time,* July 12, 1982: 73.

54. Charles Barthel, "An Angry but Obedient Daughter," (Master's Thesis, Kenrick Seminary, 1982).

55. Miller, *Harsh and Dreadful Love,* 10.

56. Ibid.

57. Often enough, however, the movement was ahead of its time, in its anticipation of pacifism, liturgical renewal, lay involvement, political radicalism, and anticonsumerism.

58. Tom Frary, "Thy Kingdom Come—The Theology of Dorothy Day," *America,* November 11, 1972: 385.

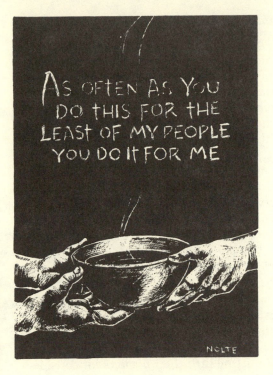

11.   THE CHICAGO CATHOLIC WORKER

Francis Sicius

IN EARLY JUNE 1936, Peter Maurin left the Catholic Worker house in New York and visited the parks, tenderloin areas, and parishes of Chicago. He was a scholar, and although the Jesuit editor of *America* called him the most well-read man he had ever met, Maurin preferred the spoken word to the written. For that reason he traveled the country teaching, sometimes preaching his views on religion, politics, and economics. Most people ignored the small, spectacled man in his wrinkled suit as he proselytized from crumpled notes he pulled from his jacket. But those who paused from their lunchtime strolls in Grant Park, or who listened simply to escape the boredom of unemployment, heard from this apparently uninteresting vagabond an intellectual synthesis that would provide the roots for an intellectual upheaval within the Catholic church in the United States.[1]

The Jesuit priests at St. Ignatius Church on the North Side were particularly intrigued by Maurin, possibly because he seemed to elicit in a simple manner the personalist philosophy in vogue in Europe. They invited Maurin to speak to their parishioners, and as he stood in the parish hall of the church, which boasted a beautiful cupola with baroque entablature, he reminded his listeners that "we need parish homes as well as parish domes." His hosts at the parish invited Maurin to spend the night, and after a good rest in an elegant suite reserved for the archbishop, Maurin traveled downtown to Lower Wacker Drive, a thoroughfare that ran under Chicago's "loop." During the Depression years it served as a "hotel" sheltering thousands of homeless people from the harsh winds blowing in from Lake Michigan. "Although you may be called bums and panhandlers," he told those that gathered there, "you are in fact ambassadors of God." His hosts that night also provided the best room they could offer: a piece of walkway near a burning trashcan.[2]

During the weeks in Chicago he spoke wherever he could. One night even the Rotarians listened to his discourses. Political disposition or economic circumstance did not matter. If they listened, he spoke. If they did not listen, he would push a copy of the *Catholic Worker* or a hand-scribbled outline into their pockets for consideration when they had time. So clear was Maurin's message in his own mind that he was sure that only a little time and thought were needed to grasp it. Maurin had a successful visit to Chicago that summer, for out of it came the beginning of that city's Catholic Worker movement, the group that emulated most closely his ideas of Catholic radicalism.

About a week after he left Chicago, a column appeared in the *Catholic Worker* entitled "Chicago Letter." It was written by Arthur Falls, a doctor, a black leader, and one of the few Chicagoans who could call themselves a Catholic Worker. When the first issue of the paper appeared in 1933, Falls had written to Dorothy Day, "Those of us who have labored with Catholics both of the clergy and laity in an effort to get them to face practical issues are more than joyful to see your publication." He did have one suggestion for the paper. He felt that it might be interesting to "see one of the workmen at the top of your page to be a colored workman." Dorothy Day accepted his suggestion, and the paper kept the same masthead until May 1985.[3]

Falls continued his correspondence with the *Catholic Worker*, and his articles on segregation, lynching, and other issues related to prejudice and racism appeared frequently in its pages. Initially this relationship was mutually beneficial. Dorothy Day was happy to have an articulate black man writing in her paper, since it did much to dispel popular myths about blacks in the 1930s; for his part, Falls was pleased to enlist a publication with a Catholic title into the civil rights movement in Chicago. More often than not, the church had proved to be more of an embarrassment to Falls than a solace. There were basic differences between the two principals, however, that would strain their accommodating relationship as the Catholic Worker became stronger in Chicago. Falls protested racism and prejudice because it prevented the *enbourgeoisement* of blacks, whereas Dorothy Day, antibourgeois to the core, viewed racism and prejudice as axioms to the capitalist "laws" of competition and supply and demand.

Nevertheless Falls had, as he said, "labored" with his coreligionists in the area of civil rights, and it was consoling to finally have a group of Catholics on his side. If his view of the Worker differed from that of Dorothy Day, it must also be said that, at least in the beginning, even Dorothy Day and Peter Maurin were not always in agreement. To note disparity is simply to help define the nature of the Catholic Worker. Cohesiveness of purpose or idea was never a strength of the movement. It is a tribute to the Catholic Worker idea that in an era that witnessed an intellectual drift toward order, collectivity, and single-mindedness, the personalism of the Worker movement attracted people who reveled in their individuality.

The first Catholic Worker group that came together in St. Patrick's Church at 718 West Adams Street at the invitation of Arthur Falls reflected the heterogeneity typical of the Worker. Some attended the meeting because they were familiar with Dorothy Day and Peter Maurin and their work in New York. But many more came simply because they noted the word *Catholic* or *Worker*. Consequently the group included one woman who after a quick inspection of the group left in a huff, exclaiming in a loud voice, "Just because I'm a Catholic doesn't mean I have to associate with niggers!" Another person at the meeting used the occasion to point out the sins that the church had perpetrated against the country's workers and explained the only refuge that remained for the working class was the Communist Party.[4]

Nevertheless, the first meeting did launch the Catholic Worker movement in Chicago. The weekly meetings continued, and in November, four months later, a Catholic Worker house was opened at 1841 Taylor Street. Since the house was primarily the creation of Arthur Falls, it reflected his personality, and therefore it differed greatly from the one run by Dorothy Day in New York. Falls boasted that the new Chicago house had a library with a good collection of books on co-ops, race relations, and other "practical issues." He also established a credit union at the house, which enabled the poor to secure low-interest loans and to save money at the rate of a nickel a week.[5] In Falls's scheme of things, this provided the poor with important lessons in thrift. Although Falls shared Dorothy Day's concern for the poor, he did not agree with her acts of charity. There would be no souplines or shelter at a Catholic Worker house started by Arthur Falls. He preferred the self-help philosophy typical of most black leaders.

As the Catholic Worker movement matured, a philosophic perspective crystalized that contrasted greatly with that of Arthur Falls, but in the 1930s the *Catholic Worker* was the only periodical that served the purpose of the intellectual Left in the Church. Since the loudest social commentator in the church at this time was Father Charles Coughlin and his *Social Justice* followers, those to the left of Coughlin were tolerant of each other's different views. For that reason the numbers associated with the Catholic Worker movement swelled very rapidly in the 1930s. On the eve of the war circulation of the paper was almost 200,000.

As the radical antibourgeois character of the Catholic Worker became clearer, however, many people began to disassociate themselves from the movement. The most noticeable groups to leave were the liberals, such as Falls, on one hand and the Christian Marxists on the other. The Catholic Worker movement was Christian and communitarian but never Marxist. Nor was it "liberal." Marxists as well as the liberal bourgeoisie built an ontology on the principle that workable systems could channel the forces of progress in time. The Catholics had no five-year plans. The "plan" was merely to emulate Christ, specifically, the Christ of peace, justice, and charity. The actualization of their Christian view put them in opposition to Marxism, bourgeois liberalism, and capitalism. They would be called anarchists, but only in a temporal sense. For they subscribed to a higher order, a spiritual realm that placed the person, acting in the personhood of Christ, as the measure of all things temporal.

Dorothy Day must have grimaced more than once as she read news of the committees, workshops, and co-ops developing in the name of the Catholic Worker in Chicago, but at least she could take consolation in the fact that the movement had finally taken root in the nation's second largest city. At first, the Taylor Street house was a loosely organized affair run by volunteers from the local high schools and colleges. The central event in the first months was the Sunday Forum. Eventually these meetings gained a reputation and attracted visitors from the University of Chicago, Loyola, Northwestern, and "Bughouse Square," Chicago's version of New York's Union Square, as leading scholars sympathetic to the Catholic Worker movement volunteered to speak.[6]

Among those who added to the excitement of these forums were

Jacques Maritain, who was leading a Thomistic revival at the University of Chicago, the Catholic sociologist Paul Hanly Furfey, and the Benedictine liturgist Virgil Michel. All these men had an important intellectual influence on the Catholic Worker as well as on the intellectual Left burgeoning in the Catholic church at this time. In addition to scholars, a number of activists also joined the Sunday discussions. John Cogley recalled one afternoon when the meeting was addressed by a young man named Walter Reuther, who had recently returned from Russia and was anxious to report on the condition of the workers there.[7] This of course was the same Walter Reuther who would become president of the United Auto Workers.

Catholic students from the local colleges and high schools were also attracted to these forums, and they played an important part in the success of the Catholic Worker movement in Chicago as elsewhere. Before the arrival of the Catholic Worker in Chicago, young Catholics discovered the social doctrine of their church through groups such as Catholic Interstudent Social Action. Founded by Martin Carrabine, a Jesuit missionary, and Sister Cecilia Himbaugh, this group awakened young Catholics to the new spirit that had been entering the Church. Students who went to these meetings eagerly absorbed the social implications of the papal encyclicals on the economy, *Quadragesimo Anno* and *Rerum Novarum*, the philosophy of Maritain, the new Catholic sociology of Furfey, and the synthesis of much of this that appeared in the *Catholic Worker*. Ed Marciniak, who was a student in 1936, remembered this era in Chicago as being intellectually exciting. "Young people were really alive," he recalled; "we would read avidly, especially every learned Catholic magazine we could locate."[8]

These students represented a new hybrid in American Catholicism. They were the first generation of Catholics to attend college on a large scale. Representing the collective struggle of their immigrant parents for upward mobility, they demanded the same quality education as their Protestant counterparts. And they also became swept up in the era that gave birth to a plethora of doctrines for social reform. Scholars in the 1930s struggled to redefine social, philosophic, and economic precepts that had been two centuries in the making.

Liberal laissez-faire capitalism had propelled the country through a dynamic century of progress, but the burden of a world war and a great economic depression had laid the idea prostrate. Although social philosophers were willing to leave the nineteenth century behind, one legacy remained. They continued to reduce the human phenomena to scientific principle. Events in Europe seemed to corroborate this assumption. Russians appeared to be prospering under their new system, as was inflation-wracked Germany and uncontrollable Italy. Europe, which had seemed corrupted beyond redemption in the 1920s, had become a successful social laboratory in the 1930s, and scholars were eager to adopt the cause of one of these theories or another. The new Catholic scholars were just as eager to adopt social theories, but they could not embrace any of the solutions emerging in Europe. Their faith, to say nothing of their Catholic intellect, recoiled at the notion of a deified state. Furthermore, they believed that humans were endowed with a spirit that elevated them above laws of ordinary matter. Therefore this new generation of Catholic scholars readily embraced the new Catholic social philosophy, particularly the philosophy of the Catholic Worker movement.

The Catholic Worker also attracted its share of characters. One who visited Taylor Street frequently and eventually moved in to direct the house until his death in 1950 was John Bowers. Bowers, whose fancy attire included a walking cane, kid gloves, and a diamond tie pin, could often be found debating the radicals who frequented Bughouse Square. He hardly looked the part. With his well-manicured mustache, Italian cigarillo clenched between his teeth, and overcoat draped over his shoulders, he looked more like a con man than anything else.[9]

Bowers announced his presence at the Catholic Worker during one of the popular Sunday Forums. After listening to someone extol the virtues of the masses, Bowers exclaimed in a high-pitched voice, "Given the chance, the masses will make asses of themselves."[10] He soon became a regular around the house and thrilled many of the group with stories from his limitless imagination. He told them he knew Mae West personally, and the Barrymores, but he wasn't talking to Lionel because of a recent argument. Just before Dorothy Day made her first visit to the Taylor Street house, Bowers revealed that he had known her since the days when they had both lived in Greenwich Village. He also was a close friend of Ernest Hemingway and Scott Fitzgerald. And he recalled long, whiskey-filled nights of singing and acting out scenes that were still merely images in the mind of their friend Gene O'Neill. But the faith of even his most avid believers was shaken when Dorothy Day arrived, for she in no way resembled Bower's description.[11]

Bowers worked as a floorwalker in Marshall Field's Department store, where he catered to the whims of the rich clientele. But this could hardly pay for his clothes or his expensive apartment in Hyde Park. The source of his income added another dimension of mystique to this dandy who preferred the company of vagabonds and radicals. Something about the Catholic Worker attracted Bowers. His visits became more frequent, and soon he gave up his worldly comforts, moved into the Taylor Street house, and took over the administration of it. Until his arrival, the house was only a part-time enterprise. Arthur Falls had his medical practice and other commitments, and the students had their responsibilities. But Bowers's presence assured that someone was always available at the house, and it became a permanent fixture in the neighborhood.

It is difficult to ascertain what motivated a man like Bowers to take on such a responsibility. His closest friend at the Catholic Worker, Tom Sullivan, who himself would become a significant part of the movement, described Bowers as a scholarly man who had made tremendous strides in the life of the spirit. Perhaps the sense of community at the Catholic Worker filled a void in the middle-aged bachelor's life. It may have been that the Catholic Worker provided what he had been seeking while hanging around Bughouse Square, attending rallies or making speeches, since at the house there were always people who had time to listen to stories.

Nevertheless there was more to the man than an initial meeting revealed. He remained at the Catholic Worker house, eventually shedding his fancy attire for the more ragged apparel of those who knocked on his door every day. Taylor Street became his final home, and Bowers became one of the minor heroes of the Worker movement. He began a day care center, organized cooking and sewing classes for the young girls in the neighborhood, and helped integrate the previously all-white St. Ignatius School, even paying the tuition himself for a number of black children.[12]

John Bowers would eventually dominate the house on Taylor Street, but during the first year it was still Falls's project. The most obvious sign of his continued influence was the ever-recurring organizational meeting. Everyone belonged to a committee. There was one on education, which reported Bowers's success with the local schoolchildren, as well as reports by individual students who at Falls's suggestion had brought up the issue of integration in their all-white classrooms. There were additional committees on liturgy, labor, and co-ops. When asked the purpose of all this, Falls responded that he hoped each committee would carry out an active program in its particular area, spreading not only the sale of the paper but the philosophy of the Catholic Worker group. He hoped to make the Catholic Worker "one of the leading civic groups in the city."[13]

Little could have been further from the hopes of Dorothy Day. At times she surely felt less than charitable toward Falls, and probably pictured this distinguished black man as no more than a Babbit in social worker's clothes. "Dorothy and I do not always see eye to eye," he once said.[14] That was probably an understatement. His attitude also disillusioned more than one idealistic student.

John Cogley, for example, had been attracted to the Worker by the stories of the hospice in New York, where young people lived a life of voluntary poverty in community and service to the poor. Such a life seemed to him to be a radical and romantic response to the challenges of other groups in the 1930s, which accused Catholics of complacency if not downright collusion with "capitalist forces of oppression." But under Falls's direction, Cogley felt that the Catholic Worker had become little more than a "conference center with religious overtones." Soon, according to Cogley, outside of the work that Bowers was doing with neighborhood children, the Taylor Street house was nothing more "than a place which sponsored forums or committee meetings five nights a week."[15] The personalist approach to injustice seemed to have been lost in the entrapments of bureaucratic procedure.

Falls cannot be blamed for his attempt to channel energetic youth to his civil rights cause. To him, the exclusion of black children from Catholic schools, black patients from Catholic hospitals, and the segregation of blacks within their Catholic parishes were real issues, which should be attacked with all his strength and all the resources he could command. Falls lived in an era when Catholic priests told blacks to go to their own Negro priests for the sacraments. This was also a time when canon law regarding the geographic division of parishes was ignored in order to put all blacks in St. Elizabeth's parish in the heart of a black ghetto.

It is no wonder that when Falls read the *Catholic Worker* position on racism he put his strength into organizing the movement in Chicago. He did it for one reason: to harness the resources of the Catholic Worker to fight racism in Chicago. Falls freely admitted that his major goal was to indoctrinate Catholic youth with church precepts regarding racism and then turn them back to their schools. He wanted them to ask their nuns and priests questions such as: "In light of the church's teaching regarding the right of every Catholic to have a Christian education, why does this school segregate Negroes?"

Falls's tactics were shrewd and to a good end, but the heart of the movement was not in it. The Worker attracted refugees from white middle-class values, and they were not going to lead a stampede of blacks back in the opposite direction. For Falls's part he was right to leave the Catholic Worker movement to its own devices, which he eventually did. For the rejection of white middle-class values represented by the Catholic Worker was a luxury blacks could not yet share.

The underlying tension at the Catholic Worker house was apparent when Dorothy Day visited there in the spring of 1937. When she arrived, Cogley noted that "she was obviously not pleased with the way things were going on Taylor Street . . . a bit of conventional social work among children and numerous committees did not coincide with Dorothy's idea of how the Catholic Worker should be running in the nation's second largest city."[16] Even Falls admitted, "Dorothy never really agreed with my concept of the Catholic Worker," but he maintained, "I thought it was the more realistic approach."[17]

Dorothy Day was forty years old when she visited the Chicago Catholic Worker for the first time. At this point in her life she had not taken on the saintly quality that would distinguish her to a later generation. In 1937 she was tall, erect, and blond. She had "beautiful slanting eyes" and a presence that demanded attention. Cogley remembered her as "strikingly attractive." While there, she went with him and his friend Sullivan to supper at an inexpensive diner. Cogley recalled it as one of the most memorable evenings of his young life. She spoke of her radical past and thrilled them with stories of Rayna Prohme, Emma Goldman, Eugene O'Neill, John Reed, Carolyn Gordon, and practically every other activist of the previous generation. Forty years later, he still had not forgotten how "glamorous the whole evening seemed."[18]

Cogley must have impressed Dorothy Day also. Before departing on the bus, her favorite means of travel, she gave him the keys to a house she had rented on Wabash Avenue, in the middle of the largest black neighborhood in Chicago. She suggested to Cogley that a Catholic Worker house there could supplement the work being done by Father Drescher at St. Elizabeth's. It is hard to know whether she acquired the house simply because it was available or because she wanted to demonstrate to Falls her concern for blacks. At any rate, Cogley felt it was the greatest day of his life. At last he was a part of the true Catholic Worker movement. "It was great to be young, and feel alive and to be participating in something so vital," he wrote later.[19]

The enthusiasm for the new house did not last long. Cogley soon realized that the pastor of St. Elizabeth's did not need his assistance. Unlike many rectories with fortresslike entrances, St. Elizabeth's was always open and there was always lunchmeat and bread on the table for hungry people in the neighborhood. The priest also ran a number of activities for the parishioners, and they knew that they could always go to him for assistance whatever the emergency. It was not long before Cogley began to see himself as the fifth wheel in a smoothly run operation. When the rent expired at the end of the summer, so did the Catholic Worker experiment on Wabash Avenue. Nevertheless, a break had been made from the original Taylor Street house, and the failure of the Wabash Avenue project was but a preface to a more successful enterprise the following spring.[20]

The split did not signal the end of the Taylor Street house. It simply meant that there were two Catholic Worker houses in Chicago. The original continued to prosper, and under Bowers's tutelage it began to take on the character of a day care center. Despite this departure, the Taylor Street house remained significant in the history of the Catholic Worker. Lasting until 1950, it surpassed all Chicago houses in longevity, and it was through this house that many Chicagoans first discovered the Catholic Worker movement.

After closing the house on Wabash Avenue in August 1937, Cogley headed for Ross, California, where he entered the Dominican friars. He remained there only a short time. On a cool morning in December Tom Sullivan stood in Dearborn Station to meet the train that brought Cogley back from California. Having left the seminary himself, he understood the many emotions that accompanied his friend, and he did not then, or ever, press the issue with Cogley. He just offered him a place to stay for as long as he needed it.[21]

Cogley moved into the YMCA but did not remain long. At the first sign that winter had subsided, he took to the road. Unemployed young men wandering aimlessly along the highways and railways of the country had become a familiar sight by 1938, but Cogley was not one of the lost and forlorn; his journey had a purpose. He had set his sights on the Catholic Worker house in New York City, where he soon joined those on Mott Street who spent their days helping in the soupline or selling the *Catholic Worker* on the street. New York's streets blossomed with idealists throughout the 1930s. Walking near Union Square, one could hear hawkers screaming, "Read the *Daily Worker!*" And frequently a nearby salesman would retort, "Read the *Catholic Worker* daily!"

In the evenings, with their long day behind them, they sat around their storefront home, sipping coffee and discussing passionately their pet theories of theology, sociology, and politics. The day's activities sapped their abundant energies and the evenings restored it. Years later Dorothy Day recalled, "Oh those early days, that early zeal, that early romance, that early companionableness, how strong we all felt it."[22]

Cogley enjoyed his stay at the Catholic Worker in New York, but soon it became apparent that he was not needed there. The recession of 1938 had swelled the number of homeless seeking shelter, and Cogley slept in a bed that might have provided a place for an unemployed laborer. Cogley had hoped to write for the *Catholic Worker*, but up to that time no one had discovered his talent. Therefore, when he received an invitation, bus ticket, and Dorothy Day's encouragement to return to Chicago to help a new Catholic Worker house there, he left.

Cogley traveled to 868 Blue Island Avenue in Chicago, where Al Reser, Marty Paul, and Ed Marciniak had started a new Catholic Worker house in an old factory. It was a large, old brick building with a second-floor loft. They convinced the owner to let them have it for $15 a month, and they also persuaded an Italian grocer in the neighborhood to give them credit for food.

On Good Friday of 1938, they opened their Catholic Worker house to a "seemingly endless line of humanity shivering from the early morning frost." They fed 350 people a breakfast of boiled oats, hot coffee, and bread, and that night they provided many of them with a place to sleep. The older men took cots donated by the Little Sisters of the Poor, and the younger ones slept on the rough wooden floor. They were content simply to be sheltered from the cold wind blowing in off Lake Michigan. "It was a bitter winter," Cogley recalled, and they took in as many as they could, wedging them in like "cigarettes in a pack." Providing shelter was difficult but not as heartbreaking as telling "another hundred outside the door, shivering and pleading, that there was no more room." Economic statistics showed that the Depression had abated by 1938, but the reality outside the Catholic Worker house proved otherwise.[23]

To raise funds, publicize their work, and promote their ideas, the Chicagoans published a journal. Edited by John Cogley and Ed Marciniak, it had a format and appearance identical to the New York *Catholic Worker*. The only difference was the word *Chicago* in the masthead. Despite the similarities to the New York paper, they disavowed any notions of competition with the original. The first editorial advised, "If you have one quarter [the price of a yearly subscription] remember, to Mott Street with it where Dorothy [Day], Peter [Maurin], and Bill [Callahan] and their gang are doing the best job of Catholic journalism in the country. But," it continued, "if you have two quarters take a chance on Blue Island Avenue, we shall do our best."[24]

They reported events at the house of hospitality, appealed for funds, reviewed movies and books, and wrote articles on personalism, church liturgy, art, and labor issues. Their circulation swelled to over four thousand, proving there was in fact a need for the type of Catholic journalism they were creating. Further proof was the letters of support, including one from Carl Sandburg and another from Dorothy Day, who told them that their paper "far outshines our own poor effort."[25]

The paper was an ambitious enterprise, and it marked the beginning of John Cogley's distinguished career as a journalist and launched Ed Marciniak into a vocation that would identify him as one of the leading advocates of human rights in Chicago. He would eventually head Mayor Daley's commission on human rights. But in 1938 they were not about the business of carefully plotting their careers, they were living their vocations as Catholic activists. This commitment gave them the fortitude to carry out their journalistic crusade, and that is just how they perceived it.

Whether they were righteously panning a movie for its anti-Catholic tone or castigating Father Coughlin for his anti-Semitism, these young men laid their Christian commitment unabashedly in newsprint for all to see. The new paper gave them national attention for the first time when John Cogley took on Father Coughlin and his radio broadcast. He told the radio priest that he ought to straighten out his "wrong-minded listeners." Some people, he warned, "are using your controversial Jewish figures to justify an un-Christian attitude toward Mrs. Cohen the delicatessan lady and Mr. Meyer the insurance salesman." Coughlin broadcast a response on his show and printed it in *Social Justice*. He told Cogley he was against only the "bad" Jews, not the good ones.[26] It was not the response Cogley expected.

The Chicago paper was never nearly as strong as Coughlin's *Social Justice*, but at least the Jews had one Catholic journal to support them during the most troubling period of their modern history. The paper also spoke out in defense of blacks at a time when few did. Urging its readers to support the antilynching bill, the *Chicago Catholic Worker* reminded them that "13,000,000 exploited, discriminated, despised black brethren were still calling out for fearless, uncompromising Christians to set the pace and light the way."[27]

Due primarily to Ed Marciniak's influence, the Catholic Worker became an important force in the industrial union movement in Chicago. On Memorial Day 1937, when policemen shot and clubbed ten workers to death outside the Republic Steel Mill, the Chicago Catholic Workers were there. They were also with the meatpackers when they began their organizing drive, and with Heywood Broun when he rallied the newspaper writers against the powerful Hearst syndicate.

The Chicagoans differed with the New York Catholic Worker on the issue of industrial unionism. "Strikes don't strike me," Peter Maurin used to say. Unions offended his romanticized concept of work. To him, labor was an art that a craftsman donated freely to the community. This concept, he believed, provided the basis for a more humanistic approach to labor relations. Capitalists had destroyed this idea of labor, however, by reducing it to a commodity, and now he feared that unionism had acquiesced in this diminution by merely trying to raise the price of the commodity.

In Chicago few were impressed with Maurin's theories, and those who were went to northern Minnesota to start a farming commune on some donated land. The rest joined Marciniak and argued that unionism was not a question of "wealth versus numbers, but rather a question of human solidarity." They believed that "the future of American labor lay in the CIO or at least in the principle of industrial unionism." They believed that Catholics should be involved in the union in-fighting and politics lest the unions fall under the wrong leadership.

The Catholic Workers were instrumental in the success of the labor movement in Chicago. Since the majority of the industrial workers were Catholic, they would never have supported unionism without the presence of Catholic leadership. Until the Catholic Worker began exerting leadership, the most visible group of union activists were the communists, but in the late 1930s Marciniak and other Catholic Workers introduced the word *Catholic* into the history of the labor movement in Chicago.[28]

Dorothy Day yielded to the enthusiasm with which the Catholic Workers immersed themselves into the Chicago labor movement. If she did not agree with them philosophically, she certainly could concur with their commitment to the working class. Another issue began to emerge, however, at the end of the decade, one that would divide Dorothy from her friends in Chicago. At the end of 1939 the war and the preparedness issue began to dominate all other discussions around the Catholic Worker. Since its inception the movement had been consistently pacifist, but given the horrors precipitated by the new regime in Germany, many in Chicago began to reevaluate their position. Dorothy Day remained adamant in her pacifism and determined to rescue her friends from the entrapments of this new call to their idealism.

Increasingly pacifism began to dominate the pages of the New York *Catholic Worker*. Reaching back into the church's calendar of saints, Dorothy Day emphasized the tradition of Catholic non-violence maintained by St. Francis of Assisi, Isidore Pelusiate, and other more obscure saints. New personalities began to influence the Worker movement. Among them was Father John Hugo, who during this period developed a clear idea of Christian pacifism. "Your pacifism must proceed from truth," he admonished Dorothy, "or it cannot exist at all." His articles began to appear regularly in the *Catholic Worker*, and they, along with Dorothy's own preoccupation with the issue, began to trouble her readers. "The pacifism you preach is false, unpatriotic and dangerous," one woman wrote. Before she would send another contribution, the reader asked Dorothy to assure her that not "one cent of what I send you will be spent for pacifist propaganda." A priest from Louisiana who had been instrumental in the labor movement and had also started a Catholic Worker house there urged Dorothy to change her stand. The Catholic Worker meant too much, he said, to too many people to become divided over one issue. Dorothy received many similar and even stronger letters, but she remained adamant.[29]

In Chicago they were also distressed over Dorothy's stand on the issue of preparedness. The *Chicago Catholic Worker* maintained editorially that "until the Pope speaks it is the right and obligation of every Catholic to form his own conscience on the issue of the war."[30] Privately, with the exception of Ed Marciniak, most Chicago Catholic Workers felt the struggle against Hitler fit the criteria for a just war. They hoped they could eventually reveal their opinion and remain at the same time part of the Catholic Worker.

In August 1940 that hope died when they received what Tom Sullivan later called "Dorothy's encyclical." In it she reiterated the pacifist position of the Catholic Worker. "There are some members of Catholic Worker groups throughout the country who do not stand with us on this issue," she pronounced. She pointed out that some had even taken it upon themselves to suppress the paper. Since there was a close connection between the personalism of the Catholic Worker and pacifism, she wanted those who were heads of Catholic Worker houses across the country to be pacifists.[31]

The decree troubled Cogley. He had not yet committed himself in either direction. Nevertheless, when he did arrive at a decision he wanted it to be a matter of conscience, not doctrinaire pacifism. The *Catholic Worker* in Chicago continued precariously for another year. During that time, because of its editorial position on the war, it was being perceived by Catholic Workers across the country as the voice of the loyal opposition. For example, Father H. A. Reinhold told Dorothy Day that the Seattle house was no longer distributing the *Catholic Worker* because of its stand on pacifism but the Workers there did continue to read and distribute the *Chicago Catholic Worker*.[32]

This undoubtedly troubled the Chicagoans and they probably sought a way out of this position. Dorothy found it for them the following year. In the summer of 1941, another letter arrived from her desk, addressed to "All Catholic Workers." It invited them to a retreat at the Catholic Worker farm in Easton, Pennsylvania. "All

Catholic Workers should come," she wrote. "We must drop every-thing listening to the Lord who will only speak if we keep silent."[33]

It was not, however, the Lord who spoke to them but the pacifist Father John Hugo. He directed the retreat, and the message was clear. It became obvious to many from the Chicago house that they could no longer be Catholic Workers, and Cogley decided that there would be no more issues of the *Chicago Catholic Worker*. At the retreat he had vigorously defended intervention, but that argument with Dorothy was over, he cared too much for her to let it fester, and he did not want the *Chicago Catholic Worker* to provide a rallying point for the "loyal opposition" within the movement.

Within months America was in the war. The debate was finished. Jim O'Gara and Tom Sullivan were drafted, Cogley enlisted, Marty Paul became a conscientious objector, and Ed Marciniak received a deferment. There was little time to contemplate the demise of their community. Before going to their assigned camps, Tom Sullivan and John Cogley visited Dorothy Day in New York. As always she welcomed the travelers and found them a place to sleep. It heartened her to see the two young men. So much had changed since the war had broken out. She tried to persuade them one more time, but Sullivan retorted, "Hitler won't be persuaded by pietistic phrases, Dorothy; the only thing he understands is a gun put to his head."[34] In September, 1943 Dorothy took leave from the Catholic Worker. In the December issue of the paper she mentioned Tom Sullivan and Jim O'Gara in the Gilbert Islands. This was one reason she had withdrawn from the work, she said, to "gather and hold in my prayers all those members of our family so dear to us." The Chicagoans she thought about were all gone, scattered throughout the Pacific and the United States in Army camps and conscientious objector compounds.[35]

To say that her pacifism resulted from her commitment to Christianity alone does not explain the passion with which she embraced it. Although most pacifists had the support of their church or community, Dorothy had little from either. The Catholic hierarchy opposed her on this issue, as did most of those within her own movement. According to Tom Sullivan, even Peter Maurin did not agree with her pacifism. Some even accused her of polishing her old socialist pacifism with her new Catholicism. Despite the attacks, she pursued her pacifist course like a saint with a vision. Perhaps she had one. The 1930s were hard years, but they represented a decade that, for the first time since the Civil War, questioned the capitalistic character of the country. The period not only witnessed a president who attacked "economic royalists," it saw the rise of idealists like the Catholic Workers who dreamt of "building the new within the shell of the old."

Dorothy knew the war would end this era. Faced with the awesome enterprise of destroying fascism, attacks against capitalism seemed petty. World War II harnessed the aberrant energy and idealism of the 1930s as workers, capitalists, statesmen, and demagogues joined forces in the crusade against the Axis powers. Dorothy Day trembled at the thought of what horror would come from this tremendous coagulation of power.

Ed Marciniak of the Chicago Catholic Worker understood Dorothy better than his colleagues. Questioning the benefits of the decline in unemployment due to the increase in war production, he pointed out the dangers to the workers on these new production lines. He commented that injured human beings were viewed as if they were "broken tractors." He noted that that was typical of the view of the industrialist, especially in time of war. If a "lost worker is merely viewed as a lost investment," he wondered what "will happen when the situation changes and it becomes profitable to take a chance on losing a worker."[36]

Perhaps too much would be sacrificed in this crusade. Given the technology at the beginning of the war, Dorothy did not have to contemplate total obliteration, but she did fear the demise of humanity. How could personhood survive in an era that had apotheosized the machine and the state? This war demanded nothing less. Dorothy Day refused to be swept up in the rapture of the crusade. She remained determined to preserve the sense of peace and community of the Catholic Worker movement. At least a glimpse of the idealism of the prior era would remain when the smoke finally settled. She threw all her strength into an effort to keep her followers out of the war, and when that failed she remained adamantly pacifist in her newspaper, even though it meant subscriptions during the war years declined from over 190,000 to under 51,000.[37] Years later when a new generation of Catholics sought a pacifist dimension to their theology, Dorothy would be vindicated, but in the 1940s she stood virtually alone.

THE WAR AND Dorothy Day's opposition to it seemed to bring the Catholic Worker movement to an end. But the influence of the movement continued in Chicago, and there appeared to be evidence that it would pass through these troubled times. Ed Marciniak received a deferment, and he continued his commitment to the labor movement in Chicago. He joined the founders of the Catholic Labor Alliance and in 1943 published a paper called *Work*. It included the same issues that had been important to the *Chicago Catholic Work-er*. In an editorial in its first edition, July 1943, Marciniak main-tained that the paper would be concerned with "all who work" and its philosophy proposed that "a return to religion, embracing a defi-nite program of action is the basic factor in the solution of social problems."[38] He could have espoused the same philosophy in the pages of the *Catholic Worker*. But he probably felt it was time to begin his own journal, free from the influence of Dorothy Day and from the turmoil that had brewed around the Worker since the war had begun.

As for the Catholic Worker in Chicago, it continued to exist dur-ing the war years through the action of a group of pacifists who were doing alternative service work at the Alexian Brothers Hospital. In 1942 Dorothy received a letter from Jim Rogan, telling her that St. Joseph House of Hospitality had a new address. "It is 1208 Webster, just one block from the Alexian hospital. We begin the new venture in fear and trembling," he told her, "because we know the great good that was done at Blue Island Avenue."[39]

Even if they could not equal their predecessors, at least Dorothy had her way: the Catholic Worker house in Chicago was run by paci-fists. And a significant group of pacifists they were. This group repre-sented the first conscientious objectors to ever work in a hospital. Before this experiment all conscientious objectors had been sent to old CCC camps to do meaningless work in a Siberia-like atmo-sphere. The success of the Chicago enterprise led to the creation of many more hospital conscientious objector groups before the end of the war. Eventually this would become the most popular and viable form of alternative service for conscientious objectors.[40]

When the war ended the conscientious objector camps closed, and so did the Catholic Worker house in Chicago. All that remained was the original house on Taylor Street. Bowers still maintained it as a day care center. Finally in 1950 this house also came to an end when Bowers died. The brash man in dandified dress who shocked many with his flippant tongue had become a quiet man in worn-out clothes, undistinguishable from those he helped. He spent his last days surrounded by cobwebs and dust, and his tattered condition symbolized the passing of an age. Dorothy Day traveled to Chicago for his funeral and remarked in the *Catholic Worker*, "I remember something he did for me years ago when I was taken ill in Chicago and he paid not only for my hospital bill . . . but for the operation on my throat. . . . He was a man of taste and culture; may God grant him a place of refreshment, light and peace."[41]

As for the others who had left the movement during the war years, they returned to Chicago with ideas intact but visions altered. John

Cogley and Jim O'Gara teamed up to begin a Catholic journal, Marty Paul went off to build a farming commune, and Al Reser and his wife took off for New Mexico to work with Native Americans. "Many people are beginning to speak of the Catholic Worker in the past tense," wrote Dorothy Day in September 1948. She was reacting to an article about the Catholic Worker written by John Cogley for *America* magazine.[42]

He was partially right, and as the new decade unfolded his conclusions regarding the worker movement seemed even more correct. In the 1950s the United States seemed to take a deep collective sigh of relief and fall into a much-needed slumber. Social upheaval had passed and the *enbourgeoisement* of America was well under way. Peace was at hand: Europe had been saved and the communists checked in Greece and Korea. It was time to relax from the tumultuous 1930s and 1940s. Those who at one time had read and supported the *Catholic Worker* preferred to ignore the issues it continued to raise and tried to forget their former association with unemployment, foreclosures, and war.

During this period of remission, a former Chicago Catholic Worker, Tom Sullivan, took over the management of the New York house. It must have been a comfort to Dorothy Day to have someone from the old crowd with her. Even Sullivan noticed that the people attracted to the movement were now different. In the 1930s he and his friends typified the problems and aspirations of their generation. The group that came in the 1950s, however, were atypical of their generation. They were unimpressed with their country's affluence, and their concern over the bomb went deeper than the fear that it might drop on their country. Their dislike of communists emanated not from McCarthy's ravings but from events such as the Stalin-Hitler pact and the murder of Trotsky. Typical of this new group was Michael Harrington, who moved into the Worker house and lived there for two years. In the introduction to his book *The Other America* he wrote, "It was through Dorothy Day and the Catholic Worker movement that I first came into contact with the terrible reality of involuntary poverty and the magnificent idea of voluntary poverty."[43]

In Chicago another disillusioned bright young man became attracted to the Catholic Worker movement. His name was Karl Meyer. He met Dorothy Day in 1957 when he joined her and her friends in a protest against the Civil Defense air raid drills that were popular throughout the decade. So impressed was he with the Worker philosophy that this Catholic convert returned to Chicago, where he was attending the University of Chicago, and opened a new Catholic Worker house there. He also became a co-editor of the *Catholic*

Worker, but more important, he presented the Catholic Worker in Chicago to a new generation of activists who would revitalize the movement.

As unemployment rose again in the late 1950s and early 1960s, and new groups such as migrant workers began to follow the paths blazed in the 1930s by industrial workers, a new generation of young Catholic activists discovered a philosophy of labor within the pages of the *Catholic Worker.* Similarly, as the civil rights struggle escalated in the early 1960s, the Catholic Worker's position on racial justice was once again relevant. But perhaps most significant, in the mid-1960s when the issue of war and peace dwarfed all others, Catholic pacifists discovered in the Worker history a tradition of nonviolent activism. Long before the first bishops' letter on the legitimacy of the conscientious objector position appeared in 1968, the *Catholic Worker* provided emotional, spiritual, and intellectual support for Catholics who refused to serve in the armed forces during the Vietnam war. Ironically, pacifism, the issue that almost buried the Catholic Worker movement in the 1940s and 1950s, was the central force behind its revitalization in the 1960s.

Karl Meyer, who started St. Stephen's House of Hospitality on Oak Street in downtown Chicago in 1958, became a nationally recognized leader of the peace movement and brought the Catholic Worker to the forefront of activist groups in the turbulent 1960s and early 1970s. He organized pickets at military installations, joined the much-heralded march to Moscow in 1961, and spearheaded the tax-resistance movement against military spending. The activities of Karl Meyer in Chicago attracted renewed attention to the Catholic Worker nationally. In 1965 when Tom Cornell and a small group of Catholics burned their draft cards in a demonstration in New York City, he pointed out that the inspiration had come from an article Meyer had written. Historian Staughton Lynd has described Meyer as one of the most effective influences on the generation of radicals and resisters that emerged in the 1960s.[44]

In 1965 Meyer went to Vietnam with a group of peace activists. Back in Chicago he told a reporter, "The Vietnamese want the Viet Cong to stay out of their villages, but they also want the United States to stop bombing them." He commented that he simply doubted the United States really wanted peace: "If we believe in peace we wouldn't bomb them." Chicago reporter Jack Mably, commenting on Meyer's trip and expulsion from Vietnam, admitted that he disagreed with Meyer more often than not. But he confessed that he admired the man because his motivation was simple: "he acts out of love for his fellow man."[45]

No comment could describe Meyer, or for that matter the rest of the Catholic Workers, any better. Mass movements did not compel him or them, but rather a simple personal commitment to humanity. For over fifty years there has been a Catholic Worker movement in Chicago. The faces have changed but the ideals have not. In a world moving toward greater centralization and depersonalization, Catholic Workers have pursued the opposite.

The Catholic church in the United States, specifically, owes the Catholic Worker a debt, as a study of the Chicago movement emphasizes. The work and ideas of John Cogley, Ed Marciniak, Jim O'Gara, and others provide the intellectual roots for current proclamations of the bishops on issues of peace and social justice. But beyond this, the history of the Catholic Worker carries a greater significance. The movement has been described as spiritual, antimaterialistic, and even overly idealistic. But another adjective is needed to complete the description.

The creation of the Catholic Worker was *instinctual*. It resulted from a basic human urge for community. Events and ideas of the nineteenth century eroded traditional forms of community that had been centuries in the making. It is no coincidence that the Catholic Worker was primarily an urban movement with a utopian urge to agrarianism. Besides the fact that most Catholics lived in the city, it was in urban America that the demise of traditional forms of community became most apparent. Therefore the city produced the first solutions to the crisis.

By the end of the nineteenth century civic clubs and professional organizations proliferated. The problem with these new manifestations of community was that they tended to be more exclusive than inclusive: the veterinarian could not join the AMA, a worker could not join the Rotarians, the Irish could not join the Italian-American club, and a black person was excluded everywhere. To those with a sense of history or humanity, these groups denied the essential purpose of their existence. Even the Catholic church, which boasted a tradition of community, failed to fulfill its historic purpose.

During this era, the church took care of its own, building protective walls around its flock. To many Catholics, this act was as abominable as the attitude of the Rotarians. It is easy to understand why many of the first Catholic Workers like Cogley, Marciniak, and Sullivan were seminary dropouts. In theory they felt their church could solve the crisis of community. But in reality they learned that priests were not being prepared to open their spiritual arms but rather to wrap them protectively around the assembled flock. The nature of the church is to be open and expansive; it does not thrive in a defensive posture. If the official church could not function as it should, then the spirit that protects the eternal church would provide another means. The new means was the Catholic Worker movement. Peter Maurin attracted idealistic Catholics in the 1930s because he elicited a new vision for the Church. His idea was Catholic, which appealed to their intellect, and communal, which appealed to their instincts.

The pursuit of community had approached a demonic frontier in the 1930s, but the Catholic Worker had no part in these illusions. Whereas Hitler bragged that he evoked a sense of community by appealing to the least common denominator, the Catholic Worker appealed to a spiritual denominator realized in the image of Christ. For many, even Christ, through the actions of his followers, had become a symbol of division. But the Christ of the Catholic Worker did not belong to a sect or denomination. To the Jew, he was the Christ of Jerusalem, to the worker he was the son of a carpenter, to the oppressed he was the author of the Sermon on the Mount.

The Catholic Workers lived the communal truth of their church. A phrase that appeared frequently in the pages of the old *Chicago Catholic Worker* was "the mystical body of Christ." Devoid of its most subtle theological implications, to the Workers this phrase simply meant that all were one in Christ. Therefore when the Jews were attacked, the Catholic Workers announced along with the pope: "Spiritually we are all Semites." When laborers were denied a living wage, Workers took up their cause, and when the war threatened to tear the mystical body apart, they struggled with the pacifist idea.

The church has come a long way philosophically and spiritually since the days before World War II when it participated in the segregation of the human community. Today the church once again opens its spiritual arms to the world. Much of this change in the church is a result of historic process but some comes from the influence of a small group of radicals who dared to call themselves Catholics. The Marciniaks, O'Garas, and Meyers who were part of the Catholic Worker in Chicago have moved on, but the movement continues to thrive in Chicago. It thrives because the words spoken by Peter Maurin in the parks and churches of Chicago still appeal to those who see their church as a quiet but powerful force of community in a world continuing to move in the opposite direction.

Notes

Note: The *Catholic Worker* is here cited as *CW.*

1. Interview with Monsignor John Hayes, Chicago, June 14, 1976.
2. Peter Maurin, *Green Revolution* (Chicago: Omega Graphics, 1976), 4, 6.

3. *Chicago Catholic Worker*, June 1936. In May 1985 a woman and child replaced the white male worker.

4. Interview with Arthur Falls, Western Springs, Illinois, June 9, 1976.

5. *CW*, December 1936.

6. Interview with Tom Sullivan, Rockville Center, New York, June 22, 1976; interview with Ed Marciniak, Chicago, October 31, 1976.

7. John Cogley, *A Canterbury Tale* (New York: Seabury Press, 1976), 10.

8. Dan Herr, "Chicago Dynamo," *Sign*, September 1962: 12.

9. Sullivan interview.

10. Ibid.

11. Interview with Jim O'Gara, New York, June 20, 1976.

12. Sullivan interview.

13. Joseph Morrison, "Chicago Catholic Worker Movement" (Master's Thesis, Loyola University of Chicago, 1938), 14.

14. Falls interview.

15. Cogley, *A Canterbury Tale*, 17.

16. Ibid., p. 11.

17. Falls interview.

18. Cogley, *A Canterbury Tale*, 11, 12.

19. Ibid.

20. Ibid., 13, 14.

21. Tom Sullivan described this incident in an obituary he wrote on Cogley for *CW*, June 1976.

22. Dorothy Day, *Loaves and Fishes* (New York: Curtis Books, 1972), 25.

23. John Cogley, "Store Front Catholicism," *America*, August 21, 1948: 447.

24. *Chicago Catholic Worker*, June 1938.

25. *CW*, September 1938.

26. Charles Coughlin, *Am I an Anti-Semite?* (Detroit: Condon Press, 1939).

27. *Chicago Catholic Worker*, January 1940.

28. Ibid., March 1940 and July 1938.

29. William D. Miller, *A Harsh and Dreadful Love: Dorothy Day and the Catholic Worker Movement* (New York: Liveright, 1973), 166–69.

30. *Chicago Catholic Worker*, November 1940.

31. Ibid., 168; Sullivan interview.

32. Miller, *A Harsh and Dreadful Love*, 168. The Los Angeles Catholic Workers had become so incensed over Dorothy Day's stand on pacifism that they burned bundles of the *Catholic Worker* when they arrived from New York. James Finn, *Pacifism and Politics* (New York: Random House, 1967), 375.

33. Miller, *A Harsh and Dreadful Love*, 188.

34. Sullivan interview.

35. *CW*, December 1943.

36. *Chicago Catholic Worker*, October 1940.

37. Nancy Roberts, *Dorothy Day and the Catholic Worker* (Albany: State University Press of New York, 1984), 119.

38.   *Work*, July 1943.

39.   *CW*, July–August 1942.

40.   Francis Sicius, "The Chicago Catholic Worker Movement, 1936–Present" (Ph.D. dissertation, Loyola University of Chicago, 1979), 209–11.

41.   *CW*, January 1950.

42.   John Cogley, "Storefront Catholicism," *America* 79 (August 21, 1946): 447.

43.   Michael Harrington, *The Other America* (New York: Macmillan, 1972), vii.

44.   Tom Cornell, "Why I Am Burning My Draft Card," *Commonweal* 83 (November 19, 1965): 203. Staughton Lynd and Michael Ferber, *The Resistance* (Boston: Beacon Press, 1971), 17.

45.   Jack Mably, *Chicago American*, April 22, 1965.

Appendix,
Contributors,
and Index

APPENDIX

Aims and Means of the Catholic Worker Movement

The aim of the Catholic Worker movement is to live in accordance with the justice and charity of Jesus Christ. Our sources are the Hebrew and Greek Scriptures as handed down in the teachings of the Roman Catholic Church, with our inspiration coming from the lives of the saints, "men and women outstanding in holiness, living witnesses to Your unchanging love" (Eucharistic Prayer).

THIS AIM REQUIRES us to begin living in a different way. We recall the words of our founders, Dorothy Day who said, "God meant things to be much easier than we have made them," and Peter Maurin who wanted to build a society "where it is easier for people to be good."

When we examine our society, which is generally called capitalist (because of its methods of producing and controlling wealth) and is bourgeois (because of a prevailing concern for acquisition and material interests, and its emphasis on respectability and mediocrity), we find it far from God's justice.

In economics, private and state capitalism bring about an unjust distribution of wealth, for the profit motive guides decisions. Those in power live off the sweat of another's brow, while those without power are robbed of a just return for their work. Usury (the charging of interest above administrative costs) is a major contributor to the wrongdoing intrinsic to this system. We note especially how the world debt crisis leads poor countries into great deprivation and a dependency from which there is no foreseeable escape. Here at home, the number of hungry and homeless and unemployed people rises in the midst of increasing affluence.

In labor, human need is no longer the reason for human work. Instead, the unbridled expansion of technology, necessary to capitalism and viewed as "progress," holds sway. Jobs are concentrated in productivity and administration for a "high tech," war-related,

This document appears in the original unedited version from *The Catholic Worker*, May 1987.

consumer society of disposable goods, so that laborers are trapped in work that does not contribute to human welfare. Furthermore, as jobs become more specialized, many people are excluded from meaningful work or are alienated from the products of their labor. Even in farming, agribusiness has replaced agriculture, and, in all areas, moral restraints are run over roughshod, and a disregard for the laws of nature now threatens the very planet.

In politics, the state functions to control and regulate life. Its power has bourgeoned hand in hand with growth in technology, so that military, scientific and corporate interests get the highest priority when concrete political policies are formulated. Because of the sheer size of institutions, we tend towards government by bureaucracy; that is, government by nobody. Bureaucracy, in all areas of life, is not only impersonal, but also makes accountability, and, therefore, an effective political forum for redressing grievances, next to impossible.

In morals, relations between people are corrupted by distorted images of the human person. Class, race and sex often determine personal worth and position within society, leading to structures that foster oppression. Capitalism further divides society by pitting owners against workers in perpetual conflict over wealth and its control. Those who do not "produce" are abandoned, and left, at best, to be "processed" through institutions. Spiritual destitution is rampant, manifested in isolation, madness, promiscuity and violence.

The arms race stands as a clear sign of the direction and spirit of our age. It has extended the domain of destruction and the fear of annihilation, and denies the basic right to life. There is a direct connection between the arms race and destitution. "The arms race is an utterly treacherous trap for humanity, and one which injures the poor to an intolerable degree" (Vatican II).

In contrast to what we see around us, as well as within ourselves, stands St. Thomas Aquinas' doctrine of the Common Good, a vision of a society where the good of each member is bound to the good of the whole in the service of God. To this end, we advocate:

Personalism, a philosophy which regards the freedom and dignity of each person as the basis, focus and goal of all metaphysics and morals. In following such wisdom, we move away from a self-centered individualism toward the good of the other. This is to be done by taking personal responsibility for changing conditions, rather than looking to the state or other institutions to provide impersonal "charity." We pray for a Church renewed by this philosophy and for a time when all those who feel excluded from participation are welcomed with love, drawn by the gentle personalism Peter Maurin taught.

A Decentralized Society in contrast to the present bigness of government, industry, education, health care and agriculture. We encourage efforts such as family farms, rural and urban land trusts, worker ownership and management of small factories, homesteading projects, food, housing and other cooperatives—any effort in which money can once more become merely a medium of exchange, and human beings are no longer commodities.

A "Green Revolution," so that it is possible to rediscover the proper meaning of our labor and our true bonds with the land; a Distributist communitarianism, self-sufficient through farming, crafting and appropriate technology; a radically new society where people will rely on the fruits of their own soil and labor; associations of mutuality, and a sense of fairness to resolve conflicts.

We believe this needed personal and social transformation should be pursued by the means Jesus revealed in His sacrificial love. With Christ as our Exemplar, by prayer and communion with His Body and Blood, we strive for the practices of:

Nonviolence. "Blessed are the peacemakers, for they shall be called children of God" (Matt. 5:9). Only through nonviolent action can a personalist revolution come about, one in which one evil will not be replaced simply by another. Thus, we oppose the deliberate taking of life for any reason, and see every oppression as blasphemy. Jesus taught us to take suffering upon ourselves rather than inflict it upon others and He calls us to fight against violence with the spiritual weapons of prayer, fasting and noncooperation with evil. Refusal to pay taxes for war, to register for conscription, to comply with any unjust legislation; participation in nonviolent strikes and boycotts, protests or vigils; withdrawal of support for dominant systems, corporate funding or usurious practices are all excellent means to establish peace.

The works of mercy (as found in Matt. 25:31–46) are at the heart of the Gospel and they are clear mandates for our response to "the least of our brothers and sisters." Houses of hospitality are centers for learning to do these acts of love, so that the poor can receive what is, in justice, theirs: the second coat in our closet, the spare room in our home, a place at our table. Anything beyond what we immediately need belongs to those who go without.

Manual labor in a society that rejects it as undignified and inferior. "Besides inducing cooperation, besides overcoming barriers and establishing the spirit of brotherhood (besides just getting things done), manual labor enables us to use our body as well as our hands, our minds" (Dorothy Day). The Benedictine motto *"Ora et Labora"* reminds us that the work of human hands is a gift for the edification of the world and the glory of God.

Voluntary Poverty. "The mystery of poverty is that by sharing in it, making ourselves poor in giving to others, we increase our knowledge and belief in love" (Dorothy Day). By embracing voluntary poverty, that is, by casting our lot freely with those whose impoverishment is not a choice, we would ask for the grace to abandon ourselves to the love of God. It would put us on the path to incarnate the Church's "preferential option for the poor."

We must be prepared to accept seeming failure with these aims, for sacrifice and suffering are part of the Christian life. Success, as the world determines it, is not the final criterion for judgment. The most important thing is the love of Jesus Christ and how to live His truth.

CONTRIBUTORS

Janice Brandon-Falcone is a Ph.D. candidate in American studies at Saint Louis University, currently writing her dissertation. She also earned an M.A. in History at Saint Louis University, where she wrote her thesis on the Catholic Worker in St. Louis during the Depression. She lives with her husband, an artist, and their daughter in the Ozark woods of southern Missouri.

Patrick G. Coy is in his fifth year as a member of the Karen Catholic Worker House community in St. Louis. He has the M.A. degree in theology from Marquette University. He served for six years as the coordinator of Peace and Justice Ministry at Saint Louis University, where he also taught. A lover of the outdoors, he is a writer and peace activist whose work has appeared in a variety of publications, including *Spirituality Today, Catholic Rural Life, Sojourners, Christian Century, St. Louis Post-Dispatch, Theology Today, Baltimore Sun, Journal of Religion and Intellectual Life,* and *National Catholic Reporter.* He is an elected member of the National Council of the Fellowship of Reconciliation, serving on its executive committee.

Daniel DiDomizio is associate professor of religious studies at Marian College in Fond du Lac, Wisconsin. He received the S.T.D. at the Institut Catholique de Paris, specializing in historical theology and spirituality. Among his areas of special interest is the relationship between spirituality and social justice. His articles have appeared in a number of publications, including *Western Spirituality: Historical Roots, Ecumenical Routes,* edited by M. Fox; *The Dictionary of Christian Spirituality; The Ecumenist; New Catholic World;* and *The Living Light.* He is active on the Ecumenical and Interfaith Commission of the archdiocese of Milwaukee and holds membership in the College Theology Society and the Catholic Theological Society of America. In 1985–1986 he held the Leo John Dehon Fellowship. He belongs to Pax Christi and the Fellowship of Reconciliation.

James Douglass has written three books on the theology of nonviolence: *The Non-Violent Cross* (Macmillan, 1968); *Resistance and Contemplation* (Doubleday, 1972); and *Lightning East to West*

(Crossroads, 1983). From 1962 to 1965 Douglass served as a theological adviser on questions of nuclear war and conscientious objection to Catholic bishops at the Second Vatican Council in Rome. Since then he has taught theology at the University of Hawaii, at Bellarmine College, and at the University of Notre Dame. In 1985 Jim and Shelley Douglass and the Ground Zero Community they helped found alongside the Trident submarine base near Seattle were given the annual Martin Luther King, Jr. award by the Fellowship of Reconciliation.

Eileen Egan, an editor of the *Catholic Worker* since 1969, spent many years in overseas development and refugee work with Catholic Relief Services. Among the honors she has received is the Pope John XXIII Medal for Peace and Justice (Ursuline College of New Rochelle). She edited *Peace Quarterly* for Pax from 1962–1970, and was a founder of Pax Christi–USA. She also edited *The War That Is Forbidden: Peace Beyond Vatican II*, a Pax publication. Besides many contributions to the *Catholic Worker*, she contributed chapters to *War or Peace*, edited by Thomas A. Shannon (Orbis Press); *The Courses of Hunger*, edited by William Byron, S.J. (Paulist Press); and *Famine*, edited by Kevin Cahill (Orbis Press). Her books include *The Works of Peace* (Sheed & Ward) and *Transfigured Night*, with E. C. Reiss (Livingston Publishers); both deal with world need and U.S. response to it. A booklet, *Dorothy Day and the Permanent Revolution*, was published by Benet Press. Her most recent book, *Such a Vision of the Street*, an account of the work of Mother Teresa of Calcutta, was published in 1985 (Doubleday). The winner of a Christopher Award, the book was released in paperback in 1986.

Marc H. Ellis is associate professor and director of the Institute for Justice and Peace at the Maryknoll School of Theology. He has worked at the Catholic Worker house in New York City (1974–1975) and written two books on Catholic Worker life and thought: *A Year at the Catholic Worker* (1978) and *Peter Maurin: Prophet in the Twentieth Century* (1981). His most recent books include *Faithfulness in an Age of Holocaust* (Amity, 1986) and *Toward a Jewish Theology of Liberation* (Orbis, 1987). He has traveled and lectured in the United States, Latin America, Europe, the Middle East, and Asia.

Geoffrey B. Gneuhs was an associate editor of the *Catholic Worker* for seven years. He has taught philosophy and ethics at Seton Hall University and Fordham University. He has a master's of sacred theology degree from Yale University. He writes and paints in New York City, where he lives.

Anne Klejment teaches U.S. history at the College of St. Thomas in St. Paul. Her research interest is Catholic war resistance and she is author of *The Berrigans: A Bibliography . . .* , *Dorothy Day and 'The Catholic Worker': A Bibliography and Index*, and "The Berrigans: Christian Nonviolent Resistance" in *Peace Heroes in Twentieth-Century America*, edited by Charles DeBenedetti.

Angie O'Gorman, originally from New York, moved to Kansas City with the staff of National War Tax Resistance in 1972. The following year she founded Holy Family House, a Catholic Worker house in Kansas City, where she lived and worked for ten years. Based partly on that experience, Angie developed a training program in nonviolent response to personal assault for Pax Christi–USA. In 1985 she spent six months in Guatemala as part of an international team accompanying members of Grupo de Apoyo Mutuo, the support group for the families of the disappeared. Currently, she is a community member of Casa Arco Iris, a sanctuary for Central American refugees in St. Louis. She holds the M.A. in religious studies from Saint Louis University.

Mel Piehl is an American historian. He has written about the Catholic Worker in *Breaking Bread: The Catholic Worker and the Origin of Catholic Radicalism in America* (Temple University Press, 1982). His article, "The Catholic Worker and American Religious Traditions," first presented at the Catholic Worker Fiftieth Anniversary at Holy Cross College, appeared in *Cross Currents*. He teaches humanities and history in Christ College at Valparaiso University.

Nancy L. Roberts is an associate professor in the School of Journalism and Mass Communication, University of Minnesota. She received the B.A. in history from Swarthmore College, and the M.A. and Ph.D. in mass communication (history) from the University of Minnesota. She is the author of *Dorothy Day and the 'Catholic Worker'* (State University of New York Press, 1984) and co-editor (with Arthur Roberts) of *'As Ever, Gene': The Letters of Eugene O'Neill to George Jean Nathan* (Associated University Presses, 1987). She has also written articles for more than fifty magazines and newspapers, including *Americana, Boston Globe, Catholic Digest, Christian Science Monitor, Catholic Life, Instructor, Midwest Art, Minneapolis Tribune*, the National Catholic News Service, *Our Sunday Visitor, Philadelphia Inquirer*, and *Salt*.

Contributors

Francis Sicius is an associate professor of history at St. Thomas University in Miami, Florida. He has written an article on the Chicago Catholic Worker for the Annals of the American Catholic Historical Society and has delivered a paper on Catholic Worker pacifism at the annual meeting of the American Catholic Historical Society. He has also recently completed a book-length manuscript on the Chicago Catholic Worker.

INDEX

Berrigan, Daniel (*cont.*):
Vietnam war and, 276; World
War II and, 275
Berrigan, Frida Fromhart, 275
Berrigan, Philip: Catonsville Nine
and, 276–300; Day and, 285–
86; goes underground, 299;
Hennacy and, 165; influence of
Catholic Worker on, 128, 275–
77; introduction, 10; Jonah
House and, 303; Merton and,
275; Plowshares movement
and, 166, 301–3; released from
prison, 187; Teilhardianism
and, 293; Vietnam war and,
276; World War II and, 275
Berrigan, Thomas, 275
Bethune, Ade, 34, 118
Bhave, Vinobha, 105
Blackfriars, 128
Blake, Simon, 92
Bloy, Leon, 49
Boillon, Pierre, 99
Bolshevik revolution, 54
Book of Ammon, The, 142
Bourgeois, 66n
Bourgeois liberalism, 340
Bourne, Randolph, 135, 155
Bowers, John, 342–43, 346,
353
Brandon-Falcone, Janice, 11, 313–
15
Brave New World, 42
Bread for the World, 314, 330
Breen, Edward J., 123
Brennan, Josephine, 190
Brethren, Church of the, 72
Brittain, Vera, 94
Brock, Hugh, 93
Brooklyn Tablet, 126
Brothers Karamazov, The, 55
Brown, John, 134
Bruderhof, 157
Brueggemann, Walter, 217
Brunini, J. G., 25
Buber, Martin, 21; *Catholic
Worker* and, 120
Burke, Senator, 78–79
Burke-Wadsworth Compulsory
Military Training Law, 77,
327
Byrne, Leo, 190

CAIP. *See* Catholic Association
for International Peace
Calcutta, Day visits, 104–5
California, Day visits, 7
Call, 116, 120
Callahan, William, 76
Calvinism movement, 181
Camara, Dom Helder, 242
Camp, Bill, 325, 328
Campion Propaganda Committee,
316, 318–19
Canada, Maurin and, 48
Canadian Social Forum, 128
Cape Canaveral, 163
Capitalism: Day on, 200, 339; dif-
ferences with Catholic Worker
movement, 340; Maurin on, 53,
200; in 1930s, 351; post-war
years, 352
Carbray, Richard, 95, 99, 100
Carnegie Steel, 138
Carrabine, Martin, 341
Carter, Anne, 330
Carter, Bolen: *Catholic Alliance*
and, 320; on Catholic Worker
movement, 330; St. Louis Cath-
olic Worker movement and, 315
Cass House in St. Louis, 247–48
Castro, Fidel, 92, 295
Catholic Action: in Boston, 315;
Day on, 205, 206; ethics and,
63; labor and liturgy and, 321;
Maurin on, 27, 30; propaganda
and, 318–19
Catholic Agitator, 128, 250
Catholic Alliance, 320, 323
Catholic Association for International Peace, 96
Catholic Church: Catholic students and scholars and, 341–
42; community and, 356–57;
laity and, 204; modernism and,
65n; nonviolence and, 349; on
pacifism, 351; racism and, 344;
role in United States, 356–57;
social doctrine and, 341–42;
state and, 286; war and, 71–72,
74, 79–80, 84, 95, 108, 110, 274
Catholic CO, 85
Catholic Family Farmer, 128
Catholic Interstudent Social Action, 341

Conscientious objection, 272–
309; Catholic camp for, 84;
Catholic Worker and, 355;
Catholic Worker movement
and, 230; Chicago Catholic
Worker movement and, 353;
Day on, 77–79, 85, 104;
Roberts on, 99; Second Vatican
Council and, 101; Selective Ser-
vice and, 84; Vishnewski and,
89
Conscription. *See* Draft
Consensus decision-making, 248–
49, 270n
Constantine, 129
Cook, Jack, 283
Cooke, Terence, 127
Cornell, Thomas: antiwar move-
ment and, 280; *Catholic Work-
er* and, 120; Catholic Worker
influence on, 128, 236; draft
board raids and, 279, 281, 282;
draft card burning and, 101,
274, 365
Corporal works of mercy. *See*
Works of mercy
Cort, John: Association of Catho-
lic Trade Unionists and, 320–
21; Catholic Worker influence
on, 128; on industrialism, 41;
labor movement and, 233
Coughlin, Charles, 340,
348
Council of Christian Pacifist
Groups, 38
Cowley, Malcolm, 116
Cowley, Peggy Baird, 116
Cox, Harvey, 5, 6
Coxey, Jacob, 135
Coxey's Army, 134–35
Coy, Patrick: introduction, 9;
nonviolence and, 254–55, 260,
265–66
Crane, Hart, 116
Cuba, Day visits, 7, 39, 92
Cullen, Michael: Catholic Worker
influence and, 236; deportation,
302; draft board raids and, 279,
285–86
Cullen, Nettie, 236
Cunningham, Adrian, 94
Cunningham, Angela, 94

Daily Catholic Worker, 27, 32
Daily Worker, 116, 346
Daley, Paul, 32
Darrow, Clarence, 140
Davisson, Zack, 247–48, 254
Dawson, Christopher, 40, 44n
Day, Donald, 120
Day, Dorothy, 69–114; air raid
drills and, xi, 296; on anarchism, 93, 141, 143, 160, 210,
307n, 326; Berrigans and, 285–
90, 295, 299, 300; Bowers and,
353; Catholic Church and, 2, 5,
70–71, 91, 100, 108, 117, 125–
27, 129, 162, 202–3, 208–10,
286, 294–95; *Catholic Worker*
and, 4, 120–29; on Church authority, 126–27; civil disobedience and, 79, 90–91, 285–86,
288, 297–99; coercion and, 257;
on community, 227–29; at
Congress of the Laity, 102; conscientious objection and, 78–
79, 85, 104; conversion, 117;
differences with Chicago Catholic Worker movement, 339,
343–45; "Dorothy's encyclical,"
350; draft board raids and, 283–
300; early views, 71; early
years, 179; editor, 120, 124–29;
eucharist and, 109–10; fasting
and, 95, 98–99; free obedience
and, 177; freedom of con-
science and, 298; Gandhi and,
296; Hennacy and, 140, 146,
149, 154, 159, 163–64; imprisonment and, 90–91, 105, 107,
299; Jews and, 80, 88; as journalist, 7–8, 73, 115–29, 202,
290; on labor, 122; on laity, 5,
120, 126–27, 204, 300; leaves
Catholic Worker movement,
85–87; on Marxism, 39, 122,
292; Maurin and, 2, 48, 117,
125, 231; as movement leader,
124–29; New York Catholic
Worker movement and, 294;
nonviolence and, 70–71, 73, 75,
80, 88, 107–10, 230, 243, 273,
278, 287, 291–92, 295–97; on
pacifism, 7, 88, 160, 246, 349–
52; peace movement and, 86–